NEW YORK

WILDLIFE ENCYCLOPEDIA

— AN ILLUSTRATED GUIDE TO —
BIRDS, FISH, MAMMALS, REPTILES, AND AMPHIBIANS

SCOTT SHUPE

Skyhorse Publishing

Skyhorse Publishing books may be purchased in bulk at special discounts for sales promotion, corporate gifts, fund-raising, or educational purposes. Special editions can also be created to specifications. For details, contact the Special Sales Department, Skyhorse Publishing, 307 West 36th Street, 11th Floor, New York, NY 10018 or info@skyhorsepublishing.com.

Skyhorse® and Skyhorse Publishing® are registered trademarks of Skyhorse Publishing, Inc.®, a Delaware corporation.

Visit our website at www.skyhorsepublishing.com.

10 9 8 7 6 5 4 3 2 1

Library of Congress Cataloging-in-Publication Data is available on file.

Cover design by Rain Saukas
Cover photos courtesy of the author

Print ISBN: 978-1-5107-2884-4
Ebook ISBN: 978-1-5107-2889-9

Printed in China

ACKNOWLEDGMENTS

The author gratefully acknowledges the following individuals who contributed to the completion of this book. In no particular order those individuals are:

Rob Mottice, Senior Aquarist at the Tennessee Aquarium in Chattanooga, TN, for help in identifing freshwater fish species photographed at that facility.

David Wilkins, Curator at the South Carolina Aquarium in Charleston, SC, for his help in identifying freshwater fish species photographed at his facility.

Larry Warner, North Carolina Aquarium on Roanoke Island, NC, for his help in identifying freshwater fish species photographed at his facility.

The staff of the North Carolina Aquarium at Pine Knoll Shores, NC, for help in identifying freshwater fish species photographed at that facility.

The staff at the Georgia Fish Center for helping identify minnow species photographed at that facility.

Dave Frymire for his photo contribution.

The staff at the Texas Fresh Water Fish Center for help in identifiying minnow species photographed at that facility.

John R. MacGregor, KDFWR, for providing a number of amphibian and mammal photographs used in this book and for providing technical information and scientific advice regarding the reptiles and amphibians.

Matthew R. Thomas, KDFWR, for help in identifiying several species of darters and minnows photographed by the author for this book as well as for his technical advice and icthyological expertise; and for providing a large number of fish photographs used in the book.

Amy Berry, Clay Hill Memorial Forest and Nature Center, for providing fish and amphibian specimens for photography.

Dr. Gordon Weddle Campbellsville University, for providing fish and amphibian specimens for photography.

Dr. Ritchard Kessler, Campbellsville University, for help collecting fish specimens for photography.

Judy Tipton for alerting me to the presence of and allowing me to photograph nesting birds in her yard.

Matt Wagner and John Hardy from the Mississippi Museum of Natural History for helping to ID fishes photographed in aquariums at that facility.

Brainard Palmer-Ball of the Kentucky Ornithological Society for help identifying fall warblers photographed by the author for this book.

Barbara Graham for taking the author spelunking in the sandstone caves of eastern Kentucky searching for bats to photograph.

Candy McNamee for guiding the author on a search for migratory birds along the Texas coast.

Karen Finch for guiding the author in a search for migratory birds in south Florida.

Dr. Tim Spier, Murray State University, for his help in collecting fish specimens for photography.

Jennifer Rader of the Kansas Department of Wildlife, Parks and Tourism for allowing me to photograph freshwater stream fishes at the Southeast Kansas Nature Center.

John Hewlett who accompanied the author in the field and helped locate and collect fish and reptile specimens for photography.

James Kiser for providing several photographs.

Loren Taylor, for help in locating contributing bird photographers.

Kate Slankard, for her help in locating contributing bird photographers.

Don Martin of Don Martin Bird Photography for contributing several of the more excellent bird photos in the book.

T. Travis Brown for several photo contributions.

David Speiser, www.lilibirds.com, for several professional-quality bird photo contributions.

Phil Myers, University of Michigan, for contribution of several small mammal photos.

Konrad Schmidt of North America Native Fish Association for contributions of several fish photos.

Jeffrey Offermann for photo contributions.

Uland Thomas for photo contribution.

Dave Neely for photo contribution.

Sterling Daniels, TWRA Wildlife Biologist, for his photo contribution.

Brian Zimmerman, www.ZimmermansFish.com, for several fish photo contributions.

Greg Lavaty for his photo contributions.

Margarete Novak for her photo contributions.

Robert Morin for his photo contributions.

Jeff Poklen for his photo contributions.

Fishingwithpole for his photo contribution.

James Harding for his photo contributions.

Missy Mandell for her photo contributions.

Nate Tesler for his photo contributions.

Chris Crippen for his photo contributions.

Twan Lenders for his photo contributions.

Tom Murray for his photo contribution.

Roger Tabor and Peter Steenstra of the US Fish & Wildlife Service for photo contributions.

US Forest Service for photo contribution.

And to any others whose names I forgot to include: my thanks—and my sincere apologies for inadverdantly omitting your name!

Last but certainly not least I would like to thank my publisher, Jason Katzman of Skyhorse Publishing.

In our negotiations Jason has not only shown patience and a willingness to compromise, but also great faith in this author. He has also exhibited extraordinary entrepreneurial courage in taking on a huge project of which this book is but a first step.

Finally, this book is dedicated to the author's three sons, Haydn, Denham, and Kyle Shupe. Though now adults, as youngsters their keen eyes, youthful enthusiasm, and unflinching companionship were responsible for the author getting many of the photographs in this book. More importantly, their presence in this world has consistently provided this author with the motivation to repeatedly bite off more than I can chew.

PHOTO CREDITS

Most of the 648 wildlife photographs that appear in this book were taken by the author. However, many of the really good photographs were contributed by several other wildlife photographers from across the United States and Canada. Those individuals were critical to the completion of this book and their remarkable photographs add much to its content. The names of those additional photographers and the number of photos each contributed appear below.

David Spieser — www.lilibirds.com — 15
Matthew R. Thomas — 13
John R MacGregor — 13
Don Martin Bird Photography — 10
Konrad Schmidt — 11
Brian Zimmerman — 11
Dave Neely — 4
James Harding — 4
James Kiser — 3
Robert Morin, Quebec Canada — 3
Jeff Poklen — 3
Fishingwithpole — 3
Phil Myers — 2
Missy Mandel — 2
Nate Tessler — 2
Chris Crippen — 2
Twan Leenders — 2
Greg Lavaty — 2
Jeffrey Offermann — 1
T.Travis Brown — 1
Sterling Daniels — 1
Uland Thomas — 1
Dave Frymire — 1
Wayne T. Helfrich — 1
James H. Harding — 1
Tom Murray — 1
Margaret Novak — 1
United States Fish and Wildlife Service, Roger Tabor — 1
United States Fish and Wildlife Service, Peter Steenstra — 1
United States Fish and Wildlife Service, Digital Files — 1
United States Forest Service — 1

Thanks also to many other photographers who offered their help but whose photographs I was not able to use due to redundancy or timing constraints. A complete list of photo credits appears in the back of this book.

TABLE OF CONTENTS

INTRODUCTION

New York's wildlife has always played an important role in the history of the human beings inhabiting the state. Native Americans depended on birds, mammals, and fish for sustenance. Early Europeans hunted and trapped in the region both for food and for profit.

Although the state's wildlife is still an important resource for trappers, hunters, and fishermen, wildlife is also increasingly important for its intrinsic, aesthetic value. Though the age-old practice of hunting and fishing is the most obvious example of how wildlife can enrich our lives, for many New Yorkers the opportunity to simply observe wildlife and experience nature also serves to enhance our existence.

In more recent history the pursuit of wildlife has evolved to encompass more benevolent activities such as bird watching, wildlife photography, etc. In fact, the numbers of Americans who enjoy these "non-consumptive" forms of wildlife-related recreation today exceed the numbers of those who hunt and fish, and the range of wildlife-related interests and activities has broadened considerably. In addition to the previously mentioned bird watching and wildlife photography can be added the activities of herpetology enthusiasts (reptiles and amphibians), freshwater aquarists, and lepidopterists (moths and butterflies), to name a few.

With interest in wildlife and nature continuing to grow throughout New York, the need for a single, simple reference to the state's wildlife has become evident. There are available a number of excellent books that deal specifically with New York's birds, reptiles, mammals, fishes, etc., but there are none that combine all the state's wildlife into a comprehensive, encyclopedic reference. This volume is intended to fill that niche. It is hoped that this book will find favor with school librarians, life science teachers, students of field biology classes, and professional naturalists as well as with the general populace.

As might be expected with such a broad-spectrum publication, intimate details about the natural history of individual species is omitted in favor of format that provides more basic information. In this sense this volume is not intended for use as a professional reference, but instead as a handy, usable, layman's guide to the state's wildlife. For those who wish to explore the information regarding the state's wildlife more deeply, a list of references for each chapter appears in the back of the book and includes both print and reliable internet references.

Embracing the old adage that a picture is worth a thousand words, color photographs are used to depict and identify each species. Below each photograph is a table that provides basic information about the biology of each animal. This table includes a state map with a shaded area showing the species' presumed range in the state, as well as general information such as size, habitat, abundance, etc. The taxonomic classification of each species is also provided, with the animal's Class, Order, and Family appearing as a heading at the top of each page.

The range maps shown in this book are not intended to be regarded as a strictly accurate representation of the range of any given species. Indeed, the phrase "Presumed range in New York," which accompanies each species range map, should be literally interpreted. The ranges of some species in the state may not be well documented. The range maps, for some species in this book may be regarded as at best an "educated guess." Furthermore, many wide-ranging species are restricted to regions of suitable habitat. Thus a lowland species like the Beaver, while found statewide, would not be expected to occur on the top of a mountain. Additionally, other species that may have once been found throughout a large geographic area may now have disappeared from much of their former range.

The compilation of species range maps is always a challenging endeavor. That challenge is further complicated by the fact that animals like birds and bats, possessed with the ability of flight, are capable of traveling great distances. Many species of both birds and bats are migratory and regularly travel hundreds or even thousands of miles annually. It is not uncommon for these migratory species to sometimes appear in areas where they are not typically found. The mechanisms of migration and dispersal of many animals is still a bit of a mystery and the exact reason why a bird from another portion of the country (or even from another continent) should suddenly appear where it doesn't belong is often speculation. Sometimes these appearances may represent individuals that are simply wandering. Other times it can be a single bird or an entire flock that has been blown off course by a powerful storm or become otherwise lost and disoriented. Whatever the cause, there are many bird species that have been recorded in the state that are not really a part of New York's native bird fauna, and their occasional sightings are regarded as "accidental."

On the other hand, some species may appear somewhere in the state once every few years dependent upon weather conditions or availability of prey in its normal habitat. Although these types of "casual species" could be regarded as belonging among New York's native bird fauna, their occurance in the state is so sporadic and unpredictable that deciding which species should be included as a native becomes very subjective. The point is that the reader should be advised that while all the bird species depicted in this volume can be considered to be members of the state's indigenous fauna, *not every bird species* that has been seen or recorded in New York is depicted in this book. However the reader can be assured that if a species is widespread, common, or otherwise likely to be encountered or observed, that species has been included in this book; as have *most* of the rarer and less likely to be seen species.

For readers who wish to delve into more professional and detailed information about the vertebrate zoology of New York, the list of references shown for each chapter in the back of this book should adequately provide that opportunity.

—Scott Shupe, 2017

CHAPTER 1
THE FACE OF THE LAND

— THE NATURAL REGIONS OF NEW YORK —

Defining and understanding the natural regions of New York is the first step in understanding the natural history of the state. Man-made political boundaries such as county lines and state borders are meaningless to wildlife, whereas mountains, rivers, or lakes can be important elements in influencing the distribution of the state's wildlife.

The major considerations used in determining and delineating natural regions are such factors such as elevation, relief (topography), drainages, geology, and climate. All these are important elements that can determine the limits of distribution for living organisms. It follows then that some knowledge of these factors is essential when involved in the study of the state's natural history.

The study of natural regions is known as *Physiography*, which means "physical geography" or literally "the face of the land." While the terms geography and physiography are closely related and sometimes used interchangeably, geography is a broader term which includes such things as human culture, resource use, and man's impact on the land, while physiography deals only with elements of geography created by nature.

The term used to define a major natural region is *"physiographic division."* Physiographic divisions are subdivided into smaller units called *"physiographic provinces."* There are several major physiographic divisions across the United States and Canada, and portions of three affect the state of New York. The three major physiographic divisions of New York are the *Appalachian Highland Division*, the *Central Plains Division*, and the *Atlantic Plains Division*. See Figure 3 on page 4.

Elevation and topography are the major defining characters of the three main provinces affecting New York, with the highest elevations and greatest topographical relief occurring in the mountainous areas of the Appalachian Highlands Division, which encompasses most of the land mass of the state. Just to the west of the Appalachian Province Division, the Interior Plains Division covers the rest of western New York. Finally, the Atlantic Plain Division is represented in New York by Long Island.

Each of New York's three major physiographic divisions are further divided into smaller "physiographic *provinces,*" which are then divided again into even smaller "physiographic *sections.*"

Figure 3 on page 4 is a map of the eastern United States showing where the major physiographic *divisions* of the eastern half of the country occur. Figure 4 on page 5 show how these major divisions in New York are subdivided into physiographic provinces.

Some appreciation of theses various divisions and provinces is helpful when it comes to discussing the distribution of some of the vertebrate species of New York. Many species may occur in only a few of the regions defined by the maps on the following page. Some may even be found in only one (or even a portion of one) of these regions. Thus the range maps given for some of the species depicted in this book my reflect one or more of the natural regions shown on the maps that follow on the next three pages.

Figure 1.
The counties of New York.

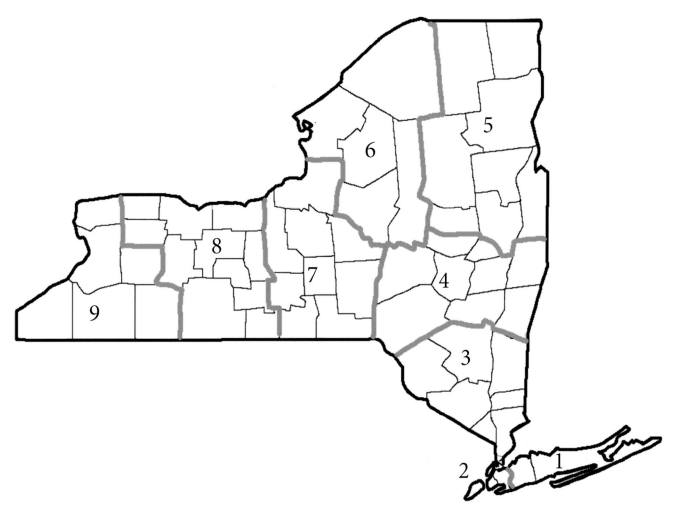

Figure 2.
The New York State Department of Environmental Conservation Regions.

Three of the major physiographic divisions shown on the map on page 4 occur within the borders of New York. The **Appalachian Highlands Division**, the **Interior Plains Division**, and the **Atlantic Plains Division.**

Figure 4 on page 5 shows how each of these divisions are subdivided into smaller *Physiographic Provinces*.

In the **Appalachian Highlands Division** the *Appalachian Plateau Province* is shown on the map above in bright green. The darker green depicts the *Ridge and Valley Province,* pea green the *Piedmont Province,* yellow the *New England Province*, and blue the *Adirondack Province*, for a total of five provinces arising from the Appalachian Highlands Division in the state of New York.

The *Interior Lowlands Province* subset of the **Interior Plains Division** is in west central New York (dark purple).

Brown depicts the *Coastal Plain Province* of the **Atlantic Plain Division**, which in New York is represented only by Long Island.

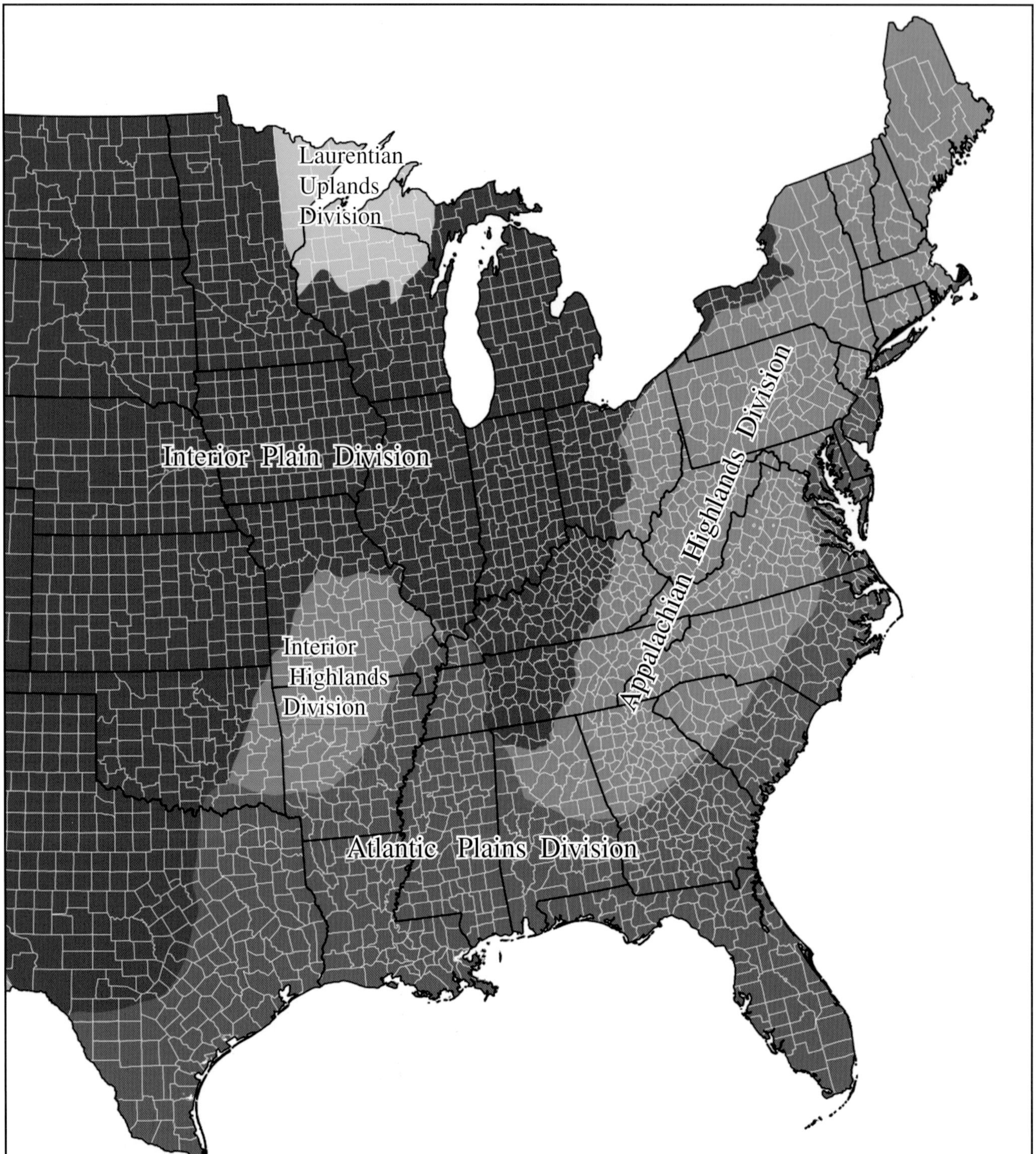

Figure 3.
Map of the eastern United States showing where the major *Physiographic Divisions* occur.
Map adapted from original produced by USGS.

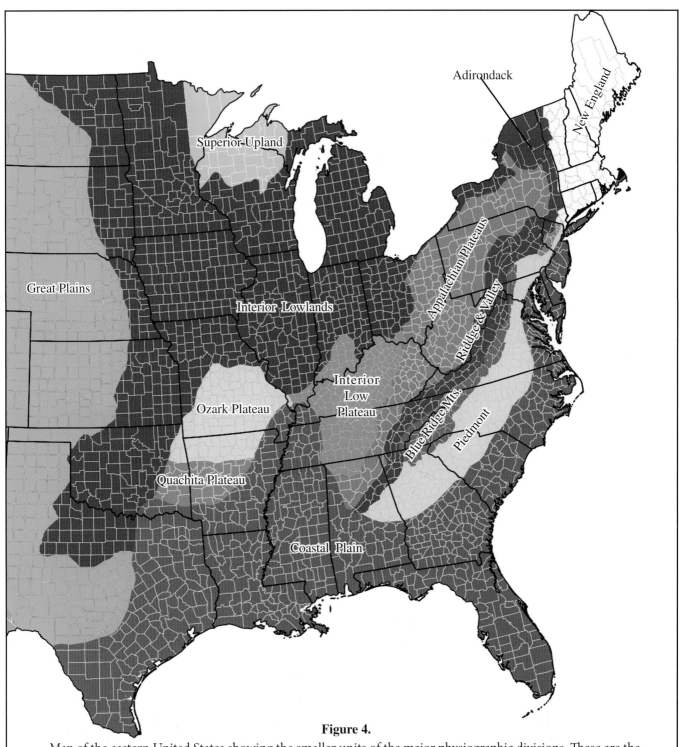

Figure 4.
Map of the eastern United States showing the smaller units of the major physiographic divisions. These are the *Physiographic Provinces* that are contained within each major division. Map adapted from original produced by USGS.

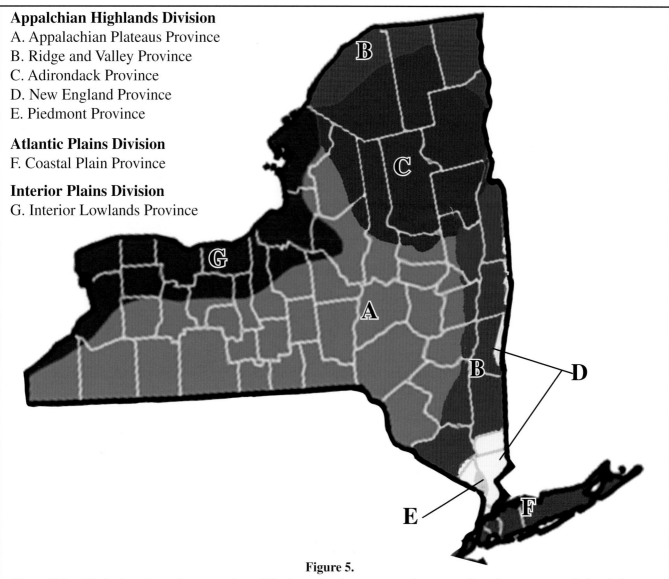

Appalchian Highlands Division
A. Appalachian Plateaus Province
B. Ridge and Valley Province
C. Adirondack Province
D. New England Province
E. Piedmont Province

Atlantic Plains Division
F. Coastal Plain Province

Interior Plains Division
G. Interior Lowlands Province

Figure 5.
Map of New York showing a close-up view of the how the three major physiographic *divisions* are subdivided into physiographic *provinces* and where each of those provinces occur in New York.

Table 1 below provides another reference for the discussion of the physiographic divisions affecting New York and their respective physiographic provinces. It should be noted that most of the provinces of the major divisions occur outside the boundaries of the state of New York. Those provinces that occur in the state of New York are shaded. Five of the six provinces of the Appalachian Highlands occur in New York, while only one province of the other two divisions occur in the state. See Figures 3 and 4 on previous pages for a visual representation of the table below.

Appalachian Highlands Division					
Appalachian Plateau P.	Piedmont P.	Blue Ridge P.	New England P.	Valley and Ridge P.	Adirondack P.

Interior Plains Division	
Interior Lowlands Province	Great Plains Province

Atlantic Plains Division	
Coastal Plain Province	Ozark Plateau Province

A written description of each of the physiographic divisions occuring in New York and their respective provinces follows:

Appalachian Highlands Division

This range of mountains, plateaus, and upland areas runs 1500 miles from Newfoundland in the north to central Alabama in the south and effectively divides most of eastern North America. These mountains constitute the second largest mountain range in the continental United States and are also one of the oldest uplifts in North America. There are a total of six smaller provinces within the Appalachian Highlands Division. The provinces that affect the state of New York as as follows:

The Appalachian Plateau Province
This is a region of older mountains that have been heavily eroded over time to produce a high plateau region that is moderately to highly dissected by rivers and streams. The entire region extends from northern Alabama to central New York and occupies the largest land mass of any of the physiographic provinces in New York. Historically this region was nearly completely covered in mature forests and the area is still mostly a heavily wooded region and most of the state's forests occur here.

The Piedmont Province
The Piedmont Province is a low plateau region on the easternmost slope of the Appalachian uplift constituting what amounts to the foothills of the Appalachian Mountain range. The Piedmont runs from east-central Alabama northeastward to New York, but only a tiny tip of the region reaches into the extreme southeastern corner of the state (see Figure 5).

The Ridge and Valley Province
This province consists of a narrow band of alternating ridges and valleys that generally have a northeast to southwest orientation. Running from Alabama to New England, for much of its length the province is sandwiched between the low hills of the Piedmont and the higher elevations of the Appalachian Plateaus (except for in the central Appalachian Highlands Division where it lies between the Piedmont and Blue Ridge provinces). In

New York it separates the New England Province from the Appalachian Plateau in the south and east, and in northern New York lies between the New England Province and the Adirondack Province.

The Adirondack Province
Endemic to the state of New York, the Adirondack Province contains the states highest elevation on Mt. Marcy. The region is well known for its boreal forests and numerous glacial lakes, as well as for the six million–acre Adirondack Park.

The New England Province
This province is contained mostly in New England to the east and northeast of the state of New York. The map on the previous page shows where this province is located in New York (in yellow). Historically this region consisted mostly of forests.

Atlantic Plains Division

The Atlantic Plains Province is divided into two provinces, the Coastal Plain and the Continental Shelf of eastern North America, which is located offshore beneath the Atlantic Ocean. The portion of the Atlantic Plain Province that occurs on land is the Coastal Plain Province.

The Coastal Plain Province
This region stretches from Cape Cod in New England to the Mexican border in south Texas, a distance of about 2200 miles. Most areas are below 500 feet in elevation. This province extends hundreds of miles inland in the Mississippi Valley. In New York only the islands of the state occur in the Coastal Plain Province.

Interior Plains Division

This is the largest physiographic division in the eastern half of the United States. It includes much of the Great Lakes region, the midwestern states, and the Great Plains region. This area includes the most geologically stable region of the United States. It is a vast plain with only moderate relief created by glacial activity and erosional action of streams dissecting the land. Only a small portion of the state of New York is affected by this division.

The portion that extends into New York is the Interior Lowlands Province.

The Interior Lowlands Province

The Interior Lowlands Province is a vast area of geologically stable bedrocks. Here the earth's crust has been little affected by the forces of plate tectonics that uplift mountains and plateaus. Most of the area is a relatively flat plain and where this province affects New York it has been subjected to the impacts of glaciation. The region of New York included in this province consists of a broad swath of land in western New York bordering lakes Erie and Huron. Relief here is slight to moderate and usually associated with the actions of rivers and streams, although in some regions glacial deposits of sand and gravel may have also contributed to its topography.

CHAPTER 2
ECOREGIONS OF NEW YORK

The maps provided in the previous chapter pertain to the "face of the land" aspects of America's and New York's natural regions. The natural topographical features of the land play an important role in determining which types of animal species live in a given area, and many species are adapted for life in a particular region, be it plains, mountains, or lowlands. But when it comes to ecoregions, an additional set of criteria comes into play. The most notable being the assemblage of plant species in a given area. Indeed, the ecoregion maps in this chapter are largely a reflection of dominant plant communities. However, many other factors are also involved in creating specific ecoregion. Included in that list of additional environmental factors are such things as precipitation amounts and temperatures (i.e., climate), soil types, geology, and hydrology.

The maps shown in this chapter are similar in many ways to the maps that depict America's physiography. In fact in some instances they are nearly synonymous. This close relationship should come as no surprise to students of natural history. Landforms, elevation, waterways, etc., have a significant impact on many of the factors that go into creating a particular ecoregion.

The ecoregion models used here are produced by the United States Environmental Protection Agency. It should be noted that in ecology, as in the study of most other scientific disciplines, different opinions exist among experts as to the definition of a particular habitat or ecoregion (such as types of forests). Man's understanding of the earth's ecology continues to evolve and not every ecologist adopts the same model or criteria in describing habitats and ecosystems. Moreover, different models may be used by different researchers based on the needs of their particular research subject.

The Environmental Protection Agency recognizes a total of fourteen "Level I Ecoregions" in the United States and Canada. Each of these Level I Ecoregions consists of several progressively smaller divisions, known respectively as Level II Ecoregions, Level III Ecoregions, and Level IV Ecoregions. The state of New York falls within two of North America's Level I Ecoregions. The regions impacting New York are known as the **Eastern Temperate Forest** and the **Northern Forest** (also known as Boreal Forest).

Figure 6 on the following page shows where the Level I Ecoregions of the North America occur. Maps on the following pages show how Level I Ecoregions are divided into Level II Ecoregions, and how Level II Ecoregions are subdivided into Level III Ecoregions. Each subsequent ecoregion has its own assemblage of plant and animal species, with that assemblage being influenced by all the factors that go into creating that particular ecoregion.

Since each ecoregion has a collection of organisms that live within that ecoregion, the range maps for some of the species depicted in this book may reflect the location of a particular ecoregion. Organisms that are dependent upon the smaller ecoregions generally tend to be more susceptible to threats, whereas organisms that are less specialized and capable of thriving in the larger ecoregions are generally much more resilient.

The designation of New York's two ecoregions as forest habitats is based on the state's *naturally occurring wildlife habitats,* i.e., the historical natural conditions found in New York prior to the changes wrought by European settlers. Obviously, today much of New York is no longer forested. Prior to European settlement, the percentage of forest cover was probably in excess of 90

Figure 6.
Level I Ecoregions of North America.
Adapted from original produced by the Commission for Environmental Cooperation.

Note: Ecoregions endemic to Mexico are not labeled.

percent. Even today the New York Department of Environmental Conservation estimates that as much as 63 percent of the state is covered in forests. Compared to other eastern states contained within the Eastern Temperate Forest Ecoregion, New York has retained a significant amount of forest. Ohio for instance has gone from being 98 percent forest (prior to settlement) to less than 30 percent today. Thus New York is truly a state consisting mainly of forest ecosytems.

Nearly all of New York's forests today are

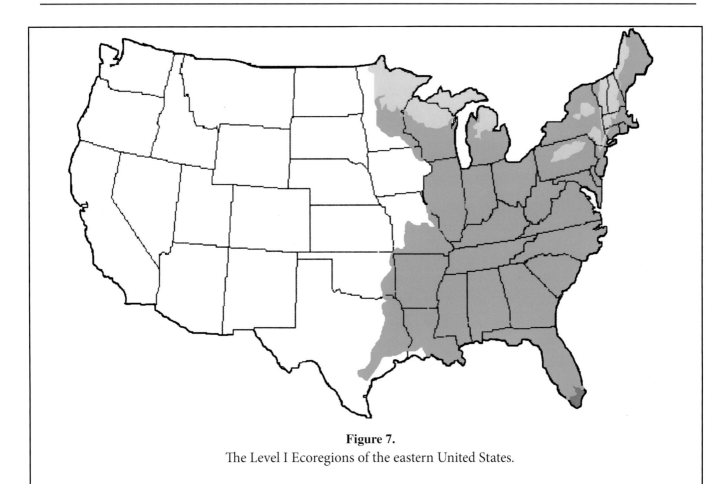

Figure 7.
The Level I Ecoregions of the eastern United States.

There are 3 Level I Ecoregions east of the Mississippi River. Blue is the **Boreal Forest**, green is the **Eastern Temperate Forest**, and purple is the **Tropical Wet Forests** of the Everglades region in south Florida. Note that the state of New York is impacted by two Level I Ecoregions (Eastern Temperate Forest and Boreal Forest).

regenerative woodlands, although some small areas of old growth still exist in the Adirondack region.

Both of New York's Level I Ecoregions are divided into progressively smaller ecoregions that more accurately reflect subtle ecological differences between regions. Figure 8 on the next page shows how the Level I Ecoregions of New York are divided into the Level II Ecoregions. Examination of that map will show that the Northern Forest Level I Ecoregions is divided into the Level II Ecoregions known as the **Mixed Wood Sheild** and the **Atlantic Highlands** ecoregions. Only one of these, the Atlantic Highlands Ecoregion, occurs in New York.

Meanwhile the Eastern Temperate Forest Level I Ecoregion is divided into five Level II Ecoregions. Of these, two occur in New York. The Level II Ecoregions found in New York are known as the **Mixed Wood**

Plains and the **Southeast Coastal Plain**, the latter of which occurs in New York only on the state's islands.

An even more finely tuned view of the ecoregions of New York is obtained by examination of the Level III Ecoregion map shown on the following page (Figure 9). Going beyond that are Level IV Ecoregions, which are even more finely tuned to the natural phenomena that goes into ecoregion designation. Among those considerations are both biotic (living) and abiotic (non-living) systems. The natural conditions involved in the abiotic aspects are such things as physiography, geology, climate, soils, and hydrology. Biotic conditions considered are plant communities and resident animal life. All these various elements are taken into consideration in ecoregion designation.

The New York Department of Environmental Conservation publication *Ecological Communites of New*

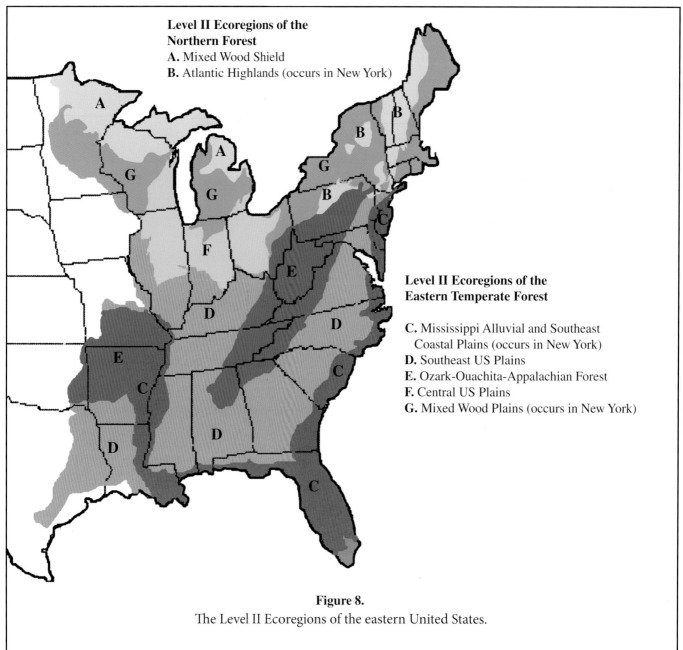

Level II Ecoregions of the Northern Forest
A. Mixed Wood Shield
B. Atlantic Highlands (occurs in New York)

Level II Ecoregions of the Eastern Temperate Forest

C. Mississippi Alluvial and Southeast Coastal Plains (occurs in New York)
D. Southeast US Plains
E. Ozark-Ouachita-Appalachian Forest
F. Central US Plains
G. Mixed Wood Plains (occurs in New York)

Figure 8.
The Level II Ecoregions of the eastern United States.

The Level II Ecoregions that occur in New York are the **Atlantic Highlands** (Level I Northern Forests), the **Southeast Coastal Plain** and the **Mixed Woods Plains** (Level I Eastern Temperate Forest).

York State, using a different, much finer model for the state's ecoregions, breaks down the various habitats of the New York into scores of ecological communites. By comparison, the ecoregion designations shown in Figures 6 through 9 are rather coarse examples of the state's natural communities.

Among the things that are readily apparent when viewing these maps of the naturally occuring regions is the fact that they have little or no relationship at all to political boundaries such as state borders or county lines. This is true both with the maps showing the physiographic provinces and for those showing the various ecoregions. Close examinatin of the maps however will reveal some correlations between physiographic and ecoregion designations.

The level III Ecoregions on the map above are further

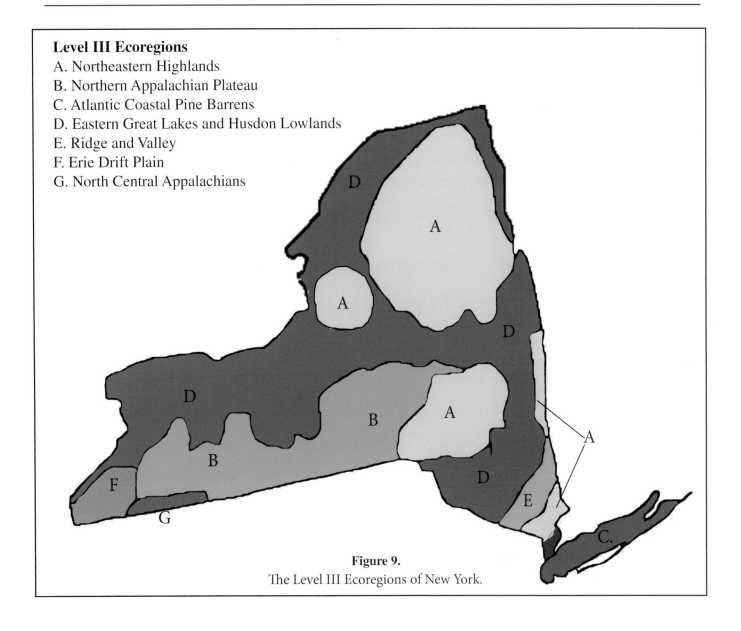

Level III Ecoregions
A. Northeastern Highlands
B. Northern Appalachian Plateau
C. Atlantic Coastal Pine Barrens
D. Eastern Great Lakes and Husdon Lowlands
E. Ridge and Valley
F. Erie Drift Plain
G. North Central Appalachians

Figure 9.
The Level III Ecoregions of New York.

refined into Level IV Ecoregions. With each subsequent hierarchical refinement the natural phenomena used to designate the ecoregion (physiography, soils, plant and animal species present, etc.) become more narrowly defined.

For those readers interested in a closer examination of the ecoregions of the state, the United States Environmental Protection Agency produces a series of downloadable PDF files of the ecoregions of North America. Included in the series of PDFs is a poster with a map and written definitions of New York state's level IV Ecoregions. Additionally, the publication *Ecological Communities of New York State*, produced by the New York Natural Heritage Program and the New York Department of Environmental Conservation, provides an extensive scientific assessment of the various habitats occuring in the state.

CHAPTER 3

THE MAMMALS OF NEW YORK

— THE ORDERS AND FAMILIES OF NEW YORK MAMMALS —

Note: The arrangement below is a reflection of how the orders and families of mammals appear in this book and may not be an accurate representation of the phylogentic relationship of the mammals.

Class - **Mammalia** (mammals)

Order - **Didelphimorphia** (opossums)

Family	**Didelphidae** (opossums)

Order - **Carnivora** (carnivores)

Family	**Procyonidae** (raccoons)
Family	**Ursidae** (bears)
Family	**Felidae** (cats)
Family	**Canidae** (canines)
Family	**Mustelidae** (weasels)
Family	**Mephitidae** (skunks)

Order - **Artiodactyla** (hoofed mammals)

Family	**Cervidae** (deer)

Order - **Lagomorpha** (rabbits and hares)

Family	**Leporidae** (rabbits)

Order - **Rodentia** (rodents)

Family	**Sciuridae** (squirrels)
Family	**Castoridae** (beaver)
Family	**Erethizontidae** (porcupine)
Family	**Muridae** (old world rats and mice)
Family	**Cricetidae** (new world rats & mice)
Family	**Dipodidae** (jumping mice)

Order - **Soricomorpha** (shrews and moles)

Family	**Soricidae** (shrews)
Family	**Talpidae** (moles)

Order - **Chiroptera** (bats)

Family	**Vespertilionidae**

Class - **Mammalia** (mammals)
Order - **Didelphimorphia** (opossums)
Family - **Didelphidae**
Virginia Opossum - *Didelphis virginiana*

Typical adult

Albino

Presumed range in New York

Typical adult

Size: About 2.5 feet from nose to tail tip. Males can weigh up to 14 pounds, females are smaller.

Abundance: Common. This is one of the most common medium-sized mammals in much of America.

Variation: Opossums can be quite variable. In most the fur is grizzled gray. Mostly white or mostly black individuals can also occur, along with a cinnamon color phase. Albino specimens like the one shown on top right are quite rare.

Habitat: Virtually all habitats within the state are utilized, including suburban and even urban areas where there is enough vegetative cover. Opossums are more common in areas altered by humans, such as farmlands and in the vicinity of small, rural communities. They are less common in areas of true wilderness.

Breeding: This is North America's only member of the mammalian subclass Marsupialia. In marsupial mammals the young are born in a highly undeveloped stage and continue their maturation in a special pouch on the mother's belly. Young Opossums are born as embryos only twelve days after conception. The newborn babies are just over .5 inch in length. At one month they are about the size of a mouse. Litters are large (up to 13) and 2 litters per year is common.

Natural History: Opossums are one of the most successful medium-sized mammals in America, which is somewhat surprising given that they are slow-moving, rather dim-witted animals that rarely survive beyond two years in the wild. They are mainly nocturnal and eat almost any palatable plant matter (seeds, grains, fruits, berries) and any type of meat they can catch or scavenge. They are known to kill and eat venomous snakes and have a strong resistance to pit viper venoms. They are well known for faking death (playing opossum) when stressed. They have strong nocturnal tendencies but they are sometimes active during the day, especially when breeding. When hard pressed they will climb to escape. In trees they use their prehensile tail to compensate for their somewhat clumsy climbing. Their greatest enemy today is the automobile. Thousands are killed nightly on highways across America. Opossums have the distinction of having more teeth than any other mammal in America. Their upper canines are often visible protruding from beneath the upper lip, giving them a rather sinister appearance. Although they are quite shy and innocuous around humans, they can give a good account of themselves in a squabble with other medium-sized carnivores. They are known to sometimes get the better of raccoons when competing for a food source. The naked ears and tail of the Opossum is vulnerable to frostbite. As a result, specimens from the northernmost portions of their range often have the top of their ears and distal portion of the tail frozen off, resulting in blunt-tailed, nearly earless specimens.

Class - **Mammalia** (mammals)

Order - **Carnivora** (carnivores)

Family - **Procyonidae** (raccoon, ringtails, coatis)	Family - **Ursidae** (bears)
Raccoon *Procyon lotor*	**Black Bear** *Ursus americanus*

Size: Up to 2.5 feet in length. Weighs 15 to 30 pounds. Record 62 pounds. Females are smaller than males and northern populations generally attain a larger size than southern populations.

Presumed range in New York

Size: Four to five feet in total length. Males can weigh over 400 pounds, females are smaller, averaging under 200. In New York the average adult male will weigh about 300 pounds. By far the largest carnivore in New York.

Presumed range in New York

Abundance: Common to very common. Can even be found in urban and suburban environments, especially if there is adequate cover in the form of trees and shrubs.

Abundance: Fairly common in suitable habitat. Today's population in New York is estimated to be around 8000 bears.

Variation: There is little variation among most specimens. A few black individuals occur occasionally. Most resemble the photo above. Some mammalogists recognize up to 25 subspecies across North America; only one occurs in New York.

Variation: Despite their name, Black Bears may be black, cinnamon, chocolate, blond, blue gray, or even white. New York specimens are invariably black in color. Cinnamon is the second most common color and occurs widely in the west.

Habitat: Found in virtually every habitat in the state. Wetlands, stream courses, and lake shores are favorite haunts. Raccoons are adaptable animals that can thrive even in cities. In some regions of America they can can actually be more common in suburbs and city parks than in remote wilderness. They are very common on Long Island.

Habitat: Throughout their range in North America, Black Bears utilize a wide array of habitats. In the deep south they use swamplands and woodlands, in the far north they are found in both boreal forests and tundra. In New York they are most common in remote wilderness but they are increasingly being seen in proximity to human-altered habitats.

Breeding: Breeds in late winter with an average of 4 (maximum of 8) young born two months later (April or May). Young begin to accompany the mother on foraging trips at about two months. They are on their own by five months. Mortality among the young can be high.

Breeding: Breeds in summer but development of the embryo is delayed until fall. 1 to 3 cubs are born in January or February in the female's winter den. Twins are common. Newborn cubs will weigh only about a pound. Females will typically breed only every other year.

Natural History: Raccoons are omnivores that feed on a wide variety of crustaceans, insects, amphibians, reptiles, small mammals, and eggs as well as grains, berries, fruits, acorns, weed seeds, and some vegetables. Although they are mainly nocturnal, they are often active by day, especially in morning and late afternoons. During particularly harsh weather they may den for days at a time. Summer dens are often tree hollows while old groundhog burrows may be used during the winter. The Raccoon is an important game animal harvested for its fur and to a lesser extent as food. When populations reach a high density they may be subjected to epidemics of canine distemper. Rabies is also well known among raccoons but it rarely poses a threat to humans.

Natural History: Young male bears will disperse for sometimes hundreds of miles, and are the first individuals to colonize a new area. A variety of plant and animal matter is eaten. The annual mast crop (acorns and nuts) is one of the most important food items in preparing for a winter hibernation that can last five months. Bears enjoy a keen sense of smell and rely more on the sense of smell and hearing than on eyesight. Most of New York's bear population resides in the Adirondacks and in the Catskills. Generally speaking, Black Bears do not pose a significant threat to humans, but attacks on humans can occur, sometimes with fatal consequences. Bears that have been fed by humans or have access to human garbage can become particularly dangerous.

Class - **Mammalia** (mammals)

Order - **Carnivora** (carnivores)

Family - **Felidae** (cats)

Bobcat *Lynx rufus*	**Canada Lynx** *Lynx canadensis*

Size: Length up to 39 inches. Weighs 15 to 35 pounds. Maximum of about 45 pounds. New York specimens are typically about 20–25 pounds for males and about 15 pounds for females.

Presumed range in New York

Size: Length up to 37 inches. Weighs 15 to 35 pounds. Maximum of about 45 pounds. No information is available on the size of New York specimens due to the fact that they are so rare.

Presumed range in New York

Abundance: Uncommon in New York.

Abundance: Extremely rare in New York.

Variation: Several subspecies occur in America but there is little variation in New York. Some specimens have more pronounced spotting to their fur and males are about one-third larger than females.

Variation: There is no variation in this species in New York. Some experts consider the population of Lynx found in the Canadian province on Newfoundland to be a distinct subspecies.

Habitat: Remote wilderness. Mountains, forests, swamps, and bogs are sanctuaries for the Bobcat in New York.

Habitat: Boreal forests are the preferred habitat of the Lynx in North America today.

Breeding: Most breeding occurs in winter or spring with an average of 3 or 4 young born two months later. Young Bobcats begin to forage with the mother by late summer and may stay with her for up to a year while perfecting hunting skills.

Breeding: Most adults will breed at about two years of age. Breeding occurs in February and March and the kittens are born in April or May. 3 or 4 young is typical but litters as large as 6 have been recorded.

Natural History: Strictly a meat eater, the Bobcat's food items range from mice to deer. Rabbits and Snowshoe Hares are a favorite prey, as are squirrels, young turkeys, and song-birds. In New York Whitetail Deer are an important element in the diet during winter months. Most (perhaps all) of the deer killed by Bobcats are either young deer or adults that have been weakened by the stress of harsh winter weather. Hunting is by ambush or by stalking to within close range and making an explosive attack. Although mainly nocturnal, Bobcats can be abroad at any time of day. Their home range can be from one to several square miles and males have larger ranges than females. Scent-marking territory with urine and feces is common. In captivity Bobcats have lived for over 20 years, but the estimate for wild cats is 12–14 years. In New York the Adirondack and Catskill areas are strongholds for this species. Although Bobcats are uncommon animals in New York, their populations are increasing and the NYSDEC has a manage-ment plan for the species that calls for a stable population of up to 8000 animals statewide. In New York the Bobcat is regarded as a game animal and a fur bearer.

Natural History: The Lynx is a true boreal species and its occurance in the eastern United States is largely restricted to the Level I Ecoregion known as "Boreal Forest" (see Figure 6). This cat is adapted to life in cold, snowy climates. It has exceptionally long legs and oversized "snowshoe-like" feet. Both are adaptations for moving through deep snow. Its prima-ry prey is the Snowshoe Hare, and the range of the Lynx in North America closely approximates the range of its primary food. Any type of small mammal or bird may be eaten, and even Whitetail Deer are sometimes killed if they are small enough or debilitated by deep snow and winter starvation. At one time the Lynx probably occurred in New York as a breeding population. Today New York represents the southern-most fringe of this species range. No confirmed breeding is known in recent times in the state, but rare sightings of this animal continue. Dispersing males travel long distances and it is reasonable to assume there will always be a few Lynx wandering into northern New York. A resurgence in Bobcats in New York may preclude the establishment of Lynx, as some evidence suggests the Bobcat is able to out-compete the Lynx.

Class - **Mammalia** (mammals)

Order - **Carnivora** (carnivores)

Family - **Canidae** (canines)

Gray Fox *Urocyon cinereoargenteus*	Red Fox *Vulpes vulpes*	Coyote *Canis latrans*

Size: Length 32 to 45 inches. Weight up to 15 pounds.

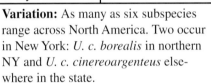
Presumed range in New York

Abundance: Fairly common.

Size: Length 33 to 43 inches. Weight up to 15 pounds.

Presumed range in New York

Abundance: Fairly common.

Size: Length up to 49 inches. Average weight about 35 pounds.

Presumed range in New York

Abundance: Fairly common.

Variation: As many as six subspecies range across North America. Two occur in New York: *U. c. borealis* in northern NY and *U. c. cinereoargenteus* elsewhere in the state.

Variation: Red Foxes can occur in several different color phases. New York specimens are typically red. Two other color phases known as the Silver Fox and the Cross Fox occur farther north.

Variation: Very dark (nearly black) individuals, tan, blond, and reddish specimens are know to occur. Most specimens in New York will resemble the photo above.

Habitat: Primarily a woodland animal that is more common in the forested regions of the state. Tends to avoid expansive open regions but may thrive where there is mosaic of woodland and farmlands.

Habitat: Although habitat generalists, Red Foxes shows a preference for open and semi-open country over deep woods. They enjoy edge areas and ecotones and have adapted well to suburban areas that have some trees and brush.

Habitat: Coyotes have adapted to all habitats in New York. They are probably most common in the Adirondacks and in the Mowhawk and St. Lawrence River Valleys, but they do occur statewide including in surburban areas.

Breeding: Dens in a burrow, hollow log or rock cave. 4 pups is usual but up to 7 is known.

Breeding: About 4–5 young are born underground, often in an old groundhog burrow, but they will dig their own hole.

Breeding: Coyotes are able to breed before their first birthday. Litter size (2–10) varies with availability of prey.

Natural History: The Gray Fox is the only American canine with the ability to climb trees. Insects are important food items in summer, with mice and rabbits becoming more important in winter. When grapes, persimmons, and other fruits are ripe they will eat them almost exclusively and in fact this is the most omnivorous canine in America. Home range can vary from a few hundred acres to over a square mile, depending upon habitat quality. Unlike the Red Fox that can be found as far north as the Arctic Circle, the Gray Fox is a more southerly animal and ranges southward into South America. Gray Foxes have lived for up to 14 years in captivity, but the average lifespan in the wild is only a few years.

Natural History: The Red Fox is one of the world's most widespread mammals and is found in Europe, Asia, north Africa, and Australia (introduced) as well as throughout North America. They are adaptable, opportunistic omnivores that will eat everything from grasshoppers to grapes. Scavenging carrion is also common. Their fur is such a good insulator that they can sleep atop a snow bank without melting the snow beneath their body. These are important fur-bearing animals and are today often reared in captivity on "fur farms." Red Fox populations in New York have probably increased since European settlement and subsequent clearing of forests for agriculture. Summer coat is paler than the luxurious winter fur.

Natural History: The Coyote is a relative newcomer to New York, having begun their invasion from the west about a half century ago. Today they range from the Pacific to the Atlantic. They are now the top predator in much of the state, occupying a niche once held by the wolf and the Cougar. They are extremely intelligent, adaptable canines that quickly learn to thrive in almost any environment. In rural areas where hunters abound they are extremely wary, but in urban areas or protected lands they may become quite bold around humans. The characteristic yipping and howling of these vocal canines has become a common nighttime sound in America. Mostly nocturnal, but also active by day. The longevity record is 18 years.

Class - **Mammalia** (mammals)

Order - **Carnivora** (carnivores)

Family - **Mustelidae** (weasels)

River Otter *Lontra canadensis*	**Fisher** *Pekania pennanti*	**Marten** *Martes americana*

River Otter

Size: Length 35–45 inches. Males can reach 30 pounds.

Abundance: Fairly common.

Presumed range in New York

Variation: As many as seven subspecies range across North America. There is very little variation in New York populations.

Habitat: Any unpolluted aquatic habitat in the state may be suitable for River Otters. They are always in association with rivers, lakes, swamps, or creeks.

Breeding: 2 or 3 young are born in an underground den often dug in a stream bank. Births are usually in the spring or summer.

Natural History: River Otters are semi-aquatic mammals that possess fully webbed toes and waterproof fur. They are excellent swimmers that prey on fish, frogs, crayfish, turtles, and small mammals. Their fur is highly valued, a fact that lead to their extirpation from much of New York and most of the eastern United States by the late 1800s. Re-stocking programs by the NYSDEC begun in 1995 have been successful and today these endearing animals can once again be found in most areas of the state where suitable habitat exists. Although there may still be parts of New York where they may not yet have colonized, it is reasonable to consider their range today as being nearly statewide. River Otters are classified as a game species by NYSDEC and limited trapping of Otters is allowed today in the northern and eastern portions of New York state.

Fisher

Size: Male can reach 4 ft. in length and 12 lbs. Female half that.

Abundance: Uncommon.

Presumed range in New York

Variation: Exhibits significant sexual dimorphism with females only half the size of males.

Habitat: The Fisher is a forest species that prefers closed canopy woodlands and avoids open areas. The bulk of the range today is mostly in the far north.

Breeding: 2 or 3 young is typical but can be more (up to 6). Nuptial den is usually a hollow in a tree. The male plays no role in rearing the young.

Natural History: By the early 1900s Fishers were nearly extirpated from New York by fur trappers and the loss of closed canopy forests as a result of logging and land clearing. The species did manage to hang on in the Adirondacks and individuals trapped there were used by NYSDEC to re-stock other regions of the state. The Fisher climbs well but is not nearly as agile in the trees as the Marten and hunting is done on the ground. Like most mustelids it is a solitary animal. All types of small mammals and birds may be prey, with Snowshoe Hares being a major food item. It is one of the few predators known to regularly kill and eat porcupines and is that animal's greatest natural enemy. The Fisher is regarded as a furbearing game species and trapping is allowed in areas of the state where the species is most abundant.

Marten

Size: Male to 27 inches and 3 lbs. Female 24 in. and 1.75 lbs.

Abundance: Uncommon.

Presumed range in New York

Variation: Females smaller than males. Fur varies from yellowish or reddish brown to black. Darkest in winter.

Habitat: Another forest species that lives mainly in mature conifer forests. In the eastern half of North America lives mostly within Boreal Forest.

Breeding: Breeding occurs in the summer but implantation of embryos is delayed and the young are not born until the following spring. 3 kits is average.

Natural History: In many respects the Marten can be regarded as a smaller, more nimble, and more arboreal version of the Fisher. The American Marten is related to the famous furbearer known as the Sable (*M. zibellina*) of Russia and northern Asia. Like that species, the fur of the Marten is luxurious and highly valued in the fur trade. This fact along with rampant logging that occurred in North America during the 1800s decimated Marten populations across most of the continent. They have semi-retractable claws like a cat and are excellent climbers. Feeds mainly on small animals, but also some berries and nuts. One of their favorite foods is the widespread Red Squirrel, as is the Red-backed Vole, both of which are species that are common in mature coniferous woodlands. Marten trapping is allowed in much of New York State.

Class - **Mammalia** (mammals)

Order - **Carnivora** (carnivores)

Family - **Mustelidae** (weasels)

Long-tailed Weasel *Mustela frenata*	Ermine *Mustela erminea*

Summer

Size: Adult males in New York average about 16 inches total length and weigh about 8 ounces. Females average 13 inches in length and weigh about 4 ounces.

Presumed range in New York

Size: Males can reach 12 inches and as much as 4 ounces. Females are about 6 to 9 inches and generally will weigh in at around 2 ounces.

Presumed range in New York

Abundance: Uncommon.

Abundance: Uncommon.

Variation: All weasels exhibit sexual dimorphism in the size of adults, with females being significantly smaller. Long-tailed Weasels in New York turn white in winter but otherwise there is no significant variation in the pelage color of New York populations. Several subspecies are recognized in North America and populations in the southwestern United States have white or creamy markings on the face.

Variation: Sexually dimorphic in size of adults. Males are nearly twice the size of females. Pelage turns all white in winter except for a black tail tip. Some mammalogists recognize as many as 19 subspecies of Ermine in North America, but there is only one subspecies in New York (*M. n. cicognanii*). There is no significant variation in pelage colors of New York populations except for seasonal molts.

Habitat: Occupies a wide variety of habitats but shows a preference for a mosaic of habitats near stream courses.

Habitat: Occupies remote northern forests and brushy edge areas, marshes, and forest openings.

Breeding: Mating occurs in mid-summer but embryo development is delayed until the following spring. 4 to 5 young is typical and babies have white fur.

Breeding: Mates in summer and experiences delayed implantation of embryos with young born the following spring. Litters number from 4 to 9.

Natural History: Long-tailed Weasels are known for being, on a pound per pound basis, one of the world's most ferocious predators. Although their prey includes animals as small as insects, they will also take prey the size of a grown Cottontail Rabbit. Mice, voles, and other rodents, along with shrews and small birds, make up the bulk of their non-invertebrate diet. Of these, voles are a favorite prey and may make up as much as one-third of the diet. They have also been known to scavenge the dead bodies of large animals such as deer. These highly active mammals have a high metabolic rate and they are active by both day and night, consuming up to a third of their body weight in a day. When an animal is killed that is too large to consume at one meal, they will cache the remains and return to finish it later. The range of this species is from northern South America to southern Canada and includes nearly all of the United States, but in many areas the population densities are quite low.

Natural History: Feeds mainly on small mammals like chipmonks, shrews, and mice. Will eat almost any kind of small vertebrate as well as insects and earthworms. Small enough to fit into the burrow of small animals like chipmonks, voles, etc. When hunting Ermine investigate hollows and crevices of trunks and stumps as well as enter the burrows of other small animals like mice and voles. They are good swimmers and climbers, so virtually no micro-habitats within their foraging range goes unhunted. They are even known to sometimes hunt in rodent tunnels beneath the snow in winter. Like all weasels, the Ermine has well-developed musk glands and scent probably plays a role in helping these solitary animals find mates. Ermine sometimes go by the name Short-tailed Weasel. Ermine range across the entire north half of North America but like other weasels they are seemingly never common and they are perhaps the least well known of New York's wild carnivores.

Class - **Mammalia** (mammals)

Order - **Carnivora** (carnivores)

Family - **Mustelidae** (weasels)	Family - **Mephitidae** (skunks)

Mink
Mustela vison

Striped Skunk
Mephitis mephitis

Size: Large males from western New York marshes can reach 23 inches and 3.5 pounds. Females 20 inches and 1.5 to 2 lbs.	Presumed range in New York	**Size:** Average length 23–31 inches, of which as much as a foot can be the tail. Average weight about 8–10 pounds.	Presumed range in New York
Abundance: Fairly common.		**Abundance:** Common.	

Variation: Males are twice as large as females. Pelage color varies from light brown to very dark brown. Mink from northern regions tend to be darker than animals from the deep south. Mink ranchers have developed a wide variety of colors ranging from white to solid black.

Habitat: Usually found near water. Swamps and marshes are the primary habitat. Found in both brackish and freshwater marshes. Also frequents creeks, rivers, and lake shores. In winter when marshes freeze over it may move into nearby woodlands.

Breeding: 3 to 6 young are born in an underground den that is often an old muskrat house. Young begin to hunt with mother at about two months.

Natural History: Mink are well known for their luxurious fur. Most mink fur sold in America today is from captive, farm-raised mink. Mink are excellent swimmers and will catch fish in stream pools. They are strict carnivores that feed heavily on amphibians and crayfish during the summer. In winter their diet turns to mammal prey such as rabbits and rodents. Muskrats are a favorite winter food of the large males who kill their formidable prey with a bite to the back of the neck. As with other members of the Mustelidae family, mink have well-developed musk glands that produce a distinct musky odor when the animal is excited, breeding, or marking territory. The range of the mink extends from the southeastern United States all the way to Alaska, including most of Canada. They range thoughout the state in New York.

Variation: Varies considerably in the amount of white in the dorsal stripes. Typical adult (shown above) has two distinct stripes down the back. In some individuals these stripes can coalesce and create a solid white back. In others, the stripes on the back may be absent entirely (see inset photo).

Habitat: Striped Skunks are found in all habitats in New York except for permanent wetlands, but they are most common in mixed habitats and edge areas. The presence of at least some woodland or brushy cover somewhere within the home range is desirable, as is a source of permanent water.

Breeding: Breeding occurs in late winter. Litter size averages 3 or 4 but can be as many as 10. Weanlings follow the mother in single file while foraging.

Natural History: The Striped Skunk's distinctive black and white color is almost as well known as its primary defense, which of course is to spray an attacker with its pungent, foul-smelling musk. The musk can burn the eyes and membranes and its odor is remarkably persistent. They can effectively project the musk up to about 15 feet and the odor can be detected hundreds of yards away. A direct hit to the face from the musk glands can cause debilitating nausea and temporary blindness. Striped Skunks dine mainly on inverte-brates and as much as three-fourths of their diet consists of insects and grubs. They possess well-developed front claws for digging and a powerful sense of smell for locating buried grubs, worms, etc. Also eats baby mice, eggs, and nestlings of ground-nesting birds. They can be particularly damaging to nesting turtles as they sniff out the nest and consume eggs.

Class - **Mammalia** (mammals)
Order - **Artiodactyla** (hoofed mammals)
Family - **Cervidae** (deer)

Whitetail Deer - *Odocoileus virginianus*		
Buck	Doe	Fawn

Size: Males up to 40 inches high at shoulder. Females about 20 percent smaller. Mature males can weigh nearly 300 pounds, females up to 150, though most are smaller. Deer from the northern states like New York have larger body size than those in the southern United States. This is due to a phenomena known as "Bergman's Rule." Larger bodies lose heat less rapidly due to the smaller ratio of body volume to surface area, thus in colder regions mammals with a larger body size tend to survive better.

Abundance: Very common. Perhaps least common in the Adirondack region.

Variation: There are as many as thirteen different subspecies of Whitetail Deer recognized in mainland North America, plus several more island races. The New York subspecies is the Northern Woodland Whitetail Deer, *Odocoileus virginianus borealis*. Young (fawns) exhibit a pattern of white spots that fade with age. Adults have reddish brown color in the summer and grayish in the fall/winter.

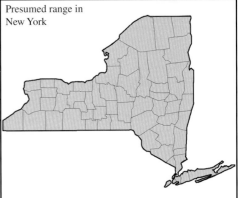

Presumed range in New York

Habitat: Found in virtually every habitat within the state and increasingly common in urban areas. Favorite habitats are a mix of woodland, brushy areas, and weedy fields, especially near farmlands. Successional areas such as regrowth of woodlands after fires or logging is also a prime habitat. In New York, deer are more common where there is a mixture of agricultural land and woodlands and increasingly in suburban neighborhoods. They are least common in mature, unbroken forests.

Breeding: Breeding begins in early fall and may continue into the winter, with the peak breeding season occurring in November. 1 to 2 (rarely 3 or even 4) young are born in the spring or early summer following a six-and-a-half-month gestation. Females (does) usually bear their first offspring at two years of age. The first pregnancy typically results in a single fawn, the second pregnancy usually is twins and the third through fifth twins or triplets (rarely quadruplets). Young lie hidden for the first few weeks and are left alone much of the time. The female will visit the hidden fawn about once every four hours to allow nursing, then moves away to avoid attracting predators. At about one month of age the young will begin to follow the mother and stay close through the summer and into the fall.

Natural History: Bucks (males) shed their antlers each year in late winter and regrow a new set by fall. Growing deer antlers are among the fastest growing animal tissue known. While growing, the antlers are covered in a spongy, fuzzy skin called "velvet." Antlers grow larger each year, up to about six or seven years of age, when they begin a gradual decline. Whitetail Deer are browsers and they feed on a wide variety of forbs, leaves, twigs, buds, crops, and mast (especially acorns). Although they are sometimes destructive to farm crops like corn or soybeans, they are an important game animal in New York with as many as 220000 harvested in 2015 for food and sport. The maximum lifespan is 20 years, but most are dead by age 10. State wildlife agencies like the NYSDEC are charged with the responsibility of protecting and managing the state's wildlife populations. In New York, this means taking into consideration not only the health and well-being of the state's deer herd, but also the cultural aspect of providing food and recreation for the state's hunting population. Additionally, considerations such as crop depredation by deer to the state's farmers or impacts on auto insurance rates by deer-auto collisions must be a part of the calculation. Thus determining how many deer of what sex should be harvested annually involves taking into consideration many factors. Happily, this animal represents one of the world's great wildlife conservation stories. Nearly wiped out by the early 1900s, the Whitetail Deer is today is perhaps as numerous in America as it was during the time of Daniel Boone. At present, the population in New York may exceed a million deer, up from a low of only a few thousand a century ago. In recent years these animals have begun to invade urban areas where deer hunting is restricted. In towns and cities they can become a nuisance.

Class - **Mammalia** (mammals)
Order - **Artiodactyla** (hoofed mammals)
Family - **Cervidae** (deer family)

Moose
Alces alces

Size: In New York mature males (Bulls) can weigh as much as 1200 pounds. They stand 7.5 feet tall at the shoulder and are 10 feet in length. Females are smaller but can still weigh 800 pounds. Bulls in their prime can have antlers that are five feet across. Animals from the western half of the continent are even larger. The largest Moose (from Alaska and northwestern Canada) can weigh as much as 1800 pounds and have an antler spread well over 6 feet. They are the largest member of the deer family and one of the largest land mammals in North America.

Abundance: Rare in New York. Restricted mostly to northern New York.

Variation: Sexually dimorphic. Males of course have antlers most of the year. Professional mammalogists recognize four different moose populations (subspecies) in North America. The moose that inhabits portions of New York state belong to the subspecies *americana,* often called the Eastern Moose.

Presumed range in New York

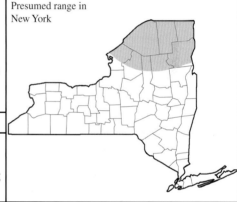

Habitat: Moose in New York are primarily a boreal forest species. Regenerative forests with large amounts of browse are preferred, as are swamps and shallow lakes with abundant aquatic vegetation. These wetland habitats are utilized mostly in summer with drier mixed conifer-hardwood forests used in winter. Forest clearings created by fire or logging are heavily used.

Breeding: Breeding activity begins as early as September. During the "rut" bulls will become vocal and emit a bellowing call to attract any nearby cows. Additional rutting activity by males includes slashing saplings and bushes with the antlers. Fights between bulls are usually brief but can on rare occasions become intense and result in injury to one or both males. Following mating the cow will give birth eight months later in late May or June. A single calf is typical, with twins being uncommon and triplets quite rare. The young calves nurse for up to six months and will usually remain with the cow until she drives them off just before giving birth to her next calf.

Natural History: Moose are holarctic in distribution and are found across all of northern North America, northern Europe, and northern Asia. In Scandanavia they go by the name "Elk." Cow moose will sometimes vigorously defend their young and they have been known to attack humans who get too close to the young with deadly consequences. Likewise, bull moose in the rut may become very agressive towards any large animal in their immediate vicinity. Most of the time however they are placid animals. The massive antlers of a mature bull are shed by mid-winter and re-grown every year. To accomplish this remarkable growth the moose must consume prodigous quantities of browse. Up to 40 pounds may be consumed daily. In many areas of their range willow and alder are favorite foods but a wide variety of tree leaves are eaten during summer months. They also love aquatic plants which grow in shallow lakes, beaver ponds, and swamps and will submerge the entire head to reach plants beneath the surface. Leaves, stems, and roots are all eaten. During winter the buds and bark of the terminal branches of deciduous trees and shrubs are eaten along with the needles of conifers such as balsam fir. Additional food items include mosses, lichens, and mushrooms. Except during the breeding season or in the case of a cow with calves, moose are mostly solitary animals. Wolves, where they are present in the ecosystem, are the biggest natural enemy of moose. In New York, Black Bears are a major threat to the young calves. But the biggest threat to moose in New York today is probably the parasitic nematode known as "Brain Worm." This devasting disease is harbored and spread by Whitetail Deer.

Class - **Mammalia** (mammals)

Order - **Lagomorpha** (lagomorphs)

Family - **Leporidae** (rabbits and hares)

Eastern Cottontail *Sylvilagus floridanus*	Snowshoe Hare *Lepus americanus*

Summer

Transitional

Size: Adult length about 14 inches. Weight up to 2.5 pounds.	Presumed range in New York 	**Size:** Total length about 16 inches. Typical adult weight about 3 pounds.	Presumed range in New York 
Abundance: Generally very common but subject to localized cyclical population fluctuations.		**Abundance:** Fairly common. Populations in many areas are cyclical on an approximately 10-year cycle.	

Variation: No variation in New York, but at least 12 very similar subspecies of this wide ranging rabbit are recognized across the United States by some mammalogists.	**Variation:** Summer pelage is brown. Winter is solid white except for black tips on the ears. Transitional fall pelage is shown in inset photo above.
Habitat: May be found in virtually any habitat within the state except for permanent wetlands. Most common in overgrown fields and edge areas. Fond of briers, brushy areas, and tall weeds.	**Habitat:** Boreal forests are the primary habitat. Within this ecosytem they favor areas with dense understory. They will move between primarily conifer woodlands in summer to mostly deciduous woodlands in winter.
Breeding: This is the most prolific of the several rabbit species in America, some populations in the south produce up to seven litters per year with as many as 5 young per litter.	**Breeding:** Capable of breeding at about one year of age. Averages about 3 young per litter and multiple litters per year is common.
Natural History: In the spring and summer Eastern Cottontails feed on a wide variety of grasses, legumes, and herbaceous weeds. Briers, sapling bark (especially Sumac) leaf buds, and other woody materials may make up the bulk of the diet in winter. During periods of deep snow they will spend the day burrowed under the snow and emerge at night. These rabbits are prey for many predators including foxes, coyotes, bobcats, and hawks and owls, especially the Great Horned Owl. The life expectancy for a Cottontail is not high, and only about one in four will live to see their second birthday. Populations are known to fluctuate, and during years when their numbers are highest good habitat may support up to nine rabbits per acre. They are an important game animal and their flesh is regarded by many as being highly palatable. Another species of Cottontail, known as the **New England Cottontail** (*Sylvilagus transitionalis*), is a very rare resident in a small area of extreme southeastern New York along the Connecticut border. The differences between the two species are indistinguishable to the lay observer.	**Natural History:** The name Snowshoe Hare is derived from the exceptionally large, heavily furred hind feet which act as natural snowshoes and allow this hare to move easily atop deep, powdery snow. The transition from brown summer pelage to all white winter pelage seen in the Snowshoe Hare is an adaptation used by a number of mammal species that live in regions where snow covers the ground all winter. In the Adirondacks region of New York a rare and engimatic all black color morph of this hare is known. Summer foods are all types of greenery including grasses, clovers, ferns, and forbs such as the Dandelion. In winter the diet switches to bark and buds of a wide variety of both conifer and deciduous trees. As the snow gets deeper, the hare, moving across the top of the snow, feeds higher and higher into the branches. Like other members of the order Lagamorpha, these hares eat their own droppings (coprophagy). This trait allow for maximum extraction of nutrients. Populations show a cyclical pattern over a 10-year period, with numbers gradually increasing to a high density then crashing suddenly.

Class - **Mammalia** (mammals)

Order - **Rodentia** (rodents)

Family - **Sciuridae** (squirrels)

Groundhog *Marmota monax*	**Eastern Chipmunk** *Tamias striatus*	**Red Squirrel** *Tamiasciurus hudsonicus*
		 Summer

Size: Length 16 to 26 inches and weighs from 6 to 9 pounds.	Presumed range in New York	**Size:** About 10 inches in length and weighing about 4.5 ounces.	Presumed range in New York	**Size:** Total length 12 inches. Tail 5 inches. Weight 6 ounces.	Presumed range in New York
Abundance: Common.		**Abundance:** Common.		**Abundance:** Common.	

Groundhog	Eastern Chipmunk	Red Squirrel
Variation: Individuals vary in color from brown to grayish, reddish, or rarely, nearly black. Most specimens in New York resemble the specimen shown above.	**Variation:** There are several subspecies nationwide and two occur in New York. The differences are very subtle. All New York Chipmunks resemble the specimen shown above.	**Variation:** Summer pelage is duller and less red and the prominent "ear tufts" are only seen in fall and winter squirrels. Otherwise there pelage color is remarkably consistant.
Habitat: Fields and woodland edges. They require some open ground within the vicinity of the burrow for foraging, as well as higher ground that is above the floodplain for locating the burrow.	**Habitat:** Deciduous forests in upland areas are the preferred habitat. It avoids wetlands and is fond of rock outcrops, stone fences, etc. Can be common in urban parks and suburbs.	**Habitat:** Like most tree squirrels, this is a forest species. Any type of northern forest may be inhabited, including deciduous and mixed, but conifer forests are where they are most common.
Breeding: Mating occurs in March or April with 2 to 4 young typical. Only one litter per year. Young remain underground until weaned at six weeks.	**Breeding:** Breeding occurs in very early spring with young born about a month later. Litters average 3 to 5 but can be as many as 8.	**Breeding:** Capable of producing two broods per year. 3 to 5 young is typical. In years of good mast crops they may produce larger litters of 7 or 8.
Natural History: These large ground squirrels dig extensive underground burrows where they retreat from danger, spend the night, and overwinter. They accumulate huge deposits of fat during the summer and fall, which sustains them during winter hibernation. During this time their metabolism slows dramatically with as few as four heartbeats per minute. They will sometimes climb small trees and bushes in springtime to eat swelling tree buds, but their primary diet is forbs and grasses. Also known by the name "Woodchuck." Their empty burrows are used as dens by a wide variety of animals, making them an ecologically important species. As they avoid extensive forests, they have benefited from human activity.	**Natural History:** While they are excellent climbers, chipmunks are true "ground squirrels," sleeping, rearing young, and wintering in an underground burrow which they dig themselves. They also will use rock crevices or hollow logs. They become less active in winter and will remain below ground living on stored nuts and seeds for long periods during harsh weather. Although Chipmunks are fairly common in much of New York they are usually absent from expansive open areas and areas of extensive agriculture. Like other squirrels, the Chipmunk is a vocal animal but its voice is less raspy, sounding at times like the chirping of a bird. Longevity is reported to be as much as eight years, but very few in the wild survive that long.	**Natural History:** Like most tree squirrels, the Red Squirrel is diurnal in habits. While most people find them to be endearing little animals, others regard them as pests and there is a widespread myth among squirrel hunters that Red Squirrels will attack and castrate the males of the more desirable (from the hunter's point of view) Gray Squirrel. Red Squirrels will store huge piles of conifer cones, usually at the base of large tree. These piles are known as "middens" and they can attain an enormous size. Piles 15 feet across and 3 feet high have been recorded. The range of the Red Squirrel includes all of Canada except the arctic and the Great Plains, and all the northern United States and south in the Appalachians to Georgia.

Class - **Mammalia** (mammals)		
Order - **Rodentia** (rodents)		
Family - **Sciuridae** (squirrels)		

Gray Squirrel *Sciurus carolinensis*	**Fox Squirrel** *Sciurus niger*	**Southern Flying Squirrel** *Glaucomys volans*

Size: 19 inches in total length. Weight about 18 ounces. 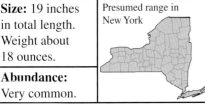 Presumed range in New York	**Size:** Length 23 inches from snout to tail tip. Weighs about 28 ounces. Presumed range in New York	**Size:** Length from 8 to 10 inches and 2–3 ounces.  Presumed range in New York
Abundance: Very common.	**Abundance:** Uncommon.	**Abundance:** Fairly common.
Variation: At least six subspecies occur in the United States and some are quite variable. Melanistic (black) populations can be found in some areas of New York and albino populations occur in a few locations. Some New York specimens may have reddish brown tails but most resemble the specimen pictured above.	**Variation:** There are a total of 10 subspecies nationwide and they range in color from solid black to reddish to silver-gray. *S. n. rufiventer* (reddish phase) occurs in New York. Most are like the specimen shown above, but a variety of color morphs may be seen in other regions.	**Variation:** Two identical species of Flying Squirrels occur in New York. Pictured above is the Southern Flying Squirrel. The very similar **Northern Flying Squirrel** (*Glaucomys sabrinus*) is an identical but slightly larger version with browner fur and a more grayish belly. It can reach 14 inches in length.
Habitat: Prefers mature deciduous forests but also found in mixed coniferous forests and second growth areas. Can be common in urban parks and lawns.	**Habitat:** Prefers open forests with trees widely spaced. Can be common in swamps. Prefers edge areas, overgrown fence rows, etc. over extensive woods.	**Habitat:** These little squirrels are dependent upon trees and live only in woodlands. They will live in suburbs if sufficient mature trees are present.
Breeding: Breeds December through February and again in June/July. 4 to 6 young per litter.	**Breeding:** Produces 4 to 6 young twice annually, breeding in winter and again in summer.	**Breeding:** Only one litter per year with up to 6 young. Nest is usually within a hollow in a tree.
Natural History: Feeds on nuts, seeds, fungi, tree buds, and the inner bark of trees as well as bird eggs and hatchlings. May sometimes even eat carrion. Like most rodents they will gnaw bones or shed deer antlers for calcium. Well known for burying and storing nuts. Frequently calls with a raspy "bark," especially when alarmed. Builds summer nests of leaves in tree crotches. Winter dens are in tree hollows. During severe weather may be inactive for several days. Poor mast years may produce mass migrations. Gray Squirrels are extremely athletic little animals and exhibit remarkable agility in trees. They are strictly a woodland animal and require a source of mast for their survival.	**Natural History:** Fox Squirrels wander frequently into open areas and spend more time on the ground than Gray Squirrels. Their home range may be ten times larger. They are generally less common than the Gray, rarely reaching the population densities of their smaller cousins. They feed on the same foods of nuts, seeds, buds, berries, etc. But the diet of Fox Squirrels also often includes the seeds of pine cones. Barks and chatters when disturbed but is overall less vocal than the smaller squirrel species which occur in New York. Although widespread across the United States, New York represents the northeastern edge of this species range in North America.	**Natural History:** Nocturnal in habits. Leaps from tree to tree and glides using flaps of skin between front and hind legs like a parachute. Flattened tail serves as a rudder while gliding. Feeds on nuts, seeds, fruits, fungi, lichens, tree buds, insects, bird eggs, and nestling birds as well as mice. Flying Squirrels are gregarious animals and several may share a den. Southern Flying Squirrels are more common in southern New York, while the northern species is mostly in northern New York, but both do occur statewide. Flying Squirrels in rural areas sometimes invade homes and attics where they can become a noisy nuisance as they scramble about in the wee hours. Longevity for captives is 10 years.

Class - **Mammalia** (mammals)

Order - **Rodentia** (rodents)

Family - **Castoridae** (beaver family)

Beaver - *Castor canadensis*	Beaver dam (top) - Beaver lodge (bottom)

Size: Up to 43 inches in total length. Can weigh up to 65 pounds. 35 to 50 pounds is average.

Abundance: Common. Least common in uplands but is present in valleys and along stream courses in mountains.

Presumed range in New York

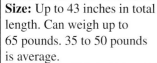

Variation: The American Society of Mammalogists recognizes 24 subspecies in North America. The status of Beavers in the eastern United States is difficult to determine due to re-introduction programs using transplanted Beavers from many regions of the country.

Habitat: Beavers are thoroughly aquatic mammals that to a great extent create their own wetland habitats. To construct their ponds and waterways they require the presence of a stream or spring run with constant or near constantly flowing water which can be dammed. Streams that are subject to fierce flooding or with exceptionally powerful flows are avoided in preference for more easily contained water flows. In addition to creating their own habitats they will use lakes, rivers, swamps, marshes, and large, deep creeks. In rivers and lakes the lodge or den is often a burrow into the bank of the lake or river. In dammed streams or swamps and marshes a stick lodge typical of the one pictured above is usual. Although they are found throughout New York in the Appalachian Highlands they are restricted to river valleys, bottomlands, and stream courses.

Breeding: Mating takes place in mid-winter with the young being born about four months later. There is only one litter per year. Baby beavers are quite precocious and are born with well-developed fur and eyes that open immediately. Four or five young, called kits, is typical. In ideal habitats more young may be produced. Young beavers are usually weaned in just two/three weeks, but the young Beavers will remain with the family for up to two years before striking out on their own to find new territories. Adult beavers may mate for life.

Natural History: Beavers are primarily nocturnal in habits, but they may be active at dawn and dusk. In remote locations where human intrusion is absent, they are observed active during the day as well. They feed mostly on the inner bark of trees, with willow being a dietary mainstay. They will also consume sedges and other aquatic vegetation, but in winter live almost exclusively on bark. The dorsal-ventrally flattened tail is hairless and scaly and along with the webbed hind feet provide these animals with powerful swimming tools. They also possess enlarged incisors which grow continually throughout life and are used to gnaw through trunks and fell trees. Most trees cut by Beavers are small saplings which are used as food, but they will also cut large trees up to two feet in diameter to open the canopy and promote the growth of new food sources. These largest of the North American rodents are famous for their dam-building abilities and they will also build elaborate living quarters known as "lodges." After many years of use these lodges may become up to 15 feet across and can house an entire extended family. They have underwater entrances for protection and a hollow "room" that is above the waterline and lined with wood chips or grasses. Other species such as Muskrats and mice may take up residence within these lodges. At one time Beaver fur was one of the most valuable natural resources in America and the pursuit of Beaver fur led to the exploration of much of the continent. Within a few decades they were nearly exterminated by trappers. They can sometimes be a pest when their dam-building activities flood farmers fields, but their wetland-creating activities benefit many scores of wetland wildlife species. In fact, the Beaver is one of the most significant players in local ecosystems throughout North America and their value to the overall ecology would be hard to overstate.

Class - **Mammalia** (mammals)		

Order - **Rodentia** (rodents)		

Family - **Erethizontidae** (porcupine)	Family - **Muridae** (old world mice and rats)	
Porcupine *Erethizon dorsatum*	**Norway Rat** *Rattus norvegicus*	**House Mouse** *Mus musculus*

Size: Maximum adult size is 50 inches in length and 40 pounds.  Presumed range in New York	**Size:** Length can be as much as 15 inches and weigh up to 12 ounces.  Presumed range in New York	**Size:** Adults about 6.5 inches and weigh about .75 ounce.  Presumed range in New York
Abundance: Uncommon.	**Abundance:** Very common.	**Abundance:** Very common.

Variation: There is no significant variation in this species in New York.	**Variation:** None in the wild. Domestic forms can be brown, gray, black, or white.	**Variation:** Wild specimens show no variation, but domesticated laboratory mice come in a variety of colors.
Habitat: In New York the Porcupine inhabits coniferous forests and mixed conifer-hardwood forests. Pure deciduous stands are also heavily used.	**Habitat:** This highly adaptable rodent can live virtually anywhere, including as a stowaway on ships, which is how it immigrated to America from Europe.	**Habitat:** A highly adaptable and successful rodent that usually associates with human habitations and man-made structures, also lives in the wild.
Breeding: Mating occurs in the fall. Single baby is born in the spring. Young are very precocial and born fully furred. Quills harden an hour after birth.	**Breeding:** The fecundity of the Norway Rat is legendary. From six to eight litters per year with up to a dozen young per litter is possible if abundant food is available.	**Breeding:** Broods can number from 5–12. Young females begin breeding at six weeks and can produce 14 litters per year.
Natural History: Except for gnawing shed deer antlers for minerals, the Porcupine is a true vegetarian. In summer they feed on a wide variety of tree leaves and buds as well as doing some ground feeding on forbs and grasses. In the fall mast is added to the diet. In winter they subsist mostly on the inner bark of tree branches. During harsh weather they may seek refuge in a tree hollow or rock crevice for a few days at a time. But their heavy winter fur provides remarkable protection against the cold and they have been known to "ride out" a blizzard perched high in a tree! The quills of the Porcupine are legendary and are more than an adequate defense against most predators. The Fisher, a large member of the Weasel family, is the only predator known to regularly kill Porcupines. The flesh of these animals is said to be palatable.	**Natural History:** Also called the Brown Rat, this species has followed man to every corner of the globe. They are responsible for an almost unimaginable degree of human suffering. Throughout the history of human civilization these rodents have destroyed crops and stored foods while spreading devastating diseases, most notably Bubonic Plague and Typhus. It is the rat's fleas and lice that are the actual vectors of these diseases. Though less of a threat to modern societies, these rats still shadow the human species. They are common in both urban and rural settings. In cities they live on human garbage, in rural areas livestock food and crops. The common laboratory rat is an albino domesticated version of this animal that has somewhat redeemed the species for humans as an experimental animal for medical and scientific research.	**Natural History:** The House Mouse has adapted to living in close proximity to humans and today they are found wherever there are people throughout the world. As their name implies, they regularly enter into houses where they can become both a pest and a health hazard. They live both in cities and farmlands. Like the Norway Rat the House Mouse originated in Eurasia and traveled around the world as a stowaway on sailing ships, eventually populating the entire globe. These mice are primarily nocturnal and their food includes nearly everything eaten by humans plus insects and fungi. Domestic versions are the familiar "white mice." Given maximum litter size and 100 percent survival of each subsequent generation, two mice in one year could result in 1800 mice! Snakes are perhaps the best means of natural control of these mice.

Class - **Mammalia** (mammals)

Order - **Rodentia** (rodents)

Family - **Cricetidae** (native mice and rats)

White-footed Mouse *Peromyscus leucopus*	**Deer Mouse** *Peromyscus maniculatus*	**Southern Bog Lemming** *Synaptomys cooperi*

Size: 7 inches total length Weighs about 1 ounce. Presumed range in New York	**Size:** 5–8 inches total length. Weighs about 1 ounce.  Presumed range in New York	**Size:** Adult is 5 inches (total length) and 1.25 ounces.  Presumed range in New York
Abundance: Common.	**Abundance:** Common.	**Abundance:** Fairly common.
Variation: Winter pelage is grayer than the brownish summer pelage. Young mice are also grayer.	**Variation:** Varies from brownish to grayish with or without a dark mid-dorsal stripe. Juveniles are always grayish.	**Variation:** Several subspecies are recognized across North America but there is little variation in New York.
Habitat: White-footed Mice prefer the woods but may also be found in overgrown fields, fence rows, etc. These mice tend to avoid open areas.	**Habitat:** Deer Mice can be found in both woodland habitats and open fields, including agricultural land and even in wide-open, harvested crop fields.	**Habitat:** Although they can found in bogs, they occupy nearly all habitat types. The presence of grasses seems to be the main habitat requirement.
Breeding: 4 to 5 young is typical. Breeding takes place in spring (March to May) and fall (as late as October). Multiple litters are produced annually.	**Breeding:** Breeding in New York probably takes place from spring to late summer. The 5 or 6 young wean at three weeks and are ready to breed at six weeks.	**Breeding:** Breeds most of year except for mid-winter. Typical litter is 3 with a maximum of 8. Young are weaned at three weeks of age.
Natural History: Mainly nocturnal in activity. Omnivorous in feeding habits and consumes a wide variety of seeds and nuts. Known to cache large stores of food in hollows. During summer months becomes quite invertivorous and is known to also eat small vertebrates on occasion. The White-footed Mouse is so similar to the Deer Mouse that professional mammalogists use measurements of the skull, tail, and hind foot to differentiate between these two sympatrically occurring species. Both these species are a major food source for a wide variety of predator species. Hawks, owls, foxes, coyotes, bobcats, snakes, and literally every other predator in the forest, including tiny, ravenous shrews, will make a meal of the *Peromyscus* mice. In this regard these handsome little mice are important elements in local ecosystems.	**Natural History:** Primarily nocturnal. They feed on a wide array of seeds, nuts, and grain as well as berries, insects, snails, centipedes, fungi, and occasionally other mice. They will cache large stores of seeds and nuts in the fall and they remain active throughout the winter. These common mice serve as prey for a variety of predators, from coyotes and bobcats to weasels, snakes, and birds of prey. They are an enigmatic species that is very difficult to properly identify. There are two morphological forms of Deer Mouse, one is a long-tailed, large-eared form that lives in woodlands, the other a short-tailed, small-eared form that lives in open fields. But both are apparently the same species! Additionally, the woodland form is nearly identical to the White-footed Mouse! Even professional mammalogists often must resort to laboratory examination for ID.	**Natural History:** Bog Lemmings often use the same burrows as other mice and vole species, as well as mole tunnels. They also make runways on the surface beneath leaf litter or grass/vegetation. Primarily nocturnal and crepuscular, they feed on green plants and berries mainly. They often occur in colonies. Bog Lemmings are mainly northern mammals that range southward into the southern Appalachians as far as east Tennessee and western North Carolina. They also occur in parts of Kentucky, Missouri, and Kansas. Though their range includes the entire state of New York, they may be very locally distributed. Some experts suspect that the Bog Lemming may be declining as a result of competition with the more common Meadow Vole. As is the case with other small mammals, this is an important prey species for many predators.

Class - **Mammalia** (mammals)

Order - **Carnivora** (carnivores)

Family - **Cricetidae** (native rats and mice)

Meadow Vole *Microtus pennsylvanicus*	Woodland Vole *Microtus pinetorum*	Southern Red-backed Vole *Myodes gapperi*

Meadow Vole — **Size:** About 6.5 inches and 1.75 ounces. Maximum of 6.75 inches.

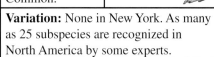

Presumed range in New York

Abundance: Common.

Variation: None in New York. As many as 25 subspecies are recognized in North America by some experts.

Habitat: Primarily fields and meadows from the northern United States to the Arctic Circle. They are perhaps least common in large, contiguous forest regions. Seems to show a preference for moist soils.

Breeding: A remarkably fecund animal, young Meadow Voles can breed within four weeks after birth. Litter size is 4 to 6.

Natural History: Generally regarded as the world's most prolific mammal. Populations in many areas are cyclical and during years of high population density there can be as many as several hundred per acre in prime habitat. Because they can be so common, these voles are an important food source for predatory species ranging from snakes and carnivorous mammals to birds of prey. They can also impact humans by eating crops, garden produce, young trees in orchards, etc. They feed on a wide variety of grasses and plants and will eat seeds, roots, and even bark. The well-maincured runways of the Meadow Vole are kept clear by constant cropping of grasses within the runway. These well-used pathways are typically hidden beneath tall grass, but they are easily discernable following a grass fire.

Woodland Vole — **Size:** Length up to 5 inches. Weight about 1 ounce.

Presumed range in New York

Abundance: Fairly common.

Variation: There are several subspecies of this widespread vole. *M. p. scalopsoides* is found in New York.

Habitat: Tolerates a wide variety of habitats as long as there is sufficient cover. Primarily deciduous woodlands and mixed deciduous/coniferous forests with a substrate of deep leaf litter.

Breeding: Breeds spring through fall with up to four litters per year. 1 to 4 young per litter. Young wean at three weeks and can reproduce at 12 weeks of age.

Natural History: Woodland Voles create networks of tunnels just below the ground or "runways" that are near the surface but beneath the leaf litter on the forest floor. These tunnel systems are utilized by other small mammals such as shrews. They rarely venture far from these tunnels, but do emerge to glean seeds, grasses, and mast. They also eat roots, especially roots of grasses, and root crops like potatoes are also eaten. Active both day and night. Their subterranean habits render them less vulnerable to many predators, but they are prey for a wide variety of carnivores, raptors, and especially snakes which are able to enter the burrow systems. Young exhibit a dark gray color. Adults are more chestnut. A similar species, the **Rock Vole** (*Microtus chrotorrhinus*), is an uncommon vole found in parts of New York.

Southern Red-backed Vole — **Size:** Length as much as 5.5 inches. Weight 1 ounce.

Presumed range in New York

Abundance: Uncommon.

Variation: Most show a characteristic reddish color on the dorsum. Occasional individuals may be uniformly gray.

Habitat: This is a northern species that ranges southward into the Appalachian Mountains as far south as North Caolina. In New York it lives statewide in heavily shaded, damp woodlands.

Breeding: May breed at any time except deep winter. Litter size varies from 2 to 8. Produces fewer but larger litters in the northern portions of its range.

Natural History: Named for the reddish color of the fur on its back. This is a generally uncommon and locally distributed vole species within its range in the United States. However, Whitaker and Hamilton, 1998 report that in the Adirondack region they are "incredibly abundant." Their distribution may be influenced by the presence (or absence) of other species such as the Meadow Vole. Like most small mammals the Red-backed Vole is primarily nocturnal and easily overlooked. The food is mostly green plants, roots, seeds, and mast. Fungi are also easten. They will cache large stores of food in underground chambers for the winter. Bark and roots will also be important food items during long winter months when this species remains active in tunnels beneath the snow.

Class - **Mammalia** (mammals)

Order - **Rodentia** (rodents)

Family - **Cricetidae** (native rats and mice)	Family - **Dipodidae** (jumping mice)	
Muskrat *Ondatra zibethicus*	**Woodland Jumping Mouse** *Napaeozapus insignis*	**Meadow Jumping Mouse** *Zapus hudsonius*

New York's two jumping mice are nearly identical. Pictured here is the Meadow Jumping Mouse. The Woodland species is very similar but has a white tail tip.

Size: Can reach 20 inches total length and weigh about 2.5 pounds.

Presumed range in New York

Abundance: Common.

Size: Length 9 inches (mostly tail). Weighs 1 ounce.

Presumed range in New York

Abundance: Fairly common.

Size: Adults are about 8 inches (mostly tail) and .66 ounce.

Presumed range in New York

Abundance: Fairly common.

Variation: There is no significant variation in this species in New York. Several subspecies across the United States.

Variation: None in New York. Some experts recognize at least five subspecies in North America.

Variation: No sexual dimorphism is noted and there are no subspecies within New York.

Habitat: Aquatic. Prefers marshland but also inhabits swamp, ponds, and lakes. Rarely in rivers or large streams. Often sympatric with the Beaver.

Habitat: The Woodland Jumping Mouse is a decidedly woodland animal. Inhabits both spruce/fir and mixed conifer/hardwood forests.

Habitat: Meadows and fields that contain dense cover. Generally avoids woodlands but may occur in edge areas. Often found near water.

Breeding: Prolific. Capable of multiple litters annually and may produce as many as 6 young per litter.

Breeding: Unlike most small rodents, this mouse breeds only once or twice annually producing 3–6 young.

Breeding: 3–6 young are born after an 18-day gestation period. Breeds about three times a year from spring to late summer.

Natural History: Primarily nocturnal but often active during daylight hours, especially in the spring. Like Beavers, Muskrats have webbed hind feet but their tail is laterally flattened rather than flattened dorso-ventrally as in the Beaver. Thus swimming Muskrats move the tail in a serpentine fashion rather than the up and down paddle-like fashion of the Beaver. Thus equipped, they are excellent swimmers and they are a thoroughly aquatic mammal. They feed on a variety of aquatic vegetation with the stems and roots of cattails being a favorite food. Many other wetland plants are eaten and they have been known to make forays into nearby meadows or fields for foods such as corn. The name comes from the presence of well-developed musk glands. These rodents are an important fur-bearer and in the recent past millions were trapped annually across America for their fur.

Natural History: A mainly boreal (northern) species that ranges southward through the Appalachian Plateau. These mice hibernate for up to six months a year in the northern parts of their range. They have very long tails and long hind legs which bestow them a remarkable jumping ability. When startled they can reportedly leap a distance of 10 feet! Food is fungi, seeds, berries, and insects. They are mainly nocturnal and they sometimes use the burrows and runways of other small rodent species. Woodland Jumping Mice can be told from the very similar Meadow Jumping Mouse by habitat preference and by the white color on the tail tip. This species enjoys the mesic woodlands found in both the Appalachian Plateau and the Boreal Forest ecoregion. Where both species of jumping mice occur sypatrically they segregate themselves by habitat preference.

Natural History: This rodent, along with the preceding species, comprise the North American representatives of the family Dipodidae. This unique family also ranges into the Old World. The Meadow Jumping Mouse is distinguished from the similar Woodland Jumping Mouse by the uniformly dark tail (as opposed to a white-tipped tail). As with the previous species they are mainly nocturnal and do not make runways of their own, but frequently use those made by *Microtus* or other small rodents. Food items are similar to the Woodland Jumping Mouse (fungi, insects, seeds, berries). Both species of Jumping Mice put on heavy layers of fat just prior to their long hibernation, but mortality during hibernation is high and many will not survive their winter sleep. The jumping mice are in a distinct family from all other North American mice (family Dipodidae).

Class - **Mammalia** (mammals)

Order - **Soricomorpha** (shrews and moles)

Family - **Soricidae** (shrews)

Masked Shrew *Sorex cinereus*	Smoky Shrew *Sorex fumeus*

Size: Adult length 3.8 inches. Weight ⅛ of an ounce.

Presumed range in New York

Abundance: Common.

Variation: Brownish in summer, grayish in winter. Young specimens tend to be browner than adults.

Habitat: Found in virtually all wild habitats. Primarily a northern species.

Breeding: 4 to 10 half-inch long young are born from spring to fall.

Natural History: Though mainly nocturnal, these shrews are active both day and night. They dart in and out of leaf litter on the forest floor or move rapidly along runways in over-grown fields. They will make chirping noises as they forage and some believe they echolocate. Known food items are snails/slugs, caterpillars, grubs, spiders, and ants. They will also eat carrion. Shrews do not hibernate, and must forage year-round. For an animal with such high food requirements, survival in winter would seem a daunting task. But dormant insects and other invertebrates are located and eaten in large quantities. In fact, shrews may be quite beneficial to man by consuming enormous quantities of injurious insects and grubs. Like other shrews their lifespan is short, believed to be only about a year and half for the Masked Shrew. Masked Shrews also frequently go by the name "Cinereous Shrew," a reference to the coppery tint that typically highlights their ashy pelage.

Size: Adult length 4.5 inches. Weight .5 ounce.

Presumed range in New York

Abundance: Uncommon.

Variation: Winter pelage dark gray, summer pelage browner. Summer pelage is April to October,

Habitat: Moist woodlands. Especially where there is abundant ground cover.

Breeding: Litter size averages 5–6. Two or three litters in warmer months.

Natural History: This is another primarily northern species that invades the southern United States as far south as northern Georgia along the Appalachian Plateau. Like other shrews it does not hibernate and will be active even in the coldest weather. Its diet is mostly insects and other inverte-brates, but salamanders are also listed as prey. The Smoky Shrew, along with other shrew species, is undoubtedly a very beneficial species to man due to the large number of larva, pupae, and adult insects consumed daily, many of which are significant pests to forest trees. The average lifespan of this species is probably less than a year and half. Females will construct a nest of shredded leaves or grass in a sheltered place beneath a rock or within a rotted log or stump. Like the other small mammals in this book, this animal is important food source for a wide variety of predators, with owls being perhaps their biggest enemy. Shrews of all varieties are secretive and are they difficult animals to study.

In addition to the two species shown above, two other shrews belonging to the *Sorex* genus can be found in New York. The **Water Shrew** (*Sorex palustris*) is aptly named as it is closely associated with streams and lakes. This is a semi-aquatic shrew that swims readily and dives below the surface to hunt aquatic invertebrates and small fish or amphibian larva. They have semi-webbed toes and wide hind feet fringed with stiff hairs. Thus equipped they can run rapidly across the top of the water for short distances without breaking the surface tension and sinking. At six inches total length it is one of America's larger shrew species. The **Rock Shrew** (*Sorex dispar*) has a longer tail than most other shrews (about 90 percent of body length) and in fact this species often goes by the name "Long-tailed Shrew." Unlike many shrews whose ranges encompass broad swaths of North America, the range of the Rock Shrew is limited to the higher elevations of the Appalachian Mountains from North Carolina to Maine. This shrew's home among forested talus ravines in remote mountains, coupled with its apparently low population densities, have made this a difficult species to study. In fact both the Water Shrew and Rock Shrew are very rarely observed, even by those who study this secretive little animal. Almost no photographs of these two species exist from New York.

Class - **Mammalia** (mammals)

Order - **Soricomorpha** (shrews and moles)

Family - **Soricidae** (shrews)

Least Shrew	Northern Short-tailed Shrew
Cryptotis parva	*Blarina brevicauda*

Size: Maximum of 3 inches and weigh about one-quarter of an ounce.

Abundance: Rare in New York.

Variation: Summer pelage is brownish, turning to slate gray during winter.

Presumed range in New York

Habitat: Grassy areas and overgrown fields primarily, but also in woodlands. Seems to avoid the wetland areas of Ohio in favor of drier habitats.

Breeding: Several litters per year is common averaging 4–5 young per litter. Breeds March through November.

Natural History: Possessing an extremely high metabolism, this tiny mammal can consume its own weight in food daily. Like many other shrews they are known to cache food items for later consumption. Animals captured for study can starve to death in just a few hours if not given access to food. Although these shrews are rarely seen due to their diminutive size and reclusive habits, they are usually a fairly common mammal throughout their very large range. Owls are a major predator and in fact the presence of these tiny mammals in a given area is often confirmed by examining owl pellets for skeleton remains. This is one of New York's smallest mammals, but not the smallest. That distinction goes to the **American Pygmy Shrew** (*Sorex hoyi*—not shown). The Pygmy Shrew is one of the world's smallest mammals. The average adult weighs about as much as a dime! These shrews are rarely observed, due perhaps more to their tiny size and secretive nature than to their relative abundance, which in New York is presumed to be rare. The shrews and moles were once classified as members of the order Insecitivora, which means "insect eater." It is an appropriate name as insects are an important item in the diet of both shrews and moles. The order Insectivora also included the old world hedgehogs and tenrecs. Recent taxonomic studies of these mammals has shown that shrews and moles are a distinct group of mammals entitled to be classified into their own order (Soricomorpha).

Size: Maximum length of 5.5 inches and weigh 1 ounce.

Abundance: Common.

Variation: Winter pelage is longer and darker and juveniles are nearly black.

Presumed range in New York

Habitat: Fond of damp woodlands and in fact cannot tolerate excessively dry conditions very well. Does avoid saturated soils however.

Breeding: Breeds in spring and fall. Up to four litters of 4–6 young per litter. Nest is shredded leaves or grasses.

Natural History: Northern Short-tailed Shrews are primarily nocturnal animals and have very high metabolic rates. They are hyperactive animals that will eat as much as one-half their body weight daily! They are known to have periods of intense activity followed by periods of lethargy, which reduces energy requirements and probably keeps them from starving. Food is a variety of insects, snails, earthworms, millipedes, etc. as well as much larger prey including mice that are as large as themselves. The Northern Short-tailed Shrew is known to possess venomous saliva with which it kills its prey. Like most shrews they have tiny eyes and their vision is quite poor. They are known to utilize echolocation. Except when breeding and rearing young, these are solitary animals. They forage beneath the leaf litter in runways and tunnels and will dig their own tunnels or use those of other small rodents. In spite of their resemblence to mice, the two groups are not all closely related. Most shrew species have scent glands that produce a musky odor. Some believe that this adaptation may make them unpalatable to predators that have a well-developed sense of smell. These are typically solitary animals and captive shrews confined together may fight to the death. Identiying shrew species can be a challenging endeavor for the average person. Expert mammalogists often identify similarly looking shrew species by examining their teeth!

Class - **Mammalia** (mammals)
Order - **Soricomorpha** (shrews and moles)
Family - **Talpidae** (moles)

Eastern Mole *Scalopus aquaticus*	Hairy-tailed Mole *Parascalops breweri*	Star-nosed Mole *Condylura cristata*

Size: Total length 6 inches. Weight 2 ounces.  Presumed range in New York	**Size:** Total length 5 inches. Weight 1.5 ounces.  Presumed range in New York	**Size:** Total length 7 inches. Weight 2 ounces.  Presumed range in New York
Abundance: Common within limited range in New York.	**Abundance:** Common. Most widespread mole in New York.	**Abundance:** Generally uncommon in New York.
Variation: Males are slightly larger than females.	**Variation:** No significant variation among New York specimens.	**Variation:** No sexual dimorphism noted. Juveniles have darker pelage.
Habitat: Except for wetlands these moles can be found in any habitat where soils are suitable for burrowing.	**Habitat:** Except for wetlands these moles can be found in any habitat where soils are suitable for burrowing.	**Habitat:** Wet meadows, swamps, mesic woodlands, and near stream courses. Even inhabits muddy habitats.
Breeding: One litter per year in early spring. 2 to 5 young.	**Breeding:** Mating takes place in the spring and 4 or 5 young is average.	**Breeding:** Breeds in late winter and litters of 2 to 7 are born in early spring.
Natural History: The most wide-ranging mole in America. Although considered a pest in suburban lawns and rural gardens, Eastern Moles actually perform some helpful tasks. The tunnels they dig help to aerate the soil and allow rainfall to penetrate more easily. They also prey heavily upon destructive grubs such as the Japanese Beetle. The pelage of the Eastern Mole is "reversible" and will lie smoothly against the skin whether mole is moving forward or backward in tight tunnels. The powerful forelegs allow this animal to burrow at an astonishing pace, and the webbed toes help move dirt aside. The eyes are tiny and covered with skin, and there are no external ears. This is an animal that is superbly adapted to a subterranean lifestyle and Eastern Moles will spend 99 percent of their lives below ground. Ranges in New York is restricted to southern tip of the state. It is replaced throughout the rest of New York by the Hairy-tailed Mole.	**Natural History:** Active year-round in both day and night but in winter utilizes deeper tunnel systems. More shallow tunnels are used in warm weather when it may sometimes leave tunnels at night to forage above ground. Feeding on earthworms and grubs, this mole has been known to consume its own weight in food daily. The tunnels of the Hairy-tailed Mole are less obvious above ground than those of the Eastern Mole. Many other small mammals such as shrews and mice are known to use the tunnels constructed by this mole. Lifespan of four years. The range of this species in New York includes all of the state except the southern tip, where it is replaced by the Eastern Mole, which fills the same ecological niche in that region of the state. The Hairy-tailed Mole is very similar to the preceding species (Eastern Mole) from which it can be told by its hairy tail.	**Natural History:** Morphologically speaking, this is surely one of America's most unusual animals. The tip of the snout is adorned with fleshy tentacles. At first glance it resembles a mole with a sea anemone (or perhaps a small octopus) attached to its nose! The fleshy tentacles are most likely tactile, and some experts cite evidence that they may also serve to detect electrical impulses emitted by fish and other aquatic animals (Whitaker and Hamilton 1998). In habits this mole is also unique among the Talpidae of New York in that they are decidedly aquatic animals. Their tunnels sometimes open directly into streams and they are excellent swimmers. Aquatic insects, worms, and even crustaceans and small fish are captured underwater. Their primary food however is earthworms and the unusual tentacled "star" on the snout undoubtedly plays an important role in locating this mole's food.

Class - **Mammalia** (mammals)
Order - **Chiroptera** (bats)
Family - **Vespertilionidae** (vesper bats)

Little Brown Bat *Myotis lucifugus*	**Northern Bat** *Myotis septentrionalis*	**Eastern Small-footed Bat** *Myotis leibii*

 Presumed range in New York	 Presumed range in New York	 Presumed range in New York

Size: All *Myotis* are somewhat small bats, ranging in size from 3 to 3.75 inches and weighing from .2 to .33 of an ounce. The Little Brown Bat is the largest (nearly 3.75 inches), with the smallest being the Eastern Small-footed Bat (3 inches).

Abundance: The four species of *Myotis* Bats found in New York range in abundance from common to rare. The rarest species is the Indiana Bat (not shown, endangered). The Eastern Small-footed Bat is regarded as a Species of Concern by the NYSDEC and is rather rare in New York. The once-common Northern Bat is a now regarded as a Threatened Species that has been hard hit by White-nose Syndrome (see Natural History section below). The Little Brown Bat is the most common bat in New York.

Variation: Most bats present an identification problem for the average person, but the *Myotis* bats can be especially confusing. Confirming the exact species usually requires looking very closely and may sometimes mean having the bat in hand. In addition to the four species of *Myotis* that range into New York, there are several other species in this genus that are found in other regions of North America.

Habitat: Although many bats are migratory and fly south during winter, this group tends to be more apt to remain in the vicinity of their summer range if adequate hibernacula can be found nearby. Most *Myotis* species will hibernate in caves but they will also use other places such as hollow trees or buildings for summer-time roosts. In summer, some species are sometimes seen roosting in clumps by day beneath the shelter of roof overhangs, roofs of picnic pavillions, inside old barns, etc. A wide variety of habitats are utilized by these bats during warmer months, including forests, fields, wetlands, and especially stream courses.

Breeding: Mating occurs in the fall with fertilization delayed until early spring. Young are born in late spring or early summer and all species form "maternity colonies" of females with young which may be in caves, buildings, hollow trees, or other structures. *Myotis* bats produce a single baby annually (except for the Southeastern Bat which can give birth to twins).

Natural History: Endangered Indiana Bats are known for their huge hibernating colonies that tend to concentrate in only a few select caves during winter. The habit many bats have of congregating in large colonies can lead to epidemics of pathogens like the "White-nose" fungus. Throughout America, many bat species are in steep decline and many once-common species have been hard hit by White-nose Syndrome. The impact of White-nose Syndrome on some of America's bat populations has been catastrophic. The Northern Bat for instance has experienced a population decline of 98 percent in New York in just the last decade. No one yet knows how much this disease and its subsequent decimation of North American bats will impact on the overall health of America's ecosystems. All bats are remarkable little animals that consume untold numbers of injurious insect species, including millions of mosquitos, and they are thus extremely useful to man. Most *Myotis* bats feed in flight on flying insects but one species (Northern Bat) feeds by gleaning insects from leaves while hovering. Some like to forage primarily over water above ponds, creeks, and wetland areas (Little Brown Bat). Some *Myotis* bats are migratory, moving south during winter months, but many will stay and hibernate near their summer breeding range.

Class - **Mammalia** (mammals)		
Order - **Chiroptera** (bats)		
Family - **Vespertilionidae** (vesper bats)		

Silver-haired Bat *Lasionycteris noctivagans*	Eastern Pipistrelle *Perimyotis subflavus*	Big Brown Bat *Eptesicus fuscus*

Silver-haired Bat

Size: Length 4 inches and weight .33 ounce. Wingspan 11 inches.

Presumed range in New York

Abundance: Uncommon.

Variation: No significant variation.

Habitat: The Silver-haired Bat is a forest species that hides in tree hollows or beneath peeling bark during daylight.

Breeding: Mates before entering hibernation. Young are born in late spring. 2 pups is typical.

Natural History: This is a widespread species that ranges from coast to coast in North America. In summer this species ranges as far north as Canada and southeastern Alaska. In fact this species is more common in summer months in northern regions than elsewhere within its range. Unlike many bat species the Silver-haired Bat is mostly a solitary animal that roosts singly, although some colony activity is reported among females with young. They are known to fly in the late afternoon or early evening well before full darkness. Silver-haireds derive their name from the "frosted" appearance of their pelage, a unique and identifying characteristic among New York bats. Food is mostly flying insects caught on the wing, but they may also feed on the ground at times. Feeding flights are mostly near water (streams, bogs, lakes, etc.). The Silver-haired is a migratory species that is seen in New York only in summer.

Eastern Pipistrelle

Size: Length 3.5 inches. Weight about .25 ounces. Wingspan 9 inches.

Presumed range in New York

Abundance: Uncommon.

Variation: No significant variation.

Habitat: Woodlands, stream courses, and edges of fields bordering woodlands are favorite hunting areas.

Breeding: Females give birth to 1 or 2 babies (pups) in late June or early July.

Natural History: Eastern Pipistrelles are widespread and common throughout the eastern United States. They will leave the roost before dark and are often seen hunting at dusk. Like many bats the females form maternal colonies where young are reared, often in buildings or sheds. Unlike many other species however, these maternal colonies are usually small, numbering only one or two dozen individuals. Hibernation begins in late fall (October) and lasts until April or May. Hibernating bats may lose as much as 25–30 percent of their body weight before emerging in the spring. Uniquely among bats, hibernating Pipistrelles accumulate water dropelets on their fur. Why this happens is not fully understood. When flying these little bats move slowly in a very erratic manner and in flight they resemble a large moth. They typically forage around the tops of trees for all manner of flying insects.

Big Brown Bat

Size: Length 4.5 inches and nearly an ounce. Wingspan 13 inches.

Presumed range in New York

Abundance: Fairly common.

Variation: No significant variation.

Habitat: Open fields, vacant lots, rural and urban areas. Sometimes seen hunting insects around suburban streetlights.

Breeding: Breeds in fall before entering hibernation. Delayed fertilization. Twins born in late spring.

Natural History: Stays year-round in New York. Winters in caves or derilect buildings. Summer roosts are usually associated with human structures (buildings, eaves, bridges). Also known to use hollow trees and abondoned mines. The primary food is reported to be beetles. This is perhaps New York's most recognizable bat species. They are the large, brown bats that are common around human habitations and they range throughout the state. They can even be seen within New York City. Roosting bats seen alone during warm weather are nearly always males. Females congregate into "maternity colonies" of up to several dozen adults to rear their young. These bats seem to tolerate cold fairly well and they remain active well into the fall. They can sometimes even be seen flying around on warm days in winter. As with other bat species they are a useful consumer of insect pests.

Class - **Mammalia** (mammals)
Order - **Chiroptera** (bats)
Family - **Vespertilionidae** (vesper bats)

<table>
<tr><td align="center">Eastern Red Bat
Lasiurus borealis</td><td align="center">Hoary Bat
Lasiurus cinereus</td></tr>
</table>

Size: Maximum 5 inches. Up to .5 ounce. Wingspan of 12 inches.

Presumed range in New York

Abundance: Uncommon in New York.

Variation: Males are conspicuously red, females are chestnut frosted with white.

Habitat: Woodlands and edge areas in both rural and urban regions.

Breeding: Litter size is 1 to 4 with the pups born in late May or early June.

Natural History: In summer this species usually roosts in trees by hanging from a limb. Usually solitary but sometimes more than one bat will roost together. Roosting bats resemble dead leaves. Trees chosen for roosting are often at the edge of a woodland bordering an open field. This is a migratory species that summers in New York and winters farther to the south. The range is quite large and includes most of the United States east of the Rocky Mountains and much of southeastern Canada. Hibernation takes place in hollow trees or beneath leaf litter on the forest floor, a very unusual tactic for a bat! Though mainly nocturnal, this species often flies in daylight, especially in late afternoon or early evening. This is one of our more handsomely colored bat species, but they are not very common in the northern portions of their range and they are an uncommon species in New York.

Size: Maximum 5.5 inches. Weight up to 1 ounce. Wingspan of 16 inches.

Presumed range in New York

Abundance: Uncommon in New York.

Variation: Females are on average slightly heavier than males.

Habitat: Another forest species that is seen in both rural and urban areas.

Breeding: Averages 2 pups born in mid-May to mid-June. Young are weaned and fending for themselves in four weeks.

Natural History: This is the largest bat species in New York. The wingspan of the Hoary Bat can be up to 16 inches! It's name comes from the white-tipped hairs of the fur on its back. Hoary Bats have the greatest distribution of any American Bat. They summer as far north as Canada and winter in the coastal plain of the southeastern United States. Most of the Hoary Bats seen in New York are seen in the Adirondack region in summer. Oddly, the sexes segregate themselves following breeding and most of those seen in the eastern United States in summer are females. Males summer farther west in the great plains, Rocky Mountains, or west coast. These bats fly higher than many other species when hunting and they also tend to roost higher, nearer the tops of trees. Like the preceding species the Hoary Bat usually roosts alone.

CHAPTER 4
THE BIRDS OF NEW YORK

— THE ORDERS AND FAMILIES OF NEW YORK BIRDS —

Note: The arrangement below is a reflection of how the orders and families of birds appear in this book rather than an accurate description of the phylogentic relationship of the birds.

Class - **Aves** (birds)

Order - **Passeriformes** (songbirds)

Family	**Tyrannidae** (flycatchers)	Family	**Polioptilidae** (gnatcatchers)
Family	**Turdidae** (thrushes)	Family	**Hirundinidae** (swallows)
Family	**Lanidae** (shrikes)	Family	**Corvidae** (crows and jays)
Family	**Alaudidae** (larks)	Family	**Vireonidae** (vireos)
Family	**Mimidae** (thrashers)	Family	**Parulidae** (warblers)
Family	**Motacillidae** (wagtails)	Family	**Icteridae** (blackbirds)
Family	**Bombycillidae** (waxwings)	Family	**Thraupidae** (tanagers)
Family	**Certhiidae** (creepers)	Family	**Sturnidae** (starlings)
Family	**Paridae** (chickadees)	Family	**Passeridae** (European sparrows)
Family	**Regulidae** (kinglets)	Family	**Calcaridae** (longspurs and snow bunting)
Family	**Sittidae** (nuthatches)	Family	**Cardinalidae** (grosbeaks)
Family	**Troglodytidae** (wrens)	Family	**Fringillidae** (finches)

Order - **Apodiformes** (swifts and hummingbirds)

Family	**Apodidae** (swifts)
Family	**Trochilidae** (hummingbirds)

Order - **Coraciiformes**

Family	**Alcedinidae** (kingfishers)

Order - **Piciformes**

Family	**Picidae** (woodpeckers)

Order - **Cuculiformes**

Family	**Cuculidae** (cuckoos)

Order - **Columbiformes**

Family	**Columbidae** (doves)

Order - **Galliformes** (chicken-like birds)

Family	**Phasianidae** (grouse)
Family	**Odontophoridae** (quail)

Order - **Caprimulgiformes**

Family	**Caprimulgidae** (nightjars)

Order - **Strigiformes** (owls)

Family	**Strigidae** (typical owls)
Family	**Tytonidae** (barn owl)

Order - **Falconiformes** (raptors)

Family	**Accipitridae** (hawks, eagles, kites)
Family	**Cathartidae** (vultures)
Family	**Falconidae** (falcons)

Order - **Pelicaniformes** (wading birds)

Family	**Ardeidae** (herons)

Order - **Gruiformes** (rails and cranes)

Family	**Rallidae** (rails)
Family	**Gruidae** (cranes)

Order - **Charadriiformes** (shorebirds)

Family	**Charadriidae** (plovers)
Family	**Scolopacidae** (sandpipers)
Family	**Haematopodidae** (oystercatchers)
Family	**Laridae** (gulls and terns)

Order - **Gaviiformes**

Family	**Gaviidae** (loons)

Order - **Podicipediformes**

Family	**Podicipedidae** (grebes)

Order - **Siluriformes**

Family	**Phalacrocoracidae** (cormorants)
Family	**Sulidae** (boobies and gannets)

Order - **Anseriformes** (waterfowl)

Family	**Anatidae** (ducks, geese, and swans)

Class - **Aves** (birds)

Order - **Passeriformes** (songbirds)

Family - **Tyrannidae** (flycatchers)

Eastern Wood Pewee *Contopus virens*	**Olive-sided Flycatcher** *Contopus cooperi*	**Eastern Phoebe** *Sayornis phoebe*

<table>
<tr>
<td>

Size: 6.5 inches.

Abundance: Common.

Variation: None. Sexes are alike.

</td>
<td>

Presumed range in New York

</td>
<td>

Size: 7.5 inches.

Abundance: Uncommon.

Variation: None. Sexes are alike.

</td>
<td>

Presumed range in New York

</td>
<td>

Size: 7 inches.

Abundance: Common.

Variation: None. Sexes are alike.

</td>
<td>

Presumed range in New York

</td>
</tr>
</table>

Migratory Status: Wintering in South America, the Eastern Wood Pewee arrives in North America in late spring (peak arrival in New York around mid-May). They are a summer/breeding resident across the state, staying throughout the summer. They begin leaving in late August with a few lingering into early October.	**Migratory Status:** Migrant in most of New York but can be seen all summer in the Adirondacks and in parts of eastern New York. Spring migrants begin to arrive in New York in May. Fall migration is mid-August through September. A boreal forest species in summer that winters from southern Mexico to South America.	**Migratory Status:** Eastern Phoebes begin to arrive in New York as early as April, perhaps a little later in the northernmost portion of the state. They are summer residents that will nest in the state. Fall migration begins late September through October. They are hardy birds that can withstand some cold and a few may linger into late fall.
Habitat: Wood Pewees are forest birds but they favor small openings in the woods or edge areas where marshes, bogs, or fields border woodlands.	**Habitat:** The summer habitat is coniferous forests of the Rocky Mountain region and northern North America where it associates with small forest openings.	**Habitat:** Woodlands and woods openings. Also in rural yards or parks in wooded regions. Can be common around rural homesteads.
Breeding: Nests are usually built high in trees in a terminal fork. Nest material consists of grasses and lichens. 2 to 4 eggs are laid.	**Breeding:** Most breeding in New York apparently occurs in the Adirondacks region. Nest is in a conifer and built of sticks, lichens, and rootlets. 3 to 4 eggs.	**Breeding:** Pheobes are early nesters. Nesting can occur by April and there will often be a second nesting later in the summer.
Natural History: These nondescript little brown birds often go unnoticed except for the distinctive call from which they derive their name. Their "pee-a-weee" song is a common summer sound in the woodlands throughout eastern North America. Like other members of the flycatcher family, they hunt flying insects from high perches, swooping out to catch their food on the wing. They are typically fairly tolerant of humans and can sometimes be closely approached. They are very similar to Eastern Pheobe, but note orange lower bill and pale wing bars on the Eastern Wood Pewee.	**Natural History:** These flycatchers are quite acrobatic in the air. They feed in typical flycatcher fashion by sallying forth from a high perch to snatch flying insects. Perch is the highest point available. Bees and wasps are reportedly a favorite food. This species avoids deep forest in favor of openings such as bogs, meadows, or second growth and may benefit from forest fires or human activities such as logging. Paradoxically, the species has been declining in recent decades. This decline is possibly tied to changes in the winter habitat in tropical America. They are federally listed as Species of Concern by the USF&WS.	**Natural History:** The Eastern Pheobe is most easily told from other Flycatchers by its habit of constantly wagging its tail down and up. Its nests are also distinctive, being constructed of mud and lined with mosses. Nests are placed beneath some form of overhang, most often the eaves of buildings. The cup-shaped nest is plastered to the surface in the manner of many swallows. These are normally tame little birds that will allow humans to approach to within a few yards before flying off only a short distance. They are very similar to the Wood Pewee but have a dark bill and they lack wing bars.

Class - **Aves** (birds)

Order - **Passeriformes** (songbirds)

Family - **Tyrannidae** (flycatchers)

Empid Flycatchers
Genus - *Empidonax* (5 nearly identical species in New York)

Acadian Flycatcher *Empidonax virescens*	**Willow Flycatcher** *Empidonax traillii*	**Least Flycatcher** *Empidonax minimus*

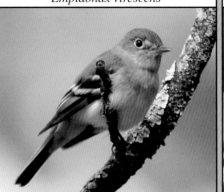  

Alder Flycatcher *Empidonax alnorum*	**Yellow-bellied Flycatcher** *Empidonax flaviventris*	

Presumed range of *Empidonax* Flycatchers in New York.

Size: Range in size from 5.25 to 5.75 inches.

Abundance: Least Flycatcher is fairly common statewide. Willow Flycatcher is a fairly common breeder throughout the state except for the Adirondack region; and the Alder Flycatcher is fairly common except in southeastern New York. Acadian Flycatcher and Yellow-bellied Flycatcher are probably the least common of the group.

Variation: Five species of *Empidonax* flycatchers may be seen in New York. All five species are so similar in appearance that even expert bird watchers have trouble identifying individual species. Most people must content themselves with calling them all "Empid Flycatchers."

Migratory Status: All the *Empidonax* flycatchers are known to breed in the state. All winter far to south, some as far as South America. They will return to New York May to mid-June. All begin to leave in August and are gone by mid-September.

Habitat: All are woodland species. Acadian and Willow Flycatchers are fond of streamside habitats, swamps, and marshes. Least Flycatchers prefer regenerative woodlands and edge areas. Yellow-bellied Flycatchers in New York summer mostly in the Adirondacks. Both the Alder Flycatcher and the Least Flycatcher summer throughout the state.

Breeding: The Acadian Flycatcher weaves a flimsy nest of grass on a low branch and lays 2–4 eggs. Willow Flycatchers build their nest in the fork of a low branch or bush and lay 2–4 eggs. Least Flycatcher nests in woodlands and usually builds its nest in a fork of a tree branch. Alder Flycatcher nests are coarsely woven cups typically placed in low bushes with 4 eggs. Yellow-bellied flycatchers hide their nests amid moss in evergreen woodlands.

Natural History: Some species, like the Acadian Flycatcher, may be less numerous in North America today due to the decline in forested habitats. The Willow Flycatcher on the other hand may be helped by the regeneration of successional forests. This genus of birds represents a good example of what biologists call "cryptic species." They are so confusingly similar in appearance that positive identification in the field can be extremely difficult. Serious birdwatchers find that the most reliable way to identify these small flycatchers is to learn their songs. In fact, Willow Flycatchers and Alder Flycatchers can be so similar in appearance that visual identification alone is unreliable.

Class - **Aves** (birds)
Order - **Passeriformes** (songbirds)
Family - **Tyrannidae** (flycatchers)

Eastern Kingbird *Tyrannus tyrannus*	Great Crested Flycatcher *Myiarchus crinitus*

Size: Length 8.5 inches.

Abundance: Common.

Variation: None.

Migratory Status: A summertime resident that nests in the state. Winters in South America.

Presumed range in New York

Habitat: Prefers open fields and pastures in rural areas. In urban settings it likes open parks and large empty lots. Commonly seen perched on fences.

Breeding: The nest is built of twigs and grass high in trees. The average clutch size is 3–5 eggs. One clutch per year. Sturdy nest is placed on limb near the top of large tree.

Natural History: The name "Kingbird" is derived from this species' aggressive defense of territory against other birds, including even large hawks! They hunt flying insects from an open perch, which is frequently a fence or power line. When flying insect prey is spotted they will launch themselves into an attack that often results in an aerial "dogfight" between bird and insect. They will also hunt flying insects by hovering. Berries are an important food item, especially mulberries, serviceberries, and blackberries. Elderberries are also eaten. These are conspicuous birds. Their charcoal gray upper parts contrast strongly with a whitish breast and belly. The bright reddish-orange blaze on the top of the head is usually not visible to the casual observer. Winters in South America, as far south as Argentina. Some populations in the eastern United States have shown declines in the last few decades, but this remains a common species. In New York this species is widespread but probably least common in the Adirondacks.

Size: Length 8.75 inches.

Abundance: Fairly common.

Variation: None.

Migratory Status: Summer resident. Winters in Central America, Mexico, or southern Florida.

Presumed range in New York

Habitat: Openings in deciduous and mixed woodlands. Edge areas and open woodlands are also used. Winter habitat is tropical forests of many types.

Breeding: Unlike most flycatchers this bird is a cavity nester, often using old woodpecker holes. 3 to 5 eggs, laid in mid-May, is typical.

Natural History: The name comes from the "crested" look of the head, which may not be readily apparent. Reddish under-side of the tail and wing primaries along with the distinctly yellowish belly contrasting with gray breast is unique among New York flycatchers. These features plus large size make it one of the more recognizable members of the flycatcher family. However, they are a rather unobtrusive species that can be easily overlooked. Food is large insects captured in flight from its perch, which is often high in the canopy. Returns to northern United States in late April from wintering grounds as far south as Central America. Forages for insects in treetops and catches flying insects on the wing. Also consumes some berries. More common in the southeastern United States than in northeast and midwest. Breeding success may be tied to woodpecker populations since old woodpecker holes are a favorite nesting site. Widespread in New York in summer but less common and less conspicuous than the Eastern Kingbird.

Class - **Aves** (birds)
Order - **Passeriformes** (songbirds)
Family - **Turdidae** (thrushes)

Robin *Turdus migratorius*	**Eastern Bluebird** *Sialia sialis*	**Wood Thrush** *Hylocichla mustelina*

Size: 10 inches.	**Size:** 7 inches.	**Size:** 7.75 inches.
Abundance: Very common.	**Abundance:** Fairly common.	**Abundance:** Common.
Variation: Females are less vivid.	**Variation:** Sexually dimorphic. See above.	**Variation:** None. Sexes alike.

Presumed range in New York (×3)

Migratory Status: Robins are most common in spring and summer months but they can be seen year-round in most of the state.

Migratory Status: Mostly a summer resident but some will remain well into the winter if the weather is mild. Migratory movements are dictated by weather.

Migratory Status: A summer resident that winters in Central America and even as far as south as northern South America.

Habitat: Virtually all habitats in the state may be utilized. Most common in areas of human disturbance, especially older suburbs. They are fond of hunting earthworms in suburban lawns.

Habitat: Field edges, woods openings, and open fields, marshes, and pastures. Savanna like habitats, i.e. open spaces interspersed with large trees, are a favorite habitat.

Habitat: Woodlands. May be found in both mature forests and successional areas. In both it likes thick undergrowth. Larger tracts of forest are favored over small, fragmented woodlands.

Breeding: The 3–4 "sky blue" eggs are laid in a nest constructed of mud and grass, often in the crotch of a tree in a suburban yard.

Breeding: Bluebirds are cavity nesters that readily take to man-made nest boxes. Two broods per summer is common in southern United States, 3 to 6 eggs per clutch.

Breeding: Nest is mud, twigs, and grass similar to that of the Robin. Nest may be in understory or at mid-level. Lays 2–5 blue-green eggs.

Natural History: Despite the fact that the Robin is a migratory species, individuals are seen in most of New York year-round. It is possible that the state's summer residents retreat south during winter and are replaced by southward moving individuals that have summered much farther to the north. In winter they are sometimes seen in large migratory flocks numbering over 100 birds. Perhaps one of the best known of America's bird species, Robins are commonly seen on both urban and rural lawns throughout America. But they are also seen in regions where few humans ever venture. Their summer range extends well into the arctic and they are common in wilderness areas of the far north during summer months. Earthworms are a favorite food.

Natural History: The Eastern Bluebirds' habit of readily adapting to artificial nest boxes has helped bring them back from alarmingly low numbers decades ago, when rampant logging of eastern forests depleted nest cavities. They are a "partially migratory" species and some individuals will move south in winter while others will stay in the vicinity of their breeding territory. As they are primarily insect eaters non-migrants are vulnerable to harsh winters. In winter Bluebirds eat many types of berries and will readily eat raisins from feeders. Their popularity among humans has lead to the establishment of The North American Bluebird Society, dedicated to Bluebird conservation. The Eastern Bluebird is the state bird of New York.

Natural History: The Wood Thrush feeds on insects, spiders, earthworms, and other invertebrates found by foraging beneath leaf mold on the forest floor. They will also feed on berries which can be an important food during fall migration. Like many songbirds this species is threatened by the fragmentation of forest habitats throughout North America. Smaller forest tracts make it easier for cowbirds to find Wood Thrush nests. Consequently nest predation by cowbirds is increasing in many areas of its breeding range. Perhaps due mainly to Brown Headed Cowbirds, this species has been in decline for several decades. The song is described as "flute-like" and it has captured the imagination of many well-known nature writers, including naturalist/writer Henry David Thoreau.

Class - **Aves** (birds)		
Order - **Passeriformes** (songbirds)		
Family - **Turdidae** (thrushes)		
Hermit Thrush *Catharus guttatus*	**Veery** *Catharus fuscescens*	**Swainson's Thrush** *Catharus ustulatus*

Size: 6.5 inches. **Abundance:** Fairly common. **Variation:** None. Sexes are alike. 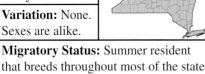 Presumed range in New York	**Size:** 7.5 inches. **Abundance:** Fairly common. **Variation:** None. Sexes are alike.  Presumed range in New York	**Size:** 7 inches. **Abundance:** Uncommon. **Variation:** None. Sexes are alike.  Presumed range in New York
Migratory Status: Summer resident that breeds throughout most of the state. Most have arrived by mid-April. Departs later than most thrushes, lingering well into the fall.	**Migratory Status:** Summer resident that breeds throughout most of the state. Most have arrived by late April. Fall departure is late August or early September. Migrates at night.	**Migratory Status:** Summer resident in the Catskills and Adirondacks. Migrant statewide. Most have arrived by late April. Fall migration is late August or early September, may last into October.
Habitat: Damp woodlands, thickets, and successional areas with heavy undergrowth.	**Habitat:** Understory of deciduous woodlands. Most common in second growth forest with thick undergrowth.	**Habitat:** Moist to wet woodlands and swamps with heavy underbrush and cool, heavily shaded woods.
Breeding: 3 to 5 blueish-green eggs are laid in a nest built just above ground level. Most will nest in the boreal forests of Canada.	**Breeding:** Breeds mostly well to the north in Canada. Nest is hidden in thickets on or near the ground. From 3 to 5 eggs are laid.	**Breeding:** Builds its moss lined nest in a tree in boreal forest. Most nesting in New York is in the Adirondacks. Lays 3–5 eggs that are blue with brown spots.
Natural History: This is the only member if the *Catharus* genus that will winter in the southern United States. Most travel to the tropics. They are rather shy but less so than other *Catharus* and they will sometimes visit feeders for suet or raisins. They feed mainly on insects found on the forest floor and beneath leaf mold, but berries are also an important element in the diet, especially in winter. The song of the Hermit Thrush is regarded by many as one of the more beautiful summer sounds in the northern forests. Unlike most other thrush species, populations of the Hermit Thrush appear stable. As with other thrush species the Hermit Thrush is known for the quality of its song. In New York they are probably least common in the lowlands around Lakes Erie/Ontario and in the Mohawk/Hudson valleys.	**Natural History:** Although the Veery is widespread in New York in the summer, they are hard to observe as they are one of the more secretive of the thrushes. They stay mostly in thick undergrowth where they feed on the ground or in low bushes on a variety of insects, earthworms, spiders, and berries. They are known to favor wetter situations than most thrushes and are said to enjoy being in the vicinity of beaver ponds. Bird watchers often confirm this bird's presence by recognizing its distinctive call, which has been described as "hauntingly beautiful." The species name *"fuscescens"* translates as "dusky," a reference to color of the plumage on the back and wings. Like other thrushes the Veery migrates at night and it is what is known as a "trans-gulf migrant," flying across the gulf of Mexico during migration.	**Natural History:** Another secretive, difficult-to-observe thrush that in migration flies by night and spends its days resting and feeding in heavy undergrowth. As with many of the thrushes, positive identification can be difficult. This species and the Gray-cheeked Thrush are easily confused. The buff-colored cheeks are a good identification character. Like others of its kind the Swainson's Thrush feeds on insects and invertebrates as well as berries. Unlike others of its genus however this thrush is known to feed higher in trees (most other thrushes feed mostly on the ground). While they can be fairly common statewide during migrations, this is one of the rarer thrushes in New York in summer. Most will pass through New York and nest farther to the north throughout the Maritime Provinces of Canada. A few will summer in the state.

Class - **Aves** (birds)

Order - **Passeriformes** (songbirds)

Family - **Turdidae** (thrushes)	Family - **Lanidae** (shrikes)	Family - **Alaudidae** (larks)

Gray-cheeked Thrush
Catharus minimus

Northern Shrike
Lanius excubitor

Horned Lark
Eremophila alpestris

Size: 6.5 inches.

Abundance: Uncommon.

Variation: None. Sexes are alike.

Presumed range in New York

Size: 10 inches.

Abundance: Uncommon.

Variation: None. Sexes are alike.

Presumed range in New York

Size: 7.5 inches.

Abundance: Uncommon.

Variation: Male is more vivid.

Presumed range in New York

Migratory Status: Nests well to the north of New York, migrants may be seen statewide in both spring and fall.

Migratory Status: Winter resident. Breeds in the far north and winters in southern Canada and northern United States.

Migratory Status: Horned Larks are year-round residents in New York, although many move south in winter.

Habitat: Summer habitats are boreal forests. Winters in South America. May be seen in woodlands throughout the state during migration.

Habitat: Summer habitat is the taiga-tundra ecoregion of the far north. In New York uses edge areas and semi-open regions near woodlands or brush.

Habitat: This is a grassland/open ground species. In New York they will use pastures and agricultural lands as well as disturbed/cleared land.

Breeding: Breeds in remote tundra and taiga in northern Canada and Alaska. Lays 3 to 6 eggs.

Breeding: Nest is proportionately large Built of twigs and rootlets lined with feathers, hair, or fur. Lays 4–6 eggs.

Breeding: Nests is on the ground and consists of a small depression lined with grasses. Lays 3–5 eggs.

Natural History: Secretive and uncommon, the biology of the Gray-cheeked Thrush is poorly known. Its summer habitats are dense spruce forests and willow-alder thickets in the far north. Breeding range extends well into the Arctic Circle and winter range is at least as far south as northern South America. Differentiating between the various thrush species can be challenging. The Gray-cheeked Thrush is easily confused with both the Swainson's Thrush and the Hermit Thrush but can be told by the gray color of the cheek. Yet another similar thrush species, the **Bicknell's Thrush** (*Catharus bicknelli),* is one of America's newest bird species, having only relatively recently been differentiated from the Gray-cheeked Thrush. Bicknell's is a rare summertime inhabitant of remote northern forests, including forests in the Adirondack region of New York. It is regarded as an endangered species in New York.

Natural History: These fierce little birds are much like a miniature raptor. They hunt mostly insects, but will also attack and kill lizards, mice, small snakes, and birds as large as themselves. Sometimes called "Butcher Bird," they kill with a powerful beak and have the unusual habit of caching food items by impaling the bodies of prey onto a thorn or fence barb. They will form permanent territories which they defend from other shrikes. An endemic North American bird, Northern Shrikes range across the northern portions of North America from the central Rocky Mountains in the west to the Great Lakes region of the Midwest and all of New England. Sadly, this unique species is declining throughout its range. Northern Shrikes are an uncommon winter resident in northern New York and rare winter visitor in southern New York. A similar species, the **Loggerhead Shrike** (*L. ludovicianus),* is very rare and endangered in New York.

Natural History: This prairie species needs open ground and has probably benefited from human activity in New York as a result of logging, land clearing, and agricultural operations. Closely cropped pastures or tilled lands are used almost exclusively in New York. Except during nesting, these are gregarious birds that are nearly always seen in flocks. They feed on small seeds and tiny arthropods gleaned from what may appear to be nearly barren ground. Harvested agricultural fields, gravel bars, and other open lands are utilized, especially in winter. Like the American Pipit, with which it sometimes associates, the Horned Lark is a species that is often overlooked by the average person. During outbreaks of severe winter weather flocks may move farther south; and indeed this species ranges as far south as central Mexico. Populations in New York appear to be in decline and it is a Species of Concern in the state.

Class - **Aves** (birds)

Order - **Passeriformes** (songbirds)

Family - **Mimidae** (thrashers)

Mockingbird	Gray Catbird	Brown Thrasher
Mimus polyglottos	*Dumetella carolinensis*	*Toxostoma rufum*

Size: 10.5 inch. **Abundance:** Fairly common. **Variation:** None. Sexes are alike. Presumed range in New York	**Size:** 8.5 inches. **Abundance:** Common. **Variation:** None. Sexes are alike. Presumed range in New York	**Size:** 11.5 inch. **Abundance:** Fairly common. **Variation:** None. Sexes are alike. Presumed range in New York
Migratory Status: A summer-only resident in northernmost New York, but is a year-round resident in the rest of the state.	**Migratory Status:** A summer-only resident in most of the state. A few will linger throughout the winter in the Coastal Plain of New York.	**Migratory Status:** A summer-only resident in most of the state. A few may linger throughout the winter in the Coastal Plain of New York.
Habitat: Prefers semi-open habitats with some cover in the form of bushes and shrubs. Found in both rural and urban environments. During colder months they are usually found in the vicinity of berry-producing plants.	**Habitat:** Edge areas, thickets, and overgrown fence rows are this birds preferred habitat. In urban areas it is often found in older neighborhoods containing landscapes overgrown with large bushes and shrubs.	**Habitat:** Edges of woods, thickets, fence rows, overgrown fields, and successional areas. Suburban lawns that have adequate cover in the form of bushes and shrubs may also be used. Avoids deep woods.
Breeding: The nest is made of sticks and is usually in a thick bush or small tree. 3 to 4 eggs are laid and more than one nesting per season is usual.	**Breeding:** The loosely constructed nest is made of sticks, vines, and leaves placed in dense bushes. 3 to 4 eggs is common.	**Breeding:** Builds a stick nest in the heart of a dense shrub, usually within a few feet of the ground. Lays 2 to 5 eggs in late spring.
Natural History: The name "Mocking Bird" is derived from this bird's habit of mimicking the calls of other birds, and they have a huge repertoire of songs. They are known to mimic the calls of everything from warblers to Blue Jays and even large hawks. New songs are learned throughout their life and the number of different songs recorded by this species is up to 150. They feed largely on insects, but in the winter will switch to berries and fruits. Mocking-birds have a reputation among rural folk as a useful bird that will chase away other pesky birds such as blackbirds and other species that can be garden pests. Appears to be expanding its range northward into southern Canada. Although found statewide, New York is near the northern limit of its range.	**Natural History:** The Gray Catbird is much more secretive than its relative the Mockingbird. Food includes all manner of insects, worms, spiders, and larva. They will also eat fruit and berries. Feeds both in the trees and on the ground. When feeding on the ground, will use the bill to flip over dead leaves. Named for their call which sounds remarkably like a meowing cat, these shy birds are often heard but unseen as they "meow" from beneath a dense shrub. Like their cousins the Mockingbirds, Gray Catbirds have a large repertoire of songs and they are accomplished mimics of other bird species. They winter along the lower coastal plain of the United States, Florida, the Caribbean, Mexico, and Central America. In New York they are least common in the Adirondacks.	**Natural History:** During warm weather the Brown Thrasher feeds on insects and small invertebrates of all types. It uses its long bill to overturn leaves and debris beneath trees and shrubs and also actively hunts in the grass of urban lawns. In winter they will eat berries and sometimes come to feeders for raisins or suet. During the breeding season males perch atop bushes or small trees and serenade all within earshot with their song. Though the Brown Thrasher lacks the repertoire of its cousin the Mockingbird, it does possess one of the most varied song collections of any bird in America. In New York the Brown Thrasher is most common in the southeastern portions of the state and in the Interior Lowlands. They are least common in the Adirondacks.

Class - **Aves** (birds)

Order - **Passeriformes** (songbirds)

Family - **Motacillidae** (wagtails)	Family - **Bombycillidae** (waxwings)	Family - **Certhiidae** (creepers)
American Pipit *Anthus rubescens*	**Cedar Waxwing** *Bombycilla cedrorum*	**Brown Creeper** *Certhia americana*

Size: 6.5 inches.

Abundance: Uncommon.

Variation: Seasonal plumage.

Presumed range in New York

Size: 7 inches.

Abundance: Very common.

Variation: None. Sexes are alike.

Presumed range in New York

Size: 5.25 inches.

Abundance: Fairly common.

Variation: None. Sexes are alike.

Presumed range in New York

Migratory Status: The American Pipit is seen in New York as a migrant only. Peak migration is mid-April and mid-Oct.

Migratory Status: Year-round resident of New York. May decrease in winter as roving flocks move southward.

Migratory Status: Year-round resident of New York. More numerous during spring and fall as migrants pass through.

Habitat: In migration the American Pipit is usually seen in expansive open areas such as harvested croplands or mudflats.

Habitat: Found both in forests and semi-open country including overgrown fields, orchards, etc. May be seen in both rural and urban settings.

Habitat: This is a forest species that prefers mature woodlands with large trees for breeding. In winter they are seen in a variety of wooded habitats.

Breeding: Breeds in tundra areas and southward into the higher altitudes of the Rocky Mountains. Lays 3 to 7 eggs in a nest on the ground.

Breeding: Builds a nest of grasses. Nest site is typically high on a tree branch. Nesting is later in the summer than most birds. Lays 3 to 5 eggs.

Breeding: The nest is nearly always built behind a piece of loose bark on the trunk of a large dead tree. 5 or 6 eggs is typical.

Natural History: The American Pipit is a hardy species that nests in America's coldest climates. They move south in the winter where they are easily overlooked. Their mottled brown winter plumage is highly cryptic, especially where they usually reside in expansive, open fields or mudflats. During migration and in winter they may be seen in the company of flocks of Horned Larks or rarely with Lapland Longspurs (another winter migrant from the far north). Characteristically wags its tail up and down. American Pipits are found throughout North America and in parts of eastern Asia. Several other related species of Pipit are found on every continent except for Antarctica. Despite being widespread they are relatively unknown birds to many. The specimen shown above is in spring plumage. Non-breeding birds are drabber, being streaked with a mottled brown.

Natural History: Waxwings are named for the peculiar red-colored waxy feathers on their wings. The name "Cedar" Waxwing comes from their propensity for Eastern Red Cedar trees where they consume large quantities of cedar berries. These birds are highly social and are usually seen in large flocks. They feed mostly on berries and wander relentlessly in search of this favored food item. In summer insects, mulberries, and service-berries are important food items. Crabapples and other fruiting trees are also favored. Large flocks are known to rove around in search of fruiting plants and to descend on a fruiting bush and consume every berry. A similar but larger species, the **Bohemian Waxwing** (*B. garrulus*) is a more northerly species that sometimes shows up in northernmost New York in late fall or winter. They are told from the Cedar Waxwing by larger size and orange undertail.

Natural History: Brown Creepers feed on small insects, spiders, etc., found in tree-trunk bark crevices. They have the peculiar foraging habit of landing on the trunk at the base of the tree and "creeping" upward, spiraling around the tree as they go. When they reach a certain height, they fly down to the base of another nearby tree and begin again. In habits, the Brown Creeper is a bit of a loner, and it is rare to see more than a pair or two in any one area. This is the only representative of the creeper family (Certhiidae) found in North America. Several other species occur in Eurasia and Africa. Population declines in regions where mature forests have been reduced suggests a dependence upon that habitat type. A nearly identical species known as the Eurasian Treecreeper occurs across Europe and northern Asia. The two species are so similar that they were long regarded as a single species.

Class - **Aves** (birds)		
Order - **Passeriformes** (songbirds)		
Family - **Paridae** (chickadees)		
Black-capped Chickadee *Poecile atricapillus*	**Boreal Chickadee** *Poecile hudsonicus*	**Tufted Titmouse** *Baeolophus bicolor*

Size: Length 5.25 inches.	Presumed range in New York	**Size:** Length 5.25 inches.	Presumed range in New York	**Size:** Length 6 inches.	Presumed range in New York
Abundance: Very common.		**Abundance:** Uncommon.		**Abundance:** Common.	
Variation: None. Sexes are alike.		**Variation:** None. Sexes are alike.		**Variation:** None.	

Migratory Status: Year-round resident.	**Migratory Status:** Year-round resident.	**Migratory Status:** Year-round resident.
Habitat: Primarily a woodland species but may be found anywhere so long as at least a few trees are present. Common in both rural and urban habitats.	**Habitat:** As its name implies this is a bird of the boreal (northern) forests. In New York it is found only in the Adirondack region.	**Habitat:** Small woodlots and successional areas. Favors edge habitats. Common in both rural and urban habitats.
Breeding: This species is a cavity nester that will use hollows in limbs, rotted fence posts, or very often, old woodpecker holes. Man-made nest boxes may also be used but natural cavities are preferred. Lays 6–7 eggs.	**Breeding:** A cavity nester that to some extent will excavate its own hole if the selected cavity needs re-sizing or remodeling. Within the cavity will construct a nest of mosses, fine fibers, hair, and fur. Lays up to 9 eggs.	**Breeding:** This species is a cavity nester that will utilize natural cavities as well as old woodpecker holes. Average of 5 eggs. Nesting in northern parts of the range usually begins in May, earlier in the south.
Natural History: Among New York's smallest songbirds, the Black-capped Chickadee is familiar bird at feeders throughout the state. They will become quite acclimated to people and with some patient coaxing they may be induced to land upon an outstretch hand containing sunflower seeds. An acrobatic little bird when searching for insect prey, they can dangle upside down from tiny branches. Their whistling song and their "chick-a-dee-dee-dee" call is distinctive and they can be quite noisy at times. In winter they will form mixed flocks with other small birds, especially their "cousin" the Tufted Titmouse. They are hyper-active, tiny birds that have high energy requirements. Exceptionally harsh winter weather and extreme cold can cause high mortality rates.	**Natural History:** This is one of the few bird species that is a year-round permanent resident of North America's great Boreal Forests. The range includes all of three Level I Ecoregions: the Boreal Forest, the Taiga, and the Hudson Plain (see Figure 6), as well as the northern half of the Northwestern Forested Mountains. In spite of the fact that this range encompass vast regions of wilderness, this species can be as tame as the preceding species, especially if acclimated to people in a place where bird seed is offered regularly. These birds seem less hyperactive than their cousin the Black-capped Chickadee, a trait that is appreciated by bird photographers. Like many other birds of the boreal regions occasional eruptions of birds well to the south of their normal range can occur.	**Natural History:** Primarily a seed eater in winter, the Tufted Titmouse is one of the first birds to find a new bird feeder. Sunflower seeds are favored, but they also love peanuts. Like Chickadees they are sometimes quite bold around humans servicing feeders and with patience can be enticed to land on an open palm holding sunflowers. In warm months they forage for small insects and spiders among the foliage of trees. They can sometimes be seen hanging upside down on a small branch or leaf as they search for prey. Their familiar song is a melodic "birdy-birdy-birdy." In winter they mix readily with Chickadees and other small birds. Their range corresponds closely to the Eastern Temperate Forest Level I Ecoregion. Recently this species appears to be expanding its range farther to the north.

Class - **Aves** (birds)

Order - **Passeriformes** (songbirds)

Family - **Regulidae** (kinglets)

Ruby-crowned Kinglet *Regulus calendula*	Golden-crowned Kinglet *Regulus satrapa*

Size: Length 4.25 inches.

Abundance: Fairly common. During periods of peak migration they can be quite common, especially during fall cold fronts.

Variation: Male has red stripe on head that is visible when excited. Spring birds and juveniles are grayer above and less yellowish below.

Presumed range in New York

Migratory Status: Rare summer resident and common spring/fall migrant.

Habitat: Summer habitat is undisturbed boreal forest from the Atlantic to the Pacific and well into Alaska. Also summers in the higher elevations of the Rocky Mountains. Winter habitats much more generalized to include deciduous and mixed woodlands as well as swamps and lowlands.

Breeding: Breeds in old growth conifers in the far north. Produces enormous clutches of up to 12 eggs. Nest is built near the tops of spruce trees or fir trees. Nest is constructed of a wide variety of materials including mosses, lichens, blades of grass, and conifer needles. Fur, feathers, or animal hair are used to line the nest.

Natural History: This is one of America's smallest songbird species, smaller even than the Chickadee. The bright red blaze on the top of the head of the male is usually not visible unless the feathers of the crown are erected. Males most often display the red feathers on the crown when issuing a challenge to other males, displaying to females, or singing their territorial song. Otherwise their bright red crown feathers will remain hidden from view. In summer they prey on arthropods and their eggs. In winter they will also feed on berries and some seeds. They are hyper-active little birds that forage throughout the canopy as well as along lower branches. Clumps of dead leaves hanging from a tree limb are like magnets to these tiny hunters who will find small spiders, insects, and other diminutive arthropods hiding within the clumps. They will flick their wings open and shut while in near constant motion. Hunting occurs mostly along the tips of smaller branches. Some studies suggest this species may be declining in the eastern United States. Some believe this decline may be due to logging and forest fragmentation in the breeding range. Birds that pass through New York in migration are true latitudinal (north-south) migrants. Populations in the living in the Rocky Mountains of the western United States migrate from high elevations to lower elevations (altitudinal migration). Most of the nesting that occurs in New York is in the Adirondacks. Like many songbirds that summer in the boreal forests of the north, Ruby-crowned Kinglets fly south for the winter. Most winter in the southern United States, but some may go all the way to tropical Mexico.

Size: Length 4 inches.

Abundance: Fairly common.

Variation: Males have orange crown.

Presumed range in New York

Migratory Status: Year-round resident.

Habitat: This is a forest species that prefers mature woodlands with large trees for breeding. In winter they are seen in a variety of wooded habitats.

Breeding: Builds its nest in the top of a spruce or fir in northern woodlands. Lays a large clutch of up to 11 eggs and may produce two broods per year. Most nesting in New York occurs in the Appalachians.

Natural History: Even smaller than its cousin the Ruby-crowned Kinglet, the Golden-crowned is a hardier bird that can tolerate colder winter weather. However, severe winter conditions can lead to near 100 percent mortality in localized areas. Amazingly, this little carnivore manages to find arthropod prey throughout the winter and does not switch to seeds and berries in colder weather. Hyperactive and always in motion, they often feed by "leaf hawking" (hovering while picking tiny insects from beneath a leaves). In winter they are often seen in small groups or mixed flocks. Though found in New York year-round, some do fly south in winter and their winter range includes nearly all of the continental United States. In summer they strongly prefer old growth conifer forests. The golden streak on the crown of the female is in the male highlighted by a bright orange center.

Class - **Aves** (birds)
Order - **Passeriformes** (songbirds)
Family - **Sittidae** (nuthatches)

White-breasted Nuthatch *Sitta carolinensis*	**Red-breasted Nuthatch** *Sitta canadensis*

Size: Length 5.75 inches.

Abundance: Common.

Variation: None.

Migratory Status: The White-breasted Nuthatch is a year-round resident of New York.

Presumed range in New York

Size: Length 4.5 inches.

Abundance: Common.

Variation: None.

Migratory Status: Mostly a year-round resident in New York. Some birds may migrate farther south in winter.

Presumed range in New York

Breeding: Nests in natural tree cavities or woodpecker holes. Averages 6 eggs per clutch.

Breeding: Cavity nesters that excavate their own nest holes in the manner of woodpeckers. Average of 6 eggs.

Natural History: Nuthatches are famous for foraging tree trunks in an upside down position. This behavior gives them the opportunity to occupy a different feeding niche from woodpeckers and other bark hunting birds that hunt from an upright position. By creeping down the trunk in an upside down position the nuthatches may see tiny prey hidden in crevices visible only from an above perspective and therefore missed by woodpeckers and creepers. This is an example of different species partitioning the same habitat by exhibiting different foraging behavior. In addition to insects they also eat seeds and are regulars at most bird feeders in the state. They will cache seeds in bark crevices and they tend to be quite territorial. Pairs will stake out a territory and typically live within that area throughout the year. One of four species of nuthatch found in North America and the only one that may often be a full-time inhabitant of deciduous woodlands. Other species occupy boreal forests, southern pine forests, and western pine forests.

Natural History: These birds have a tendency to make "irruptive" migrations far to the south in winter every few years and the exact mechanism of their irruptive movements remains something of a mystery. It is believed to be related to cone production in northern coniferous forests where this species usually lives. During the spring and summer the Red-breasted Nuthatch feeds entirely on small arthropods. Seeds are the staple food during winter and Sunflower seeds are a favorite item at bird feeders. They will wedge seeds into bark crevices to hold them fast while using the beak to hammer open the shell in characteristic "nuthatch" fashion. They will glean insects from bark in the same upside down manner as their larger cousin the White-breasted Nuthatch. Unlike many cavity nesters the Red-breasted Nuthatch seems to avoid using man-made nest boxes. They are also one of the few birds other than woodpeckers to excavate their own den. It may take over two weeks to excavate their nest hole. They will reportedly line the entrance of the nest cavity with resin from conifers, possibly to deter other cavity nesters or potential predators.

Class - **Aves** (birds)

Order - **Passeriformes** (songbirds)

Family - **Troglodytidae** (wrens)

Carolina Wren *Thryothorus ludovicianus*	Marsh Wren *Cistothorus palustris*	Sedge Wren *Cistothorus platensis*

Carolina Wren

Size: 5.5 inches.

Abundance: Fairly common.

Variation: None.

Presumed range in New York

Migratory Status: Carolina Wrens are a year-round residents in New York.

Habitat: Carolina Wrens are very flexible in habitat choices. They can be seen in remote wilderness or in suburban backyards.

Breeding: A nest of fine twigs and grass is built in a sheltered place, often provided by man. Eggs number 3 to 6. Will produce at least two clutches per year.

Natural History: The Carolina Wren adepts well to human-influenced habitats and is well known for building its nest in an old pair of shoes or in a vase of flowers left on the back porch for a few days. They will become quite tame around yards and porches and frequently endear themselves to their human neighbors. They are voracious consumers of insects, spiders, and caterpillars and help control insect pests around the home. They are also incessant singers whose musical song serves as a dawn alarm for many residents throughout the state. They range across most of the southern two-thirds of New York south of the Adirondack region and are most common in the southeastern portions of the state and Long Island. Although vulnerable to exceptionally harsh winters, Carolina Wrens are expanding their range northward, perhaps in response to climate change.

Marsh Wren

Size: 5 inches.

Abundance: Uncommon.

Variation: None.

Presumed range in New York

Migratory Status: Summer resident in New York.

Habitat: Pastures, marshes, and lowland meadows as well as open, grassy edges of wetlands or ponds. Coastal salt marshes are widely used in winter.

Breeding: Nest is low in grasses or small bush. Nest is built of grasses woven into a ball with an entrance hole in the side. Several unused "decoy" nests are built. 7 eggs is typical.

Natural History: Marsh Wrens winter well to the south of New York and summer throughout most of the state. They may be seen anywhere in the state where suitable habitat exists from mid-May to October. These are secretive birds that can be very difficult to observe, even in areas where they are common; and they are not common in most of New York. They spend most of their time hidden in thick stands of cattails or other vegetation deep in the marsh. Like most wrens they will sing continuously in the breeding season and most birdwatchers confirm their presence by learning to recognize their song. They will build one or more "decoy" nests that are never used and they are also known to destroy the eggs of other birds that may be nesting in the vicinity of their own nests. Fresh water marshes of cattail and sedges are a favorite breeding habitat in New York.

Sedge Wren

Size: 4.25 inches.

Abundance: Rare in New York.

Variation: None.

Presumed range in New York

Migratory Status: Spring/fall migrant through New York.

Habitat: This is a wetland species that enjoys marshes and wet meadows. Unlike the Marsh Wren it does not occupy cattail marsh but prefers grassy areas.

Breeding: Nest is built low to the ground, often in a clump of sedges or a small bush. 6 or 7 eggs is typical and some may produce two broods per year. Nesting occurs in western New York.

Natural History: This is another secretive species that is difficult to observe. Like the Marsh Wren it winters well to the south of New York but it is a rare summer resident in western New York. The natural history of this species is poorly known, but it is known that nesting dates vary considerably from one region of the country to another. Nesting can occur from May to as late as September. Some birds may produce two broods per year in two different regions. The diet is spiders and insects. Sedge Wrens winter in coastal plain of the southeastern United States from the Carolinas all the way to northwestern Mexico. Fall migration begins in September and most birds are usually gone from the northern portions of their range by late October. Spring migration in the midwest begins in April and continues into early May. Listed as Threatened Species by the NYSDEC.

Class - **Aves** (birds)

Order - **Passeriformes** (songbirds)

Family - **Troglodytidae** (wrens)

House Wren *Troglodytes aedon*	Winter Wren *Troglodytes troglodytes*

Family - **Polioptilidae** (gnatcathers)

Blue-gray Gnatcatcher *Polioptila caerulea*

Size: Length 4.75 inches.	Presumed range in New York 
Abundance: Very common.	
Variation: None.	

Size: Length 4 inches.	Presumed range in New York 
Abundance: Failrly common.	
Variation: None.	

Size: Length 4.25 inches.	Presumed range in New York 
Abundance: Common.	
Variation: Sexes very similar.	

Migratory Status: A spring/summer resident that begins to arrive in New York in May and departs in the fall.

Migratory Status: Year-round resident in southern New York. Summer resident in the Adirondacks.

Migratory Status: One of the earliest returning summer migrants, arriving in New York as early as mid-April.

Habitat: Prefers open and semi-open habitats. These wrens readily associate with humans and are most common in small towns and suburbs. They can also be common in more natural habitats.

Habitat: Mature, old growth forests are the primary summer habitat, often near a stream or bog. Deciduous and mixed woodlands are utilized in winter, but conifers are preferred.

Habitat: Occupies a wide variety of forested or successional habitats. Most common along wooded streams and bottoms. Shows a definite preference for deciduous woodlands.

Breeding: A cavity nester, the House Wren readily takes to artificial nest boxes. In fact, this species may owe its increase in population to man-made "bird houses." Lays up to 8 eggs.

Breeding: Breeds mainly in boreal forests. Nest is often constructed in the root wad of an upturned tree. A wide-spread breeding bird in New York state. Lays 5 to 9 eggs.

Breeding: Nest is a cup-like structure built with lichens and plant fibers glued together with spider web. Nest usually placed at mid-level near the terminus of a branch. 4 to 5 eggs is average.

Natural History: Although the House Wren may be seen anywhere in New York, it is least common in the Adirondack region of the state, but some breeding does occur there. They are more common today than in historical times, as they favor open and semi-open habitats over dense forests (thus their relative scarcity in the Adirondacks). They also have a strong affinity for human-altered habitats and settlements. They feed on a wide variety of insects, spiders, snails, caterpillars, etc. When feeding large broods of young they catch huge quantities of arthropod prey daily. House Wrens range from coast to coast across America and northward into the prairie provinces of Canada. House Wrens are one of the most studied of America's bird species.

Natural History: Much shyer and more secretive than other wrens, the Winter Wren skulks about under dense bushes and shrubs where it tends to stay close to the ground. This species has likely declined since presettlement times due to the destruction of ancient forests. Like other wrens, these birds are strictly carnivorous and feed on a wide variety of small insects, larva, arachnids, amphipoda, etc. As with many other invertivorous birds, they are vulnerable to exceptionally harsh winters. Their stubby, upturned tail makes identification easy, but they are more often heard than seen as they are persistent, loud singers. Winter Wrens are holarctic in distribution, being found in Europe and northern Asia as well as North America. Widespread in New York in summer.

Natural History: As their name implies, gnatcatchers feed on tiny prey. Any type of small arthropod is probable food item. They hunt the tips of tree branches and sometimes pick off prey while hovering. Despite their small size they will chase away larger birds and will mob predators such as hawks, snakes, or house cats. The gnatcatchers are a unique family that is probably most closely related to the wrens. Like many small songbird species the Blue-gray Gnatcatcher is often the victim of nest parasitism by the Brown-headed Cowbird, which lays its eggs in other birds' nests. Despite cowbirds, they seem to be a thriving species and their range has been expanding northward in recent times. They winter as far south as Central America and the Carribean.

Class - **Aves** (birds)

Order - **Passeriformes** (songbirds)

Family - **Hirundinidae** (swallows)

Barn Swallow *Hirundo rustica*	**Cliff Swallow** *Petrochelidon pyrrhonota*	**Bank Swallow** *Riparia riparia*

Barn Swallow	Cliff Swallow	Bank Swallow
Size: 7 inches. **Abundance:** Very common. **Variation:** Male is more vivid.  Presumed range in New York	**Size:** 5.5 inches. **Abundance:** Fairly common. **Variation:** None.  Presumed range in New York	**Size:** 5.25 inches. **Abundance:** Uncommon. **Variation:** None.  Presumed range in New York
Migratory Status: A summer resident that returns to the state in early April.	**Migratory Status:** Summer resident. Arrives in New York in May.	**Migratory Status:** Summer resident. Begins to arrive in New York in April.
Habitat: Open and semi-open habitats. Most common in agricultural areas but found virtually everywhere in the state. Least common in the Adirondacks.	**Habitat:** Open areas near large bodies of water are the preferred habitat for this species. Breeding habitat was historically limited to regions with cliff faces.	**Habitat:** Open country near large rivers. In migration may be seen in a wide variety of habitats but most often observed in valleys, near lakes, etc.
Breeding: Nest is bowl shaped and made of mud and grasses plastered to roof joists of a barn or eaves of buildings, beneath concrete bridges, etc.	**Breeding:** Conical mud nests are plastered beneath sheltered overhangs of concrete structures such as bridges or dams. 4 eggs is typical.	**Breeding:** Historically nested in high, steep banks along major rivers. Nest hole is dug by the parents and may be as much as 2–3 feet deep. 4 to 6 eggs.
Natural History: A familiar bird to all who grew up on rural farmsteads. Barn Swallows are common throughout most of North America in summer, and birds that summer in the United States winter in Central and South America. The Barn Swallow breeds throughout the northern hemisphere and European breeders winter in the Mediterranean, Africa, and the Middle East; while Asian breeding birds winter throughout southeast Asia to Australia. Thus this is one of the most widespread bird species in the world. Its long association with humans throughout the world has led to the invention of many legends. Barn Swallows nesting in your barn was considered by American pioneers as good luck, while destroying a nest in the barn would cause the milk cow to go dry. Flying insects are the main food including pesky flies and even wasps. This is the world's most common swallow species.	**Natural History:** The Cliff Swallow is primarily a western species that nested historically on cliff faces in the Rocky Mountains. They are more numerous in New York today than even a few decades ago. Man-made structures such as dams and bridges have likely helped this species expand its range in the eastern United States and into New York. These birds are colony animals that seem to always nest in groups. In the east there seems to be a preference for nesting near water, and colony size varies from a few dozen to a few hundred nests. Farther west, where the species is more common and widespread, colonies consisting of several thousand nests are known. Like other swallows they feed almost entirely upon airborne insects, and they are adept at locating swarms of airborne prey. In New York this species is least common in heavily wooded regions such as the Adirondacks.	**Natural History:** Although widespread across America during migration, this species is perhaps one of the least common swallows in New York. Like many swallows the Bank Swallow often nests in large communities. Nest colonies are usually associated with large river systems. Despite being somewhat uncommon in New York, these birds are found throughout the world, in fact they are one of the most widespread bird species on Earth. The natural nesting habitat has always been riverbanks and bluffs, but today this species utilizes the banks created by man-made quarries or road cuts through hillsides. During migration Bank Swallows can be seen in the company of other species of migrating swallows. Food is exclusively flying insects caught on the wing, mostly flies, flying ants, small beetles, and mayflies. Since these swallows love open country, they are least common in New York in the Adirondack region.

Class - **Aves** (birds)
Order - **Passeriformes** (songbirds)
Family - **Hirundinidae** (swallows)

Northern Rough-winged Swallow *Stelgidopteryx serripennis*	Tree Swallow *Tachycineta bicolor*	Purple Martin *Progne subis*

Size: Length 5.5 inches.	Presumed range in New York 	**Size:** Length 5.75 inches.	Presumed range in New York 	**Size:** Length 8 inches.	Presumed range in New York
Abundance: Fairly common.		**Abundance:** Very common.		**Abundance:** Fairly common.	
Variation: None. Sexes are alike.		**Variation:** Immatures are glossy gray.		**Variation:** Sexually dimorphic (see above).	

Migratory Status: Summer resident. Winters in south Florida and in Central America. In New York April to Oct.	**Migratory Status:** A warm-weather bird that arrives in New York in early spring after wintering well to the south.	**Migratory Status:** Summer resident. The first arriving birds are males and they may arrive as early as April.
Habitat: Mainly open and semi-open areas, but can be found in forested regions along rivers or cliffs.	**Habitat:** Open and semi-open habitats. Fond of being near water, including small farm ponds and Beaver swamps.	**Habitat:** Inhabits both rural areas and suburbs. Artificial nest boxes near water in open areas are attractants.
Breeding: Nests in crevices in rock faces, cliffs, etc. Today often uses man-made situations such as road cuts, quarries, etc. Not a colony nester. Lays 4 to 8 eggs.	**Breeding:** A cavity nester, Tree Swallows will use old woodpecker holes or tree hollows. They also use artificial nest boxes and sometimes nest in close proximity to Purple Martins.	**Breeding:** Originally nested in natural cavities but today nearly all use artificial nest sites. 3 to 6 eggs is typical but may lay as many as 7 or 8. Purple Martins are colony nesters.
Natural History: As with other swallows the Rough-winged Swallow feeds by catching flying insects in mid-air. All swallows in America are diurnal hunters whose predatory role is replaced at dusk by the bats. Although this swallow is found from coast to coast across America it is not extremely common anywhere. Unlike the similar Bank Swallow, Rough-winged Swallows are not known to dig their own burrow and availability of nest burrows may be one reason why these swallows tend to be solitary nesters. They will use burrows dug by other species of birds or small mammals as well as natural cavities in cliff faces. They are also known to use man-made structures. In mountainous regions this species is usually associated with river valleys.	**Natural History:** Tree Swallows are probably more numerous in New York today than in historical times due to the activities of man. Human activities have benefited this species by creating more open lands and also by creating more ponds and lakes throughout the landscape. The proliferation of artificial nest boxes has also helped (they take readily to bluebird boxes); and the resurgence of Beaver populations is also credited with helping this species. Flying insects are the primary food items, but the species also eats bayberries during the winter. They are also known to eat snails during the breeding season to obtain calcium for eggshell production. The Tree Swallow winters along the southeastern coastline of the United States, Florida, Mexico, and the Caribbean.	**Natural History:** Our largest swallow and perhaps the most beloved bird in America. Many people anxiously await the return of Purple Martins each spring to nest boxes erected in their yard. This bird's relationship with humans extends at least as far back as the 18th century and today there are at least two national organizations dedicated to Purple Martin enthusiasts. House Sparrows and Starlings sometimes take over "martin houses" unless the landowner is vigilant. Mainly a warm weather species that is dependent upon flying insect prey, Purple Martins are vulnerable to spring cold fronts in the more northern reaches of the summer range. This species is so adapted to nesting in man-made nest boxes that today it is rare to find one nesting in natural cavities.

Class - **Aves** (birds)

Order - **Passeriformes** (songbirds)

Family - **Corvidae** (crows and jays)

American Crow *Corvus brachyrhynchos*	Fish Crow *Corvus ossifragus*	Common Raven *Corvus corax*

American Crow
Corvus brachyrhynchos

Size: 19 inches.

Abundance: Common.

Variation: None. Sexes are alike.

Presumed range in New York

Migratory Status: This is one of New York's year-round birds, but some may move south in winter.

Habitat: Occurs in virtually all habitats including urban areas. Favors regions where there is a patchwork of woods and open spaces. Also common in agricultural areas where waste grain is an important food source.

Breeding: Crows build a bulky stick nest high in the fork of a tree, well hidden by thick foliage. The nest is quite large and may be 2 feet across. 4 eggs is typical.

Natural History: Crows are omnivores that will eat virtually anything, including the young and eggs of other birds. They are among the most intelligent and resourceful of birds. They may be seen in pairs, small groups, or large flocks numbering in the hundreds. Highly adaptable, crows have fared well in human-altered habitats and the species is more common today than prior to European settlement. As a testament to the crow's intelligence, in rural areas where hunting is commonplace, they are extremely wary of humans; while in protected parks and urban regions they will become quite accepting of the presence of humans, often haunting the parking lots of fast food restaurants in search of scraps. Longevity record for a wild bird is 17.5 years.

Fish Crow
Corvus ossifragus

Size: 15 inches.

Abundance: Uncommon.

Variation: None. Sexes are alike.

Presumed range in New York

Migratory Status: Year-round in coastal areas, but a summer-only resident in inland regions of New York.

Habitat: Mainly a coastal species that favors estuaries, salt marsh, beaches, and dunes. Often invades inland areas along river valleys and in the vicinity of large lakes. Habitat can include urban parks, golf courses, and suburbs.

Breeding: Large stick nest is placed in a tree crotch. Averages about 4 eggs. A single clutch is produced annually. Un-mated adults are known to bring food to nestlings of mated birds.

Natural History: Identical to the American Crow but smaller. They are often seen in the company of their larger cousin and when seen together the Fish Crow can be distinguished by its smaller size. Expert bird watchers can identify this species by its call, which is higher pitched than that of the American Crow. A southern species that historically was found in coastal areas and lowlands of the lower coastal plain, the Fish Crow has expanded its range northward over the last few decades. They are also increasing in inland areas, including in New York. All members of the *Corvus* genus are omnivorous, and the Fish Crow is no exception. In addition to all types of edible vegetable matter they will eat baby birds and bird eggs as well as any small animal caught.

Common Raven
Corvus corax

Size: 24 inches.

Abundance: Fairly common.

Variation: None. Sexes are alike.

Presumed range in New York

Migratory Status: Ravens are non-migratory year-round residents in New York.

Habitat: Ravens today inhabit both remote wilderness and urban environments. They have experienced a population boom in recent years and can today been seen nearly statewide, including rarely in New York City.

Breeding: Nest consists of sticks and twigs placed in a tall tree or a ledge on a cliff face. Rarely may nest on man-made structures such as water towers. 3 to 7 eggs per clutch.

Natural History: Like their relatives the crows, the ravens are intelligent, highly adaptable birds. They are found mostly in the western United States and in the boreal forests of the far north, but they have been recorded from most counties in New York. A few decades ago they were an uncommon bird in the state and their range in New York was restricted to the Adirondacks and the Catskills. Today they are presumed to occur statewide (or nearly so). They are consummate opportunists that will consume a wide variety of plant and animal matter ranging from carrion to human garbage. They are also known for their aerial antics and flight maneuvers and for their playful mischievousness. They are equally at home in remote wilderness or regions of significant human habitation.

Class - **Mammalia** (mammals)
Order - **Passeriformes** (songbirds)
Family - **Corvidae** (crows and jays)

Blue Jay *Cyanocitta cristata*	**Gray Jay** *Perisoreus canadensis*

Size: Length 11 inches.	Presumed range in New York 	**Size:** Length 11.5 inches.	Presumed range in New York 
Abundance: Common.		**Abundance:** Uncommon.	
Variation: None.		**Variation:** None in New York.	
Migratory Status: Although Blue Jays in some populations may migrate, they can be seen year-round in New York.		**Migratory Status:** Gray Jays are non-migratory year-round residents throughout their range.	

Habitat: State-wide from dense woodlands to semi-open farmlands. They can also be common in suburban and urban neighborhoods. The presence of at least some trees seems to be a requirement.	**Habitat:** Coniferous forests of northern North America and high mountain ranges are the home of the Gray Jay. They are a truly boreal species whose range extends well above the Arctic Circle.
Breeding: Builds a stick nest fairly high up on a tree branch, often in a fork. Lays an average of 4 eggs. Blue Jays in the southern United States may produce more than on clutch per year. Probably only one per year in New York.	**Breeding:** This species is unique among passerine birds in that it nests in late winter. More amazing is the fact that it nests in winter in areas where temperatures can drop well below zero. Young are hatched as early as late February.
Natural History: The Blue Jay's handsome blue, black, and white feathers and distinctive crest make it one of the most recognizable birds in the state. They mainly eat insects, acorns, and grains, but also eat eggs and young of other songbirds. They will aggressively mob much larger birds like hawks and owls, as well as snakes and house cats. Members of this family are relatively long-lived. The record lifespan for a wild Blue Jay is 18 years, but a captive specimen was reported to have lived for 26 years. An endemic American bird, Blue Jays are found throughout the eastern half of the United States from about the Rocky Mountains eastward. They also range northward into Canada but well below the Arctic Circle. Although they are common and widespread across the eastern half of North America, they never seem to be exceedingly plentiful. Small flocks of a few to a dozen is most common. They may be very common in suburban areas with large trees. May be vulnerable to mosquito-borne avian diseases.	**Natural History:** Anyone who has experienced the long, frigid winters of the remote wilderness "north country" where the Gray Jay makes its home has to admire the survival capacity of this plucky little bird. Finding food in winter in such a place seems a daunting challenge. Not only does the Gray Jay thrive in this harsh environment, it actually chooses to raise its young here during the fiercest time of year. How it manages to find enough food for itself and its brood in mid-winter is a bit of mystery. One tactic utilized by the Gray Jay is storage of large amounts of food from spring through fall. Food caches are then retrieved throughout the harsh winter. Food is anything edible, from berries and seeds to small animals and carrion. Gray Jays are ever alert for food opportunites and they will shadow humans who venture into their wilderness homes hoping to pick up a few scraps. In fact, birds that may have never seen a human can sometimes be enticed to take food from the hand.

Class - **Aves** (birds)

Order - **Passeriformes** (songbirds)

Family - **Vireonidae** (vireos)

Yellow-throated Vireo *Vireo flavifrons*	White-eyed Vireo *Vireo griseus*	Blue-headed Vireo *Vireo solitarius*

Size: Length 5.5 inches.	**Size:** Length 5 inches.	**Size:** Length 5.5 inches.
Abundance: Fairly common.	**Abundance:** Uncommon.	**Abundance:** Uncommon.
Variation: None.	**Variation:** None.	**Variation:** None.

Presumed range in New York    Presumed range in New York    Presumed range in New York

Migratory Status: A long-range migrant that winters as far away as northern South America. Returns to New York in early May.	**Migratory Status:** Winters from the lower coastal plain of the United States into Mexico, Cuba, and Bahamas. Returns to southern New York around early May.	**Migratory Status:** Summer resident and spring/fall migrant. Breeding birds return to New York around late April. Most will leave by the end of September.
Habitat: A woodland bird that will inhabit a wide variety of forest types excluding stands of pure conifers. In New York it is least common in the Adirondack region.	**Habitat:** Dense thickets and early successional hardwoods are favored. May also be seen in later stage successional deciduous woodlands and in overgrown fields with small saplings and thickets.	**Habitat:** This vireo likes expanses of mature forests, and is also partial to conifers for its summer habitat. It thus summers mostly to the north of New York in the boreal forests of Canada.
Breeding: The nest is a woven basket usually suspended from the fork of a small branch at the mid-story level. 4 eggs is typical.	**Breeding:** Nest is a woven, hanging basket held together with silk from caterpillars or spiders placed in a fork very low to the ground. 3 to 5 eggs.	**Breeding:** Nest construction is similar to other vireos. A tightly woven cup is suspended from a horizontal fork. 4 eggs is typical.
Natural History: The nest is usually located in a branch overhanging a forest opening such as a lane or a stream. Feeds on a wide variety of arthropods with caterpillars being a mainstay. Also eats small amount of berries and seeds in the fall. The biology of this species is not as well understood as with many other vireos, but it is known that it has decreased in numbers in areas of deforestation. As with many small woodland songbirds, the nest of the Yellow-throated Vireo is subject to parasitism by cowbirds. The summer range of this species coincides closely with the Eastern Temperate Forest Level I Ecoregion. The winter range is from southern Mexico to northern South America. Migrants regularly fly across the Gulf of Mexico.	**Natural History:** This is the only vireo with a white iris, making identification easy. Nest parasitism by Brown-headed Cowbirds is estimated to be as high as 50 percent, with no young surviving in parasitized nests. Highly insectivorous. Caterpillars are a favorite food item. Will also eat fruit. New York represents the northernmost extension of this species range in the eastern United States, and it is seen only in the southern tip of the state. Like the previous species, nest parasitism by Brown-headed Cowbirds posses a potential threat. Deforestation contributes to the problem. Brown-headed Cowbirds tend to avoid deep woods in favor of more open habitats. Loss of large tracts of woodland makes life easier for the cowbirds and more difficult for the species which they parasitize.	**Natural History:** Also known as the Solitary Vireo. Most Blue-headed Vireos summer in Canada and in the higher elevations of the Appalachians. They winter from the lower coastal plain of the southeastern United States all the way to Central America. They are quite common in peninsular Florida throughout the winter. Food is mostly insects, with moths and butterflies and their larva being a major portion of the diet. Most foraging is done in trees well above the forest floor. As is the case with many of America's migrant songbirds, the Blue-headed Vireo is highly dependent upon large tracts of forest. Deforestation negatively impacts local populations; but forest regeneration in many areas of its summer range has helped this species in recent years.

Class - **Aves** (birds)		
Order - **Passeriformes** (songbirds)		
Family - **Vireonidae** (vireos)		

Red-eyed Vireo *Vireo olivaceus*	**Warbling Vireo** *Vireo gilvus*	**Philadelphia Vireo** *Vireo philadelphia*
		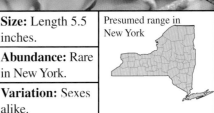

Size: Length 6 inches. **Abundance:** Very common. **Variation:** Male is larger.	Presumed range in New York	**Size:** Length 5.5 inches. **Abundance:** Uncommon. **Variation:** None.	Presumed range in New York	**Size:** Length 5.5 inches. **Abundance:** Rare in New York. **Variation:** Sexes alike.	Presumed range in New York

Migratory Status: A summer resident that winters in the Amazon Basin. Peak arrival in New York is in mid-May.

Migratory Status: Peak appearance in New York early to mid-May. Winters in Mexico and Central America.

Migratory Status: Migrant throughout the state. Some will nest and spend the summer in the Adirondack region.

Habitat: Although a woodland species, the Red-eyed Vireo is very generalized in its habitat requirements. Mature forests, regenerating woodlands, and forest fragments are all occupied.

Habitat: Although this species likes mature trees in its habitat, it avoids dense forest in favor of areas with a mosaic of small woodlands. Riparian woodlands are also utilized.

Habitat: Philadelphia Vireo can be found in large tracts of forest, but it seems to favor successional woodlands over mature. Uses mixed conifer and deciduous woodlands.

Breeding: 2–4 eggs are laid. May have two broods per summer with second brood fledging in late August.

Breeding: Nesting takes place in mid-summer. Nests are placed high in trees. 4 eggs is typical.

Breeding: The breeding range of the Philadelphia Vireo is mostly in Canada. Clutch size is typically 4 eggs.

Natural History: This is one of the most common summer songbirds in the forests and woodlots of eastern North America, but it is not readily observed due to its habit of staying high in the forest canopy. It is however regularly heard, as it sings incessantly throughout the spring. While on their breeding grounds they are primarily insectivorous feeders, but they do consume some fruits while wintering in the tropics. The population health of the Red-eyed Vireo may be due to its less stringent dependence upon large tracts of forest. This species can subsist happily in small woodlands and regenerative areas. However, in these habitats it is more susceptible to the parasitic nesting of the Brown-headed Cowbird. Most Red-eyed Vireos nesting in New York will have departed by mid-September. Red eye color is unique among vireos.

Natural History: The Warbling Vireo is least common in New York in the heavily forested Adirondack region. They are widespread, however, in most of the rest of the state. Like the similar Red-eyed Vireo, they are persistent singers that are more often heard than seen. They feed by gleaning small insects and other arthropods from canopy foliage. A few seeds and berries are also sometimes eaten. This is one of the most widely distributed members of the North American Vireonidae family. Their breeding range extends from coast to coast across the northern two-thirds of the United States as well as much of Canada. By contrast, the winter range is much smaller and restricted to the western half of Mexico and western Central America from northern Costa Rica northward. Visual identification of vireos on this page can be a challenge.

Natural History: The Philadelphia Vireo migrates through most of New York each spring but it does not nest in most of the state. Some nesting does occur in the Adirondacks and the higher elevations of Tug Hill. They are a somewhat rarely observed bird and are difficult to distinguish from the more common Warbling Vireo, but they usually have more yellowish wash below. They are also very similar to the Red-eyed Vireo and their song also closely resembles that species. Their food is mostly caterpillars. As with many other neotropical migrant songbirds that can be seen in New York, this species is a trans-gulf migrant that makes epic non-stop flights across the Gulf of Mexico during migration. The payoff for these perilous journeys is a breeding habitat that is rich in insect foods and less competition from other bird species.

Class - **Aves** (birds)

Order - **Passeriformes** (songbirds)

Family - **Parulidae** (warblers)

Canada Warbler *Cardellina canadensis*	Wilson's Warbler *Cardellina pusilla*	Yellow-breasted Chat *Icteria virens*

Size: 5.25 inches.

Abundance: Fairly common.

Variation: Females have less black.

Presumed range in New York

Migratory Status: Summer resident. Peak arrival is mid-May. Fall departure is late August or early September typically. Winters from southern Mexico to northern South America.

Habitat: Favors moist northern forests with thick understory shrubs. In New York they are more common nesters in the higher elevations.

Breeding: Nest is on the ground and hidden amid dense vegetation. In Canada nest is often placed amid carpet of moss. 4 or 5 eggs is typical.

Natural History: As its name implies, the bulk of this warbler's breeding range (over 80 percent) is in Canada. However, they do migrate through all of New York and breeding has also been documented nearly statewide. Migration is at night and they pass quickly through southern states en route to breeding grounds farther to the north. Loss of breeding habitat in North America as well as wintering habitat in South America is probably to blame for the fact that this is generally and uncommon warbler species. Future threats include the Woolly Adelgid, an alien insect that is decimating hemlock forests throughout the Appalachians. Formerly this species was placed in the genus *Wilsonia*.

Size: 4.75 inches.

Abundance: Fairly common.

Variation: Black "cap" more prominent in males.

Presumed range in New York

Migratory Status: A passage migrant in most of New York. Very rare summer resident in the Adirondacks. Most spring migrating birds will have passed through the state by the end of May.

Habitat: Summer breeding habitat is in the boreal forests of Canada, pacific northwest, northern Rockies, and Alaska. Winter habitat is tropical forests.

Breeding: Nest is on the ground. Uniquely, the nest of this warbler is usually placed in a small depression. From 2 to 7 eggs may be laid.

Natural History: Wilson's Warbler is more common in the western half of America than in New York. Although they may migrate through any part of the state, the bulk of this species population occurs and migrates to the west. But some will travel though the state and nesting has been recorded in the Adirondacks. Though they are probably more numerous in the pacific states than they are in the eastern United States, some studies indicate that they are recently declining in the west. Most blame the loss of riparian habitat for decline in western populations. They range as far north as the Arctic Ocean in summer and as far south as Panama in winter. The species name *"wilsonia"* is for early naturalist and ornithologist Alexander Wilson.

Size: 7.5 inches.

Abundance: Rare in New York.

Variation: None. Sexes alike.

Presumed range in New York

Migratory Status: Summer resident in extreme southeastern New York and in western New York. Winters in southern Mexico and throughout Central America. Arrives in New York in mid-May.

Habitat: This warbler likes overgrown fields, second growth areas, and early successional regenerating woodlands. It avoids the deep woods.

Breeding: Nests low to the ground in brier thickets or a dense shrub such as a multiflora rose. Nest is cup-like. Lays 2 to 5 eggs.

Natural History: The Yellow-breasted Chat is America's largest wood warbler and some question its status in the family Parulidae. They are fairly common in suitable habitats throughout the southern United States in summer months but are very rare in New York. They are not easily observed due to their secretive nature and preference for dense vegetation. Foods are a wide variety of arthropods with a preference for crickets, grasshoppers, caterpillars, and spiders. They are also known to eat some fruits and berries. These birds are probably more numerous today than prior to deforestation. Their breeding range in eastern North America corresponds closely to the Eastern Temperate Forest level I Ecoregion. A NYSDEC Species of Special Concern.

Class - **Aves** (birds)

Order - **Passeriformes** (songbirds)

Family - **Parulidae** (warblers)

Cape May Warbler *Setophaga tigrina*	Hooded Warbler *Setophaga citrina*	Northern Parula *Setophaga americana*
	 Male / Female	

Cape May Warbler	Hooded Warbler	Northern Parula
Size: 5 inches.	**Size:** 5.25 inches.	**Size:** 4.5 inches.
Abundance: Uncommon.	**Abundance:** Fairly common.	**Abundance:** Fairly common.
Variation: Females lack chestnut cheek patch.	**Variation:** Female lacks black "hood" on head.	**Variation:** Females lack black on breast.

Presumed range in New York

Migratory Status: Widespread migrant in spring and fall and very rare summer resident in the Adirondack region. A late spring migrant, with passage in New York peaking in mid- to late May. Fall migration begins in late August.

Habitat: This is another species that summers in boreal forests, primarily in the vicinity of spruce bogs and other forest openings. Winter habitat is mostly in the West Indies.

Breeding: Nest is near the trunk in the top of a spruce or fir. 5 or 6 eggs are laid in early to mid June. One clutch per year. Most breed farther north in Canada.

Natural History: On summer breeding grounds in northern forests the Cape May Warbler spends its time high in the trees. Feeds heavily on Spruce Budworm caterpillars. Their breeding cycle corresponds to the timing of maximum availability of budworm caterpillars and the population density of this species is known to be closely tied to the presence of this food source. In years of heavy budworm infestations they will rear large broods. On wintering grounds they are known to feed heavily upon nectar and fruits. They have a specialized tubular tongue for extracting nectar from flowers and juices from fruit. Has nested in the Adirondacks (rare).

Migratory Status: After wintering in Central America and parts of the Caribbean, the Hooded Warbler returns to New York in late April through mid-May Leaves for wintering grounds by September.

Habitat: A forest species. Range in New York restricted to the southern half of the state. Habitat requirments are woodlands with dense understory. Most common in western New York.

Breeding: Cup-shaped nest of grasses, bark, and dead leaves is woven into two or more upright limbs of a small bush near the ground. Nest sites are usually associated with dense shrubs. 4 eggs.

Natural History: Like many small, woodland birds the Hooded Warbler is more likely to be heard than seen. On their breeding grounds in the eastern United States they require large tracts of woodlands, and they have declined in areas where intensive agriculture or development has resulted in the loss of this habitat. This handsome little warbler is a good example of why the protection of extensive tracts of forest can be so important in the conservation of neotropical migrant songbirds. With the largest eyes of any warbler, this species is adapted to a life spent in heavy shade. Some females exhibit varying amounts of black "hooding" seen in males.

Migratory Status: Summer resident. Winters from south Florida to Central America. Arrives in New York in April and begins to leave in August or September. All are gone by early October. Migrates at night.

Habitat: Habitat is forest. Mostly bottomland woods or swamps or along streams and rivers. Also moist ravines in the mountains. In New York is most common in the Adirondack region.

Breeding: Nests high in trees. Sycamores, Baldcypress, and Hemlocks are reported as favorite nest trees in the south. In the deep south nests are often built in Spanish moss. 4 or 5 eggs.

Natural History: The Northern Parula feeds by gleaning tiny arthropods from tree branches. They tend to feed and spend much time in the middle and upper story of the forest. This habit coupled with their small size make them difficult to observe even in areas where they may be common. The summer range of this species includes most of the eastern United States east of the Great Plains region. They nest from southern Florida to southern Canada. The species appears to be thriving but like all neotropical migrants it is subject to threats by human-induced activites such as insecticide use and habitat alterations such as logging.

Class - **Aves** (birds)

Order - **Passeriformes** (songbirds)

Family - **Parulidae** (warblers)

Yellow Warbler *Setophaga petechia*	Black-throated Blue Warbler *Setophaga caerulescens*	Cerulean Warbler *Setophaga cerulea*

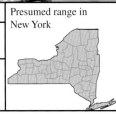

Size: 5 inches.

Abundance: Common.

Variation: Sexually dimorphic. See above photos.

Presumed range in New York

Size: 5.25 inches.

Abundance: Fairly common.

Variation: Females are drab olive on back.

Presumed range in New York

Size: 4.75 inches.

Abundance: Rare.

Variation: Female is blueish green.

Presumed range in New York

Migratory Status: Summer resident. Winters in Mexico and Central America. Most birds nesting in New York arrive in early to mid-May.

Migratory Status: Summer resident in most of New York. Absent as nester in the Interior Lowlands but can occur there as a migrant. Winters in the Caribbean.

Migratory Status: Winters in the Andes Mountains. Flies across the gulf to southeastern United States coast then northward into interior, arriving in New York by mid-April.

Habitat: Thickets of willow or buttonbush in wet lowlands are the classic habitat for this species. Riparian woodlands and mesic upland woods are also used.

Habitat: Summer habitat consists of large, contiguous tracts of mature forests. Both hardwood and mixed forest are used, but mainly northern forests types are inhabited in summer.

Habitat: Summer habitat is primarily deciduous forests. Both bottomland forest and moist mountain slopes. In New York this species is most common in the west and in the southeast.

Breeding: Nest is built in the upright fork of a sapling and averages 4 or 5 eggs. Nest is a cup-like structure made mostly from grasses. Breeds throughout most of the state.

Breeding: Nest is strips of bark lined with finer materials such as moss. Usually placed in an upright fork of dense shrub. Clutch size typically 4. Apparently does not breed on Long Island.

Breeding: Nest is a tight cup woven around forked branches in the mid to upper canopy level. Average clutch size is 3 or 4 to as many as 5. Breeding habitat includes thick understory.

Natural History: This is one of North America's most wide-ranging of the warblers. Their summer breeding range encompasses the entire northern two thirds of North America, from the Atlantic to the Pacific and extends as far north as the Arctic Circle. Although they may be seen statewide in New York, this species is much less common in the Adirondack Mountains. Feeds on a variety of insects and other arthropods and uses a variety of foraging techniques including gleaning of leaves and branches, flying from perch to seize airborne prey, and picking insects from leaves and branches while hovering. Caterpillars are an important food item during breeding. This species shows a strong affinity for willow trees.

Natural History: This species forages mostly in shrubs and branches at the mid-story level for caterpillars and other small arthropod prey. Deforestation and forest fragmentation in both summer and winter habitats are the greatest threats. These threats may be compounded by habitat degradation from alien species like the Woolly Adelgid. The summer range of this species in North America is contained to the east of the Mississippi River, and the bulk of the population summers from the Appalachians eastward. In the Appalachians they range as far south as northern Georgia. Food is a variety of small invertebrate prey with caterpillars constituting a significant element in the diet.

Natural History: The Cerulean Warbler hunts high in the canopy, gleaning tiny invertebrates from small branches and leaves. Searches both upper and lower surface of leaves for food. Like many species dependent upon forests, this warbler experienced significant population declines following the European settlement of America. Listed as a Species of Concern by NYSDEC, Cerulean Warbler populations have declined significantly from historical times and that sad trend seems to be continuing even today. Loss of mature forests in the United States coupled with habitat loss on winter grounds is blamed. Even in areas where they occur, they are difficult to observe due to their habit of staying high in the canopy.

Class - **Aves** (birds)

Order - **Passeriformes** (songbirds)

Family - **Parulidae** (warblers)

Magnolia Warbler *Setophaga magnolia*	**Yellow-rumped Warbler** *Setophaga coronata*	**Blackpoll Warbler** *Setophaga striata*

Size: 5 inches. **Abundance:** Fairly common. **Variation:** See above photos.	Presumed range in New York	**Size:** 5.5 inches. **Abundance:** Common. **Variation:** See above photos.	Presumed range in New York	**Size:** 5.25 inches. **Abundance:** Uncommon. **Variation:** See above photos.	Presumed range in New York

Migratory Status: Migrant in the coastal plain of the southeastern tip of the state. Summer resident throughout the rest of the state.

Habitat: Summer habitat for most is in spruce forests in Canada and in the northeastern United States. Thickets of young conifers are preferred. Winters in Mexico, Central America, and Caribbean.

Breeding: Nests in evergreen trees. The nest is usually well concealed amid dense vegetation. 4 eggs laid. Nest is always in a conifer such as spruce, fir, or in the southern Applachians, hemlock.

Natural History: Feeds on insects (including large numbers of caterpillars) that are caught near the ends of branches in dense conifer trees. Known to feed on the Spruce Budworm and may enjoy greater survival of offspring during years of budworm outbreaks. Leaves Central American wintering grounds in February and arrives in New York from late May to early June. Fall migration begins in September and may last into October. Fall migration routes generally more easterly than spring. The various warbler species that nest in the northern forests of America usually avoid competition by partioning habitats. This species uses dense understory thickets, another will forage mostly in the treetops, another at mid-level, etc.

Migratory Status: Mostly a spring/fall migrant in southeastern New York but is a common summer resident/breeder in the rest of the state.

Habitat: Primary summer habitat is conifer and mixed conifer/deciduous forests. Mostly in mountainous regions. Outside its breeding range this warbler is a habitat generalist.

Breeding: Breeds in the boreal forest of northern North America. Nest is built on the branch of a conifer. Clutch size is usually 4 or 5 eggs. One clutch per year. Vulnerable to cowbirds.

Natural History: There are two morphologically distinct forms of this common warbler, one in the eastern United States and one in the western United States. Hybrids between the two forms sometimes occur. The form seen in New York is sometimes called the "Myrtle Warbler." In summer feeds mainly on insects, but if bad weather necessitates it is capable of surviving on berries during the winter. Unlike most warblers that will winter in the tropics, the Yellow-rumped is a hardy species and in mild winters can be seen as far north as southern IL, IN and OH in the Midwest and NJ on the east coast. Populations of this bird seem fairly stable and it is probably in less jeopardy than many other warbler species.

Migratory Status: Mostly a spring/fall migrant. A few will summer in the Adirondacks or in the Catskills. Arrives in mid-May to early June.

Habitat: Summer breeding habitat is mostly taiga and tundra-taiga transition zones; often well above the Arctic Circle. Winter habitat is South American forests.

Breeding: Nest is an open cup built on a branch near the tree trunk, usually in a spruce and often only a few feet off the ground. Eggs number 3 to 5. Young fledge as early as within 8 to 10 days.

Natural History: This is one of the great long distance migrants among America's songbird species. In fall migration some may travel non-stop over the Atlantic Ocean from Newfoundland (Canada) all the way to South America. Considering that this is a bird that weighs less than one-half ounce, that is a remarkable feat of endurance. Although they are not rare in New York during the spring migration, they tend to stay hidden high in the forest canopy. The fall migration is mostly along the east coast or offshore. In both its summer range and winter habitats it tends to use remote regions, thus this is a rarely seen bird in New York except by those who train themselves to look for it during spring migration.

Class - **Aves** (birds)

Order - **Passeriformes** (songbirds)

Family - **Parulidae** (warblers)

Bay-breasted Warbler *Setophaga castanea*	Pine Warbler *Setophaga pinus*	Black-throated Green Warbler *Setophaga virens*

Spring Male

Fall Male

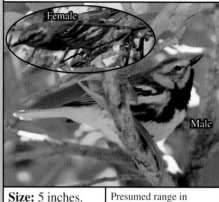
Female / Male

Size: 5.5 inches.

Variation: Female resembles fall male. See photos above.

Presumed range in New York

Abundance: Uncommon.

Migratory Status: Summer resident in the Adirondack region of New York. Spring/fall migrant statewide. Arrives in May. Fall migration begins in August.

Habitat: Summer habitat is spruce/fir woodlands. Mainly in Canada. During migration it is found in a variety of habitats. Winter habitats are tropical forests of Central and South America.

Breeding: Nests in dense conifer trees on horizontal limb. Nest is cup shaped and made of woven twigs, pine needles, and grasses. Average clutch size is 5 or 6 eggs.

Natural History: This long-distance migrant is not commonly seen by residents of New York, as migrants they pass through rather quickly and the few that summer in the state do so in the Adirondack Mountains. They migrate later than most other warblers and don't appear until mid to late May. Their primary food in summer is the Spruce Budworm caterpillar, and their populations may rise and fall with the availability of this insect. Populations have declined possibly due to spraying of Canadian forests to control spruce budworms. These birds are less common today than decades ago. They winter from southern Central America to northwestern South America.

Size: 5.5 inches.

Variation: Females and immatures are drabber, less yellow.

Presumed range in New York

Abundance: Fairly common.

Migratory Status: Summer resident in New York from April through October. However a few may linger into late fall or very early winter.

Habitat: Pine forests are the primary habitat, but they are also seen in deciduous and mixed woodlands, especially during migration. Their affinity for pine trees is nothing short of legendary.

Breeding: Builds its nest high in pine trees. 3 or 4 eggs is typical. An early nester, eggs are usually laid by late May. Breeding range is limited to regions where pines trees occur.

Natural History: This species is always found in association with pine trees. The Pine Warbler winters in the southern United States and this is the only warbler whose range is contained entirely within the United States and Canada. It is also the only one of its kind to regularly change its diet from insects to seeds in the winter, thus it is one of the few warblers seen at bird feeders. These birds can reach high densities in winter in the southern pine forests, when resident populations are supplemented by northern migrants. Pine Warblers are much more tolerant of cold weather than other warblers, perhaps because they are able to switch from insects to seeds as a food source.

Size: 5 inches.

Variation: Females have less black on the throat.

Presumed range in New York

Abundance: Uncommon.

Migratory Status: Summer resident throughout the state. Uncommon to rare on Long Island. Seen in New York from May through August/early September.

Habitat: This warbler requires significant tracts of unbroken forests. Except for migration, it is an inhabitant of conifer and mixed conifer/deciduous forests, especially those containing hemlock.

Breeding: Very rare as a breeder on Long Island, but is a widespread breeder in most of the state. Most nests are in conifers such as hemlock or pine. Only the female incubates the 4 or 5 eggs.

Natural History: Like others of its kind, this small, handsome warbler faces many threats. Red Squirrels are reportedly an important nest predator in the boreal forests of Canada and New England. Another major threat may come from other birds like the Blue Jay, and from the common and widespread Woodland Rat Snake, an excellent tree climber that is always on the hunt for bird nests. Sharp-shinned Hawks are a threat to the adults, while Brown-headed Cowbirds parasitize the nest. Human activities such as forest fragmentation threaten populations as a whole. Add to that the impact of Woolly Adelgid insects on hemlock trees and you have an uncertain future for this species.

Class - **Aves** (birds)

Order - **Passeriformes** (songbirds)

Family - **Parulidae** (warblers)

Blackburnian Warbler *Setophaga fusca*	**Palm Warbler** *Setophaga palmarum*	**American Redstart** *Setophaga ruticilla*

Size: 5 inches.

Variation: Orange of males is yellowish on females and immatures.

Presumed range in New York

Abundance: Fairly common.

Migratory Status: Summer resident in most of New York. Migrant only in southernmost New York and Long Island.

Habitat: Summers mostly in mature coniferous and mixed forests. Migration habitat is highly variable. Birds that breed in the Appalachians favor groves of Eastern Hemlock.

Breeding: Nest is usually in a conifer and well concealed amid foliage. Average of 4 to 5 eggs. Not known to produce more than a single brood.

Natural History: The beautiful blaze of orange coloration on the head, throat, and breast of the Blackburnian Warbler is unmistakable. However, this is a difficult species to observe due to the fact that it is primarily a treetop dweller. Like many members of the warbler family, the migratory range of this bird in the United States coincides closely with the Eastern Temperate Forest Level I Ecoregion. Loss of forest in much of this region may make migration for warblers more difficult as they must find places to rest and forage on the long flight to breeding grounds farther north. Forest fragmentation on wintering grounds in South America may also be a threat. Insects (especially caterpillars) are primary food.

Size: 5.5 inches.

Variation: Varies seasonally, but winter-plumaged birds are not seen in New York.

Presumed range in New York

Abundance: Fairly common.

Migratory Status: A fairly common migrant throughout the state. Very rare summer resident in the Adirondacks.

Habitat: Summer habitat consists of bogs and woods openings in boreal forests. Transient in a variety of habitats during migration. Winter habitat is open woodlands, mangroves, and thickets.

Breeding: Nests of moss is on the ground in a northern bog, usually at the base of a conifer tree. Clutch size is 4 or 5. Many nest in remote wilderness.

Natural History: This species nests in the boreal forests of Canada and winters along the southeastern United States coast (including all of Florida) and throughout the Caribbean. Unlike most warblers that spend most of their time high in the canopy, the Palm Warbler is a decidedly terrestrial species that hunts primarily on the ground or in low shrubs. It is one of the most northerly wintering of the warblers, with many staying in the southeast United States or Florida (thus the name Palm Warbler). Their summer habitats are very far to the north, many summer well into northern Canada. Food is mainly insects, mostly caught on the ground. Includes grasshoppers, beetles, lepidopterans, flies, and bee larva. Some berries and nectar may also be eaten.

Size: 5.75 inches.

Variation: Sexually dimorphic (see photos above). Juvenile like female.

Presumed range in New York

Abundance: Common in eastern New York.

Migratory Status: Summer resident throughout most of New York. Mostly a migrant in western portion of the state.

Habitat: Prefers deciduous woodlands over conifers. More common in second growth areas and riparian thickets. Larger woodlands are preferred over small woodlots.

Breeding: The nest woven of thin fibers of grass or bark strips and placed in the crotch of an upright branch or trunk. Usually 4 eggs.

Natural History: The striking bright orange-on-black colors of the male flash like neon in the heavily shaded forests where this species makes its home. They are active little birds that display their bright colors by regularly spreading their tail feathers and drooping their wings. They hunt tiny insects among the foliage and often catch flying insects in mid-air. In New York this species is least common as a breeder in the Interior Lowlands region adjacent to lakes Erie and Ontario, although it may be see there as a migrant. Small numbers winter in coastal Louisiana, the lower Rio Grande valley, and the everglades region of south Florida. Most winter from northwestern Mexico to northern South America. Clearing of tropical forests is a threat.

Class - **Aves** (birds)

Order - **Passeriformes** (songbirds)

Family - **Parulidae** (warblers)

Prairie Warbler *Setophaga discolor*	Chestnut-sided Warbler *Setophaga pensylvanica*	Black-and-white Warbler *Mniotilta varia*

Size: 4.75 inches. **Variation:** Females less vividly marked, juvenile birds are paler. Presumed range in New York	**Size:** 5 inches. **Variation:** Females and juveniles are less vividly colored. Presumed range in New York	**Size:** 5.75 inches. **Variation:** Sexually dimorphic (female less vividly marked). Presumed range in New York
Abundance: Fairly common.	**Abundance:** Common.	**Abundance:** Common.
Migratory Status: Summer resident. Spring migrants arrive in mid-May, with fall migration begining in August.	**Migratory Status:** Summer resident throughout New York. Arrives in early May. Fall migration begins in late Aug.	**Migratory Status:** Summer resident and spring/fall migrant. Arrives in mid-April, departs in September.
Habitat: Semi-open habitats. Old, overgrown fields, shrubby successional areas, second growth woodlands, and cedar glades. Absent to very rare in intensive agricultural areas. Uses coastal dunes during winter.	**Habitat:** The Chestnut-sided Warbler is a bird of successional areas and shrubby second growth. Forest edges, early regenerative timber harvest areas, and forest clearings are favored for nesting. In migration also seen in mature woods.	**Habitat:** Found in a wide variety of forest types, but mature and second-growth deciduous forests are the primary habitat. Mixed conifer-hardwood forests are also used. Likes woodlands with dense understory.
Breeding: Widely scattered breeding throughout the southern and southeastern part of the state. An average of 4 eggs (3 to 5) are laid.	**Breeding:** Nests fairly low to the ground in thick cover of dense sapling growth. 3 or 4 eggs are laid in late spring or early summer.	**Breeding:** Nest is constructed of dry leaves, dead grasses, and the bark of grapevines. Placed on the ground at the base of tree or stump. Lays 3 to 5 eggs.
Natural History: In spite of the name, this is not a prairie species. They are in fact birds of the Eastern Temperate Forests. Insects, spiders, slugs, and other soft-bodied arthropods are listed as food items. Feeds from the ground all the way up to treetops, but mainly gleans lower bushes and shrubs. Tail-bobbing is a common behavior in this species. The Prairie Warbler winters farther north than many warbler species. While some fly as far as the Yucatan Peninsula, others stay in the northern Caribbean or Florida. They can be fairly common in the Florida Everglades during winter. Despite having benefited from clearing of forests the last century, there are unexplained declines in some populations in recent years.	**Natural History:** This is one of the few warbler species that has benefited from deforestation. They are probably more common now than they were in the days prior to the European settlement of America. Despite their overall increase in population, they are negatively impacted by modern agricultural practices. The clearing of fence rows and overgrown field corners, and conversion of successional habitats into cropland, eliminates their preferred habitat. They are thus absent from most areas of intensive agriculture escept as a migrant. Winter range is in Central America. Migrating birds fly at night. But flights across the Gulf of Mexico will continue well into the following day, as that perilous journey can last for 18 hours.	**Natural History:** Feeds by plucking tiny creatures from tree bark and branches. Its feeding habits is more similar to that of woodpeckers, nuthatches, and creepers than to most warblers. This species is dependent upon deciduous and mixed conifer forests, and it can be sensitive to deforestation. But overall it does not appear to have been significantly impacted throughout its wider range. While this species can be seen throughout the state, it nests mostly in the eastern half on New York. The peculiar genus name "Mniotilta" means "moss plucker" and is probably derived from this species' habit of foraging among clumps of spanish moss in the southern United States, where it is an abundant spring migrant.

Class - **Aves** (birds)

Order - **Passeriformes** (songbirds)

Family - **Parulidae** (warblers)

Tennessee Warbler *Oreothlypis peregrina*	Orange-crowned Warbler *Oreothlypis celata*	Nashville Warbler *Oreothlypis ruficapilla*

Size: 4.75 inches. **Variation:** See photos. Sexual and seasonal plumage changes. Female like fall male. *Presumed range in New York*	**Size:** 5 inches. **Variation:** Female slightly duller, less yellow below. Varies regionally. *Presumed range in New York*	**Size:** 4.75 inches. **Variation:** Little variation. Sexes and immatures are all quite similar. *Presumed range in New York*
Abundance: Common.	**Abundance:** Uncommon in New York.	**Abundance:** Fairly common.
Migratory Status: Mostly a spring/fall migrant that passes through the state. Some nesting has been recorded in the Adirondack region. Most will arrive in mid-May and depart in September.	**Migratory Status:** A spring/fall migrant. Most migrate to the west of New York in spring, but migration routes are presumed to include all of the state. Spring migration is late April/early May.	**Migratory Status:** Summer resident in most of New York. Migrant on Long Island. Spring migration peaks in mid May. Fall migration is more prolonged, from late August through October.
Habitat: Summer habitat is the boreal forest. Winter habitat in Central America is semi-open forest and forest edges. In migration may be seen anywhere.	**Habitat:** Summers in northern woodlands (Canada and Rocky Mountains) where it prefers habitats with significant understory. Also found old weedy fields, brier thickets, etc. during migration.	**Habitat:** Summer habitat includes tamarack bogs and boreal forests. Prefers second growth and open woodlands with shrubby undergrowth. Avoids the deep woods.
Breeding: Nest is on the ground at the base of a tree or among upturned roots. Clutch size ranges from 3 to 8.	**Breeding:** Breeds in northern Canada and as far north as Alaska and well into the Arctic Circle. Western subspecies breeds along west coast. Lays 4–5 eggs.	**Breeding:** Nests on the ground under bushes or in hummocks of grasses or sphagnum moss. Clutch size ranges from 3 to 6.
Natural History: The numbers of this species passing through New York each spring and fall fluctuates depending upon the previous year's abundance of its primary summer food, the Spruce Budworm. In the northern forests of Canada in good budworm years, this is one of the most common bird species. In years of diminished budworm populations, the population of these birds also crashes. This relationship provides a valuable insight into the intricate interdependencies of unrelated organisms. This is an inconspicuous bird as it feeds high in trees and migrates later in the spring after trees are fully leaved. Thus it is difficult to detect despite being common.	**Natural History:** Like most warblers, this species is highly insectivorous, but in winter it also eats some fruit and is known to feed at the sap wells created by sapsucker woodpeckers. Feeds deliberately in the lower branches of trees and in bushes. These can be very common birds on their northern breeding grounds, but are seen in New York only briefly during migrations. Orange streak on crown from which it derives its name is not typically visible in the field. Winters across the southern United States from the Carolinas to California, and south to northernmost Central America. Ornithologists recognize four subspecies of this rather variable warbler and their ranges can overlap.	**Natural History:** This warbler species has benefited from human alterations to the American landscape (they prefer logged-over, second growth habitats). However, some human alterations have also had a very negative effect. As with many other migrant songbirds, they are vulnerable to towers, power lines, and antennas. No one knows exactly how many birds are killed during migration each year by flying into these obstacles, but some estimate the number to be in the millions. Insects are eaten almost exclusively by this warbler. Summers in northern United States and Canada, winters in Mexico. Two subspecies are recognized, an eastern race (east of the Mississippi River), and a western race.

Class - **Aves** (birds)		
Order - **Passeriformes** (songbirds)		
Family - **Parulidae** (warblers)		

Ovenbird *Seiurus aurocapilla*	**Louisiana Waterthrush** *Parkesia motacilla*	**Worm-eating Warbler** *Helmitheros vermivorus*

Size: 6 inches. **Abundance:** Common. **Variation:** None.	 Presumed range in New York	**Size:** 6 inches. **Abundance:** Fairly common. **Variation:** None.	 Presumed range in New York	**Size:** 5.5 inches. **Abundance:** Uncommon. **Variation:** None.	 Presumed range in New York

Migratory Status: Summer resident that winters from south Florida to southern Central America. Arrives in New York in May and leaves in September.	**Migratory Status:** A summertime resident that arrives early (mid- to late April), and departs early (July–Aug.). Winters from Mexico to northern South America.	**Migratory Status:** Summer resident. Winters in the Caribbean and in Central America. They are seen in New York from late April through September.
Habitat: Mature, contiguous forests. Seems to prefer upland woods. A substrate of abundant leaf litter is an important element to this bird's habitat.	**Habitat:** Forested streams are the preferred habitat. In migration they may also be seen along the edges of swamps or small woodland ponds.	**Habitat:** This is a woodland species, but it seems to avoid lowland forests. More common in rugged regions with steep slopes.
Breeding: Nest is on the ground and is constructed of leaves and grass. Nest is unique in that it has a domed roof with an opening in front. 3 to 6 eggs.	**Breeding:** Nesting can occur as early as May in Ohio. 4–6 eggs are laid in a nest placed in tree roots along a the banks of a stream.	**Breeding:** Nests are built on the ground in deep woods and are often hidden beneath overhanging vegetation. 4–5 eggs is typical.
Natural History: This large warbler is a ground dweller, and is usually observed on the ground or in low foliage. Food is a wide variety of insects and arthropods taken mostly on the ground among the leaf litter. The song of the Ovenbird is distinctive and has been variously described as "emphatic" and "effervescent." Often two nearby birds will sing at once, with their overlapping songs sounding like a single bird. This species has experienced a decline in the last few decades. Forest fragmentation and Brown-headed Cowbird nest parasitism may be to blame. The name "Ovenbird" is derived from the fact that the nest is shaped rather like the old fashioned brick ovens that had a domed roof and opened to the front.	**Natural History:** This species is famous for its incessant "tail bobbing" behavior. The entire rear half of the body constantly wags up and down when foraging in streamside habitats. Requires ecologically healthy stream habitats and this species may be a barometer of overall stream health. *Similar Species:* The **Northern Waterthrush** (*P. noveboracensis*) is so similar to the Louisiana Waterthrush that most casual observers will not be able to tell them apart. The Northern is more widespread in New York (statewide). Northern Waterthrush breeds mostly around bogs and beaver ponds in boreal forests (but scattered breeding occurs through southern New York as well). Both associate with wetland habitats.	**Natural History:** Although the Worm-eating Warbler may occur throughout most of southern New York, it is much more common in the southeastern tip of the state. This is a species that specializes in feeding amid low bushes, searching the dead leaf clusters and low-hanging foliage for insects, spiders, and primarily, caterpillars. Like many of America's neotropical migrant songbirds, the Worm-eating warbler is highly dependent upon deciduous forests for breeding habitat. They need large tracts of woodland. They winter in Mexico, Central America, and the West Indies. Despite their name, earthworms are not an important item in their diet. Caterpillars however are a dietary mainstay. It is the only bird in its genus and its closest relatives are in tropical America.

Class - **Aves** (birds)

Order - **Passeriformes** (songbirds)

Family - **Parulidae** (warblers)

Prothonotary Warbler *Protonotaria citrea*	**Common Yellowthroat** *Geothlypis trichas*	**Kentucky Warbler** *Geothlypis formosa*

Size: 5.5 inches. **Variation:** Sexes similar but color of female is less vivid.  Presumed range in New York	**Size:** 5 inches. **Variation:** Females lack the prominent black mask.  Presumed range in New York	**Size:** 5.5 inches. **Variation:** Black hood much reduced on female or totally absent.  Presumed range in New York
Abundance: Very rare in New York.	**Abundance:** Very common.	**Abundance:** Rare in New York.
Migratory Status: A very rare summer resident. New York represents the extreme northern extension of range. May be seen from late May to early August.	**Migratory Status:** Summer resident. Seen in New York from late April through early fall. Winters from south Florida to Central America.	**Migratory Status:** Arrives in New York in early to mid-May. Leaves for the tropics in August or early September.
Habitat: Prothonotary Warblers always nest near water. They are most common in swamps and marshes but can also be seen along lake shores, riparian areas, and in the vicinity of small ponds.	**Habitat:** Likes thick vegetation in wetland areas. Cattails and sedges in marshes and swamp edges are especially favored. Avoids deep woods but may be seen around edges of woods.	**Habitat:** Throughout its summer range the Kentucky Warbler enjoys deciduous bottomland forests and wooded riparian habitats. Within this habitat it requires dense undergrowth.
Breeding: Unlike other warblers that build a nest, the Prothonotary Warbler nests in tree cavities. They will also use artificial nest boxes. Lays 4 or 5 eggs.	**Breeding:** The nest is woven from wetland grasses among cattails or sedges. 4 to 6 eggs are laid in late May or early June. Cowbird parasitism occurs.	**Breeding:** A ground nester. The nest is constructed of dead leaves and grasses and is usually well hidden. 4 to 5 eggs are laid.
Natural History: The dredging and draining of swamplands throughout the eastern United States significantly reduced breeding habitat for this warbler in the first half of the 20th century. Loss of wetlands in the United States has stabilized somewhat in the last few decades, but the species now faces threats from habitat loss on its wintering grounds in northern South America. Much of the swampland habitats in the United States disappeared with settlement. In New York today this warbler occurs very sporadically in the southern part of the state. It has recently benefited from the placement of artificial nest boxes in its range. Feeds on aquatic insects, snails, and tiny crustaceans. Will also eat fruits and nectar.	**Natural History:** The Common Yellowthroat is one of the more abundant warblers in America and their summer range includes most of North America south of the arctic. They do avoid the desert southwest and dry southern plains, not surprising since they are mainly a wetland-loving species. They feed low to the ground on almost any type of tiny invertebrate. Their behavior when foraging is rather "wren-like" as they negotiate dense stands of cattails, reeds, and tall grasses. They tend to stick to heavy cover and when flushed make short flights into deep cover. All of New York's Common Yellowthroats move south in the fall, but a few have been recorded in the state as late as November or very rarely, early December.	**Natural History:** Kentucky Warblers are abundant and widespread summer resident birds in suitable habitats throughout much of the eastern United States. They become increasingly scarce northward and the southern tip of New York represents the northernmost extension of their range. Like other small warblers they are easily overlooked. The Cornell Laboratory of Ornithology (birds online) website reports that this species appears to be in decline. Destruction of mature tropical forests may be to blame. It is also possible that fragmentation of large forest tracts in North America could be a threat. A handsome warbler, it feeds low to the ground on a wide variety of invertebrates.

Class - **Aves** (birds)

Order - **Passeriformes** (songbirds)

Family - **Parulidae** (warblers)

Mourning Warbler	Connecticut Warbler
Geothlypis philadelphia	*Oporornis agilis*

Size: Length 5.25 inches.

Abundance: Fairly common.

Migratory Status: Summer resident in all but the southern portion of New York. Spring/fall migrant throughout the state. Arrival is later than most, in late May.

Presumed range in New York

Variation: Female has less contrasting head color.

Habitat: The Mourning Warblers' summer/breeding habitat is mostly in the boreal forests and bogs of Canada. In New York they are most likely to be seen in dense regenerative woodlands. Usually seen on or near the ground.

Breeding: Nests on the ground in dense vegetation or a clump of grass. Lays an average 4 eggs. Breeds in all but the southern portion of the state.

Natural History: This warbler likes second growth areas with lush undergrowth. It prefers these conditions both in its summer breeding grounds in boreal forests as well as its wintering grounds in tropical forests. Thus it is one of the few neotropical migrant warblers that has actually benefited from man's insatiable appetite for wood products. This is a secretive bird that "skulks" in dense thickets. Unlike many neotropical migrant songbirds that make long-distance flights across the Gulf of Mexico, this warbler is a "circum-gulf" migrant that follows the coastline north. Some experts put this species in the same genus as the Connecticut Warbler (*Oporornis*). And indeed the two are quite similar morphologically. Other experts (relying more on DNA sequencing) insist it is more closely related to the previous two species in the genus *Geothlypis*.

Size: Length 5.75 inches.

Abundance: Rare.

Migratory Status: The Connecticut Warbler is a fall-only migrant in New York. It summers in Canada and winters in South America. Fall migration in late August and September.

Presumed range in New York

Variation: Females are duller without gray head of male.

Habitat: Summer/breeding habitat is boreal forest. There it prefers edges of coniferous woodlands bordering wetland habitats like tamarack bogs and muskeg. Winter habitat is forests in Central and South America.

Breeding: Nest is hidden in thick undergrowth on or near the ground. 3 to 5 eggs are laid in late June. Young birds fledge in late July or early August. Breeds in Canada.

Natural History: This shy warbler is rarely observed. In part due to its secretive nature (migrating birds are typically observed low to the ground in dense undergrowth). In addition, it occurs in New York only briefly during fall migration. Finally, this is one of the rarest of America's warblers. Despite its name, this species is quite rare in Connecticut, where it may only occasionally be seen during fall migration. Due to its secretive nature and relative rarity, this is one of the least understood and least commonly observed of America's warbler species. Spring and fall migrations take different routes. Spring migrants move up the Florida Peninsula and fan out across the southeast toward the Mississippi River, following it north into the northern United States and Canada. Fall migrants move eastward across Canada and then fly south along the United States eastern seaboard.

Class - **Aves** (birds)

Order - **Passeriformes** (songbirds)

Family - **Parulidae** (warblers)

Blue-winged Warbler *Vermivora cyanoptera*	Golden-winged Warbler *Vermivora chrysoptera*

Size: Length 4.75 inches.

Abundance: Fairly common.

Variation: Little variation. Females and juveniles are less vividly colored with less prominent black eyeline and an olive crown. Pictured above is male.

Presumed range in New York

Migratory Status: Winters in southern Mexico and Central America. Breeds and summers in most of New York except the Catskills and the Adirondacks. May be seen as a migrant everywhere except in the Adirondack region.

Habitat: Overgrown weed fields with ample brushy undergrowth and early successional woodlands constitute this bird's primary habitat. Least common in areas of intensive agriculture. Avoids dense, mature woodlands.

Breeding: Nest is near the ground in or under a low bush. From 4 to 6 eggs are laid in May or early June. One clutch.

Natural History: A shrub land specialist, the Blue-winged Warbler has experienced an upswing in populations as a result of deforestation by pioneering European settlers of eastern North America. In recent years there has been a decline in their numbers in the northeastern United States as forests have begun recovering from the rampant logging of the last century. In New York they are least common in the Catskills and nearly absent from the Adirondacks. These birds sometimes hybridize with the similar Golden-winged Warbler and produce at least two additional forms of difficult-to-identify hybrid birds. One hybrid type goes by the name "Brewster's Warbler," the other by the name "Lawrence's Warbler." Although they have benefited from the presence of second growth from logging activites, they do not fare well where there has been extensive clearing for modern agriculture.

Size: Length 4.75 inches.

Abundance: Rare.

Variation: Sexual and ontogenetic variation. Females and juveniles are similar. They show less prominence of black cheek patch and wingbars. Above is a male.

Presumed range in New York

Migratory Status: A rare summer resident and migrant that occurs sporadically throughout the state. The first spring migrants begin to arrive in southern New York by the second week of May. Fall migration peaks in September.

Habitat: Second growth woodlands and overgrown fields. This species is another shrubland specialist that benefits from logging or forest fires. Summer range is mostly in the boreal forest and in the Appalachian Mountains.

Breeding: Nests on the ground near the ground at the base of a bush, hidden in thick grass and weeds. 4–5 eggs.

Natural History: This is a declining species in New York and a NYSDEC Species of Special Concern. Among the factors believed to be contributing to the disappearance of this bird are the maturation of regenerative woodlands, Cowbird nest parasitism, and hybirdization with the more common Blue-winged Warbler. Oddly, the species seems to be expanding its range farther to west while diminishing in numbers in the east. They winter in a variety of forest habitats in Mexico, Central America, and northern South America from sea level to 7000 feet. Like many other warblers, this species is a trans-gulf migrant, flying across the Gulf of Mexico in spring. Foraging birds glean tiny insects, spiders, etc. from the ends of branches. Moths and their caterpillar larva are also listed as major food items. Most nature lovers regard males of this species as being among New York's most attractive birds.

Class - **Aves** (birds)

Order - **Passeriformes** (songbirds)

Family - **Icteridae** (blackbirds)

Brown-headed Cowbird *Molothrus ater*	Red-winged Blackbird *Agelaius phoeniceus*	Common Grackle *Quiscalus quiscula*
	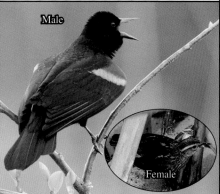	

Size: 7.5 inches.

Abundance: Common.

Variation: See photos above. Sex dimorphism.

Presumed range in New York

Size: 9 inches.

Abundance: Very common.

Variation: See photos above. Sex dimorphism.

Presumed range in New York

Size: 12.5 inches.

Abundance: Common.

Variation: Bronze and purple color morphs.

Presumed range in New York

Migratory Status: The cowbird can be seen in most of the state year-round, but they are mainly a summer resident in northern New York. They are least common in the state in mid-winter and most common in early spring/summer.

Migratory Status: These birds are seen throughout the year in southernmost New York but they are mostly summer residents throughout most of the state. Even in northern parts of the state, however, they may be seen in winter.

Migratory Status: Grackles are seen year-round in southern New York and they are summer residents in the north. Harsh winter weather may result in some birds leaving the state altogether in winter.

Habitat: Open fields and agricultural areas primarily, but can also be common in towns and suburbs. Inhabits edge areas and woods openings but avoids deep forest.

Habitat: The Red-winged Blackbirds' favorite habitat is marsh or wet meadows. They are also found along roadside ditches and the edges of ponds in open areas.

Habitat: Grackles favor agricultural areas and open fields/croplands. They are also common in urban areas where they inhabit lawns, parks, etc. In winter roosts in large flocks in small woodlots.

Breeding: Female cowbirds lay their eggs in the nest of other bird species, a unique nesting strategy known as "brood parasitism" (see below). As many as 40 eggs may be laid in dozens of songbird nests.

Breeding: The nest of the Red-winged Blackbird is a woven basket usually suspended from two or three cattail blades and is most often positioned over water. 2 to 4 eggs are laid. Young are fed enormous quantities of insects.

Breeding: Grackles often nest in groups that may consist of a dozen or more pairs. The nest is built in the upper branches of medium-sized trees and several nests can be in the same tree, or in adjacent trees.

Natural History: This species is unique among North American birds in that the adults play no role in rearing their young. Instead the female lays an egg in another species' nest and the adoptive parents rear the young cowbird, usually to the detriment of their own offspring. The disappearance of extensive forest tracts has allowed the cowbird to parasitize many more woodland songbirds than was possible prior to settlement. As a result, this species continues to increase in numbers and now poses a real threat to many smaller songbird species.

Natural History: In winter Red-winged Blackbirds often join large mixed flocks that can include all the birds shown on this page. Males sing conspicuously in spring. Like the other blackbirds on this page, the Red-winged has benefited from human alterations to America's natural habitats, thriving in open land and agricultural areas. Food is almost entirely insects, and along with the Common Grackle this species plays an important role in insect control. The bright red and yellow "epaulets" on the wing of the male are greatly reduced in winter.

Natural History: Grackles are known for forming large flocks during the winter that will roost communally and can number in the thousands. When these large congregations move into a town or neighborhood they can become a messy nuisance, but their reputation for spreading disease is exaggerated. Throughout most of the year they are busy consuming millions of insect pests. In harsh winter weather they may descend on backyard bird feeders in large flocks that overwhelm the regular residents, creating consternation among backyard birdwatchers.

Class - **Aves** (birds)

Order - **Passeriformes** (songbirds)

Family - **Icteridae** (blackbirds)

Boat-tailed Grackle *Quiscalus major*	**Rusty Blackbird** *Euphagus carolinus*	**Bobolink** *Dolichonyx oryzivorus*
	 Spring-Summer Plumage / Fall - Winter Plumage	 Breeding male

Size: 16.5 inches	 Presumed range in New York	**Size:** 9 inches.	Presumed range in New York	**Size:** 7 inches.	 Presumed range in New York
Abundance: Uncommon.		**Abundance:** Rare.		**Abundance:** Fairly common.	
Variation: Males are larger. Female is more brownish.		**Variation:** Seasonal plumage variations. See photos.		**Variation:** Females and winter males are brownish/sparrow-like.	

Migratory Status: Mostly a year-round resident, but may migrate farther south in harsh winters.

Habitat: In New York this species is found along the coast. Inhabits salt marsh, beaches, dunes, and areas near the coast on Long Island and Staten Island. In Florida they can be found in inland areas throughout the Peninsula.

Breeding: Nest is built in a small bush or tree, usually in salt marsh. 3 to 5 eggs is probably typical. May produce two broods annually in the deep south.

Natural History: This is the largest blackbird found in New York. They are an endemic American bird that ranges along the eastern coastlines from New York to eastern Texas. This species has been expanding its range northward since at least the 1930s, and they first appeared in New York as recently as 1982. Like many blackbirds this species seems able to adapt well to human activities. They will live in urban regions where predators are rare and food is abundant in dumpsters and around fast food parking lots. They are omnivorous birds that will eat a variety of plant materials as well as insects and other invertebrates such as small crabs or small reptiles and amphibians.

Migratory Status: Early spring and late fall migrant throughout New York. A few may winter in the downstate area.

Habitat: Wintering Rusty Blackbirds favor wetland habitats. Floodplain forests, edges of swamps, and woods bordering marshes make up the bulk of this bird's winter habitat. Summers in wet boreal woodlands and tundra edges.

Breeding: Breeding occurs far to the north (as far as the arctic). An average of 4 eggs are laid in a bulky nest of twigs, lichens, and grass.

Natural History: In the last few years Rusty Blackbirds have garnered the attention of birdwatchers and conservationists concerned about an apparently significant decline in the population of this species. The loss of wet woodlands to agriculture throughout much of their wintering grounds in the southern United States may be partly to blame. Unlike many blackbirds that regularly intermingle with other species, the Rusty Blackbird seems to remain mostly segregated from the large winter flocks of grackles, cowbirds, starlings, and Red-wingeds. These birds summer far to the north and are seen in New York mostly in winter or during migration periods. Food is insects, seeds, grains, etc.

Migratory Status: Both a spring/fall migrant and a summer resident. Most begin to arrive in New York in mid-May.

Habitat: Bobolinks are open country birds and they are usually seen in open, grassy areas. These birds are probably more common in New York today than in pre-settlement, as they benefit from the creation of pasture and hayfields.

Breeding: Females breed with a number of males and a clutch of 5 eggs may have several fathers. Nest is woven of grasses and placed on the ground.

Natural History: Bobolinks are one of the greatest migrators of America's birds. They will nest in the northern United States and Canada and winter in southern South America in the open grasslands of the Pampas region of Uruguay and Argentina. Thats a round trip of nearly 20000 miles! They are uncommon to rare as a nesting bird in the southern portions of the state and in the Adirondacks. This species has experienced population declines in the last half century, but has recently benefited from CRP programs. Food items include seeds, grains, and many invertebrates during breeding. Many people are surprised to learn that these handsome birds are in the blackbird family.

Class - **Aves** (birds)

Order - **Passeriformes** (songbirds)

Family - **Icteridae** (blackbirds)

Eastern Meadowlark	**Baltimore Oriole**	**Orchard Oriole**
Sturnella magna	*Icterus galbula*	*Icterus spurius*

Male | Female

Juvenile Male

Male | Female

Juvenile Male

Size: 9.5 inches.

Abundance: Uncommon.

Migratory Status: Summer resident.

Presumed range in New York

Variation: Females are slightly smaller and duller in color, but differences are barely noticeable.

Habitat: Open, treeless pastures and fields that are kept closely grazed or mowed. They like short grasses and avoid overgrown areas. In winter they are often seen in harvested croplands or emerging wheat fields.

Breeding: Nest is on the ground and well hidden beneath overhanging grasses or under the edge of a grass tussock. 3 to 5 eggs.

Natural History: As might be expected of a bird that loves open spaces, the Eastern Meadowlark is least common in New York in the forested regions of the state. Even in forests, however, this bird can be found in areas where there are large expanses of open habitat. They feed mostly on insects in warmer months, with grasshoppers and crickets being a dietary mainstay in the summer. During winter they will eat seeds and grain. They tend to occur in small flocks during the winter, but pair off and scatter in the breeding season. In New York they are most common in the agricultural regions in central part of the state. A few may overwinter, especially along the coastlines where the modifying effects of large bodies of water keep temperatures on the milder side.

Size: 8.75 inches.

Abundance: Common.

Migratory Status: Summer resident.

Presumed range in New York

Variation: Significant sexual dimorphism (see photos above). Immature male less vividly colored (inset photo).

Habitat: Savanna-like habitats are preferred. Pastures with scattered large trees, parks and lawns in urban areas, or farms and ranches in rural areas. During migration may be seen in a variety of habitats.

Breeding: The nest is an easily recognizable "hanging basket" woven from grasses and suspended from a tree limb. 4 to 6 eggs is typical.

Natural History: These handsome orange and black birds are a favorite with backyard birdwatchers. They will come to nectar feeders and fruits such as oranges, and they relish grape jelly. In addition to nectar and fruit they feed heavily on insects. In some areas of their range they have adapted well to human activities. Small town neighborhoods and city parks in urban areas are among their habitats today. Their occurance is widespread across the state except for the Adirondacks. Although they are fond of semi-open habitats and avoid dense forests, they do like the presence of some mature trees in their habitat. Thus, they may decline from areas where intensive agriculture reduces the presence of woodland patches and large trees.

Size: 7 inches.

Abundance: Uncommon.

Migratory Status: Summer resident.

Presumed range in New York

Variation: Significant sexual and ontogenic plumage variation. Immature males resemble female (see photos).

Habitat: This species shows a preference for semi-open habitats and narrow strips of woodland bordering rivers and streams. Their name comes from the fact that they are fond of orchards and they will often nest fruit trees.

Breeding: The nest is a rounded basket woven from grasses and suspended from a forked tree branch. 4 eggs is typical, but can be as many as 6.

Natural History: Like the larger Baltimore Oriole, Orchard Orioles will eat fruit. They also feed on a wide variety of arthropods gleaned from tree branches and leaves, as well as from weedy fields. Immature males resemble females but have a large black throat patch. These birds are somewhat gregarious and they often occur in flocks on tropical wintering grounds. They are also known to nest in small colonies where ideal habitat exists. Spraying for insects in orchards can be dangerous for these insect and fruit eaters as it can be for other bird species, many of which are highly susceptible to insecticides. This bird is quite common in New York City and on Long Island. It is much less common throughout the rest of its range in the state.

Class - **Aves** (birds)

Order - **Passeriformes** (songbirds)

Family - **Thraupidae** (tanagers)

Scarlet Tanager *Piranga ludoviciana*	Summer Tanager *Piranga rubra*
	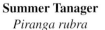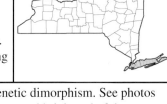

Size: Length 7 inches.

Abundance: Common.

Migratory Status: A summer resident that breeds widely in the state. Begins to arrive in May. Leaves for wintering grounds in September.

Presumed range in New York

Variation: Sexual and ontogenetic plumage variations. Juvenile males resemble females for the first year of their lives. See photos above.

Habitat: The summer habitat for the Scarlet Tanager closely coincides with the Eastern Temperate Forest Level I ecoregion. It prefers large tracts of unbroken woodlands.

Breeding: The thin, saucer-like nest of the Scarlet Tanager is placed on the fork of an outer branch. 4 eggs is typical. Only one brood is produced.

Natural History: The male Scarlet Tanager is one of the most strikingly colored songibrds birds in New York. Unfortunately, this species' dependence upon larger tracts of forested land means that its future is uncertain. Forest fragmentation leads to vulnerability to cowbird nest parasitism. Throughout much of the midwest, where deforestation and fragmentation of forests has been rampant, this species is in decline. In New York it is still common throughout the state, especially where large amounts of woodland remain. Food in summer is mostly insects (including wasps and hornets). Winters from Panama to northwestern South America. These birds are more easily seen than heard, as they tend to stay high in the canopy.

Size: Length 7.75 inches.

Abundance: Very rare in New York.

Migratory Status: Well named, this bird is seen in America only during summer. It winters in the tropics. Spring arrival is usually early May.

Presumed range in New York

Variation: Sexual and ontogenetic dimorphism. See photos above. The mottled yellow-green and bright red of the juvenile male entering its second year can be seen in early spring.

Habitat: Like their cousins Scarlet Tanagers, Summer Tanagers are birds of the eastern forests. However, this species is more likely to occupy fragmented forests and edge areas.

Breeding: The rather flimsy nest is on a terminal fork of a branch that is usually low over an opening such as a creek bed. The typical clutch size is 3 to 4.

Natural History: Summer Tanagers feed on a variety of woodland insects and larva, but they also eat some berries and fruits. One of their primary food items however is bees and wasps, a fact that makes them an attractive species to have around the rural homestead. Immature males resemble females their first summer. By the following spring they begin transformation into the bright red plumage of the adult male. During this transformation they are one of the most colorful birds in America's woodlands (see photos above). Southernmost New York represents the most northerly portion of their summer range. About the only place they can be seen in the state is in New York City parks and on Long Island.

Class - **Aves** (birds)

Order - **Passeriformes** (songbirds)

Family - **Sturnidae** (starlings)	Family - **Passeridae** (European sparrows)

European starlings
Sturnus vulgaris

House Sparrow
Passer domesticus

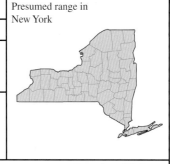

Size: Length 8.75 inches.

Abundance: Very common.

Migratory Status:
A non-migratory, year-round resident.

Variation: Breeding plumage iridescent dark purple, non-breeding has white speckles. Juveniles are drab.

Presumed range in New York

Size: Length 6.25 inches.

Abundance: Very common.

Migratory Status:
A non-migratory, year-round resident.

Variation: Males have distinctive gray crown with black face mask. Females are a plain drab brown. See photos.

Presumed range in New York

Habitat: Urban and suburban areas as well as farms and ranches. Starlings are closely tied to human activity and are rarely seen in true wilderness. By contrast, they can be quite common in large cities and small towns.

Habitat: The House Sparrow's name comes from its affinity for human habitations. These are mostly urban birds and when they do occur in rural areas it is always near farms and homesteads.

Breeding: Nest is made of grass, leaves, etc. stuffed into a cavity. Often uses cracks or holes in man-made structures. Also old woodpecker holes. Clutch size is typically 5 eggs.

Breeding: House Sparrow build bulky nests of grass, feathers, paper strips, etc. placed in hollows or crevices of barns, outbuildings, or even occupied homes. 5 to 6 eggs on average.

Natural History: The Starling is one of the most familiar birds in America, but ironically it is a non-native species. All the Starlings in America are descendant from a handful of birds released in New York City in the 1890s. Contrary to popular belief, the Starling is not related to the blackbirds. Instead they belong to the same family as the old world mynas. These birds have enjoyed remarkable success since being introduced to North America and they are now found throughout the continent. They represent a real threat to many of our native species, especially those that nest in cavities. In winter they often join grackles and blackbirds in large mixed flocks that can become messy nuisance in urban and suburban areas. Along with the blackbirds, these birds are sometimes regarded as a threat to humans due to the avian-borne disease Histoplasmosis. In truth, this threat is exaggerated.

Natural History: A European immigrant, the House Sparrow was released into the United States about 150 years ago. They have spread across the continent and they are now perhaps the most familiar bird species in America. They roost communally in dense vegetation. Roosting sites are often in yards or foundation plantings next to houses. They are common scavengers around outdoor restaurants and fast food parking lots. They are often considered to be a nuisance bird, but their tame demeanor endears them to many. Despite being extremely common in urban areas, they are quite rare in wilderness. These highly successful birds may nest up to four times in a season. Despite their common name, House "Sparrow," they are not closely related to sparrows. They belong to an old world family known as the Weaver Finches. This is one of the most abundant birds in New York's urban regions.

Class - **Aves** (birds)

Order - **Passeriformes** (songbirds)

Family - **Passerellidae** (sparrows)

Swamp Sparrow *Melospiza georgiana*	Song Sparrow *Melospiza melodia*	Lincoln's Sparrow *Melospiza lincolnii*

<table>
<tr><td>Size: Length 5.75 inches.</td><td rowspan="3">
Presumed range in New York</td><td>Size: Length 5.5 inches.</td><td rowspan="3">
Presumed range in New York</td><td>Size: Length 5.5 inches.</td><td rowspan="3">
Presumed range in New York</td></tr>
<tr><td>Abundance: Fairly common.</td><td>Abundance: Very common.</td><td>Abundance: Uncommon.</td></tr>
<tr><td>Variation: No significant variation.</td><td>Variation: Light and dark color morphs.</td><td>Variation: No significant variation.</td></tr>
</table>

Migratory Status: Mainly a summer resident and a migrant, but may be seen year-round in southern and western New York.

Habitat: Summers in wetlands. Swamps, marshes (including salt marsh), and wet meadows. More diverse habitats may be used in winter, including upland fields.

Breeding: Nest is made of grasses and placed in cattails, grasses, or low bush. 3 to 6 eggs, 4 on average.

Natural History: Secretive and elusive, the Swamp Sparrow is less familiar to New Yorkers than most of its kin. They will visit feeders during the winter, but they are rarely a commonly seen bird at feeders. These birds are highly dependent upon wetlands for breeding, and they may be negatively impacted by loss of wetlands. At this time however populations appear stable. Although they can be quite common in summer habitats and in the bayous of of the deep south in winter, they do not flock and are nearly always seen singly. There are three distinct subspecies of Swamp Sparrow recognized by professional orinithologists but the differences between the races is rather slight. Most laymen cannot distinguish subspecies.

Migratory Status: Year-round resident throughout the state. Most common in winter in the southern half of New York.

Habitat: Overgrown fields, dense underbrush, and rank weeds are the preferred habitat of the Song Sparrow throughout their range. They are especially common in edge habitats.

Breeding: Nests are built low to the ground in weeds or shrubs. 4 eggs is typical.

Natural History: Both the common and scientific names of the Song Sparrow are references to its distinct and melodic song. Primarily seed eaters, these sparrows migrate in response to heavy snow cover, and they are common at bird feeders throughout the southern United States each winter. Sharp-shinned and Cooper's Hawks are major predators of adults, and the young and eggs are vulnerable to a variety of snake predators. However, they remain a thriving species. There are dozens of subspecies nationwide with light and dark color morphs. Most New York specimens resemble the photo above. One of the earliest and most comprehensive studies of bird biology was conducted on this species.

Migratory Status: Spring and fall migrant throughout the state. Summer resident in the Adirondacks.

Habitat: Summer habitat is boreal regions of Canada and northern Rockies where it occupies damp woodlands with dense brush such as willow. Spruce bogs and wetlands are favored.

Breeding: Nests on the ground amid sedges or at the base of willow in boreal wetlands. Lays 3 to 5 eggs.

Natural History: Lincoln's Sparrows are less common in New York than other sparrows. In addition they are shy and secretive and tend to stick to heavy cover. Add to this the fact that they are a transient species in most of New York and sightings are uncommon. During migration they are believed to be fairly widespread across the state. When excited they will raise the feathers on the back of the head giving them a "crested" look. Due to their secretive habits the biology of these sparrows is not well understood. Feeds on insects in summer and seeds in winter. Unlike many sparrows they rarely visit feeders except during periods of harsh winter weather. Very similar to the Song Sparrow, but has finer streaking on the breast.

Class - **Aves** (birds)
Order - **Passeriformes** (songbirds)
Family - **Passerellidae** (sparrows)

Chipping Sparrow *Spizella passerina*	**Clay-colored Sparrow** *Spizella pallida*	**Field Sparrow** *Spizella pusilla*

Size: 5.5 inches.

Abundance: Very common.

Variation: Winter plumage more subdued.

Presumed range in New York

Migratory Status: A summer resident that returns in April.

Habitat: Edge areas and woods openings. Thrives in human altered habitats including farmsteads, suburban yards, and parks.

Breeding: Breeds earlier than most other songbirds. Nests may be complete and eggs can being laid as early as late April in southern New York.

Natural History: Chipping Sparrow move to the deep south in winter. Nesting has been recorded throughout New York, but they are least common as breeding birds in the northern parts of the state and they are rare as a breeder in the Adirondack region. They adapt well to the human disturbance of natural habitats and they are undoubtedly more common today than prior to settlement. They can be quite common in New York in areas of intensive agriculture and also in urban/suburban environments. In fact, this is one of the most common sparrows in the state during summer months. The Chipping Sparrow feeds mostly on the seeds of grasses and forbs, and does most of its foraging on the ground. Insects are eaten during the breeding season and are fed to the young. They can also be a common bird at feeders.

Size: 5.5 inches.

Abundance: Rare in New York.

Variation: Non-breeding birds paler.

Presumed range in New York

Migratory Status: Summer migrant and rare summer breeder.

Habitat: This is an open country species that prefers grasslands. In New York uses abandoned fields taken over by weeds, grass, and brush.

Breeding: Typically nest is close to the ground in grassy or brushy environments. 4 eggs is typical. Very few nests have been recorded in New York.

Natural History: This species is a newcomer to the eastern United States, with the first observations occuring in Ohio 1940s and the first confirmed nesting there in 1994. The core range for this species is in the Great Plains region. Range expansion eastward into the Great Lakes region apparently began in the 1920s. Despite the fact that the Great Plains ecosystem is one of the most damaged of all America's natural habitats, this species continues to maintain healthy population numbers and it is one of the more common birds in the northern plains of Canada and North Dakota in summer. Winter range includes south Texas and Mexico. Sometimes flocks with other sparrows and has been known to hybridize with the Field Sparrow. There are a few widely scattered sightings of this species across the state, but they are rare in New York.

Size: 5.75 inches.

Abundance: Common.

Variation: Immatures have streaked breasts.

Presumed range in New York

Migratory Status: Mostly a summer resident. A few may be seen in winter.

Habitat: Open and semi-open areas with good cover in the form of weeds and taller grasses. Also shrubby, early regenerative woodland areas.

Breeding: Nest is on the ground usually at the base of a clump of grass or in a low bush. Two broods per year is common. 2 to 5 eggs.

Natural History: Another species that has adapted well to man-made changes in natural landscapes, the Field Sparrow is probably more numerous today than in historical times. Unlike many sparrows however, the Field Sparrow is a "country" sparrow that prefers rural regions over towns and suburbs. Although they are seen statewide in summer, most will move south in winter. A few may persist through the winter in the southernmost parts of New York and in the western tip of the state. Food is mostly grass seeds. Insects are also eaten, especially during the breeding season. Very similar to the American Tree Sparrow, but has all pink bill instead of dark upper mandible. Although still a common species the Field Sparrow has experienced population declines in recent years, perhaps due to habitat changes in much of its range.

Class - **Aves** (birds)

Order - **Passeriformes** (songbirds)

Family - **Passerellidae** (sparrows)

American Tree Sparrow *Spizelloides arborea*	**Vesper Sparrow** *Pooecetes gramineus*	**Savannah Sparrow** *Passerculus sandwichensis*

Size: 6.25 inches.	**Size:** 6.25 inches.	**Size:** 5.5 inches.
Abundance: Common.	**Abundance:** Uncommon.	**Abundance:** Fairly common.
Variation: No variation among adults.  Presumed range in New York	**Variation:** Immatures are similar but drabber.  Presumed range in New York	**Variation:** Highly variable with 28 subspecies.  Presumed range in New York

Migratory Status: Winter resident. November through March.

Migratory Status: Seasonal migrant and summer resident.

Migratory Status: Summer resident. April to October.

Habitat: In winter they use overgrown fields, edge areas, brushy patches with weeds, and grasses. Summer habitat is open tundra and taiga.

Habitat: This is a bird of open country. its natural habitats are grasslands and today it also uses agricultural fields. Prefers dry areas.

Habitat: Pastures, grasslands, mowed areas in vacant lots, and cultivated fields are used. Also uses salt marsh, tundra, and bogs.

Breeding: Nest is on the ground. 4 to 6 eggs. These hardy sparrows will nest as far north as the Arctic Circle and well above the tree line.

Breeding: Nest is on the ground in open fields, sometimes concealed by grass tussock. 3 to 5 eggs. May to produce two broods per year.

Breeding: Nests on the ground beneath overhanging vegetation. 4 to 5 eggs is typical. Nesting in New York is mostly in western and central regions.

Natural History: The American Tree Sparrow is a northern species that is only seen in New York in winter when heavy snow cover in the northern regions pushes migrating flocks southward. Like most sparrows, seeds are the staple food in winter. Seeds are also eaten in summer months but insects are more important, especially when rearing young. Seeds of a wide variety of grasses and weeds are consumed, and this species is regularly seen at bird feeders in northern states. Despite its name this species can be found in summer on treeless, arctic tundra. Winter migrants begin to arrive in the northern United States by late October or early November. Degree of southerly movement can be dictated by weather conditions. These are cold-tolerant birds and most will begin to head back north in very early spring (March).

Natural History: The Vesper Sparrow is more common in the western region of North America. They are uncommon as a breeding bird in New York with most breeding confined to the western portions of the state. They are declining in the eastern portions of their range which includes much of the Midwest and Great Lakes region; and they have experienced significant declines in New York. They winter across the southern United States and southward to northern Central America. This species enjoys open country and agricultural regions and is absent in much of the more heavily wooded regions of the state. The sparrows are a group that presents a difficult identification challenge for beginning bird watchers, and the Vesper Sparrow is one that closely resembles several other sparrow species. The presence of white outer tail feathers is diagnostic.

Natural History: This is one of the most widespread sparrow species in America. Between breeding range, winter range, and migration routes, the Savannah Sparrow may be seen anywhere on the continent. In New York they are least common in the Adirondack region and in the southeastern tip of the state. They feed on arthropods in summer and seeds in winter. The name comes from the Georgia town of Savannah (where the first specimen was described) rather than from the habitat type. As with many grassland animals the Savannah Sparrow has experienced population declines in areas of intensive agriculture or urbanization. Delaying cutting of hayfields has shown to benefit by allowing young time to fledge. This is a highly variable species with light and dark color morphs. Most New York specimens resemble photo above.

Class - **Aves** (birds)

Order - **Passeriformes** (songbirds)

Family - **Passerellidae** (sparrows)

Henslow's Sparrow *Ammodramus henslowii*	Grasshopper Sparrow *Ammodramus savannarum*	Nelson's Sparrow *Ammodramus nelsoni*

Size: 5 inches.	 Presumed range in New York	**Size:** 5 inches.	 Presumed range in New York	**Size:** 5 inches.	 Presumed range in New York
Abundance: Rare.		**Abundance:** Uncommon.		**Abundance:** Rare.	
Variation: None.		**Variation:** None.		**Variation:** None.	

Migratory Status: Summer resident that winters in the lower coastal plain of the southeastern United States Spring arrival is probably late April or early May.	**Migratory Status:** Summer resident. Arrives in late April and departs in late August through September. The winter range is in the southeastern United States, Mexico, and California.	**Migratory Status:** Spring/fall migrant. Probably more commonly observed during fall migration in October. Very rare as winter resident on coast.
Habitat: Undisturbed, overgrown grassy/weedy fields in open areas. Unmowed hayfields and re-claimed strip mines are also used.	**Habitat:** A grassland species, the Grasshopper sparrow likes short and mid-grass prairie. In New York it is most common in the western region.	**Habitat:** Primary habitat is marshes, both fresh (in summer) and brackish/salt marshes (winter). Also may use grassy fields during migration.
Breeding: Nest is on the ground in thick grass and well concealed. 2 to 5 eggs are laid in May. Double-broods are known.	**Breeding:** Nest is on the ground and well hidden beneath overhanging grass. Two broods per summer is usual with 4-5 eggs per clutch.	**Breeding:** Nest is a cup-like structure placed amid and supported by upright grass stems. 3 to 5 eggs is typical, with a minimum of 2 and maximum of 6.
Natural History: Henslow's Sparrow is nowhere a common species and in New York its relative scarcity and secretive nature make it one of the least familiar birds in the state. This is a species in decline throughout its range, not surprising since the tallgrass prairies that once provided ample nesting habitat are all but gone. Restoration of tallgrass prairies in midwestern states may help. Modern agricultural practices that have eliminated natural grasslands are a major threat to this species. Insects, especially grasshoppers and crickets, are important food items in the summer. In winter eats mostly seeds, especially small grass seeds. Snakes are reported to be a major predator on nests, along with a variety of carnivorous mammals.	**Natural History:** In many ways similar to the preceding species, but more common. It uses grasslands with shorter grasses and more areas of bare ground. its name is derived from the sound of its song which mimics the buzzing sound made by some types of orthopteran insects. Throughout its range (which includes most of the United States east of the Rocky Mountains) it is a rather inconspicuous bird. Though unfamiliar to most New Yorkers, in the high plains region of the north-central United States it is commonly seen (and heard). Feeds entirely on the ground. Food is mostly grasshoppers and other insects in summer. In winter eats both insects and seeds, especially tiny grass seeds. Avoids dense forest regions like the Adirondacks and Catskills.	**Natural History:** Nelson's Sparrow winters along the southeastern coastline of the United States from the Chesapeake Bay to Texas. Most spend the summer in the Canadian plains or along the southern shore of Hudson Bay. A few will pass through coastal regions of New York en route to and from summer breeding grounds in coastal New England, Nova Scotia, and New Brunswick. Until recently this species was considered conspecific with the Salt Marsh Sparrow. This species requires large tracts of undisturbed marshland or grassland habitat and both habitats have experienced significant alteration or outright destruction. Subsequently, loss of grassland habitat in central Canada and loss of coastal marshes poses a significant threat to this species.

Class - **Aves** (birds)
Order - **Passeriformes** (songbirds)
Family - **Passerellidae** (sparrows)

Saltmarsh Sparrow *Ammodramus caudacutus*	Seaside Sparrow *Ammodramus maritimus*	Fox Sparrow *Passerella iliaca*

Size: 5 inches. **Abundance:** Uncommon. **Migratory Status:** Summer resident. 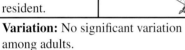	**Size:** 6 inches. **Abundance:** Uncommon. **Migratory Status:** Year-round resident. 	**Size:** 7 inches. **Abundance:** Fairly common. **Migratory Status:** Fall and winter resident. 
Presumed range in New York	Presumed range in New York	Presumed range in New York

Variation: No significant variation among adults. | **Variation:** Several color morphs occur in other regions. Little variation in New York. | **Variation:** A variable species with reddish, grayish, and sooty brown morphs.

Habitat: The Saltmarsh Sparrow is an endemic bird of the salt marshes of the eastern United States. It lives exclusively in tidal influenced marshes from Maine to Florida.

Habitat: Lives in salt and brackish water marshes along the Atlantic coastline of North America. Ranges from southern New England to Mexico. In New York restricted to coastal regions.

Habitat: The Fox Sparrow is a lover of dense cover and thickets. Thick weeds and shrubs bordering woodlands or thickets. A mixture of brier, saplings, weeds, regenerating timberlands, etc.

Breeding: Nest is a woven cup of coarse grasses placed amid upright stems of marsh grasses. 4 eggs is typical and two broods per year is common.

Breeding: Nest is a cup woven from blades of dried grass. Coarse grass stems make up the outer nest with finer grasses used as liner. 2 to 5 eggs.

Breeding: Nests are low to the ground or even on the ground. Breeding is in the boreal forests of Canada and in the northern Rockies. Usually 4 eggs.

Natural History: The Saltmarsh Sparrow and the Nelson's Sparrow are very similar and the two were once considered to be the same species. Most Saltmarsh Sparrows in New York are summer residents that winter in coastal marshes farther to the south, but a few can be found in the state year-round. Female Saltmarsh Sparrows may mate with several males resulting in a clutch of eggs with more than one father. Apparently only the female cares for and feeds the young. Flooding is an inherent threat to nesting in tidal marshes and exceptional tides or storm surges can destroy nests. Re-nesting is common if nest is destroyed. Adults feed on both invertebrates and seeds, but the young are reared on animal foods only. Mostly insects, spiders, amphipods, and snails.

Natural History: Several subspecies of the Seaside Sparrow are recognized. At least one subspecies, the Dusky Seaside Sparrow of central Florida coastlines, is extinct and another, the Cape Sable Seaside Sparrow of the Everglades region, is endangered. The coastlines of North America have been subjected to two centuries of man-made alterations. Harvesting of salt grass hay, draining projects aimed at creating cattle pasture, or filling marshes for development have had major impacts. Ditching to drain marshes as part of mosquito control is another serious threat, along with the widespread spraying of insecticides to kill mosquitos. Future threats may be loss of marshes to coastal erosion as climate change brings sea level rise and more frequent storms.

Natural History: The Fox Sparrow is widespread across the North American continent, summering in the far north (Canada, Alaska, and the northern Rockies) and wintering across much of the southern United States. Several distinct subspecies are recognized. They feed on a variety of insects and other arthropods in summer and subsist mainly on seeds in winter. They can be an occasional to regular visitor at bird feeders. Unlike many other sparrows, the Fox Sparrow is never seen in large flocks and it is rare to have more than one or two (rarely three) at a time visiting feeders. This widespread species exhibits a number of regional color morphs. Most Fox Sparrows seen in New York will resemble the reddish morph specimen shown above.

Class - **Aves** (birds)

Order - **Passeriformes** (songbirds)

Family - **Passerellidae** (sparrows)

White-throated Sparrow *Zonotrichia albicollis*	White-crowned Sparrow *Zonotrichia leucophrys*

White-striped morph - adult

White-striped morph - juvenile

Adult

Juvenile

Size: Length 6.75 inches.

Abundance: Common.

Variation: Two adult morphs. One has bright white eye stripe, other has tan. Immatures have brownish stripes breast.

Presumed range in New York

Size: Length 7.75 inches.

Abundance: Fairly common.

Variation: First year birds have chestnut and beige head stripe as opposed to black and white (see photos above). Sexes alike.

Presumed range in New York

Migratory Status: A summer resident of northernmost New York and a year-round resident in much of the rest of the state.

Migratory Status: Mostly a spring/fall migrant throughout the state.

Habitat: Brushy thickets, fence rows, weedy fields, edge areas, and regenerative woodlands. Both in upland and lowland areas. Can be seen in both rural and urban areas but always in the vicinity of bushes, shrubs, tall weeds, or other cover.

Habitat: They may be seen in any area where there are weeds, grasses, or brush in sufficient amount to provide good cover for roosting and escape from predators. Woodland edges and overgrown fence rows are best.

Breeding: Breeds in a broad band across Canada and the northeastern United States, as well as northern Great Lakes states (MI, WI, MN). Nest is on the ground in open areas, forest edges, etc. 4 eggs is typical. As many as 7 recorded.

Breeding: Breeds in boreal regions, tundra, and mountain meadows. Nest is in a low bush with about 4 eggs. Breeds very far to the north in northern Canada and Alaska. Will summer well into the Arctic Circle beyond the tree-line.

Natural History: This is one of New York's more common sparrows. In early spring the White-throated Sparrow serenades the fields and woodlands with its distinctive whistling song. As these birds are ground foragers, snow cover is one of the most important conditions that influence migratory patterns. Feeds mostly on insects in summer and switches to seeds in winter. When feeding, uses both feet with a backwards thrusting motion to clear away leaf litter. They are well represented at bird feeders throughout the state in winter and can be common even within New York City in parks. A short-distance migrator, this species winters mostly within the United States.

Natural History: Similar in many respects to the White-throated Sparrow to which it is closely related. Ranges farther west (all the way to the Pacific) and farther north. The White-crowned Sparrow produces multiple broods (as many as four per season in some western populations). Most will have at least two broods annually. Some summer well into the arctic tundra and make annual migrations of over 4000 miles up and down the continent. Eats insects and seeds in summer, mostly seeds in winter. Forages on the ground near cover. Less common than the White-throated Sparrow, but still a familiar bird at feeders in many regions. This is one of the most highly studied songbirds in America.

Class - **Aves** (birds)

Order - **Passeriformes** (songbirds)

Family - **Passerellidae** (sparrows)

Dark-eyed Junco *Junco hyemalis*	Eastern Towhee *Pipilo erythrophthalmus*

Size: Length 6 inches.

Abundance: Common.

Migratory Status: A winter resident throughout the state and a year-round resident in western New York, the Adirondacks, and Catskills.

Presumed range in New York

Variation: Highly variable. Several different color morphs nationwide. Most birds seen in New York are the typical "Slate-colored" morph shown in top photo.

Habitat: Occupies a wide variety of habitats in winter, but is most fond of semi-open areas or woods openings. Summer habitat is boreal forests.

Breeding: Nesting in New York occurs regularly in the more heavily forested regions of the state. Although seen in the southern portion of the state in winter, it does not nest there. Nest is on the ground, often concealed in a clump of ferns. 4 eggs is usual.

Natural History: Juncos are a familiar winter-time bird at feeders throughout the United States. They arrive with the colder weather fronts and are often associated with snow-storms. In fact a common nickname in much of America is "Snowbird." Northern migrants arrive in much of the southern United States in October/November and most head back north by mid-March. Those that summer in the southern United States do so only at the highest elevations in the Appalachian Mountains (above 3500 feet). The combined summer, winter, and migratory ranges of the Dark-eyed Junco includes nearly all of the North American continent except Florida.

Size: Length 8 inches.

Abundance: Common.

Migratory Status: Mostly a summer resident but a few may linger through the winter in the coastal regions of the state. Mostly April through October.

Presumed range in New York

Variation: Sexually dimorphic. Males are black on back, head, and wings whereas females are reddish brown. No seasonal variation.

Habitat: Succesional woodlands, overgrown fields/fence rows, edges of stream courses, and woodlots where honey-suckle, briers, weeds, and saplings are predominant.

Breeding: Nests are low to the ground or even on the ground. Nesting in New York can occur throughout the state except for in the Adirondack region. Nest is often on the ground amid leaf litter and dead grasses. Also frequently builds nest in dense vegetation above ground. Usually 4 eggs.

Natural History: Our largest member of the sparrow family. Sometimes called "Rufous-sided Towhee." It's "tow-wheee" song is a familiar sound beginning as early as March. The widespread range of the Eastern Towhee corresponds closely to the Eastern Temperate Forest ecoregion, but they normally do not occur in dense populations. Most bird feeders in rural areas will have a pair, but rarely more than two pairs. When feeding on the ground it uses both feet in unison to throw ground litter backwards and uncover hidden food items. The similar Spotted Towhee (*P. maculatus*) replaces the Eastern Towhee in the western half of America.

Class - **Aves** (birds)

Order - **Passeriformes** (songbirds)

Family - **Calcaridae** (longspurs)

Snow Bunting *Plectrophenax nivalis*	**Lapland Longspur** *Calcarius lapponicus*

Size: Length 6.75 inches.

Abundance: Fairly common in winter.

Migratory Status: Winter migrant/resident that arrives in late October and departs in March.

Presumed range in New York

Size: Length 6.25 inches.

Abundance: Fairly common in winter.

Migratory Status: A winter resident and migrant from the far north that is usually seen in New York in winter.

Presumed range in New York

Variation: Breeders are strikingly black and white. Winter plumage is off-white with dark brown wings and tail and rusty brown highlights on face.

Variation: Seasonal and sexual plumage differences. Birds seen in New York are usually in winter plumage (see above). Winter females are less vivid.

Habitat: Winter habitat is mostly harvested crop fields. Also weedy patches around field edges, roadsides, farmsteads, etc. Summer habitat is rocky areas in tundra.

Habitat: Winter migrants in New York use very open areas with nearly bare ground. Large acreage harvested crop fields are the primary habitat for flocks wintering in the United States.

Breeding: One of the most northerly breeding songbirds in the America. Builds its nest in rock crevices in the high arctic. Lays 4 to 6 eggs.

Breeding: Nests on the ground in arctic tundra. In places it may be the only nesting songbird. Eggs (3 to 7) are not laid until early June.

Natural History: After summering as far north as the shores of the Arctic Ocean, Snow Buntings will move south to winter as far south as the northernmost United States. In years of exceptional snowfall or extreme cold they may be seen as far south as Kentucky. They are obviously very cold hardy birds, but they can be susceptible to winter die-offs if deep snows conceal their food source of seeds and grain. In New York they can be seen in mixed flocks with Lapland Longspurs and Horned Larks. Circumpolar in distribution, there are some indications are that this species is recently experiencing a sharp drop in North American populations.

Natural History: This hardy longspur breeds and summers in arctic tundra and is circumpolar in its distribution. It is very common on its breeding grounds where it is sometimes the only songbird present. In winter they move far to the south, but are not very abundant east of the Mississippi River. Changes wrought on the landscape by modern agriculture have made for more hospitable habitat for this species in New York. On breeding grounds they eat dipterous insects (flies, mosquitos) and seeds. Winter diet is mostly seeds and waste grain. In winter they are often seen together with mixed flocks of Snow Buntings and Horned Larks.

Class - **Aves** (birds)

Order - **Passeriformes** (songbirds)

Family - **Cardinalidae** (grosbeaks)

Indigo Bunting *Passerina cyanea*	**Northern Cardinal** *Cardinalis cardinalis*	**Rose-breasted Grosbeak** *Pheucticus ludovicianus*

Size: Length 5.5 inches.	Presumed range in New York	**Size:** Length 8.75 inches.	Presumed range in New York	**Size:** Length 8 inches.	Presumed range in New York
Abundance: Common.		**Abundance:** Common.		**Abundance:** Common.	
Migratory Status: Summer resident.		**Migratory Status:** Year-round resident.		**Migratory Status:** Summer resident.	

Variation: Pronounced sexual dimorphism (see photos above). Immature males resemble females but with varying amounts of blue mottling.

Variation: Pronounced sexual dimorphism. Male bright red, female buff-tan with reddish wings, crest, and tail (see photos above).

Variation: Sexually dimorphic. Female drab brown, males striking black and white with rose-colored breast (see photos above).

Habitat: Edge areas, fence rows, brushy/weedy cover, and overgrown fields or early successional woodlands.

Habitat: From undisturbed natural areas to suburbs, the Northern Cardinal favors edge areas with shrubs and brush.

Habitat: A forest species primarily, but enjoys edge areas and regenerative woodlands with thick shrubby cover.

Breeding: Two broods are common. Lays 2 to 4 eggs in a nest of woven grasses that is usually placed in thick cover only a few feet above the ground.

Breeding: Nest is usually in a thick shrub or bush. About 4 eggs on average. Most nesting is from mid-April to August. Two broods per year.

Breeding: 3 to 5 eggs are laid in a nest of twigs, grass, and plant fibers. Nesting begins in late May. May rarely produce two broods per year.

Natural History: Indigo Buntings are common in summer throughout New York. Probably more so today than in historical times when more of the state was covered in forest. The neon blue color of the male makes it one of the most striking of North American birds. These birds are found throughout the eastern United States in summer, generally ranging from the short grass plains eastward to the Atlantic and as far north as southern Canada. They are most common in the southeastern United States. Their annual migration may encompass up to 2500 miles and many make the long flight across the Gulf of Mexico. Seeds and berries are the primary food with insects eaten during the breeding season.

Natural History: Conspicuous and highly recognizable, the Northern Cardinal enjoys the distinction of being the state bird for a total of seven states. They are mainly seed and berry/fruit eaters, but they will eat insects and feed insects to the young. They are common birds at feeders throughout their range, especially during winter, and they are equally abundant in rural and urban regions. In the last century they have expanded their range farther to the north into the Great Lakes region and New England. Today they are seen throughout much of the United States east of the Rockies. The southern extent of their range is northern Central America. Throughout their range they are often known by the name "Redbird."

Natural History: Many Rose-breasted Grosbeaks seen in New York in the spring and fall may be passage migrants. But nesting is widespread throughout the state and many will reside throughout the summer. Many others nest well to the north of New York and pass through again in the fall en route to wintering habitats in Central and South America. Food in summer about 50/50 insects and plant material such as seeds, fruits, flowers, and buds. During migration they are readily attracted to bird feeders where sunflower seeds are a favorite food. Birdwatchers throughout the state enthusiastically await the return of migrant songbirds each spring, and the Rose-breasted Grosbeak is a favorite.

Class - **Aves** (birds)

Order - **Passeriformes** (songbirds)

Family - **Fringillidae** (finches)

Goldfinch *Spinus tristis*	Purple Finch *Haemorhous purpureus*	House Finch *Haemorhous mexicanus*

Male / Male - winter

Male / Female

Male / Female

Size: 5 inches.

Abundance: Very common.

Migratory Status: A year-round resident.

Presumed range in New York

Size: 6 inches.

Abundance: Fairly common.

Migratory Status: A year-round resident.

Presumed range in New York

Size: 6 inches.

Abundance: Common.

Migratory Status: A year-round resident.

Presumed range in New York

Variation: Exhibits sexual and seasonal plumage variations. See above. Female resembles winter male.

Variation: Significant plumage differences between the sexes. See photos above.

Variation: Plumage differences between males and females make sexes easily recognizable. See photos above.

Habitat: Edge areas and successional habitats, fence rows, overgrown fields, and floodplains in open and semi-open areas.

Habitat: Summer habitat is moist coniferous forests. In winter they are seen in almost all habitats across the eastern half of the United States.

Habitat: As implied by the name, House Finches are usually associated with human habitation. Found both in cities and rural areas.

Breeding: 4 to 6 uniformly white eggs are laid. Nest is a tightly woven cup of grasses usually wrapped around a triad of upright branches.

Breeding: Nest of twigs, roots, and grasses is built in a fork on the outer portion of a branch of a conifer. 3 to 6 six eggs per clutch. Two broods per year.

Breeding: Typical woven nest of grasses is usually placed in dense evergreen shrub, cedar, or conifer tree. Lays 3 to 5 eggs and multiple broods are common.

Natural History: This well-known species is widespread across North America. The transition of the male Goldfinch into its strikingly yellow breeding plumage in spring is a profound example of what is known as a prealternate (or springtime) molt. The Goldfinch is a common visitor to bird feeders and is especially attracted to thistle seeds. Unlike many other species that eat seeds in winter and insects in summer, the Goldfinch is mainly a seed eater. Weed seeds, grass seeds, and especially seeds from forbs like thistles, sunflowers, and coneflowers are consumed. This species is apparently immune to parasitism by the Brown-headed Cowbird, as young cowbirds cannot develop on a diet that contains no insects.

Natural History: The Purple Finch seems to be a declining species in the eastern United States. Competition with the House Finch may be to blame. Although Purple Finches are seen in New York all winter, some may move well south in some years, all the way to the Gulf Coast in years of poor cone production. Seeds are the major food item, including seeds of trees (elm, maples, ash) and seeds of fruits. Buds are also eaten. Insects are also consumed. As with most other seed eaters, the Purple Finch will frequent bird feeders in winter. Easily confused with the House Finch, but is larger headed and has a heavier bill. In summer they are uncommon in the southeastern part of the state, but they can be common there in winter and during migration periods.

Natural History: House Finches have extended their range into the eastern United States over the last few decades. Originally native to the southwestern United States, the first House Finches appeared in New York in the 1940s with an intentional release on Long Island. Today they are found throughout the United States. Primarily a seed eater, these birds can be very common at urban feeders. Weed seeds, fruit, buds, and flowers are also reported to be eaten. Birds seen at feeders sometimes exhibit signs of a disease (Mycoplasmal conjunctivitis) that causes swelling of the eyes with occasional blindness or death. Similar to and easily confused with the less common Purple Finch, which has a larger head and lacks dark streaking on the belly of the males.

Class - **Aves** (birds)

Order - **Passeriformes** (songbirds)

Family - **Fringillidae** (finches)

Common Redpoll *Acanthis flammea*	**Evening Grosbeak** *Coccothraustes vespertinus*	**Pine Siskin** *Spinus pinus*
	 Male Female	Male Female

Size: 5 inches.	Presumed range in New York 	**Size:** 8 inches.	Presumed range in New York 	**Size:** 5 inches.	Presumed range in New York 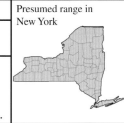
Abundance: Variable.		**Abundance:** Fairly common.		**Abundance:** Common.	
Migratory Status: Winter migrant/winter resident.		**Migratory Status:** Year-round in north, winter elsewhere.		**Migratory Status:** Year-round in north, winter elsewhere.	

Variation: Shows varying amounts of reddish or pinkish on breast and throat. Females are darker. Juveniles have brown streaks.	**Variation:** Female is gray-brown with yellowish wash on nape, sides, and belly. Male has bright yellow throughout and bright yellow stripe on forehead.	**Variation:** Males have a yellowish wash, females are heavily streaked with brown. See photos above. Juveniles resemble females.
Habitat: Summer habitat is in the far north where they occupy edge areas of coniferous forests, open subarctic tundra, arctic tundra, and taiga.	**Habitat:** Boreal-type forests of conifer and mixed conifer/deciduous. Summer habitat includes the forested regions of Canada and the Rocky Mountains.	**Habitat:** Pine Siskins prefer coniferous woodlands but in winter they are often seen in mixed or even pure hardwood forests.
Breeding: Nest is on a branch (forest) or in low vegetation (tundra). Lays 5 eggs. May double brood in good years.	**Breeding:** Saucer-like nest of twigs and rootlets is placed high in a tree at or near the trunk. Lays 3–4 eggs.	**Breeding:** Nest is woven of grasses, twigs, rootlets, etc. and lined with mosses or fur. 3 to 4 eggs is typical.
Natural History: Circumpolar in distribution (northern hemisphere), this is one of the world's most northerly songbirds and some will stay through the winter in the far north. Many will move south, some into New York. Very rarely they may be seen as far south as Arkansas or Tennessee. Though some Common Redpolls may be seen every winter in northern New York, they only approach being a fairly common bird in years of major eruptions. These eruptions are thought to be associated with poor cone production in boreal forests, which is the major winter food source for this species in boreal regions. In addition to conifer seeds they also eat small seeds produced by other trees and shrubs such as birch, willow, and alder. Grass seeds and insects are also eaten.	**Natural History:** The Evening Grosbeak is a northern species. The main food in winter is the seeds of trees like maples, Box Elder, etc. as well as conifer seeds and weed seeds. In a year of exceptionally poor seed production they will migrate southward great distances in a phenomena know to birdwatchers as an irruption. In irruption years they may rarely be been seen as far south as the southern United States. During these rare irruption events they might be seen far to the south of their normal range. However, in typical winters the Great Lakes region represents the southern edge of their winter range. Thus sightings of this bird in more southerly regions is rare and usually elicit excitement from the local birdwatching community.	**Natural History:** The Pine Siskin is a coniferous forest species, though it is also found in mixed deciduous/coniferous woodlands and in pure deciduous woods during winter irruptions. It is mostly a bird of the far north and the Rocky Mountains. They sometimes range as far south as the Gulf Coast in winter. In New York they can be seen throughout the year in the northern part of the state. In winter they are seen statewide but their erratic movement means they may be common in one area and rare in another. Feeds on seeds of coniferous trees, grass seeds, and weed seeds and will regularly visit feeders in winter and where thistle seeds are favored. Insects are also eaten during breeding. They are often seen in the company of Goldfinches.

Class - **Aves** (birds)

Order - **Passeriformes** (songbirds)

Family - **Fringillidae** (finches)

Pine Grosbeak *Pinicola enucleator*	**White-winged Crossbill** *Loxia leucoptera*	**Red Crossbill** *Loxia curvirostra*

Size: 9 inches.

Abundance: Rare in New York.

Migratory Status: Winter migrant.

Presumed range in New York

Size: 6.5 inches.

Abundance: Rare in New York.

Migratory Status: Winter migrant.

Presumed range in New York

Size: 6.5 inches.

Abundance: Uncommon.

Migratory Status: Mostly a winter resident.

Presumed range in New York

Variation: Significant sexual dimorphism (see phtos above). Also exhibits some geographical variation. New York specimens resemble photos above.

Variation: Pinkish wash of male is replaced by greenish-yellow on female. Juvenile birds are heavily streaked with brown.

Variation: Males show a decidedly reddish color. Females are more yellowish. Juveniles are heavily streaked with dark brown.

Habitat: A species of the boreal forest, the Pine Grosbeak favors areas of open coniferous forest or in the vicinity of forest clearings.

Habitat: Coniferous forests. Chiefly dominated by spruces, fir, and tamarack. Partitions habitat with Red Crossbill which favors pine/hemlock/fir forests.

Habitat: Most birds seen in New York in winter use taiga forests in Canada as their summer habitat. May utilize mixed forests in winter.

Breeding: Nest is a bulky structure built amid dense foliage of a conifer. 3 to 4 eggs is usual, can be as many as 5.

Breeding: Nest is well hidden amid foliage and situated on limb of a spruce or other conifer. 2 to eggs is usual.

Breeding: Nest is made of twigs and lined with lichens, grass, or conifer needles. 3 eggs are usual.

Natural History: This large finch endears itself to bird lovers both by its beautiful plumage and by its relative tameness. The fact that it is largely an animal of remote wilderness forests of the far north further enhances its attraction to wildlife watchers. Pine Grosbeaks feed on a wide variety of seeds, both coniferous and deciduous in origin. They will also eat fruits like crabapples as well as cranberries, blackberries, and rose hips. Smaller seeds from herbaceous plants are also consumed and they will eat sunflower seeds at feeders. In winter they often consume the dormant buds of both deciduous and coniferous trees. Adults rarely eat animal matter, but small arthropods are fed to young along with vegetable matter. This is another periodically irruptive species in winter, but it never goes too far south.

Natural History: Like its cousin the Red Crossbill, this species has a bill that is uniquely adapted to extracting seeds from cones. The White-winged Crossbill shows a decided preference for seeds of various species of spruce and Tamarack. By contrast, the Red Crossbill includes fir, pine, and hemlock in its diet. They forage in flocks, and by multiplying the number of foraging birds they are able to more quickly ascertain which trees are bearing more food-producing cones. The crossbills represent a good example of a highly specialized morphological character (the scissor-like bill), which evolved to take advantage of a plentiful but difficult-to-access food source. The downside of this specialization is a bill shape that makes it difficult to capitalize on other common food sources.

Natural History: The unique scissor-like beak of the crossbills is an adaptation for feeding on the seeds of conifers. The curved, crossed beak is used to pry open cones enough to allow the tongue to scoop out the seed. Seeds of pine, hemlock, spruce, and fir are the primary foods, but a variety of other seeds are also eaten and they will visit feeders for sunflower seeds. Their foraging habits are nomadic and small flocks wander through the forests searching for cone-bearing trees. Like many other boreal species they are prone to nomadic "irruptions." In years of poor cone production they may show up well south of their normal range. In a typical year northern NY, northern WI, and northern MI, represents the southernmost edge of their range in the eastern United States.

Class - **Aves** (birds)

Order - **Apodiformes** (swifts and hummingbirds)		Order - **Coraciiformes** (kingfishers)
Family - **Apodidae** (swifts)	Family - **Trochilidae** (hummingbirds)	Family - **Alcedinidae** (kingfishers)

Chimney Swift *Chaetura pelagica*	**Ruby-throated Hummingbird** *Archilochus colubris*	**Belted Kingfisher** *Megaceryle alcyon*
	 Male 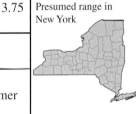 Female	Male  Female 

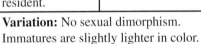

Size: Length 5.5 inches.	**Size:** Length 3.75 inches.	**Size:** Length 13 inches.
Abundance: Fairly common.	**Abundance:** Common.	**Abundance:** Uncommon.
Migratory Status: Summer resident.	**Migratory Status:** Summer resident.	**Migratory Status:** Year-round resident.

Presumed range in New York (shown in all three columns)

Variation: No sexual dimorphism. Immatures are slightly lighter in color.

Variation: Female lacks ruby throat patch. See photos above.

Variation: Female has a rust-colored band across belly (see inset above).

Habitat: Mainly seen in open and semi-open country and in urban/suburban areas.

Habitat: Woodlands. Both deciduous and mixed forests are utilized. Edge areas and open fields are used for feeding.

Habitat: Kingfishers require water and they haunt creeks, rivers, lakes, swamps, and farm ponds.

Breeding: Nest is a flimsy cup plastered to the inside of a chimney or hollow tree. 2 to 5 eggs are laid.

Breeding: Nest is a tiny cup of fine plant fibers and lichens glued together with spider webs. 2 eggs is typical.

Breeding: Kingfishers nest in burrows they excavate into vertical banks of dirt or sand that are at least 8 feet high.

Natural History: This is a species that has benefited from human population expansion. Historically, the Chimney Swift nested mainly in hollow trees. These birds require a vertical surface within a sheltered place for nesting. When people began to build houses and large structures like schools, churches, and factories equipped with chimneys, their populations exploded. Today they are less common than a few decades ago when most dwellings and other buildings had chimneys. Some nesting in natural hollows still occurs. Swifts have long, narrow, pointed wings that allow for extreme maneuverability and these birds feed entirely on the wing. Small flying insects are their prey. During migration they are sometimes seen in large flocks that can contain over 1000 birds. In most regions, the greatest population densities occur in the vicinity of major cities.

Natural History: The tiny hummingbirds are ounce for ounce one of the world's greatest travelers. Many fly across the Gulf of Mexico each year during migration! Considering that they weigh barely more than .1 of an ounce that is a remarkable feat of endurance. The range of the Ruby-throated Hummingbird includes all of the Eastern Deciduous Forest Level I Ecoregion, as well as portions of the Boreal Forest and Great Plains Ecoregions. Nectar is the major food item for hummingbirds and they show a preference for red, tubular flowers. They possess a highly specialized beak and tongue for reaching nectar deep within flowers. They will also eat some small, flying insects caught on the wing, and are known to pluck tiny invertebrates from foliage or small spiders from their webs. These birds will readily use artificial nectar feeders containing a one-to-four mix of sugar water.

Natural History: The Belted Kingfisher is one of the most widely distributed birds in North America. In fact they range throughout the continent from Alaska and northern Canada south to Panama. Although widespread with breeding records from every county in the state, they are widely dispersed. The presence of suitable nesting habitat in the form of vertical earthen cliffs may be a limiting factor in their abundance. Human activities such as digging of quarries and road cuts through hills and mountains may have helped this species in modern times by providing the requisite vertical banks for nest sites. Small fish are the primary food item. They are known for diving headfirst into the water from either a perch or while hovering to catch fish near the surface. In addition to fish will eat mollusks, crustaceans, insects, amphibians, and baby birds or even small mammals.

Class - **Aves** (birds)

Order - **Piciformes** (woodpeckers)

Family - **Picidae** (woodpeckers)

Pileated Woodpecker	Northern Flicker	Red-headed Woodpecker
Dryocopus pileatus	*Colaptes auratus*	*Melanerpes erythrocephalus*

Size: Length 16.5 inches.

Abundance: Uncommon.

Migratory Status: Year-round.

Presumed range in New York

Size: Length 12.5 inches.

Abundance: Fairly common.

Migratory Status: Year-round.

Presumed range in New York

Size: Length 9.25 inches.

Abundance: Uncommon.

Migratory Status: Year-round.

Presumed range in New York

Variation: Male has a red cheek patch.

Variation: Male has black "mustache."

Variation: No sexual variation.

Habitat: A forest species, the Pileated Woodpecker prefers mature woodlands. It is also seen in semi-open areas where large tracts of woods occur nearby. Floodplain forests are a favorite habitat.

Habitat: Semi-open areas and open lands with at least a few large trees. Farmlands, older urban neighborhoods and parks are also used. Least common in dense, mature woodlands.

Habitat: Savanna-like habitats with widely spaced, large trees are the preferred habitat of the Red-headed Woodpecker. They seem to show a preference for areas near lake or rivers.

Breeding: Nest is a hollow cavity excavated into the trunk of a tree (usually a dead tree, but sometimes living). Nests are usually fairly high up. 4 eggs.

Breeding: Nest is usually excavated in a fairly large diameter dead tree. Also known to use natural hollows. Averages 6 to 8 eggs.

Breeding: Nest hole is usually in a dead tree but it is also fond of using utility poles. 5 eggs is typical and some may produce two broods per summer.

Natural History: By far America's largest woodpecker, Pileated Woodpeckers play an important role in the mature forest ecosytem. Their large nest cavities are utilized as a refuge by many other woodland species including small owls, Wood Ducks, bluebirds, and squirrels. In the boreal forests the Pine Marten is reported to use their holes. Using their powerful, chisel-like beaks to break apart dead snags and logs, they also help accelerate decomposition of large dead trees. In addition to mast and fruit such as wild cherries, they eat insects, mainly Carpenter Ants and beetle larva. In New York this species is most common in heavily forested areas and they are least common in the coastal regions such as Long Island and Staten Island.

Natural History: In addition to feeding on insects (mainly ants) usually caught on the ground, the Flicker also eats berries and in winter, grains (including corn). Two distinct subspecies of Northern Flicker occur in North America. The "Yellow-shafted Flicker" is native to New York and the rest of the eastern United States. In the Rocky Mountain west the "Red-shafted Flicker" occurs. The two are distinguished by the dominant color on the underneath side of the wing, which is visible only in flight. As with New York's other large woodpecker (Pileated), the Northern Flicker is regarded as a "keystone" species that is important to other species which use its excavations for shelter and nesting. Thus recent declines in the population of this species is cause for concern.

Natural History: Once regarded as very common, this handsome woodpecker has declined significantly in the last century. It eats large amounts of acorns and other mast, especially in fall and winter, and may move about in fall and winter in search of areas with good mast crops. Insects are regularly eaten in warmer months and some may be caught on the wing, but they also commonly forage on the ground. In New York this woodpecker is probably more common in the western half of the state and is uncommon in much of the heavily forested regions. Overall this species has experienced a nationwide population decline. The Red-headed Woodpecker was apparently well known to many native Americans, and was a war symbol of the Cherokee.

Class - **Aves** (birds)

Order - **Piciformes** (woodpeckers)

Family - **Picidae** (woodpeckers)

Red-bellied Wood Pecker *Melanerpes carolinus*	**Downy Woodpecker** *Picoides pubescens*	**Hairy Woodpecker** *Picoides villosus*

Male / Female

Male / Female

Male / Female

Size: 9.75 inches.

Abundance: Fairly common.

Migratory Status: Year-round resident.

Presumed range in New York

Size: 6.75 inches.

Abundance: Very common.

Migratory Status: Year-round resident.

Presumed range in New York

Size: 9.25 inches.

Abundance: Fairly common.

Migratory Status: Year-round resident.

Presumed range in New York

Variation: Female has gray crown.

Variation: Male has red spot on nape.

Variation: Male has red spot on nape.

Habitat: A woodland species that inhabits all forest types in the eastern United States. Semi-open and open woods are favored.

Habitat: Occupies a wide variety of habitats throughout the state. From wilderness to farms and urban areas.

Habitat: A forest species that likes woodlands with larger, more mature trees. Also in parks and neighborhoods.

Breeding: Nests in holes excavated by the adults. 4 to 5 eggs are laid in mid April to early June.

Breeding: Nests is usually excavated in a dead limb. Eggs range from 3 to as many as 8. Eggs hatch in 12 days.

Breeding: Nest hole may be in dead snags or living trees with heart rot. 4 eggs is typical.

Natural History: Feeds on all types of tree-dwelling arthropods as well as seeds, nuts, fruit, and berries. This species has been expanding its range farther north for several years and today they are found in most of the state south of the Adirondacks (though they are still rare in Catskills). These woodpeckers are known to take over the nest holes of the endangered Red-cockaded Woodpecker where their ranges overlap in the southern United States. Conversely, the introduced Starling sometimes takes over the nest hole of the Red-bellied Woodpecker. Due to its fairly large size and its tendency to be quite vocal year round, the Red-bellied Woodpecker is a fairly conspicuous bird in both rural and urban areas. Because both males and females have a significant amount of red on the head they are often misidentified as the Red-headed Woodpecker. Like other woodpeckers they will come to bird feeders for suet or sunflower seeds.

Natural History: Ranging across all of North America except the far north and the desert southwest, the Downy is one of the most widespread woodpeckers in America and in many areas it is also the most common woodpecker. These appealing little woodpeckers are well-known and frequent visitors to bird feeders where they eat suet and seeds. Arthropods are the most important food item making up as much as 75 percent of the diet. Fruit and sap is also eaten. Like other woodpeckers, the Downy's nest holes in dead limbs and trunks may be utilized by a wide array of other species as a home and shelter. Many small cavity nesting birds may use old woodpecker holes and mice, lizards, snakes, treefrogs, spiders, and insects can often be found using their abandoned nests. They are very similar to the Hairy Woodpecker, but they are smaller and have a thinner beak.

Natural History: The range of the Hairy Woodpecker closely coincides with that of the smaller Downy Woodpecker. The two are often confused but the Hairy is a much larger bird and has a heavier, longer bill. Like the Downy, this woodpecker excavates nest holes that may be used by a variety of other species, making it an important species in forest ecosystems. A wide variety of insects and other arthropods are eaten along with seeds and fruits. This species can be seen at feeders throughout the state, and although it is less common than its smaller cousin it can often be seen in the company of the smaller Downy Woodpecker. When both are seen together, size differences become more apparent. The Hairy Woodpecker varies somewhat geographically in both size and coloration. Specimens shown above are typical for the eastern United States.

Class - **Aves** (birds)

Order - **Piciformes** (woodpeckers)

Family - **Picidae** (woodpeckers)

Black-backed Woodpecker *Picoides arcticus*	Three-toed Woodpecker *Picoides dorsalis*	Yellow-bellied Sapsucker *Sphyrapicus varius*
		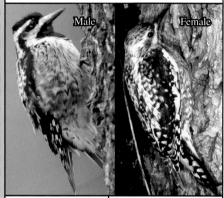 Male Female

Black-backed Woodpecker — *Picoides arcticus*

Size: 9.5 inches.

Abundance: Rare in New York.

Migratory Status: Year-round resident.

Presumed range in New York

Variation: Male has yellow crown.

Habitat: A boreal forest species that seeks regions where fire or disease has killed large numbers of trees.

Breeding: Nest hole may be excavated in a live or dead tree. Male does most of the excavating. Lays 2 to 6 eggs.

Natural History: The Black-backed Woodpecker appears to be a species that has evolved to take advantage of the natural wild fires that periodically re-configured the North American Boreal Forest. Its solid black back blends in well as it forages on the trunks of burnt trees and wood-boring beetles that infest fire-killed trees are a major food item. Thus this species is vulnerable to fire suppression programs that were until recently practiced by state and federal agencies like the United States Forest Service. Some populations of this bird are regarded as being at risk and are under consideration for protection locally as threatened or endangered. In recent decades forest managers have begun to take a more natural approach to forest management that allows naturally caused wildfires to burn themselves out, a management philosophy that should ultimately prove to be a benefit to this unusual woodpecker species.

Three-toed Woodpecker — *Picoides dorsalis*

Size: 8.75 inches.

Abundance: Very rare in New York.

Migratory Status: Year-round resident.

Presumed range in New York

Variation: Male has yellow crown.

Habitat: Boreal and montane coniferous forests. In New York has been reported to associate with beaver ponds.

Breeding: Nest hole may be excavated in a live or dead tree. Both sexes work at excavating hole. Lays 3 to 7 eggs.

Natural History: This is New York's rarest woodpecker species. They are seen in New York only in the Adirondack region, and are rare even there. Thus most New Yorkers will never see this species in the wild unless they make a serious effort to do so, and even then they may be disappointed. In many ways the Three-toed Woodpecker is a smaller version of the Black-backed Woodpecker. Both are forest fire specialists that haunt regions where stands of fire-killed trees are dominant. The Three-toed differs from the Black-backed in food choice, focusing mainly of bark beetles (the Black-backed favors wood-boring beetles). As with the previous species, this species is vulnerable to outmoded forest management practices such as fire suppression, salvage logging of trees in burned areas, and the cutting of insect-infested trees by forest managers.

Yellow-bellied Sapsucker — *Sphyrapicus varius*

Size: 8.5 inches.

Abundance: Fairly common.

Migratory Status: Year-round resident.

Presumed range in New York

Variation: Female has white throat.

Habitat: This woodpecker occupies a wide variety of woodland habitats, both deciduous and coniferous.

Breeding: Nest is an excavated hole in dead tree or a living tree with heart rot. Clutch size ranges from 2 to 7 eggs.

Natural History: The Yellow-bellied Sapsucker is unique among American woodpeckers in that it creates feeding opportunities by drilling small holes into the bark of trees. These holes, called "sap wells," fill with sap which the sapsucker then drinks. Sapsuckers regularly visit the "sap wells" to maintain them and defend them from other sapsuckers. Many other bird species benefit from the sapsuckers activities, especially the Ruby-throated Hummingbird, which will also drink sap from the woodpeckers' holes. The sap also attracts insects which in turn feed many species of insectivorous birds. In addition, the nest holes excavated by the sapsucker may be used by other birds, flying squirrels, etc. Though widespread across New York during migration periods, they are not a breeding bird in the southeastern part of the state. They are, however, common as a breeder in northern and central New York.

Class - **Aves** (birds)

Order - **Cuculiformes** (cuckoos, anis, and roadrunner)

Family - **Cuculidae** (cuckoos)

Black-billed Cuckoo *Coccyzus erythropthalmus*	**Yellow-billed Cuckoo** *Coccyzus americanus*

Size: Length 12 inches.

Abundance: Fairly common.

Migratory Status: Summer resident. Migrates later than most songbirds. Arrives in New York late May to early June.

Presumed range in New York

Variation: Sexes alike. Juvenile lacks red eye ring.

Habitat: Successional areas, thickets, and mature woodlands with some open areas. Shows a preference for being near water (riparian areas, lakes, etc).

Breeding: Breeds throughout New York but is uncommon in the Adirondacks. Clutch size averages 2 to 4 eggs.

Natural History: Although once common, the Black-billed Cuckoo has declined in abundance over the past several decades. Widespread use of pesticides may be to blame. Caterpillars are a primary food and pesticide-depleted caterpillar numbers result in a scarce food source for the birds. Ironically, large flocks of these handsome birds once acted as a natural control of caterpillars and historical observers reported seeing flocks of Black-billed Cuckoos descend on a tree full of caterpillars and eat every caterpillar on the tree! Today it is rare to see more than one or two of these birds at a time. Cicadas are another important insect food, and in years of cicada outbreaks cuckoos (and many other bird species) will produce larger clutches and success-fully rear more young. Of New York's two cuckoo species, this one is slightly more common.

Size: Length 12 inches.

Abundance: Fairly common.

Migratory Status: Summer resident that arrives in late May or early June. Departs in October.

Presumed range in New York

Variation: Sexes alike. Juveniles have darker bills.

Habitat: Favors open woodlands, edge areas, regenerative woodlands near open fields, overgrown fence rows, etc. Uses similar habitats on winter range in the tropics.

Breeding: Breeds from early June through the summer. Nest is flimsy and placed in thick vegetation. 2 to 4 eggs.

Natural History: The Yellow-billed Cuckoo is one of the latest arriving of New York's neotropical migrant songbirds. They often go by the nickname "Raincrow" and folklore states that they call right before a rain. Like our other cuckoo, their numbers have diminished significantly in modern times. Caterpillars are an important food and widespread pesticide use is likely the major contributing factor in their decline. These are secretive birds that are heard more often than seen. Their call is quite distinctive and is heard most frequently during the "dog days" of mid- to late summer. The young of this species develop rapidly and may leave the nest within 17 days of hatching. In New York this species is less common than the Black-billed Cuckoo, but it is still a fairly widespread and observable species except in the Adirondacks, where it is rare or absent.

Class - **Aves** (birds)
Order - **Columbiformes** (doves)
Family - **Columbidae** (doves)

Rock Pigeon *Columba livia*	**Mourning Dove** *Zenaida macroura*

Size: Length 13 inches.

Abundance: Very common.

Migratory Status: A year-round, non-migratory, resident bird.

Variation: Highly variable. Can be almost any color.

Presumed range in New York

Size: Length 12 inches.

Abundance: Very common.

Migratory Status: Year-round in southern half of state, summer only in north.

Variation: No variation among adults.

Presumed range in New York

Habitat: Farms and ranches in rural areas and parks and downtown streets in urban environments.

Habitat: Agricultural areas and open lands with short grass or areas of bare ground. Open to semi-open areas.

Breeding: Nests on man-made ledges and beneath overhangs in cities. Bridges and barns are used in rural areas. Multiple nesting with 2 eggs per clutch.

Breeding: Builds a flimsy nest of small sticks in sapling or low branch usually from 6 to 15 feet above ground. 2 eggs is usual with multiple broods per year.

Natural History: Although the Rock Pigeon is about the same overall length as the Mourning Dove, the pigeon is a much stockier, heavier bird that weighs over twice as much as the Mourning Dove. Despite the fact that this familiar bird ranges from coast to coast across North America, the Rock Pigeon is not a native species. It was introduced into North America by the earliest European settlers in the 1600s. Pigeons followed the first settlers into the west colonizing towns and settlements and living in close proximity to rural farms and livestock. Today they are one of the most familiar urban birds in America and are also common around farms and ranches. Young pigeons known as "Squab" are eaten in many places throughout the world. Rock Pigeons are incredibly variable and can exhibit almost any color or pattern. This specimen shown above is probably the most typical color and pattern.

Natural History: Although these birds are found year-round southern New York, they are summer-only residents in the north. Mourning Doves are regarded as a game species throughout much of the United States. The United States Fish and Wildlife Service estimates that as many as 20 million are killed each fall during America's dove seasons. While that seems an appallingly high number, the Mourning Dove is actually one of the most numerous bird species in America and the total population is estimated at around 350 million birds! Seeds are the chief food item. They will eat everything from the tiniest grass seeds to every type of seed crop produced by man, including corn, wheat, sorghum, millet, and sunflower as well as peanuts and soybeans. This abundant species may face competition from the invasive Eurasian Collard Dove, which continues to expand its range across America. Although not yet seen in New York, it gets closer every year.

Class - **Aves** (birds)

Order - **Galliformes** (chicken-like birds)

Family - **Odontophoridae** (quail)

Family - **Phasianidae** (grouse)

Northern Bobwhite *Colinus virginianus*	Spruce Grouse *Falcipennis canadensis*	Ruffed Grouse *Bonasa umbellus*

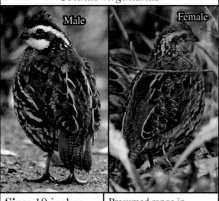

Size: 10 inches.	**Size:** 16 inches.	**Size:** 17 inches.
Abundance: Rare in New York.	**Abundance:** Very rare in New York.	**Abundance:** Fairly common.
Migratory Status: Year-round resident.	**Migratory Status:** Year-round resident.	**Migratory Status:** Year-round resident.

Presumed range in New York (for all three)

Variation: Female has tan eye stripe and throat patch. Male's is white.

Variation: Sexually dimorphic (see photos above).

Variation: Two color morphs. Red and Gray. Male has larger "ruff" on neck.

Habitat: Small woodlands, edge areas, and overgrown fields bordering agricultural land are the favorite habitats. Requires tall clumped grasses or shrubs/vines which provide overhead cover as a protection against Cooper's Hawks.

Habitat: Strictly a boreal forest species. Range includes all of Canada (except for the Great Plains, tundra regions, and Marine Forests of the west coast). An obligate of conifers. Especially (but not exclusively) spruce woodlands.

Habitat: Forests. Mainly successional forests, forest clearings, and disturbed woodlands. Most common in mixed forests. Ideal habitat has both mature and regenerative woods adjacent. Is especially fond of Aspen woodlands.

Breeding: Ground nester. Clutch size averages about 15 eggs but nest failure due to predation is high. Multiple nestings are common.

Breeding: Nest is on the ground. Usually situated in a small depression and often near the base of conifers. Nest always has overhead cover. 4 to 6 eggs.

Breeding: Nest is on the ground in woodland. Usually placed near the base of a tree, stump, or beneath downed trees. 9 to 14 eggs.

Natural History: Bobwhite have always been an important game bird in the United States. In recent decades, however, the species has experienced significant population declines, especially in the northern portions of its range. New York has always been on the northern fringe of this species range. Today it is considered extirpated everywhere except Long Island. Modern agricultural practices that eliminated fence rows and created expansive crop fields are the main factor contributing to the decline. Through fall and winter Bobwhites will stick together in family groups known as a "covey." In spring adults pair off for breeding with the resultant offspring and their parents producing the next fall's covey. Mortality through the winter is high and survivors from more than one covey will often join together.

Natural History: The Spruce Grouse often goes by the name "Fool Hen." This uncomplimentary moniker comes from the fact that they often behave in a remarkably tame manner. Early pioneers and homesteaders across the great northern wilderness often relied on the "Fool Hen" for sustence during hard times, sending the children out into the woods with sticks to kill a few birds for supper. In warm seasons when the land is free of snow they feed mainly on the ground, eating green shoots and new leaves, flowers, fungi, berries, and to a lesser extent animal matter. In winter they exist mainly on conifer needles. During winter they spend less time on the ground and much more time in the trees. Their biggest natural enemy is the Goshawk, which specializes in hunting birds of the grouse family.

Natural History: Mainly a bird of the northern forests, the Ruffed Grouse ranges southward in the Appalachian chain as far as northern Georgia. In New York they are found everywhere except the extreme southeastern portion of the state. The name comes from the "ruff" of feathers around the neck which are erected by the males during courtship displays. At this time the male also produces a deep, resonant sound similar to that produced by blowing across the top of a soda bottle. Known as "drumming," the sound carries quite a distance in the spring forest. This species has declined in some regions since the European settlement of America. The decline in populations of this species seems widespread in the southern Appalachians, but numbers seem stable farther north.

Class - **Aves** (birds)

Order - **Galliformes** (chicken-like birds)

Family - **Phasianidae** (grouse)

Wild Turkey *Meleagris gallopavo*	**Ring-necked Pheasant** *Phasianus colchicus*

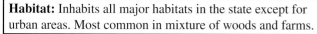

Size: Up to 47 inches.

Abundance: Fairly common.

Migratory Status: A year-round, non-migratory, resident bird.

Variation: Sexually dimorphic (see photos above).

Presumed range in New York

Habitat: Inhabits all major habitats in the state except for urban areas. Most common in mixture of woods and farms.

Breeding: Nests on the ground in thick cover such as thickets, honeysuckle, Multiflora Rose, or tall grasses. Lays up to 14 eggs.

Natural History: The courtship of the male Wild Turkey includes a "strutting" display that involves spreading the tail feathers, drooping the wings, and producing a low-frequency "drumming" sound. When attempting to attract females in the spring breeding season males become quite vocal and regularly emit a loud "gobble" that can be heard for a mile. The saga of the disappearance and resurgence of the Wild Turkey in America is one of wildlife management's greatest success stories. In pioneer days turkeys were found throughout much of America but by the early 1900s they had disappeared from many areas, including New York. Re-stocking efforts by state wildlife agencies aided by sportsmen groups have been highly successful and Wild Turkeys are now found in suitable habitats throughout America and all of New York except the most urbanized areas.

Size: Up to 35 inches.

Abundance: Uncommon.

Migratory Status: A year-round, non-migratory, resident bird.

Variation: Sexually dimorphic (see photos above).

Presumed range in New York

Habitat: Prefers a mosaic of crop lands interlaced with cover such as wetlands, grassy patches, overgrown fence rows.

Breeding: Nests on the ground in thick cover such as tall grasses, cattails, etc. Lays up to 15 eggs. Rarely, two females will use the same nest.

Natural History: Ring-necked Pheasants are an alien species from Asia that were introduced into America in the late 1800s. The species has thrived in the Great Plains region where adequate natural habitats still exist. In New York they are most common in the agricultural regions in western part of the state. But they are widespread (though not common) across New York where suitable habitat exixts. Despite repeated stocking efforts to bolster the population for hunters, this species appears to be in decline in New York in recent years. Modern agricultural practices may be a contributing factor in the decline. This is a popular game bird throughout its range in America and sportsmen are actively involved in attempts to restore this bird in many areas. The conservation organization "Pheasants Forever" raises money for habitat restoration.

Class - **Aves** (birds)

Order - **Caprimulgiformes**		Order - **Strigiformes** (owls)
Family - **Caprimulgidae** (nightjars)		Family - **Tytonidae** (barn owl)

Common Nighthawk *Chordeiles minor*	**Whip-poor-will** *Antrostomus vociferus*	**Barn Owl** *Tyto alba*

Size: Length 9.5 inches.	Presumed range in New York 	**Size:** Length 12 inches.	Presumed range in New York 	**Size:** Length 16 inches.	Presumed range in New York
Abundance: Rare.		**Abundance:** Uncommon.		**Abundance:** Uncommon.	
Variation: No significant variation, sexes alike.		**Variation:** No significant variation, sexes alike.		**Variation:** Males are lighter with less buff below.	

Migratory Status: Spring and fall mostly. A few still summer in the state.	**Migratory Status:** Summer resident. May through September.	**Migratory Status:** Mostly summer. Birds in southeast New York are year-round.
Habitat: Open and semi-open areas. Can be seen around cities and towns but also in rural areas.	**Habitat:** Forest edge, power-line cuts through wooded areas and xeric woods. Favors thickets for daytime roosting.	**Habitat:** Prefers open and semi-open habitats. Often found around farms and small towns.
Breeding: No nest is constructed and 2 eggs are laid on bare gravel. May nest on flat, gravel-covered rooftops.	**Breeding:** Nests on the ground amid leaf litter. No nest is built and the eggs (usually 2) are laid on the ground.	**Breeding:** Nested in hollow trees or in caves historically. Now uses old buildings or barns. As many as 11 eggs.
Natural History: These birds sometimes go by the nickname "Bullbat." They are most common in urban areas but they are also seen in open and semi-open rural areas. Like our other nightjars the Common Nighthawk feeds on the wing, but unlike the others this bird is active both at night and at dawn and dusk, or sometimes on cloudy days. Around towns and cities they chase airborne insects attracted to streetlights at night. This is one of the great travelers of the bird world. Nighthawks are usually seen in flight, but they will occasionally be spotted resting atop a fence post in open country. They often migrate in large flocks. This species was formerly much more common in New York, including in the vicinity of the state's major cities. It has experienced a severe decline in recent years.	**Natural History:** Few animals exhibit a more cryptic color and pattern than this species. When resting on the forest floor during the day they are nearly invisible. Like the Nighthawk, this species has been declining throughout its range for several years. A very similar species, the **Chuck-wills-widow** (*A. carolinensis*) is a very rare species in New York that is sometimes seen in summer on western Long Island. It is smaller (9.75 inches) and grayer than the Whip-poor-will. The two are easily differentiated by their songs, usually described as *whip, prrr-weel* for the Whip-poor-will and as *chuk-wills wee-dow* for the Chuck-will's-widow. Both calls are usually repeated rapidly and at times incessantly. Equipped with a very large mouths for feeding on moths and other large flying insects, they are nocturnal and catch most of their food in mid-air.	**Natural History:** The Barn Owl is one of the most widespread owl species in the world, being found throughout most of North America south of Canada, all of Central and South America, most of Europe and sub-saharan Africa, parts of southern Asia, and all of Australia. In spite of its wide range they are usually not common anywhere. In New York they are a rare species. Small rodents are the primary prey, especially mice and voles. When feeding a large brood of young a pair of Barn Owls may catch over two dozen mice in a single night. Like other owls their hearing is so acute they can catch mice unseen beneath leaves by homing in on rustling sounds. Ironically, man's attempts to control rodents with poisoned baits may be in part responsible for the demise of rodent-eating species like the Barn Owl, which is vulnerable to secondary ingestion of rodent poisons.

Class - **Aves** (birds)		
Order - **Strigiformes** (owls)		
Family - **Strigidae** (typical owls)		
Snowy Owl *Bubo scandiacus*	**Great Horned Owl** *Bubo virginianus*	**Barred Owl** *Strix varia*

Size: 24 inches.  Presumed range in New York	**Size:** 23 inches.  Presumed range in New York	**Size:** 21 inches.  Presumed range in New York
Abundance: Rare in New York.	**Abundance:** Fairly common.	**Abundance:** Fairly common.
Migratory Status: Winter migrant.	**Migratory Status:** Year-round resident.	**Migratory Status:** Year-round resident.

Variation: Females and juveniles have extensive black barring. Adult males are nearly pure white below with reduced dark bars and spots dorsally.	**Variation:** Males are slightly smaller and have a larger white patch on throat. There are a total of 10 subspecies in North America.	**Variation:** No sexual variation. Three subspecies are known in America with a fourth in central Mexico, the Northern Barred Owl (*S. v. varia*) occurring in New York.
Habitat: Summer habitat is the high arctic and open tundra. Birds that wander south in winter favor expansive open fields, beaches, and airports.	**Habitat:** Woodlands, semi-open, and open habitats are all utilized, but most common in mosaic of upland woods and fields.	**Habitat:** Woodlands primarily. Especially in bottomlands, swampy areas, and riparian corridors, but also upland woods.
Breeding: Nest is on the ground in open tundra. Often built atop small mounds or ridges. Lays 5 to 15 eggs.	**Breeding:** One of the earliest nesting birds in New York. Nest is often an old hawk nest. 2 eggs is usual.	**Breeding:** Nest is usually in tree cavities but known to nest tree crotches or old hawk nests. Usually 2 eggs.
Natural History: A true icon of northern wilderness, the sight of a Snowy Owl is often met with excitement by nature lovers. Winter migrants appear fairly regularly in the state and in rare winters they can be seen as far south as the Ohio River in the midwest. Every now and then large numbers of these giant owls appear in winter in the northern United States in a phenomenon known as an "irruption." The exact cause of these irruptions are not completely understood, but they may relate to unusually successful breeding seasons. One of this bird's primary food items is lemmings. Populations of these rodents vary considerably from year to year in what amounts to a boom-bust cycle. In years of abundant lemmings many more young owls are produced than in years of poor lemming numbers.	**Natural History:** This widespread species occurs throughout the Americas from Alaska to southern South America. In the United States specimens from the western portions of the country are much paler than those seen in the east. The Great Horned Owl is the ecological counterpart of the Red-tailed Hawk, hunting much the same prey in the same regions, with the hawk hunting by day and the owl at night. These powerful predators eat a wide variety of small animals. Rabbits are a favorite food item. They are also known to eat larger mammals like muskrats, groundhogs, and even skunks! They can be a problem at times for those who raise chickens and leave them out in the open at night. But they also consume many rodents. Once regarded as a varmint, they are now federally protected.	**Natural History:** The Barred Owl ranges throughout the eastern half of the United States from the eastern edge of the great plains eastward. The eight-noted call of the Barred Owl is described as "Hoo-hoo-hoo-hoo, hoo-hoo-hooaahh." In addition the species is capable of a wide array of hoots, screeches, and coarse whistles. Small vertebrates are the main prey, especially rodents like voles, mice, and flying squirrels. Birds, lizards, small snakes, and amphibians are also eaten. In the eastern United States the range of the Barred Owl closely coincides with that of the Red-shouldered Hawk and the two predators are often regarded as ecological counterparts occupying the same niche at different times. In New York this species is most common in the Adirondacks and Catskills regions.

Class - **Aves** (birds)		
Order - **Strigiformes** (owls)		
Family - **Strigidae** (typical owls)		

Short-eared Owl *Asio flammeus*	**Long-eared Owl** *Asio otus*	**Northern Saw-whet Owl** *Aegolius acadicus*

Size: Length 15 inches.	Presumed range in New York 	**Size:** Length 15 inches.	Presumed range in New York 	**Size:** Length 8 inches.	Presumed range in New York 
Abundance: Rare in New York.		**Abundance:** Uncommon.		**Abundance:** Fairly common.	
Variation: Little variation. Females tend to be slightly darker.		**Variation:** Female darker, more rusty face, and larger.		**Variation:** Immature has buff belly, dark facial disk.	

Migratory Status: Mostly a winter-time resident or winter migrant, but some breeding has been recorded in New York.	**Migratory Status:** Mostly a summer resident in northern New York but found year-round in the southern half of state.	**Migratory Status:** Year-round resident, but some birds may move south in winter.
Habitat: These are open-country birds and the primary habitat is prairie, marsh, and tundra. In forested regions they haunt fields, pastures, meadows, etc.	**Habitat:** Prefers open and semi-open woodlands and riparian habitats in open regions. Breeds and summers in boreal regions and mountains.	**Habitat:** Spruce-fir-pine-dominated forests in the north and in the Rocky Mountain west. In the east uses mostly mixed deciduous/conifer forests.
Breeding: Nest is on the ground. A slight depression is scraped out by the owl and lined with grasses. 5 or 6 eggs is typical.	**Breeding:** Usually nests in trees in abandoned stick nests built by hawks, crows, or other large bird species. 5 or 6 eggs is typical.	**Breeding:** Uses old woodpecker holes almost exclusively for nesting. 5 or 6 eggs is typical with a survival rate to fledging of about 50 percent.
Natural History: In New York the Short-eared Owl is most likely to be seen in open regions during winter. The food is mostly small rodents. Voles are the most significant item in their diet. Rodent prey is located mostly by sound while flying low and slow over open, grassy fields. Most hunting is done at night or dusk and dawn, but these owls are more diurnal than most and may hunt during the day. The erectile feathers on the face that form the "ears" are not usually visible unless the owl is agitated or defensive. This species appears to be in decline in much of America. The daytime counterpart of the Short-eared Owl is the Northern Harrier, which occupies the same habitats and is distributed across much of the same regions of North America.	**Natural History:** Although this rare owl could possibly be seen anywhere in the state, sightings are uncommon due to their secretive nature. They are most likely to be seen in southern New York where they are year-round residents, but they can be seen in northern New York in winter. Their name comes from the well-developed feather tufts on the head which are erected when resting. These "ear tufts" are folded against the head and not visible on owls in flight. Long-eared Owls during winter can sometimes be seen in small flocks that roost in close proximity to each other. Although they primarily are a northern species, a few may move far south in winter. Their food is almost exclusively small mammals, mostly voles and mice of the *Peromyscus* genus.	**Natural History:** Small mammals (mice, voles, and shrews) make up the bulk of this little owl's diet. Mice of the genus *Peromyscus* make up as much as three-fourths of the food consumed. Insects are oddly not listed as a major food item, but songbirds are known to be eaten. Small and secretive, the Saw-whet Owl roosts in thick evergreens and is typically silent except during the breeding season. Thus these birds are difficult to observe in the wild. Within its range in the Rockies and Appalachians, seasonal migration is mostly vertical, with the owls moving to lower elevations in winter. These uncommon breeding birds in New York, but some nesting does occur in widely scattered localities around the state, mostly in the Adirondacks.

Class - **Aves** (birds)

Order - **Strigiformes** (owls)	Order - **Falconiformes** (raptors)
Family - **Strigidae** (typical owls)	Family - **Accipitridae** (hawks, eagles, kites)

| **Eastern Screech Owl** *Megascops asio* | **Red-tailed Hawk** - *Buteo jamaicensis* |

Typical

Light morph

Size: Length 8.5 inches.	Presumed range in New York	**Size:** Total length 19 inches. Wingspan to 49 inches. Weight 2.5 pounds.	Presumed range in New York
Abundance: Common.		**Abundance:** Common throughout the state.	
Migratory Status: Year-round.		**Migratory Status:** Year-round resident. Numbers may be supplemented in winter with migrants from farther north.	

Variation: Two distinct color morphs occur in New York. A reddish brown phase and a gray phase (inset). Gray is more common in mountains.

Variation: Highly variable. Can vary from nearly solid dark brown to very pale. Most adult birds are like the typical adult specimen pictured on top left above. Females are about 20 percent larger than males. Juveniles have brownish tails with dark crossbars. Some experts recognize as many as 16 subspecies.

Habitat: All types of habitats within the state may be used, including suburban areas and in the vicinity of farms. Favors edge areas, fence rows, etc.

Habitat: Found in virtually all habitats within the state. Likes open and semi-open areas and is least common in continuous forest, although they do occur there. Favors a mosaic of woodlands, farmland, fencerows, overgrown fields, etc. They will also hunt grassy areas along roadsides, including busy interstates.

Breeding: Nest is in tree hollows and old woodpecker holes. 4 to 6 eggs are laid and young fledge by mid-June.

Breeding: In New York the large stick nest is usually built high in trees. Nest is usually situated in place that is remote from human activities. Lays 2 to 4 eggs. Young fledge at six weeks. Old nest are used by the Great Horned Owl.

Natural History: The eerie call of the Screech Owl is often described as "haunting and tremulous." Despite being at times vocal birds, these small owls often go unnoticed. They may even live in suburban yards and small towns, especially if older, large trees with hollow limbs and trunks are present. They feed on insects such as crickets and grasshoppers and on a wide variety of small vertebrate prey including mice, voles, and songbirds that are plucked from their roosts at night. These wide-ranging birds are found through-out the eastern United States as from the Altlantic to the Rocky Mountains and from southern Canada to Florida and Mexico. Birds in the northern portions of their range can be negatively impact-ed by severe winters with deep snow.

Natural History: This is the most common and widespread large *Buteo* hawk in America. Their range includes all of North America south of the arctic and much of the Caribbean and Central America. The Red-tailed Hawk is generally regarded as the daytime counterpart of the Great Horned Owl, hunting by day many of the same species in the same habitats utilized by the owl at night. "Red-tails" prey mostly on rodents (mice, voles, and ground squirrels). Much larger prey like rabbits may also be taken on occasion. In some areas ground-dwelling birds like pheasants and quail are taken, and they have been known to attack large flocks of blackbirds. In summer they also take large snakes such as the Woodland Rat Snake (*Pantherophis*). Large examples of these snakes (which are strong constrictors) have been known to turn the tables and end up killing a hungry hawk. During winter these large hawks sometimes resort to eating carrion and can sometimes be seen feeding on roadkill. In much of the eastern United States the Red-tailed Hawk is often known by the nickname "Chicken Hawk" in the mistaken belief that they prey on chickens. Although they may catch a few chickens occasionally, their main food is rats, mice, and other rodents, making them an overall useful species to man. Their habit of perching conspicuously in dead trees, snags, and power poles along highways makes them one of the more easily observed hawk species. Historically, all hawks were regarded as varmints and they were shot on sight by uninformed individuals. By the 1950s many were becoming scarce in America. Since the passage of the Migratory Bird Treaty Act in the early 1970s, Red-tailed Hawks have become common.

Class - **Aves** (birds)

Order - **Falconiformes** (raptors)

Family - **Accipitridae** (hawks, eagles, kites)

Broad-winged Hawk *Buteo platypterus*	Rough-legged Hawk *Buteo lagopus*	Red-shouldered Hawk *Buteo lineatus*
	 Light morph	 Adult Juvenile

Size: 16 inches.	**Size:** 21 inches.	**Size:** 17 inches.
Abundance: Fairly common.	**Abundance:** Uncommon.	**Abundance:** Uncommon.
Migratory Status: Summer resident.	**Migratory Status:** Winter migrant.	**Migratory Status:** Summer resident.

Presumed range in New York (three maps)

Variation: First-year plumage is mottled brown (similar to juvenile Red-shouldered Hawk on this page). | **Variation:** Two distinct color morphs, a dark (nearly black) phase and a lighter morph with paler head and shoulders. | **Variation:** Four subspecies. Ours is the eastern race (*B. l. lineatus*). Female larger. Young are brownish (see above).

Habitat: Favors large tracts of unbroken woodlands in upland areas. Least common in the Interior Lowlands of western New York. | **Habitat:** This is a northern species that summers as far north as the arctic. Favors tundra in summer and farmlands and prairies in winter. | **Habitat:** Woodlands of all kinds, but especially likes woods bordering swamps or rivers, or along wooded creek-sides. Less common in uplands.

Breeding: Stick nest is in a tree crotch, usually in deep woods. Lays 2–3 eggs on average. | **Breeding:** Nests well to north in arctic or subarctic regions of tundra and tiaga. Clutch size (3–7) is prey dependent. | **Breeding:** Bulky stick nest is in the fork of a tree about 20–40 feet high and often near water. 2 to 4 eggs in April.

Natural History: A decidedly woodland raptor whose breeding range in North America closely mimics the Eastern Temperate Forests Level I Ecoregion. In New York this species is much more common in the regions which are more heavily forested. They may be seen as a migrant throughout the entire state but the lack of large tracts of forest in the Interior Lowlands province precludes most nesting in that region. They are less conspicuous than most hawks except during the migration when they band together in large flocks known as "kettles." Extremely large flocks that may contain 200 birds are usually seen during fall migrations. Hunts by scanning for prey from a perch. Food includes insects, but consists mostly of small vertebrates like rodents as well as a large amount of reptile and amphibian prey, including lizards and small snakes. | **Natural History:** The Rough-legged Hawk is an arctic species that moves south in winter, often as far south as northern Virginia in the east as as far as Texas in the west. Their migrations are sporadic depending upon weather, snow cover, and prey availability, but every winter at least a few can be seen in New York. They prey primarily on small mammals, and lemmings are an important food on the breeding grounds. During years of high lemming populations more eggs will be laid and more young fledged. In winter they take mice, voles, and shrews mostly. Hunts by soaring and hovering over open country. They can face into the wind and remain in a stationary hover for over a minute. While these are fairly large hawks, they have relatively small feet and small beaks, and are thus unable to take the larger prey taken by hawks like the Red-tailed Hawk. | **Natural History:** The Red-shouldered Hawk is the daytime counterpart of the Barred Owl, and the two species often occur in the same territory. These are vocal birds. Their call, described as "kee-ah, kee-ah, kee-ah" is rapidly repeated about a dozen times. They can be fairly tame if unmolested and their raucous calling will not go unnoticed when the nest is nearby. They feed on a wide variety of small vertebrates but mostly eat reptiles, amphibians, and rodents. The range of the Red-shouldered Hawk coincides closely with the Level I Ecoregion known as the Eastern Temperate Forest. However, a disjunct population (subspecies *elegans*) is found on the west coast of North America in the Mediterranean California Ecoregion. Although breeding is widespread across the state they do not breed on Long Island, though they can be seen there in the winter. |

Class - **Aves** (birds)
Order - **Falconiformes** (raptors)
Family - **Accipitridae** (hawks, eagles, kites)

Golden Eagle *Aquila chrysaetos*	Bald Eagle *Haliaeetus leucocephalus*	Osprey *Pandion haliaetus*

Size: 30 inches.  Presumed range in New York	**Size:** 31 inches.  Presumed range in New York	**Size:** 30 inches. Presumed range in New York
Abundance: Very rare in New York.	**Abundance:** Uncommon.	**Abundance:** Fairly common.
Migratory Status: Winter migrant.	**Migratory Status:** Year-round resident.	**Migratory Status:** Summer resident.
Variation: Sexes are alike in appearance but female is about 20 percent larger. Juvenile birds have white in tail.	**Variation:** May not acquire the characteristic white head and tail until their fourth annual molt at five years of age.	**Variation:** No variation in plumage of adults and immatures. Females are slightly larger than males.
Habitat: Rugged mountains, deserts, and open plains of the western United States and rugged regions of Canadian tundra.	**Habitat:** Bald Eagles are usually associated with lakes and large rivers and such as the Hudson and Delaware.	**Habitat:** Typically seen in the vicinity of the state's large lakes and rivers and along the coast.
Breeding: A large stick nest up to 6 feet across is usually built on the face of a steep cliff. Usually lays 2 eggs.	**Breeding:** Extremely bulky stick nest is re-used and gets larger each year. Usually only 2 eggs per clutch.	**Breeding:** Bulky stick nest is often built on man-made structures like bridges and power line towers. 2 to 4 eggs.
Natural History: Although they are slightly smaller than the Bald Eagle, Golden Eagles are probably the most fearsome hunting bird in America. Ground squirrels and other small mammals make up the bulk of their prey, with larger species like jackrabbits and the young of wild sheep, goats, and Pronghorn also being taken. They are sometimes persecuted by sheep ranchers in western North America, who blame them for killing young lambs in the spring. Indigenous to the entire northern hemisphere, in America the Golden Eagle is found mostly in the west. Like many large raptors they are capable of significant seasonal movements. Although very rare east of the Great Plains, they may sometimes show up almost anywhere in North America, including New York, especially during winter months.	**Natural History:** One of the great conservation success stories, Bald Eagles were highly endangered just a few decades ago. Stringent protection, banning of the pesticide DDT, and a widespread education campaign has lead to a remarkable recovery. They first began to recover as a breeding species in the mid 1980s following extreme conservation efforts by NYSDEC and the USF&WS. Though uncommon they are increasing in New York. Bald Eagles feed largely on fish and carrion but are also capable hunters. Some birds specialize in hunting migratory waterfowl in winter, picking off birds wounded by hunters. Bald Eagles wander widely in the winter and may be seen virtually anywhere in the state, but they are nowhere numerous. Most nesting is along major rivers and lakes. Adopted as the national emblem of the United States by Congress in 1782.	**Natural History:** Subsists mainly on fish. Hunting tactics consist of a steep dive that ends with the Osprey plunging feet first into the water, allowing them to catch fish up to three feet below the surface. Most fish caught in freshwater are non-game species, thus they have little to no impact on sport fisheries. Like the Bald Eagle, Osprey populations in the mid–United States plummeted dramatically in the first half of the 20th century. The same types of conservation efforts that restored the Bald Eagle (including re-introduction programs) have brought Osprey numbers back to respectable levels. Once regarded as an endangered species, the Osprey has recovered enough to have recently been de-listed. New York now boasts healthy populations of nesting Ospreys and they continue to increase across the state.

Class - **Aves** (birds)

Order - **Falconiformes** (raptors)

Family - **Accipitridae** (hawks, eagles, kites)

Northern Goshawk *Accipiter gentilis*	Sharp-shinned Hawk *Accipiter striatus*	Cooper's Hawk *Accipiter cooperii*

Size: Length up to 2 feet.	Presumed range in New York	**Size:** Length 9–13 inches.	Presumed range in New York	**Size:** Length 14–19 inches.	Presumed range in New York
Abundance: Uncommon.		**Abundance:** Fairly common.		**Abundance:** Fairly common.	
Migratory Status: Year-round.		**Migratory Status:** Year-round.		**Migratory Status:** Year-round.	

Variation: Females are larger. Juveniles are heavily streaked with dark brown as with other *Accipiter* hawks.	**Variation:** Ontogenetic plumage variation (see photos). Females are as much as twice the size of males.	**Variation:** First-year birds are brown with streaked breast. Females are about 30 percent larger than males.
Habitat: A bird of coniferous and boreal forests. In winter sometimes uses mixed deciduous/conifer woodlands.	**Habitat:** Forests and thickets. Found in both rural and urban areas where vegetative cover is present.	**Habitat:** Woodlands, regenerative areas, and edge habitats are favored. Can also be seen in tree-lined urban yards.
Breeding: Large stick nest can be 3 feet across, usually built in the largest tree in the area. 2 to 4 eggs on average.	**Breeding:** Pine trees are a favored locale for placing the nest. Lays as many as 8 eggs, with 5–6 being the average.	**Breeding:** Stick nest is built high in tree and eggs are laid in April or May. Clutch size averages 4–6.
Natural History: This is a bird of wilderness. It inhabits most of Canada and the Rocky Mountains. Their primary food consists of several species of grouse, but they also take smaller birds as well as squirrels, rabbits, and animals as large as the Snowshoe Hare. Known for fearlessness, the Goshawk has been known to attack humans who venture to close to its nest. It is equally couragous on the hunt and will crash headlong into thickets in pursuit of fleeing prey. This characteristic coupled with its speed and large size have made the Goshawk a favorite bird among those who practice the ancient art of Falconry. Although this species is widespread across the northern half of North America, they are an uncommon bird even within their core range. In New York they are most common the northernmost section of the state.	**Natural History:** A relentless hunter of small songbirds, the Sharp-shinned Hawk is sometimes seen raiding backyard bird feeders, and they are known to pluck baby songbirds from nests. These small raptors are capable of rapid, twisting flight while pursuing their small songbird prey through woodlands and thickets. In New York they are more common during migration periods when birds that summer farther north move southward. Although many are breeding residents in the state, some nest far to north, some as far north as the edge of the arctic. The Sharp-shinned Hawk is a widely distributed species that ranges across all of North America south of the arctic region and southward all the way to southern Central America. In New York they are a fairly common breeding bird throughout the state except for Long Island and New York City.	**Natural History:** Feeds almost exclusively on birds and is known to haunt backyard bird feeders. These hawks are a major predator to the Bobwhite, an important game species that is in decline throughout most of its range. Cooper's Hawks are fierce hunters that will fearlessly attack birds as large or larger than themselves, including grouse, waterfowl, and domestic chickens. Although quite widespread and fairly common, they are not as observable as the *Buteo* hawks. Cooper's Hawks tend to stay in wooded areas and thickets with heavier cover than their bulkier cousins. These birds are fast fliers and capable of great maneuverability, an adaptation to hunting in forests and thickets. They have adapted well to human activities and they sometimes exist in urban areas, especially in parks and heavily wooded neighborhoods.

Class - **Aves** (birds)

Order - **Falconiformes** (raptors)

Family - **Accipitridae** (hawks, eagles, kites)	Family - **Cathartidae** (vultures)	
Northern Harrier *Circus cyaneus*	**Turkey Vulture** *Cathartes aura*	**Black Vulture** *Coragyps atratus*

Size: Length 18 inches.

Abundance: Fairly common.

Variation: See photos above.

Presumed range in New York

Size: Length 26 inches.

Abundance: Common.

Variation: None.

Presumed range in New York

Size: Length 25 inches.

Abundance: Uncommon.

Variation: None.

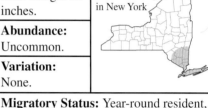
Presumed range in New York

Migratory Status: Year-round in southeast and western New York. Summer only in northern and central NY.

Habitat: Open country. Pastures, agricultural fields, wet prairies, grasslands, and especially marshes.

Breeding: Nests on the ground in thick grass. Builds a nest of grasses and weed stems. Lays 4 to 6 eggs.

Natural History: The range of the Northern Harrier is holarctic and includes Europe and northern Asia as well as North America. Unlike most diurnal raptors that hunt entirely by sight, the Northern Harrier mimics the technique used by owls and hunts largely by sound. A special "parabola" of feathers surround the face and direct sound waves to the ears. It hunts by flying low to the ground with a slow, buoyant flight that resembles a giant butterfly. Food is mostly small mammals and birds but reptiles and amphibians are also listed as food items. Roosting and nesting on the ground and hunting as much by sound as by sight, the Northern Harrier is unique among America's diurnal raptors. They are also commonly called Marsh Hawks, an appropriate moniker, and in historical times before the draining of so many of America's marshes, this was a more common species.

Migratory Status: Year-round resident in the southeastern tip of the state. Summer resident elswhere.

Habitat: Seen in all habitats throughout the state. Less common in urban areas and regions of intensive agriculture.

Breeding: Nests on cliff faces, in large tree hollows, or on the ground in hollow logs. Almost always lays 2 eggs.

Natural History: The absence of feathers on the head and neck of vultures is an adaptation for feeding on carrion. Vultures may stick the head deep inside a rotting carcass and feathers would become matted with filth. The bare skin on the neck and face on the other hand is constantly exposed to the sterilizing effects of sunlight. Turkey Vultures are one of the few birds with a well-developed sense of smell, and food is often located by detecting the odor of rotting flesh. Sight is also important and they are quick to notice a fresh carcass on a roadway. Newly mowed fields and other disturbed areas within their range are closely scanned for small animals victimized by machinery. Highly social, they roost communally, sometimes with Black Vultures. Vultures have benefited from a constant supply of road-killed animals and both species of vulture seen in New York are expanding their ranges.

Migratory Status: Year-round resident, but some birds will go south in harsh winters.

Habitat: Found in a wide variety of habitats within it's range. In New York restricted to southeastern tip of state.

Breeding: No nest is built and the 2 eggs are laid on a bare surface. The nest site is often in a derelict building.

Natural History: America's vultures are named for the color of the skin on the face. Turkey Vultures have reddish skin (like a turkey), Black Vulture has dark gray or black facial skin. Black Vultures also have shorter tails and lesser wingspan, giving them a much "stubbier" look than the Turkey Vulture. Vultures were once regarded as a threat to livestock by spreading disease. In fact, the powerful digestive juices of the gut of vultures destroy bacteria. Both the Turkey Vulture and the Black Vulture have the unappealing habit of defecating on the legs and feet as a way of disinfecting the feet (which can become quite nasty and the birds feed on rotted carcasses). Black Vultures lack the well-developed sense of smell of Turkey Vultures, but they do have keen eyesight. Both vulture species in the eastern United States are expanding their ranges, perhaps due to a constant food supply provided by roadkill.

Class - **Aves** (birds)

Order - **Falconiformes** (raptors)

Family - **Falconidae** (falcons)

American Kestrel *Falco sparverius*	Merlin *Falco columbarius*	Peregrine Falcon *Falco peregrinus*

Size: 10 inches.	**Size:** 11 inches.	**Size:** 17 inches.
Abundance: Fairly common.	**Abundance:** Uncommon.	**Abundance:** Uncommon.
Migratory Status: Year-round resident.	**Migratory Status:** Mostly migrant.	**Migratory Status:** Year-round and migrant.
Presumed range in New York	Presumed range in New York	Presumed range in New York
Variation: Sexually dimorphic. Male has gray wings, female brown.	**Variation:** Male has blue-gray back, female and immatures have brown back.	**Variation:** Juvenile birds have dark streaks on the breast rather than bars.
Habitat: Throughout America the Kestrel is seen in open country. Least common in regions of dense forest.	**Habitat:** Habitat is open regions. Most likely to be seen along major river valleys or along the coast.	**Habitat:** Prefers cliffs in remote wilderness areas but has adapted to living among skyscrapers in many cities.
Breeding: Usually nests in tree cavities or old woodpecker holes within trees situated in open fields. May also nest in man-made structures. 4 to 5 eggs.	**Breeding:** Most breeding is far to the north in Canada, but some breeding occurs in New York in the Adirondacks. Uses old crow or hawk nests and cliffs.	**Breeding:** Nests on ledges of cliff faces and on man-made structures like skyscrapers and bridges. 4 eggs is typical, sometimes up to 6.
Natural History: While the Kestrel is a fairly common bird in open regions throughout New York, there has been some decline in populations in the eastern United States in recent years. They are widely known by the name "Sparrow Hawk," but that name is properly applied to a european member of the *Accipiter* clan. The Kestrel is not a hawk, but a true falcon. They are widespread throughout North and Central America and as many as 17 subspecies are recognized. They are often seen perched on power lines and poles along roadways in rural farmlands throughout the state, but they are uncommon in the heavily forested regions of New York. Insects are the major food in summer (especially grasshoppers). In winter they eat small mammals and rarely, small birds. Hunts both from a perch and by hovering over open fields.	**Natural History:** The Merlin is seen in New York mostly during migration (or as very rare summer resident/breeder in the Adirondack region). These small falcons are only slightly larger than the Kestrel and they are easily confused with that species. The facial markings of the Merlin are less distinct than the Kestrels. Summering mostly far to the north of New York and wintering along coastlines they are, like most falcons, prone to wander widely and they may be seen anywhere in the state. They seem to be increasing in population in New York. Food is mostly small birds. Shorebirds seem to be a favorite target and Merlins can often be seen flying fast and low above beaches and dunes as they attempt to surprise a flock of feeding sandpipers. In inland areas they will use the same tactic on mudflats in river valleys or lake shores.	**Natural History:** Falcons are fast-flying birds and the Peregrine is among the fastest. Hunts pigeons, waterfowl, grouse, etc. Hunting technique usually involves soaring high above and diving in on birds in flight, or diving towards resting birds and panicking them into flight. Once airborne, no other bird can match the Peregrine's speed. Diving Peregrines may reach speeds approaching 200 mph, making them perhaps the fastest animal on Earth. In New York this species currently breeds mostly along the Hudson River valley and in the vicinity of Lake Champlain. However, the name "peregrine" means "wanderer," and these birds may be seen almost anywhere in the state. Once nearly extirpated by DDT contamination, populations of the Peregrine Falcon have recovered dramatically and they continue to increase in numbers.

Class - **Aves** (birds)

Order - **Pelicaniformes** (wading birds)

Family - **Ardeidae** (herons)

Great Blue Heron	Great Egret	Snowy Egret
Ardea herodias	*Ardea alba*	*Egretta thula*

Size: 47 inches.

Abundance: Fairly common.

Variation: See Natural History below.

Presumed range in New York

Size: 39 inches.

Abundance: Fairly common.

Variation: Breeders acquire plumes.

Presumed range in New York

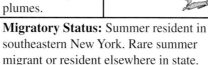

Size: 24 inches.

Abundance: Fairly common.

Variation: Breeders acquire plumes.

Presumed range in New York

Migratory Status: A year-round resident in southeastern New York. Summer resident elsewhere in the state.

Migratory Status: Summer resident in southeastern New York. Rare summer migrant or resident elsewhere in state.

Migratory Status: Summer resident in southeastern New York. Rare summer migrant along the Hudson River.

Habitat: Along rivers and streams, swamps, marshes, ponds, and wet meadows and floodplains.

Habitat: Along major streams, lakes, swamps, and marshes. Also low-lying areas subject to flooding.

Habitat: Along major streams, lakes, swamps, and marshes. Also low-lying areas subject to flooding.

Breeding: Often nests in colonies. Nest is a platform of sticks in tree or bush above water. Nesting occurs statewide except in NYC and on Long Island. 3 to 4 eggs is typical.

Breeding: Most nesting in New York occurs in the vicinity of Long Island. Sporadic nesting occurs elsewhere in New York. Nest is a platform of sticks in tree or bush above water. Lays 3 or 4 eggs.

Breeding: Nesting in New York occurs only on islands in the southeast. They will nest in colonies with other heron species. Nest is made of sticks and twigs. 3 to 5 eggs is average.

Natural History: The largest heron in North America, the Great Blue Heron will eat almost anything it can swallow. Fish and frogs are major foods, but it also eats snakes, salamanders, small mammals, and even small turtles. Birds are sometimes eaten, including other, smaller heron species. All food items are swallowed whole. Large prey is killed by stabbing repeatedly with the beak or by bashing against a hard object. Smaller prey is often swallowed alive. Hunts both day and night and reportedly has good night vision. Great Blue Herons are found throughout most of the United States and much of Canada, including in riparian habitats in desert regions. Sexes are alike but juveniles will have streaked breast and neck and are duskier overall than adults. A solid white subspecies is found in parts of southern Florida.

Natural History: This heron species (along with the Snowy Egret and several other herons) was nearly hunted to extinction during the last half of the 19th century. The long, wispy feathers (known as "plumes") were once used to adorn the hats of fashionable ladies. The plumes are most pronounced during the breeding season. Thus the catastrophic impact of the plume hunters was magnified as hunters killed birds at their nesting colonies. Killing of parent birds doomed nestlings as well. Efforts to save this and other plume bird species lead to some of Americas earliest laws to protect wildlife. Today this species is still a symbol of conservation efforts and is the logo of the National Audubon Society. It is also known by the names Common Egret or Great White Egret. As with many other herons, it often nests in colonies.

Natural History: As with several other heron species, the Snowy Egret during breeding season sports long "plume" feathers on the back. As with other plume bird species, the Snowy Egret was nearly wiped out by the feather trade of the late 1800s. Today the species has recovered to healthy numbers but remains under threat due to its dependence upon coastal wetlands. This species feeds on smaller prey such as worms, insects, crustaceans, amphibians, and small fish. It is an active feeder that often chases prey through the shallows rather than using the stealth method employed by its larger cousins. It also often feeds by swishing its feet in the mud to disturb benthic organisms. Can be distinguished from the similar Great Egret by its smaller size and by its bright yellow feet.

Class - **Aves** (birds)		
Order - **Pelicaniformes** (wading birds)		
Family - **Ardeidae** (herons)		

Little Blue Heron *Egretta caerulea*	**Cattle Egret** *Bubulcus ibis*	**Green Heron** *Butorides virescens*

Size: Length 24 inches. **Abundance:** Rare in New York. **Migratory Status:** Summer.  Presumed range in New York	**Size:** Length 19 inches. **Abundance:** Very rare in New York. **Migratory Status:** Summer  Presumed range in New York	**Size:** Length 19 inches. **Abundance:** Fairly common. **Migratory Status:** Summer.  Presumed range in New York
Variation: First-year birds have white plumage (see inset photo).	**Variation:** Orange on crown and throat more pronounced during breeding.	**Variation:** Juvenile birds are browner above and have streaked throat.
Habitat: Wetlands. In New York seen only in wetlands around New York City and Long Island.	**Habitat:** Unlike other herons, these birds are usually seen in open pastures and fields in association with cattle.	**Habitat:** Usually seen in the vicinity of wetlands or rivers and streams. Also common around lakes and small ponds.
Breeding: Builds a stick nest platform in bushes and low trees in wetlands. Lays 2 to 5 eggs.	**Breeding:** Stick nest built in trees or bushes. Nests in large colonies. 3 or 4 eggs is average.	**Breeding:** Usually nests singly rather than in colonies. Nest is a stick platform in a tree fork. Lays 3 to 5 eggs.
Natural History: Even within the heart of its range along the lower coastal plains of the southeastern United States, the Little Blue Heron is generally less common that other heron species. In New York it is a rare bird. In addition, the dark plumage of adults and its rather secretive nature make it one of the least observable herons. Like most herons, it is an opportunistic feeder that eats almost anything it can swallow. Food is mostly frogs, fish, crustaceans, and insects. It is a daytime hunter that hunts by stalking slowly through wetland habitats. The transitional plumage of the juvenile Little Blue Heron is unique, and produces for a brief time a white bird with blue splotches. Blue increases throughout the molt ending in a solid blue adult. The range map above approximates the range of summer breeders. Some post-breeding dispersal may occur into more northerly regions of the state in late summer.	**Natural History:** The Cattle Egret is one of our most interesting heron species. Originally native to Africa, Cattle Egrets began an inexplicable range expansion in the early 1800s. They first migrated across the Atlantic to South America and then appeared in North America around 1950. The first sighting in Ohio was in 1958. The species continues to expand its range and is today a rare summer migrant in southernmost New York. Their name is derived from their habit of associating with cattle herds in pastures. Before expanding their range out of Africa they associated with herds of Cape Buffalo, Hippopotamus, and wild ungulates. They feed mostly on insects that are disturbed by the large grazers they follow through pastures and grasslands. The map above shows the approximate range of summer migrants in New York. The potential for this species to continue to expand northward in the state exists.	**Natural History:** In many areas the Green Heron often goes by the name "Shy-poke." This is one of America's most familiar herons and its range encompasses all of the eastern United States as well as the west coast. It also ranges southward throughout Central America. When flushed it nearly always emits a loud "squawking" alarm call. Feeds mostly in shallow water and often feeds from a perch on a floating log or a limb just above the water's surface. Hunts by stealth and may remain frozen for long periods as it watches and waits for prey. Fish is the primary food item with small frogs probably being the next most common prey. Amazingly, this species has been reported to catch insects and worms to use as bait for luring in fish. While the Green Heron is one of our most common wading birds, it is dependent upon wetlands. Sadly, wetlands are among our most threatened wildlife habitats.

Class - **Aves** (birds)

Order - **Pelicaniformes** (wading birds)

Family - **Ardeidae** (herons)

Yellow-crowned Night Heron *Nyctanassa violacea*	**Black-crowned Night Heron** *Nycticorax nycticorax*	**Least Bittern** *Ixobrychus exilis*

Size: Length 25 inches.	Presumed range in New York	**Size:** Length 25 inches.	Presumed range in New York	**Size:** Length 13 inches.	Presumed range in New York
Abundance: Rare in New York.		**Abundance:** Uncommon.		**Abundance:** Uncommon.	
Migratory Status: Summer.		**Migratory Status:** Summer		**Migratory Status:** Summer.	

Variation: Juveniles are heavily streaked with brown and white.	**Variation:** Juvenile birds are heavily streaked with brown (see inset).	**Variation:** Male has black cap and black back. See both sexes above.
Habitat: Swamps and marshes. Favors heavier cover than many herons.	**Habitat:** Wetlands, river valleys, and in the vicinity of lakes and impoundments.	**Habitat:** Favors marshes with dense growths of tall grasses and sedges.
Breeding: Breeds very sparingly in southeastern tip of New York. Flimsy stick nest is fairly high in a tree, usually over water. 3 to 5 eggs.	**Breeding:** Nests in colonies that are usually situated over swamps or on an island. Colonies may contain hundreds of birds, with 3 or 4 eggs per nest.	**Breeding:** Nest is a well-concealed platform built amid dense growth of cattails or other sedges/grasses. Up to 6 eggs are laid.
Natural History: These birds are often active at night, hence the name "night heron." Food is mostly crustaceans. Crabs are important foods in coastal regions, while crayfish are eaten in freshwater areas. A classical ambush predator, the Yellow-crowned Night Heron does most foraging from a stationery position, sitting like a statue and waiting for prey to wander into striking range. They will also stalk slowly and methodically with slow, deliberate movements that are largely undetectable to prey. Diet may be supplemented with fish and invertebrates, but this heron is mainly a crustacean specialist. Has recovered nicely from low numbers decades ago and now seems to be expanding its range farther to the north. Although they are very rare in New York in general, they can be fairly common locally in coastal areas of the state in summer months. Leaves early for wintering grounds in the deep south.	**Natural History:** Although the Black-crowned Night Heron may be locally common near breeding colonies, it is widely scattered and uncommon in New York. Surprisingly, this is a widespread species that is found not only in much of the United States, but in fact throughout most of the world. They can be found on every continent except Australia and Antarctica. As its name implies this species is often active at night. The food is primarily fish. However, the list of known foods is quite long and includes insects, leeches, earthworms, crustaceans, gastropods, amphibians, snakes, small turtles, small mammals, and even birds! Prefers to feed in shallow water along the margins of weedy ponds, marshes, and swamps. Most breeding in New York occurs in the southeastern tip of the state. A few breed in widely scattered locales along the Lake Ontario shore and in the Niagra River and Hudson River valleys.	**Natural History:** This smallest of American herons is also a secretive bird that often stays hidden in dense marsh grasses and sedges. When alarmed they point their bill skyward and freeze, mimicking the vertical vegetation of their habitat. These small herons move with ease through thick stands of marsh vegetation. When flushed they fly only a short distance just above the vegetation before dropping back down. Despite their seemingly weak flying abilities, they migrate great distances from wintering areas in south Florida and the Carribean to summer breeding grounds that may be as far north as New Brunswick. They have very long toes for grasping stems of grass and sedge. Feeds on small fish, insects, crayfish, and amphibians. The biggest threat to this and other herons is loss of wetland habitat. Where habitat persists these birds will thrive and they even live in wetlands surrounded by urban areas.

Class - **Aves** (birds)

Order - **Pelicaniformes** (wading birds)	Order - **Gruiformes** (rails and cranes)	
Family - **Ardeidae** (herons)	Family - **Rallidae** (rails)	

American Bittern *Botaurus lentiginosus*	**Clapper Rail** *Rallus crepitans*	**Virginia Rail** *Rallus limicola*

Size: 26 inches.

Abundance: Uncommon.

Migratory Status: Summer resident mostly.

Presumed range in New York

Size: 14.5 inches

Abundance: Fairly common.

Migratory Status: Mostly a summer resident.

Presumed range in New York

Size: 9.5 inches.

Abundance: Uncommon.

Migratory Status: Summer resident mostly.

Presumed range in New York

Variation: None. Sexes alike.

Variation: None. Sexes alike.

Variation: None. Sexes alike.

Habitat: Large freshwater marshes are used in summer, coastal marshlands in winter.

Habitat: An obligate of salt marsh that ranges along America's coastlines from Massachussets to northern Mexico.

Habitat: Primarily a marsh dweller. In migration may visit ponds, swamps, or wet meadows.

Breeding: Nest is in dense emergent vegetation of the marsh and is well hidden. 3 to 5 eggs is typical. Most breeding occurs in northwestern New York.

Breeding: Nest is built in the marsh amid emergent vegetation. Some nests may be inudated by high tides. Clutch size can range from 4 to 16 eggs.

Breeding: Builds a nest platform of aquatic vegetation a few inches above water level. Nest is usually well hidden among vegetation. Lays 8 or 9 eggs.

Natural History: The biology of this species is not well known. Presumably they may be seen anywhere in New York during migration, but they are probably most likely to be seen in the marshes bordering Lake Ontario. Few people will ever see one, as they are usually quite secretive. Hunts by stealth and may remain motionless for long periods of time. The eyes of this heron are situated with a downward slant, better facilitating the bird's ability to see into the water. When startled they will throw the head back and point the beak straight up. The streaked brown pattern of the neck and breast is remarkably cryptic amid the vertical stalks of marsh grasses and sedges. Like most herons, an opportunistic feeder. Eats fish, amphibians, crayfish, small mammals, and some insects. During migration they will sometimes stop at very small ponds that are heavily vegetated with cattails. Mainly a summer resident, but some overwinter the state's coastal marshes.

Natural History: Rails are well adapted to life in the marsh. They move with ease through thick grasses and rarely fly except when migrating. They can run quite fast through the grass and rarely offer more than a glimpse. They can also swim and dive beneath the surface, using the wings to swim underwater. Despite the fact that rails are listed as a game bird by most state wildlife agencies, almost no one hunts them, due probably to their scarcity and secretiveness. Few people not actively seeking this secretive bird will ever see one as they typically remain hidden in thick marsh grasses. At low tide they can sometimes be glimpsed as they emerge onto bare mudflats and they can easily be heard calling within the marsh. They feed mostly on aquatic insects and their larva, spiders, and other invertebrates. Some plant material is also eaten. A few Clapper Rails may overwinter in New York's salt marshes, but most will move farther to the south in winter.

Natural History: Although generally uncommon in the state, the Virginia Rail is the most common breeding rail in New York. Nesting has been recorded widely across the state in suitable habitats. Still, this is not a common bird in New York and this fact coupled with its secretive nature means that it is a species that remains unfamiliar to most residents. Similar in many ways to the Clapper Rail, but this species is an obligate of large freshwater marshes. They are sometimes seen in brackish marshes, especially in winter, but they nest mostly in freshwater environments. Food is mostly small aquatic invertebrates including insects, crustaceans, and mollusks. Small vertebrates such as frogs, small fish, or small snakes are also eaten. Like the Clapper Rail this species is listed as a game bird with legal hunting seasons by most state wildlife agencies, but very few hunters take advantage of the opportunity to hunt this extremely elusive species.

Class - **Aves** (birds)

Order - **Gruiformes** (rails and cranes)

Family - **Rallidae** (rails)

American Coot *Fulica americana*	**Common Gallinule** *Gallinula chloropus*	**Sora** *Porzana carolina*

American Coot	**Common Gallinule**	**Sora**
Size: 15 inches. **Abundance:** Uncommon. **Migratory Status:** Summer in western New York. Winter in southeastern New York.  Presumed range in New York	**Size:** 14 inches. **Abundance:** Uncommon. **Migratory Status:** Summer resident. Late April to September. Presumed range in New York	**Size:** 9 inches. **Abundance:** Uncommon. **Migratory Status:** Summer resident. April to September.  Presumed range in New York
Variation: Sexes alike. Juvenile paler gray with yellowish beak.	**Variation:** Sexes alike. Juvenile is paler gray without red bill and forehead.	**Variation:** Juvenile lacks black on face and throat. Sexes are alike.
Habitat: Rivers, lakes, large ponds, marshes, and wetlands.	**Habitat:** Freshwater wetlands and lake shores with abundant vegetation.	**Habitat:** Primarily a marsh dweller. Favors heavily vegetated wetlands.
Breeding: Breeds mostly to the north and to the west of New York, but does nest sporadically across the state. Nest is a platform built amid emergent vegetation. About 6 eggs are laid.	**Breeding:** Nest is a platform of vegetation slightly above the waterline and usually well concealed. Most nesting in New York is in the western part of the state. Will lay as many as 10 eggs.	**Breeding:** Builds a nest platform of aquatic vegetation a few inches above water level. Nest is well hidden in dense upright plants. Does not breed on Long Island. Lays 8 to 11 eggs.
Natural History: During migration and in winter American Coots gather in large flocks on open water and behave more like ducks than rails. During the breeding season they act more like rails and live among cattails and reeds in freshwater marshes. But they are not as elusive as the rails and are usually easily observed even in summer. They are considered a game species, but rarely hunted, as most waterfowl hunters regard them as a "trash" species. They sometimes go by the nickname "Mud Hen." Although the feet are not webbed as with ducks and geese, their long toes are equipped with lateral lobes which flare out when swimming and create an ample surface for pushing against the water. Thus they are good swimmers. They feed both on land (on grasses) and in the water (aquatic plants, algae, and aquatic invertebrates). Small fish and small amphibians are also taken.	**Natural History:** Sometimes known as the Common Moorhen, but that name is properly reserved for a very similar bird that lives in Europe. Although these birds may be seen in suitable habitat throughout much New York, they are an uncommon bird in the Empire State and they are also rather secretive. Farther south in places like Louisiana and Florida they can be quite common and usually more observable. They feed largely on seeds of aquatic plants but also eats animal matter including most predominately snails and insects. Although similar to the American Coot in size and appearance, the Common Gallinule is rarely seen in the open and prefers to stay close to heavy cover. Additionally, they don't form large flocks as do American Coots. However, they can be quite tame and approachable within the heart of their range in Florida and the lower Coastal Plain.	**Natural History:** The Sora is one of the more observable of America's rails. Still, it is fairly secretive, especially during fall migration. They are usually observable on both breeding and wintering grounds, but catching a glimpse of this species in New York can be difficult. They are vocal birds, however, and their whinnying call can be heard for a long distance. They feed on a variety of aquatic invertebrates but also eat seeds of aquatic plants, particularly wild rice. Soras have exceptionally long toes, an adaptation that allows for walking across floating vegetation. Although the Sora is one of the most common and widespread rail species in America, their dependence upon wetlands renders them vulnerable. America's wetlands remain under a constant assault from land developers and agricultural interests. As with other American rails, the Sora is regarded as game species.

Class - **Aves** (birds)

Order - **Gruiformes** (rails and cranes)	Order - **Charadriiformes** (shorebirds)	
Family - **Gruidae** (cranes)	Family - **Charadriidae** (plovers)	
Sandhill Crane *Grus canadensis*	**Killdeer** *Charadrius vociferus*	**Semipalmated Plover** *Charadrius semipalmatus*

Juvenile

Young

Summer

Winter

Size: Length 42 inches.	Presumed range in New York	**Size:** Length 10.5 inches.	Presumed range in New York	**Size:** Length 7.25 inches.	Presumed range in New York
Abundance: Rare in New York.		**Abundance:** Common.		**Abundance:** Fairly common.	
Variation: Juveniles splotched with rusty brown.		**Variation:** None. Sexes are alike.		**Variation:** Seasonal plumage variations.	

Migratory Status: Very rare resident in western New York Rare migrant through much of the state.	**Migratory Status:** Year-round resident in southeastern New York. Summer resident elsewhere in the state.	**Migratory Status:** Spring/fall migrant that passes through New York in April/ May and again in July to September.
Habitat: Open lands, farm fields, mudflats, marshes, and shallow water areas. In migration uses harvested crop fields.	**Habitat:** Open lands. Mudflats, agricultural fields, lake shores, sandbars, and even gravel parking lots.	**Habitat:** Winter habitat is along coastlines. Summer habitat is open tundra. Migrants favor mudflats and shorelines.
Breeding: Most breeding in occurs in the Interior Lowlands of western New York where it is a newcomer as a breeding bird. Typically lays 2 eggs on a platform nest built of vegetation.	**Breeding:** Lays 4 eggs directly on the ground. Nest is often in gravelly or sandy situations in wide-open spaces. Young are very precocial and they will run about within hours of hatching.	**Breeding:** Nests on the ground, usually near water. Nesting grounds are in northern Canada and Alaska. 4 eggs. Chicks are precocious and able to feed themselves immediately.
Natural History: Standing over three feet tall, the Sandhill Crane is one of the largest birds seen in America. Populations were seriously depleted by the beginning of the 20th century, but the species has recovered dramatically in the last few decades. The largest populations are seen west of the Mississippi River and number tens of thousands. Eastern populations have been slower to recover but are now reasonably healthy. Several states treat them as a game species and have regulated hunting seasons. Some conservationists question the wisdom of hunting seasons on this species. They often form into large flocks that roost together and can be vulnerable to natural disasters like tornados.	**Natural History:** Although the Killdeer is found state-wide, they are much less common in the Adirondacks and Catskills regions where open habitats are rare. This is a species that has likely benefited significantly from human activities such as agriculture and land clearing. The creation of open spaces where there was once forest has resulted in a habitat boom the Killdeer. They are found all over North America south of the Arctic Circle. They were once hunted for food and their populations suffered a serious decline in the days of "market hunting." They feed on the ground and earthworms are a major food source along with grasshoppers, beetles, and snails. A few seeds are also consumed.	**Natural History:** Most Semipalmated Plovers migrate along the coasts of North America, but a few travel overland and they are regularly seen in New York. Most sightings will likely be along the Atlantic coast or Great Lakes as they tend to favor shorelines and other open spaces. The food of the Semipalmated Plover is mostly invertebrate animals plucked from the mud. They hunt these "benthic" organisms along the edges of marshes, lakes, seashores, etc. Aquatic food items include insect larva (especially fly larva), polychaete worms, crustaceans, and small bivalves. On dry land these plovers will eat spiders, flies, and beetles. Most foraging is done along water's edge or in very shallow water or on exposed mudflats.

Class - **Aves** (birds)		
Order - **Charadriiformes** (shorebirds)		
Family - **Charadriidae** (plovers)		

Piping Plover *Charadrius melodus*	**Black-bellied Plover** *Pluvialis squatarola*	**American Golden Plover** *Pluvialis dominica*

Size: 6.25 inches.	Presumed range in New York 	**Size:** 11.5 inches	Presumed range in New York 	**Size:** 10.5 inches.	Presumed range in New York 
Abundance: Rare.		**Abundance:** Fairly common.		**Abundance:** Uncommon.	
Migratory Status: Summer resident.		**Migratory Status:** Migrant/ winter resident.		**Migratory Status:** Migrant, mostly in fall.	

Variation: Seasonal plumage variations. Winter birds are extremely pale gray, nearly white.	**Variation:** Seasonal plumage variations (see above). Both plumages may be seen in New York.	**Variation:** Sexes similar with seasonal plumage variations (see above). Both plumages may be seen in New York.
Habitat: Habitat in New York is sandy beaches on Long Island. In winter uses beaches farther south.	**Habitat:** Beaches are the preferred winter habitat. Inland migrants will use shorelines, mudflats, and bare fields.	**Habitat:** Beaches are the preferred winter habitat. Inland migrants will use shorelines, mudflats, and bare fields.
Breeding: Nest is a scrape on sand or gravel, often near a clump of grass in an elevated place on the beach. 4 eggs.	**Breeding:** Nest is a shallow cup scraped into the arctic tundra and lined with lichens. 4 eggs are laid.	**Breeding:** Nest is a scrape on tundra soil. 4 eggs are laid and young are highly precocial, able to walk immediately.
Natural History: The Piping Plover is a federally endangered species that breeds primarily on sandy beaches along America's Atlantic coastline. Wide-spread coastal development and near complete utilization of beaches by man has made successful nesting in these habitats very problematic for the Piping Plover. In recent years conservation efforts which attempt to mitigate human interference may the only hope for the species. Closing of beaches to human activity where nesting occurs along with erecting predator exclusion fences around nests are two conservation actions that are regularly taken by conservation teams up and down America's Atlantic coast. Recent political trends aimed at decimating environmental regulations may spell doom for this and many other species facing similar threats across America.	**Natural History:** Black-bellied Plovers occur in both the new and old worlds and in fact they are one of the most widespread shorebirds in the world. They occur throughout much of the old world as well as most of the western hemisphere. North American birds winter along both coastlines from just south of Canada to South America, including the Caribbean. Summers are spent within the Arctic Circle of Alaska and Canada. During migration they are seen mostly along America's coastlines and in the great plains region. Unlike many shorebirds, the Black-bellied Plover exhibits nocturnal tendencies and will often feed at night. Food items are marine worms and small mollusks plucked from the mud at low tide. On the breeding grounds in the far north they will eat insects, small freshwater crustaceans, and berries. Climate change may threaten tundra nesting habitat.	**Natural History:** Like the similar Black-bellied Plover, the American Golden Plover is a long-distance traveller that nests in the arctic and spends its winters in southeastern South America. Its epic migrations sometimes include extensive flights over vast expanses of open ocean. Many migrate through inland regions and they are known for their propensity to appear almost anywhere during migrations. Food items include some plant material as well as a wide variety of invertebrate prey. The American Golden Plover was hunted relentlessly during the days "market hunting" throughout the 1800s. Tens to perhaps hundreds of thousands were killed annually. Today they are still legally hunted hunted in some South American countries. Some scientists have expressed concern about changes on tundra breeding grounds due to climate change.

Class - **Aves** (birds)

Order - **Charadriiformes** (shorebirds)

Family - **Scolopacidae** (sandpipers)

Sanderling *Calidris alba*	Pectoral Sandpiper *Calidris melanotos*	Dunlin *Calidris alpina*
 Winter / Summer		

Size: Length 8 inches.	Presumed range in New York	**Size:** Length 8.5 inches.	Presumed range in New York	**Size:** Length 8.5 inches.	Presumed range in New York
Abundance: Fairly common.		**Abundance:** Common.		**Abundance:** Fairly common.	
Migratory Status: Absent in summer.		**Migratory Status:** Spring/ fall migrant.		**Migratory Status:** Spring/ fall migrant.	

Variation: Significant seasonal variation (see photos above). | **Variation:** Male breeding plumage is darker brown and more vivid. | **Variation:** Significant seasonal plumage changes (see photos above).

Habitat: Shorelines. In winter lives on the beach. During migration frequents lake shores and river bars. | **Habitat:** Migrants use wet meadows, flooded fields, marshes and lake or pond shorelines, as well as mudflats. | **Habitat:** During migration uses flooded agricultural fields, mudflats, and seasonally flooded lowland pastures.

Breeding: Nests on arctic tundra on bare ground. Lays 4 eggs. | **Breeding:** Nests on the ground in the Arctic Coastal Plain. 4 eggs. | **Breeding:** Another high arctic breeder. Lays 4 eggs on ground in open tundra.

Natural History: Unlike most members of the sandpiper family, which are more likely to be found on mudflats, the Sanderling is commonly found on seashores. Except during migration or when breeding, these birds inhabit sandy beaches throughout the Americas. Any person who has been to the seashore has probably been amused by watching this species running back and forth in front of the waves. On beaches it feeds by running just in front of oncoming wave and chasing right behind receding wave, picking up tiny marine crustaceans, bivalves, and polychaetes. On the breeding ground it will eat both terrestrial and aquatic invertebrates and insects. Most Sanderlings migrate along the coastlines of America or through the great plains. Some can be seen inland in New York however, mostly along the shores of the Great Lakes.

Natural History: Breeding males of this species perform displays in which they erect the feathers of the breast, droop the wings, raise the tail feathers, and emit soft "hooting" sounds. They are the only member of the sandpiper family that vocalizes in this manner. They also perform flight displays above the heads of grounded females. These birds are remarkable travelers that breed in the high arctic and winter in the Pampas region of southern South America. Some individuals will cross the Arctic Ocean to breed in Siberia, then migrate back to South America, a round-trip journey of over 18000 miles each year! The food is mostly small mud-dwelling invertebrates. In New York this species is most likely to be seen during migration in flooded crop fields in agricultural regions or where receding waters leave mudflats.

Natural History: The Dunlin winters along both coasts of North America where it haunts estuaries and inter-tidal regions. A few may be seen in winter along New York Coastlines but most move farther south. In southern Louisiana and gulf coastal Texas it often uses rice fields in winter. Various clams, insects, worms, and amphipods are picked from the mud or plucked from vegetation with its moderately long, probing bill. Like other shorebird species it is usually seen in flocks, sometimes numbering in the thousands or even tens of thousands. In the early 1800s market hunters killed these birds in enormous numbers. Using cannon-like shotguns known as "punt guns" that were loaded with bird shot, a single blast could kill scores of shorebirds in a closely packed flock. Today's threats include pesticides and other contaminants and loss of wintering habitat.

Class - **Aves** (birds)
Order - **Charadriiformes** (shorebirds)
Family - **Scolopacidae** (sandpipers)
The "Peep" Sandpipers Genus - *Calidris* (five species in Ohio pictured below)

Least Sandpiper *Calidris minutilla*	**White-rumped Sandpiper** *Calidris fuscicollis*	**Semipalmated Sandpiper** *Calidris pusilla*
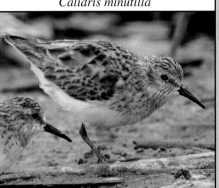		

Baird's Sandpiper *Calidris bairdii*	**Western Sandpiper** *Calidris mauri*	Presumed range of the "peep" Sandpipers in New York

Size: Least Sandpiper 6 inches. Semipalmated Sandpiper 6.25 inches. Western Sandpiper 6.5 inches. White-rumped and Baird's Sandpipers both reach 7.5 inches.

Abundance: The Least Sandpiper and the Semipalmated are probably the most commonly seen of the "Peep" Sandpipers in New York. White-rumped is common in the state in fall, along with the Western. Baird's is a rare species in seen only in the vicinity of Lake Erie.

Migratory Status: All are seasonal migrants in New York. All but the Least and Semipalmated are more commonly seen during fall migration from late July through September.

Variation: All five of these species exhibit seasonal plumage changes. All are comparably paler in winter than in summer.

Habitat: The name "Mudpiper" would be a more appropriate name for these birds as they favor mudflats and flooded fields over sandy beaches. All can be seen along the coastlines but many migrate through the interior of North America.

Breeding: All "peep" sandpipers nest on the ground in the barren arctic tundra. 4 eggs is typical.

Natural History: These five species are all similar in their natural history and are confusingly alike in appearance. While serious birders and professional ornithologists take pride in being able to correctly identify any species, most casual observers are satisfied with calling these homogeneous birds simply "peeps." Food habits and feeding methods are also similar in these sandpipers, with mud-dwelling benthic invertebrates making up the bulk of the diet in winter and during migration. Aquatic insect larva and some terrestrial insects are eaten on the breeding grounds. The hordes of mosquitos for which the arctic tundra is famous in summer make up a high-protein smorgasbord for both the adult birds and the newly hatched young. All the sandpipers are known for their epic migrations. Some species travel non-stop for a thousand miles or more over open ocean. Flights lasting as long as five days have been reported. Quite a feat of endurance for birds that can weigh as little as .75 to 1.5 ounces! Recent population declines have been reported for the Least Sandpiper and the Semipalmated Sandpiper. By contrast, the Western Sandpiper (despite being uncommon in New York) is one of the most abundant shorebirds in America with a total population estimate of 3.5 million birds.

Class - **Aves** (birds)
Order - **Charadriiformes** (shorebirds)
Family - **Scolopacidae** (sandpipers)

Stilt Sandpiper *Calidris himantopus*	Red Knot *Calidris canutus*	Purple Sandpiper *Calidris maritima*

Size: Length 8.5 inches.	Presumed range in New York	**Size:** Length 10.5 inches.	Presumed range in New York	**Size:** Length 12 inches.	Presumed range in New York
Abundance: Uncommon.		**Abundance:** Uncommon.		**Abundance:** Uncommon.	
Migratory Status: Mostly a fall migrant.		**Migratory Status:** Spring/fall migrant.		**Migratory Status:** Winter resident.	

Variation: Winter birds are much paler, more grayish.	**Variation:** Winter birds are drab gray brown with off-white breast and belly.	**Variation:** Seasonal plumage variations. Winter birds uniformly gray.
Habitat: Ponds, marshes, flooded fields, and lake shorelines. Uses salt marsh and brackish marshes in winter.	**Habitat:** Summer habitat is arctic tundra. Winter and migration habitat is intertidal areas and beaches/coastlines.	**Habitat:** Rocky seacoasts of the North Atlantic. Jetties, breakwaters, anywhere there are rocks and waves.
Breeding: Nests in lowland areas near the Arctic Ocean. Lays 4 eggs.	**Breeding:** Nest on tundra all the way to the Arctic Ocean. 4 eggs is typical.	**Breeding:** Breeds on islands of the Arctic Ocean in northernmost Canada.
Natural History: The Stilt Sandpiper gets its name from its long legs. The long legs are an adaptation that allow it to feed in deeper water than most other *Calidris* sandpipers. its body shape and habit of feeding in deeper water rather than on mudflats is unusual for its genus and mimics the yellowlegs sandpipers (genus *Tringa*, next page). The migratory routes for this sandpiper are mainly west of the Mississippi River, but many will use the Atlantic coastal flyway. They nest along the northernmost coast of North America and will spend the winter in the interior of the South American continent. As with many other sandpiper species, the Stilt Sandpiper shows a remarkable fidelity to the nest site. After migrating thousands of miles from South America they often return to the same exact spot on the arctic coastline to lay their eggs.	**Natural History:** This is North America's largest member of the *Calidris* genus. Like many other Sandpiper species, the Red Knot is a remarkable traveller, with some covering nearly 10000 miles in a round-trip journey from southern South America to the arctic and back each year. Some birds may fly non-stop for thousands of miles across great expanses of ocean, mountains, and deserts. Nesting is on the most northerly land masses in North America including northern Greenland and Canada's Arctic Archipelago. During the North American winter, they will be enjoying summer in the southern hemisphere as far south as Terra del Fuego on the southern tip of South America. Along the way these world travelers will sometimes stop for a brief rest somewhere in New York, usually along the coast.	**Natural History:** This sandpiper should be call a "rockpiper." They favor rough, rocky shores where they are quite fearless and navigate with amazing capability among waves breaking against the rocks. Here they sally forth between waves to pick tiny marine orgainisms from seaweed or rock crevices. Feeds both day and night. They will also sometimes feed on mudflats. They spend their summers on islands in the Arctic Ocean where they feed and nest in Tundra habitats. In winter they move south onto the Atlantic coast. They are reported to be fairly tame and approachable and when flushed only fly a short distance. Both traits tend to endear them to birdwatchers. Wintering birds begin to show up in New York by late October and a few may linger until early May.

Class - **Aves** (birds)
Order - **Charadriiformes** (shorebirds)
Family - **Scolopacidae** (sandpipers)

Greater Yellowlegs *Tringa melanoleuca*	**Lesser Yellowlegs** *Tringa flavipes*	**Solitary Sandpiper** *Tringa solitaria*

Size: Length 14 inches.

Size: Length 10.5 inches.

Presumed range in New York

Size: Length 8.5 inches.

Presumed range in New York

Abundance: Greater Yellowlegs is usually the less common of the two, but both species are fairly common.

Abundance: Fairly common.

Migratory Status: Both species are transient spring and fall migrants but the Greater may also be seen in winter along the coast. Spring migration is in late April and May. Fall peak for Greater is August/September. Lesser begins fall migration as early as July.

Migratory Status: Spring (April and May) and fall (July–October) migrant.

Variation: Speckled appearance is less prominent on winter adults and juveniles of both species.

Variation: Summer plumage has more distinct white spotting on the back.

Habitat: Both species are seen in a wide variety of wetland habitats during migration, including mudflats, flooded agricultural field, and marshes.

Habitat: Pond margins, lake shores, and along creeks and rivers.

Breeding: Greater breeds in northern bogs, Lesser in drier, more upland habitats. Both species nest on the ground and 3–4 eggs is the typical clutch size for both.

Breeding: Nests in trees and uses old songbird nests. 3 to 5 eggs, usually 4.

Natural History: These two related species are frequently seen together. When seen together they are easily recognized by size. When not in found in mixed flocks they are best identified by the shape of the bill. Greater's bill is longer and ever so slightly upturned at the tip. The Greater Yellowlegs is the least social of the two, and although it is seen in small flocks it can also be seen singly. Both species were once heavily hunted and during the days of market hunting both species experienced steep population declines. Hunting still occurs in some areas of their migratory range, especially in the Caribbean. Both spend the summer in the boreal regions of Canada and Alaska and winter from the Gulf Coast of the southeastern United States southward into South America. Food items for the Greater include both aquatic and terrestrial invertebrates as well as some small aquatic vertebrates like small frogs or fish. Lesser's food items are mainly invertebrates, both aquatic and terrestrial, but some small fish are also eaten. Both feed mostly by wading in shallows, but the Lesser is a more active feeder, wading rapidly and picking food from both the surface and the water column. It will also feed in this manner in terrestrial habitats such as grassy shorelines or meadow areas. Greater feeds both diurnally and at night, when it employs a sweeping motion of the bill back and forth through the water, apparently catching food by feel. The major threat to both species today is probably loss of habitat, both on wintering grounds in South America (loss of wetlands) and on summer range in North America, i.e., logging in boreal forests (Greater), and loss of wetlands in Alaska (lesser).

Natural History: As implied by their name, the Solitary Sandpipers are nearly always seen alone during migration. In this respect they differ markedly from most other members of their family. They also differ in their nesting habits, as they are the only North American member of the Scolopacidae family that nests in trees. When feeding it wades in shallows and plucks its food from the surface or beneath the water. Rarely probes the mud with its bill. Food is mostly invertebrates, both aquatic and terrestrial. Insects make up the bulk of the terrestrial foods. They also take aquatic insects and their larva, small crustaceans, snails, and some vertebrate prey such as small minnows or tadpoles. Due to their solitary habits and the fact that they breed in trees in remote boreal forests, little is known about their population status, but it appears to be stable.

Class - **Aves** (birds)		
Order - **Charadriiformes** (shorebirds)		
Family - **Scolopacidae** (sandpipers)		

Willet *Tringa semipalmata*	Upland Sandpiper *Bartramia longicauda*	Short-billed Dowitcher *Limnodromus griseus*

Willet — *Tringa semipalmata*

Size: 15 inches.

Abundance: Rare in New York.

Migratory Status: Summer resident/migrant.

Presumed range in New York

Variation: No sexual dimorphism but does exhibit seasonal plumage variations. Winter plumage (not seen in New York) lacks brown speckling.

Habitat: In migration uses pond banks, mudflats, lake shores, riverbanks, and flooded fields.

Breeding: Lays 4 eggs in nest on the ground. Nesting in New York occurs along the Atlantic coast.

Natural History: The Willet is a true "shorebird" that is quite familiar to those who frequent America's seashores. Both coasts of America are home to Willets during the winter, and some will nest in coastal marshes. Others fly into the interior of North America and nest as far north as the central Canadian prairie. Crustaceans, mollusks, insects, small fish, and polycheate worms are listed as food items. Feeds both day and night. In the 1800s they were hunted for food and for their eggs which were also eaten, resulting in a significant decrease in populations. Today these are fairly common shorebirds whose population appears stable at an estimate of about a quarter of a million birds. In addition to birds that breed on Long Island, migrants can sometimes be seen in western New York.

Upland Sandpiper — *Bartramia longicauda*

Size: 12 inches.

Abundance: Uncommon.

Migratory Status: Summer resident.

Presumed range in New York

Variation: Fall and juvenile plumages are slightly paler than breeding adults, but the differences are not significant.

Habitat: An obligate of grasslands and prairies. Migrants will also use pastures and fields.

Breeding: Nest is a shallow scrape on the ground lined with grass. 4 eggs.

Natural History: The bulk of the Upland Sandpiper's summer range is in the northern Great Plains. A few summer very sparsely east of the Mississippi River and into New York. Unlike most other members of the sandpiper family, the Upland Sandpiper avoids coastal areas in favor of prairies and grasslands well into the interior of the continent. Historically, these birds were much more numerous. Market hunting in the late 19th century saw countless numbers of dead Upland Sandpipers shipped by rail from their nesting grounds on the northern plains to markets in the east. At the same time they were being hunted mercilessly on their winter habitats in the Pampas of South America. Even more devastating to their populations was the conversion of the Native American prairie to cropland. Amazingly, the species survives. They are uncommon and declining in New York.

Short-billed Dowitcher — *Limnodromus griseus*

Size: 11 inches.

Abundance: Fairly common.

Migratory Status: Spring/fall migrant.

Presumed range in New York

Variation: Breeding birds are rich brown. Winter birds uniformly gray with whitish belly. Sexes are alike (see photos above).

Habitat: In inland migrations dowitchers use mudflats and lake shores. Many migrate along the coasts.

Breeding: Breeds in bog and muskeg habitats of northern Canada and Alaska. Both species lay 4 eggs.

Natural History: The nearly identical **Long-billed Dowitcher** (*Limnodromus scolopaceus,* not shown) can also be seen in New York during spring and fall migrations, though it is much less common than the Short-billed Dowitcher. Distinguishing between the two in the field is difficult even for experts. The Long-billed is slightly larger at 11.5 inches. It migrates earlier in the spring and later in the fall than the Short-billed. In New York, the Long-billed is seen mostly in the fall. The Short-billed is more common and may be seen anywhere in the state. Like many shorebirds both species of dowitcher were heavily hunted during the days of market hunting. At that time, it was not known that the two similar dowitchers constituted two distinct species. The existence of two species was not finally confirmed until 1950.

Class - **Aves** (birds)

Order - **Charadriiformes** (shorebirds)

Family - **Scolopacidae** (sandpipers)

Woodcock *Scolopax minor*	**Wilson's Snipe** *Gallinago delicata*	**Ruddy Turnstone** *Arenaria interpres*

Size: 11 inches.	**Size:** 10.5 inches.	**Size:** 9.5 inches.

Presumed range in New York

Woodcock

Size: 11 inches.

Abundance: Fairly common.

Migratory Status: Summer resident.

Variation: No plumage variations. Females are significantly larger.

Habitat: Swamps, regenerative woodlands, thickets, and weedy fields in bottomlands or uplands with moist soils.

Breeding: Nest is on the ground and not concealed. Lays 4 eggs as early as late February.

Natural History: The Woodcock is unique among American sandpipers in that it is strictly an inland species. It is also one of the most common members of its family that breeds widely throughout the state. Woodcock are known for their elaborate courtship flights that consist of an upward twisting corkscrew accompanied by a twittering call. The long beak is used to probe moist soils for invertebrates. Among its unique features are a flexible upper bill that aids in extracting the favorite food, earthworms, and eyes which are situated far back on the head, allowing for backward vision while feeding. One of the most remarkably cryptic of the sandpipers, Woodcocks are nearly impossible to detect when motionless on the forest floor. Woodcock are classified as a game bird and hunted in many areas.

Wilson's Snipe

Size: 10.5 inches.

Abundance: Fairly common.

Migratory Status: Summer resident.

Variation: No significant sexual or seasonal plumage differences.

Habitat: Mudflats, flooded grassy fields, marshes, river bars, water-filled ditches, temporary pools, and grassy pond banks.

Breeding: Most nesting in New York is in northern and western New York. Lays 4 eggs in nest on ground within marsh or swamp.

Natural History: As with other members of the sandpiper family, the beak of the Wilson's Snipe contains sensory pits near the tip which help to locate invertebrate prey hidden in the mud. It also shares the Woodcock's rearward-positioned eyes for watching behind and above while feeding. This is another highly camouflaged species that is nearly invisible when immobile. It is one of the most common and widespread members of the sandpiper family that often relys on its cryptic coloration when approached. Sitting quietly until nearly trod upon it will burst from the grass with a twisting, erratic flight while emitting a raspy call. Like the Woodcock the Wilson's Snipe is regarded as a game bird, but few people hunt them. Mostly a summer resident, but a few may be seen in winter in the Coastal Plain Province in the southeast.

Ruddy Turnstone

Size: 9.5 inches.

Abundance: Uncommon.

Migratory Status: Mostly a seasonal migrant.

Variation: Seasonal plumage variations. Breeding plumage shown above.

Habitat: Winters on sandy beaches along both coasts. May use lake shores, mudflats, or river banks during inland migrations.

Breeding: Breeds in the arctic tundra and coastlines from Siberia and Alaska across Canada to Greenland.

Natural History: Most Ruddy Turnstones travel up and down America's coastlines during migration, but a few migrate through inland regions of the continent. This is one of the most northerly ranging birds in America, traveling to the northernmost extreme of the continent to breed each summer. Its name comes from its habit of using its beak to overturn pebbles and stones on beaches in search of small invertebrate prey. It also feeds on ocean carrion found on beaches. On the breeding grounds the primary food source is mosquitos and other dipteran insects. The unusual genus (*Arenaria*) contains only two species and their position in the phylogeny of the shorebirds is unclear. In New York they are most commonly seen in along the Atlantic coastline or very rarely along the shores of the Great Lakes. A few may overwinter along the coast.

Class - **Aves** (birds)
Order - **Charadriiformes** (shorebirds)

Family - **Scolopacidae** (sandpipers)		Family - **Haematopodidae** (oystercatchers)

Spotted Sandpiper
Actitis macularia

Whimbrel
Numenius phaeopus

American Oystercatcher
Haematopus palliatus

Size: 7.5 inches.	**Size:** 17.5 inches.	**Size:** 17.5 inches.
Abundance: Fairly common.	**Abundance:** Rare in New York.	**Abundance:** Fairly common.
Migratory Status: Summer resident. April to October.	**Migratory Status:** Spring and fall migrant.	**Migratory Status:** Summer resident, arrives in April.

Presumed range in New York

Variation: Winter birds lack the spots on the breast and are grayer on the back. Most Spotted Sandpipers seen in New York will be in summer plumage.

Variation: Several subspecies are recognized but differences are slight. No significant variation between sexes and juveniles resemble adults.

Variation: No variation. Sexes alike. On young chicks the bill is not fully developed until about six weeks. Young are fledged at about four weeks.

Habitat: In migration uses edges of ponds, lake shores, stream courses, and river bars.

Habitat: In New York they use coastal marshes mostly. Also may be seen bare fields or mudflats in Interior Lowlands.

Habitat: Habitat in New York is beaches and dunes primarily. Winter habitat includes mudflats and salt marshes.

Breeding: Nests on the ground in grassy situations. Nests near water across the state. Lays 2 to 4 eggs.

Breeding: Nests in Alaska, the Yukon, Northwest Territory and near Hudson Bay in Manitoba. 3–4 eggs on ground.

Breeding: Nest is a scrape on bare sand, gravel, or shell substrate usually in marsh islands. Lays 3 eggs.

Natural History: Unlike most sandpipers that exhibit strong flocking tendencies, the Spotted Sandpiper is always seen singly or in very small groups. This is one of the most widespread sandpipers in America and one of the few that nests in the lower forty-eight. The distinctly spotted breast along with a habit of constantly bobbing up and down makes the Spotted Sandpiper one of the most recognizable members of the Scolopacidae family. Feeds on a wide variety of aquatic and terrestrial invertebrates, especially dipteran (fly) larva. Also eats significant quantities of mayflies, crickets, grasshoppers, caterpillars, beetles, mollusks, crustaceans, and worms. In New York this species is a widespread nester across the state using lake shorelines and islands or gravel bars in rivers.

Natural History: Like many shorebirds, the Whimbrel is a wide-ranging and highly travelled species. In the western Hemisphere they range from the Arctic Ocean (in summer) to the coasts of South America (winter). In the old world they occur in summer across Scandinavia to northeastern Siberia and in winter south to parts of Africa, southeast Asia, and Australia. They are very rare in New York but being great travellers, a few will pass through the state duriing migration. They sometimes stop briefly in western New York in the spring and forage in flooded fields or mudflats. In fall migration they can sometimes be seen on the coast on beaches, marshes, or mudflats. The unusual downcurved bill of the Whimbrel may be adpated for capturing its favorite food, marine invertebrates in the intertidal zone.

Natural History: The commmon name Oystercatcher aptly describes the feeding habits of this unusual species. The laterally flattened bill is adapted for prying open the shells of mollusks like oysters and mussels. The technique involves stalking through shallows in search of mollusks with shells open and quickly inserting the blade-like bill into the open bivalve. It then stabs with the bill until the abducter muscle is severed allowing the shell to be pried open and the contents extracted. This species is completly dependent upon beaches and coastal dunes as habitat. Human encroachment and coastal development have ravaged these habitats for decades and today this is one of America's most threatened natural habitats. In the year 2000 a population census revealed the entire population of American Oystercatchers to be only around 10000 birds.

Class - **Aves** (birds)
Order - **Charadriiformes** (shorebirds)
Family - **Laridae** (gulls and terns)

Black Skimmer *Rynchops niger*	Glaucus Gull *Larus hyperboreus*	Great Black-backed Gull *Larus marinus*

Black Skimmer
Rynchops niger

Size: Length 18 inches.

Abundance: Fairly common.

Migratory Status: Summer resident.

Presumed range in New York

Variation: Sexes are alike. No significant variation among adult birds. Young birds at hatching have upper and lower mandibles of equal length.

Habitat: New York habitat is bays, salt marsh, and coastal regions. May rarely fly inland to use freshwater lakes.

Breeding: Colony nester on coastal dunes or marsh islands. Nest is a scrape in sand or on mats of vegetation. 4 eggs.

Natural History: Another seaside bird with a distinctive bill. The lower mandible is significantly larger than the upper, which allows the Black Skimmer to snatch small fishes from the quiet waters of inlets, bays, and especially tidal pools in marshes and intercoastal areas. Flying just centimeters above the surface with bill slightly agape the longer lower mandible plows the surface and any small fish encountered slides upward on the lower bill to be instantly caught by the upper bill snapping closed. These are highly social birds that nest in colonies and when resting are always seen in large flocks. Nesting colonies are often in the company of nesting terns, and it is possible that some protection from predators may be afforded to the Skimmers by the terns that can be very aggressive when defending their nests.

Glaucus Gull
Larus hyperboreus

Size: Length 27 inches.

Abundance: Rare in New York.

Migratory Status: Winter migrant.

Presumed range in New York

Variation: Juveniles are dusky or white and have a pinkish bill with a black tip. Adults are pure white on head, breast, and belly with pale gray wings.

Habitat: Northern coastlines of both coasts in winter. Arctic coasts in summer.

Breeding: Nest is on the ground in open tundra. Often on ledges or atop steep cliffs. Usually lays 3 eggs.

Natural History: This is a northern gull that breeds far to the north on arctic coasts. Winters on northern coastlines, both Pacific and Atlantic and also throughout the Great Lakes region. In New York they are seen around the Great Lakes and along the coast in winter. As with most gull species they are opportunistic predators as well as unashamed scavengers. The list of food items includes most types of aquatic organisms that are small enough to be swallowed as well as terrestrial foods such as the eggs and chicks of other birds that may be nesting nearby. There are two other similar gull species that nest in the arctic and can be seen in New York in the winter. They are the **Thayer's Gull** (*Larus thayeri*), rare in winter on the Great Lakes, and the **Iceland Gull** (*Larus glaucoides*), rare in winter on both the Great Lakes and along the Atlantic coast.

Great Black-backed Gull
Larus marinus

Size: Length 30 inches.

Abundance: Uncommon.

Migratory Status: Year-round resident.

Presumed range in New York

Variation: Age-related plumage varition significant. Juveniles are mottled brown on the wings and the back. Adults have jet black wings and back.

Habitat: A gull of the Atlantic coastline from Nova Scotia to Florida. Winter habitat includes the Great Lakes.

Breeding: Nests in the far northeastern coastline of North America. 3 eggs is typical. Nest is a scrape on the ground.

Natural History: At 30 inches in length and with a nearly five-and-a-half-foot wingspan, the Great Black-backed Gull is the largest and heaviest gull in America. By the early 1900s the Great Black-backed Gull had become a very rare bird in America due to egg collecting and feather hunting. Today the species is recovering and may be expanding its range. Like all gulls it is an oportunistic feeder and it may have benefited from utilizing human refuse as food source. Another very similar but smaller gull species, the **Lesser Black-backed Gull** (*Larus fuscus*), can also be seen along the coasts of New York in winter, though it is much less common. The Lesser Black-backed Gull is a much smaller gull at 21 inches in length, but has the same color pattern as the Great Black-backed Gull.

Class - **Aves** (birds)

Order - **Charadriiformes** (shorebirds)

Family - **Laridae** (gulls and terns)

Ringed-billed Gull *Larus delawarensis*	Herring Gull *Larus argentatus*	Bonaparte's Gull *Chroicocephalus philadelphia*

Size: 17.5 inches.

Abundance: Very common.

Migratory Status: Year-round in west, winter on coast, migrant statewide.

Presumed range in New York

Variation: Juveniles are brownish gray, two-year-olds resemble adults but with greenish legs and bill.

Habitat: Primarily in the vicinity of lakes, rivers, and coast, but also in rural crop fields and in urban areas.

Breeding: Nest is usually on the ground on sandbars or rocky beaches. May nest on rooftops in urban areas. Lays 2 to 4 eggs.

Natural History: The Ring-billed Gull is one of the most common and widespread gull species in America. Most population estimates put their number in the millions, and they may be increasing. This is the gull commonly seen around inland lakes in summer and along coastal beaches in winter. They are also seen in urban parking lots or hanging around fast food restaurants ready to swoop in and grab a dropped french fry. They are common in garbage dumps and may be seen foraging with starlings and other urban birds around dumpsters. These are highly gregarious birds that travel in flocks and nest in colonies. Food is almost anything, from carrion to insects, fish, rodents, earthworms, and human refuse. Extremely large breeding colonies exist on Lake Ontario.

Size: 25 inches.

Abundance: Common.

Migratory Status: Year-round on coast and in west, winter inland.

Presumed range in New York

Variation: Highly variable as juvenile. Younger birds are dark brownish gray with dark eyes and get lighter with age.

Habitat: Coastlines, offshore islands, barrier islands, beaches, and shorelines in general. Both salt and freshwater.

Breeding: Nest is on the ground in a bowl-shaped scrape lined with vegetation. Also nest on rooftops in urban areas. 2 or 3 eggs are laid.

Natural History: Like the smaller Ring-billed Gull, the Herring Gull is an opportunistic feeder that will eat almost anything, including human garbage. This fact may account in part for their population rebound in recent decades. Like other gull species, they are gregarious and they often nest in large colonies. Only about 50 percent of the young gulls hatched each year reach adulthood, but the species seems to be thriving. Their numbers were drastically reduced during the 1800s but they have recovered completely and may be more numerous now than in historic times. The presence of man-made garbage dumps that serve as a smorgasbord for these birds may explain their recent population expansion. They are widespread in their distribution and are common on both of America's coastlines.

Size: 13.5 inches.

Abundance: Fairly common.

Migratory Status: Winter resident on coast. Migrant elsewhere.

Presumed range in New York

Variation: Summer plumage adults have a black head. Juveniles resemble winter adults.

Habitat: Frequents coastlines and large rivers and larger lakes inland. Summer habitat is wetlands in boreal forests.

Breeding: The only gull that nests in trees, using conifers bordering remote lakes in Canada and Alaska. Typically lays 3 eggs.

Natural History: Many people tend to lump all gull species together and refer to them all as "seagulls." Most species, however, including the Bonaparte's Gull, are often inland birds during the breeding season. Like other gulls, many Bonaparte's Gulls will spend the winter along America's coastlines and sometimes far out to sea. Small to moderately large flocks can be seen on inland rivers and lakes in throughout New York during migration and in winter. One of America's smallest gulls, they feed mostly on small fish such as shad and shiners, but like other gulls they are highly opportunistic feeders and will eat a wide variety of insects and other invertebrates. Unlike other gull species, however, they are not typically seen around towns or dumps. They will gather in large flocks for migration.

Class - **Aves** (birds)		
Order - **Charadriiformes** (shorebirds)		
Family - **Laridae** (gulls and terns)		

Laughing Gull *Leucophaeus atricilla*	**Little Gull** *Hydrocoloeus minutus*	**Forster's Tern** *Sterna forsteri*

Size: Length 14.5 inches. **Abundance:** Common. **Migratory Status:** Summer resident.	**Size:** Length 11 inches. **Abundance:** Very rare. **Migratory Status:** Winter migrant/resident.	**Size:** Length 14 inches. **Abundance:** Uncommon. **Migratory Status:** Summer resident.
Variation: Black "hood" reduced in winter to a black "smudge" behind the eye. Juveniles uniformley dusky on back and wings.	**Variation:** Adult birds in breeding plumage all black head. Non-breeding adults and juveniles have black reduced on the head a black blotch behind eye.	**Variation:** Exhibits both seasonal and age-related plumage variations. Juveniles resemble winter adults (see photos above).
Habitat: Migrants use lakes, rivers, marshes, flooded fields, and pastures.	**Habitat:** New York habitat is along the Atlantic coast and around Lake Erie.	**Habitat:** Marshes. Both fresh and salt. Also beaches and coastlines.
Breeding: Nests along coastlines in large colonies that can contain 50000 birds. In New York a large colony nests at JKF airport.	**Breeding:** There are only a few dozen records of this species breeding in America. Nest is in marsh on floating mats of vegetation. Lays 3–4 eggs.	**Breeding:** Breeds both along the Gulf Coast and on inland marshes in the center of the continent. 1 to 4 eggs in nest of matted vegetation within marsh.
Natural History: Birds seen in New York are invariably in summer plumage (shown above). Familiar birds to residents of Long Island, these hand-some and engaging gulls are quite well known to anyone that frequents New York's beaches and coastline. They will become quite bold in attempts to snatch anything edible from their human neighbors on the beach. They are ubiquitous around boat docks and they regularly follow boats at sea. They often select low-lying islands for their breeding colonies. In winter they move south along the coast and can be seen from North Carolina to the Carribean and Central and South America. The name comes from their call which mimics the sound of laughter.	**Natural History:** A native of the old world, the Little Gull apparently become established in North America as recently as a few decades ago. They are most common along the northeast coast of the United States, but are rare even there. In New York this species can be also be seen on Lake Erie in winter. Very few studies have been conducted into the natural history of this species in North America and less in known about it than any other gull in America. It usually occurs in small flocks or in the company of other gull species such as the Bonaparte's Gull. At only 11 inches long it is the world's smallest gull species. It feeds on small fishes and insects and will also scavenge. Probably consumes aquatic invertebrates as well.	**Natural History:** This species is most common in New York around Long Island, but it can also rarely be seen in the vicinity of the Great Lakes. They can be seen statewide during migration, usually frequenting the state's major river systems and large impoundments or natural lakes. They are sometimes seen in the company of gulls and other tern species, especially in winter along the coastlines of America where gulls and terns are both extremely common. These medium-sized terns feed almost exclusively on small fish that are captured by diving from above. When "fishing" they fly back and forth over water with the bill pointed downward and plunge headlong into the water. They are graceful fliers that sometimes hover when schools of fish are located.

Class - **Aves** (birds)

Order - **Charadriiformes** (shorebirds)

Family - **Laridae** (gulls and terns)

Common Tern	Caspian Tern	Black Tern
Sterna hirundo	*Hydroprogne caspia*	*Chlidonias niger*

Size: 15 inches.	**Size:** 21 inches.	**Size:** 9.75 inches.
Abundance: Common.	**Abundance:** Uncommon.	**Abundance:** Uncommon.
Migratory Status: Summer resident.	**Migratory Status:** Spring/fall migrant.	**Migratory Status:** Mostly a fall migrant.

Presumed range in New York

Variation: First-year juveniles and winter birds have white foreheads and all black bill. White on forehead reduced on second-year juvenile in summer colors.

Variation: In winter birds the black cap becomes mottled with white. Juveniles are similar to winter adults. Sexes are alike.

Variation: In winter and in juvenile birds the dramatic black color of the breast and belly is replaced by white. Transitional birds are blotched.

Habitat: Migrating birds usually associate with major rivers and large lakes. Islands and dunes are frequently used.

Habitat: Mainly coastal birds in winter, they use rivers, large lakes, and marshes in migration.

Habitat: Habitat in is shallow, fresh-water marshes, salt marshes, and tidal mudflats.

Breeding: Nests mostly in Canada and along the Atlantic coastline. A few nest in on man-made platforms in Great Lakes marshes. Lays 2 or 3 eggs.

Breeding: North American populations nest both on coasts and large bodies of water in the interior of the continent. 1 to 3 eggs.

Breeding: Nest is built upon floating vegetation or muskrat platforms. Nests can be vulnerable to flooding. 2 or 3 eggs is typical.

Natural History: The Common Tern is well known to conservationists. They are symbolic of the fight to save many of America's bird species from wanton slaughter. From the early European settlement of North America to the late 1800s, unregulated over-hunting of America's wildlife nearly wiped out many species. Millions of herons, egrets, waterfowl, and shorebirds were killed for food and for the millinery trade. At the same time America's large mammal species also suffered dramatic population declines. Today many wildlife species, including terns, have recovered dramatically, but tern populations are still below historical numbers nationwide. Common Tern nesting colonies in New York are afforded strict protections.

Natural History: The world's largest tern and also the most widespread. Found all over the world, the Caspian Tern breeds on every continent except Antarctica. Despite its wide range it is not as common in North America as many other terns. Feeds almost entirely on fish. Feeds by hovering and diving. When diving often submerges completely. Food is mostly fish. This is the only large tern regularly seen inland. They are found along the southern coastlines as well and in winter stay along the coasts. They are also seen inland in winter throughout the Florida peninsula. Nesting has been recorded in New York in eastern Lake Ontario and northern Lake Champlain. These large terns are known to live up to 26 years.

Natural History: Winters along coastlines from Central America to northern South America. There is a European subspecies that winters in Africa. Like most terns these birds are highly social and usually seen in flocks. Unlike other terns however they feed heavily on insects, especially in summer. This is the only tern seen in New York that has a dark breast and belly. Although the number of Black Terns today is estimated to be in the hundreds of thousands, this figure is paltry compared to the size of the population that existed before modern agricultural practices destroyed much of their breeding habitat. Though mainly a seasonal migrant in New York, some nesting has been recorded in large marshes in upstate New York.

Class - **Aves** (birds)

Order - **Charadriiformes** (shorebirds)	Order - **Gaviiformes**	
Family - **Laridae** (gulls and terns)	Family - **Gaviidae**	

Least Tern
Sternula antillarum

Common Loon
Gavia immer

Red-throated Loon
Gavia stellata

Size: 9 inches.	Presumed range in New York 
Abundance: Uncommon.	
Migratory Status: Summer resident.	

Size: 35 inches. | Presumed range in New York

Abundance: Fairly common.

Migratory Status: See below.

Size: 25 inches. | Presumed range in New York

Abundance: Uncommon.

Migratory Status: Winter mostly.

Variation: No variation in New York. Birds that nest on coasts may be a distinct subspecies from inland nesters.

Variation: Sexes are alike but exhibits significant seasonal plumage changes. See photos above.

Variation: Exhibits seasonal plumage changes but most seen in New York will be in winter plumage (see above).

Habitat: Beaches and dunes are the main habitat, both in summer and winter. Also uses islands on inland rivers. May frequent inland lakes in summer.

Habitat: Highly aquatic. In inland areas such the Common Loon lives on lakes. They may also be seen along the coast in winter.

Habitat: Thoroughly aquatic. In inland areas in summer or on migration they may be seen on lakes and rivers. In winter they use mostly coastlines.

Breeding: Breeding in New York occurs on protected beaches on Long Island. Nest is a scrape with 2–3 eggs.

Breeding: Nests is built on small islands in northern lakes. Usually lays 2 eggs. Chicks often ride on adult's back.

Breeding: Breeds in small ponds in remote tundra. Nest is a large mound of aquatic vegetation. 2 eggs.

Natural History: The Least Tern is, as its name implies, our smallest tern species. They are widespread in distribution along America's coastlines and a distinct population also nests inland on major rivers in the middle of the continent. All winter along southeastern coastlines and some as far south as the Caribbean and Central America. In the 1800s these birds were killed and skinned to adorn women's hats. This bird's habitat (sandy beaches and dunes) is also highly valued real estate for humans. Thus coastal development is a major threat to the species today. They are regarded as a Threatened Species in New York and inland nesting populations are federally endangered. The food of the Least Tern is mostly small fishes, usually caught in shallow waters. They will also eat crustaceans and insects.

Natural History: On lakes and marshes in the far north the call of the Common Loon echoes through the wilderness. The sound is so distinctive and unique that it has inspired many poetic depictions. "Haunting," "ethereal," and "lonely" are words that are often used in conjunction with describing its yodeling cry that can carry for a great distance. They call both day and night on the breeding grounds in the northern half of the continent, but they are rarely heard calling on their winter range. Remarkable swimmers, they dive beneath the surface and propel themselves through the water with their powerful webbed feet. Fish caught in this manner are the main food item. In New York the Common Loon is a summer resident in the northern portion of the state and a winter resident on the coast. Migrants may be seen statewide on rivers and lakes.

Natural History: These birds occur mostly along the coastline of New York in winter. A few overwinter on Lake Ontario and migrants are seen in spring and fall on both the Great Lakes of New York. They also migrate through the Adirondack region and may breifly drop into lakes there, but rarely do they stay for long. In winter plumage they are very similar to the Common Loon but are smaller and have white spots on the back. These are mostly northern birds that summer all the way to the Arctic Ocean. They are circumpolar in distribution and occur throughout Scandinavia. The legs of loons are situated very far back on the body which works well for propelling through water, but makes movement on land very difficult. This species appears to be in decline in North America. No explanation for this decline is known at this time.

Class - **Aves** (birds)

Order - **Podicipediformes** (grebes)

Family - **Podicipedidae**

Red-necked Grebe *Podiceps grisegena*	**Pied-billed Grebe** *Podilymbus podiceps*	**Horned Grebe** *Podiceps auritus*

Red-necked Grebe

Size: 18 inches.

Abundance: Uncommon.

Migratory Status: Winter resident mostly.

Presumed range in New York

Variation: Winter plumage is gray and white (similar to Horned Grebe photo).

Habitat: Summers on shallow lakes, marshes, and bays of large lakes across Canada and Alaska. Winters in marine habitats. Bays, esturaries, and offshore.

Breeding: Nesting is on northern lakes. 4 to 5 eggs is typical (as many as 9).

Natural History: By mid-winter most of these grebes are along the coasts. Some will linger in the Great Lakes into winter, especially on Lake Ontario. But in severe winters when the Great Lakes freeze over, large numbers may irrupt southward and at these times they may be seen on open water well to the south of their normal range. They are circumpolar in distribution in the northern hemisphere. The grebes are known for their elaborate courship displays and "dances." As many as a dozen different postures may be displayed during one of these courtship dances. The pair often engage in mutually responsive movements that gives the appearance of two highly choreographed dancers. Feeding is done entirely in the water. Most feeding is in shallows but they are capable swimmers and divers and may feed in deep water. Food items include fish, crustaceans, and aquatic insects. Migration includes inland regions but winter residents use Great Lakes and coast.

Pied-billed Grebe

Size: 13 inches.

Abundance: Fairly common.

Migratory Status: Mostly a summer resident.

Presumed range in New York

Variation: Winter birds are grayer and lack the prominent dark ring on bill.

Habitat: Completely aquatic, the Pied-billed Grebe uses everything from large lakes to small farm ponds. Also open-water areas of swamps and marshes.

Breeding: Nests on floating platform among emergent vegetation. 4–8 eggs.

Natural History: A night-time migrator, this little grebe evades potential threats by submerging and they sometimes swim with just the head sticking out the water. They feed on a wide variety of small fish and other aquatic vertebrates as well as crustaceans and insects. This is the most widespread and common grebe in North America and they range from coast to coast. They are most common during summer in the "Prairie Pothole" habitats of the west-central United States and Canada. In winter they move as far south as Central America. They can be seen all winter across the southern half of the United States, but tend to concentrate along the Gulf Coast in winter. Although they are mostly a summer-time bird in New York, some will linger into winter along the coast. These little grebes are almost never seen in flight as they escape threats by diving and swimming. When threatened they can swim for long distances underwater and re-surface hundreds of yards away.

Horned Grebe

Size: 14 inches.

Abundance: Fairly common.

Migratory Status: Winter resident/migrant.

Presumed range in New York

Variation: Winter plumage (shown) is usually seen in New York.

Habitat: In New York this species uses the larger lakes as well as large marshes with open water and coastal areas. Not usually seen on small ponds.

Breeding: Nests on floating platform among emergent vegetation. 5–7 eggs.

Natural History: As is the case with other grebes (and loons), their adaptations for an aquatic lifestyle include the legs being positioned far back on the body. The legs can also be flared outward to a remarkable degree to facilitate underwater swimming maneuvers. As a result of this adaptation, these birds are very clumsy on land and walk with difficulty. Breeding on marshes and lakes in the northernmost portions of the continent, these birds are a transient migrant in much of New York. Breeding birds (seen in New York in spring migration) are handsomely marked with chestnut neck and flanks and golden brown head stripe that flares out to form "horns." The specimen shown above is in winter plumage and is typical of fall migrants and winter residents. Food is small fish, crustaceans, insects, etc. Their summer range is to the west and north of New York, but their winter range includes coastal regions of the state.

Class - **Aves** (birds)

Order - **Suliformes** (tropical sea birds)

Family - **Sulidae** (boobies and gannets)

Family - **Phalacrocoracidae** (cormorants)

Northern Gannet *Morus bassanus*	Great Cormorant *Phalacrocorax carbo*	Double-crested Cormorant *Phalacrocorax auritus*

Northern Gannet
Morus bassanus

Size: 37 inches.

Abundance: Fairly common.

Migratory Status: Winter resident/migrant.

Presumed range in New York

Variation: Sexes are alike. Juveniles are gray-black above with scattered white spots.

Habitat: Closely tied to the sea, Northern Gannets ply the waters of the continental shelf. They come to land only to breed on cliffs or remote islands.

Breeding: Colony breeder. Colonies are often large and dense and usually situated on a cliff. Lays a single egg.

Natural History: Though mainly a marine species, the Northern Gannet sometimes shows up far inland in New York as migrant on the Great Lakes or Lake Champlain. These birds are native to both sides of the North Atlantic, and are found from France to Norway on the European side of the ocean. In North America they summer in maritime provinces of Canada and winter along the coast as far south as Texas. They are fairly common in the Long Island Sound in winter. Although they may range many miles out into the ocean, they are not a true pelagic (open ocean) bird. They feed by diving from height of up to 120 feet and may reach speeds of over 100 mph in a dive. A variety of marine organisms may be eaten opportunistically but he main food is fish and squid. Among the most common fish eaten are mackeral and herring. Monogamous and mates for life.

Great Cormorant
Phalacrocorax carbo

Size: 3 feet.

Abundance: Fairly common.

Migratory Status: Winter resident/migrant.

Presumed range in New York

Variation: Sexes alike. Juvenile birds have a brownish neck and a whitish belly.

Habitat: Summer habitat is rocky coastlines in the far north. Winter habitat is shallow coastal waters, inlets, jetties, etc.

Breeding: Nest colonially. Known to share breeding colony with other species. Lays 4 eggs.

Natural History: America's largest cormorant, the Great Cormorant has a rather small geographic range in North America. But it is very widespread throughout much of the rest of the globe. In fact it is the most wide-ranging cormorant in the world, being found in Europe, Africa, Asia, and much of the south pacific, including Australia and New Zealand. In America it is restricted to the Atlantic coastline from the Carolinas (rare) to Greenland. In New York this species is fairly commmon along the coast in winter. Unlike New York's other cormorant species (Double-breasted Cormorant), this species is mainly marine in its habitats and rarely ventures far inland. They do range up the Hudson Valley as far as Albany. Confirmed fish eaters, cormorants have a bad reputation with fishermen who see them as competitors. For the most part, cormorants eat non-commercial species.

Double-crested Cormorant
Phalacrocorax auritus

Size: 33 inches.

Abundance: Common.

Migratory Status: Mostly summer.

Presumed range in New York

Variation: Juveniles are much browner and have whitish throat and breast. Breeding plumage has white crest.

Habitat: Lakes, rivers, estuaries, and swamplands. In New York they are most common on the islands in around New York City and in all large lakes.

Breeding: Large colonies nest on islands. Bulky nest of sticks and floating debris. Lays 2 to 4 eggs.

Natural History: Cormorants are rarely seen far from water. They are thoroughly aquatic birds that have webbed feet and frequently submerge and swim underwater in search of fish. Their exclusive diet of fish and their uncanny aquatic abilities have caused these birds to come into conflict with man. Occurring in large flocks, they will concentrate in areas where food is most readily available. Under natural conditions they catch a wide variety of fish species and thus do not impact significantly upon fisheries. However, around fish farms or hatcheries they can become quite a nuisance. Nearly wiped out by the pesticide DDT a half century ago they have made an incredible comeback. In some regions they have come to be seen as an ecological problem by crowding out other colonial nesting bird species and impacting negatively on fish stocks.

Class - **Aves** (birds)
Order - **Anseriformes** (waterfowl)
Family - **Anatidae** (ducks, geese, and swans)

Mallard *Anas platyrhynchos*	**Black Duck** *Anas rubripes*	**Northern Pintail** *Anas acuta*

Mallard		Black Duck		Northern Pintail	
Size: 23 inches. **Abundance:** Very common. **Migratory Status:** Both year-round and migrant.	Presumed range in New York	**Size:** 23 inches. **Abundance:** Uncommon. **Migratory Status:** Both year-round and migrant.	Presumed range in New York	**Size:** 25 inches. **Abundance:** Fairly common. **Migratory Status:** Mainly a winter resident and migrant.	Presumed range in New York

Variation: Pronounced sexual plumage variation (see photos above).

Variation: Sexes are very similar, females have a darker bill than males.

Variation: Profound sexual dimorphism (see photos above). Male larger.

Habitat: Found in aquatic situations everywhere, from deserts to tundra to southern swamplands, ponds, lakes, etc.

Habitat: Fond of estuaries and coastal marshes. Inland will use other aquatic habitats (lakes, marshes, swamps, etc.).

Habitat: Open country. In New York this species is most common in the western and southeastern portion of the state.

Breeding: Nests on the ground in close proximity to water. Lays up to 13 eggs and will re-nest if nest is destroyed.

Breeding: For breeding favors coastal marshes and beaver ponds and bogs in boreal forests. Lays up to 14 eggs.

Breeding: Breeds in marshes, potholes, and tundra in the northern and western portions of the continent. 3–12 eggs.

Natural History: By far the most familiar duck in America. The Mallard has been widely domesticated but it is also the most common wild duck in the United States. Many parks and public lakes around the country have semi-wild populations that are non-migratory. Highly adaptable, this is the most successful duck species in America, perhaps in the world. It is the source of all breeds of domestic duck except the Muscovey and they are thus an important food source for humans. They are also a highly regarded game bird and they are hunted throughout North America. They range throughout the northern half of the globe and their range in the western hemisphere closely coincides with the North American continent. Mallards are one of the most common breeding ducks in NY. Between wild ducks and semi-tame populations in urban parks, breeding probably occurs in every county.

Natural History: The Black Duck is very similar to the Mallard in size, shape, and voice, and the two species are known to hybridize. In appearance and other traits however they are quite different. This is one of the few puddle ducks that does not range throughout the continent, being restricted to the eastern half of America. Like many of America's duck species, the Black Duck has been impacted negatively by human-related changes to the landscape and environment in America. Drainage of wetlands, urbanization along northeastern coastlines, and deforestation have hit this species harder than most other ducks and the population has declined significantly in the last half-century. Interbreeding with the more adaptable Mallard may also be a threat to this uniquely American Duck. They may be seen throughout the state as a migrant or winter or as a breeding bird. They winter mainly along the coast.

Natural History: Northern Pintail populations are in decline. Modern agricultural practices on the great plains of the United States and Canada are the greatest threat. They are also highly susceptible to droughts in the prairie regions, which limit breeding habitat. Food is mostly plant material but some aquatic invertebrates are also eaten. On wintering grounds, waste grain from farming operations has become an important food source. In recent decades the species has benefited from a number of conservation efforts by state and federal agencies as well as private organizations, most notably Ducks Unlimited, an organization funded by duck hunters. Conservation efforts that have recently benefited the species are reduced hunter harvest and changing agricultural practices in the prairie pothole region. Though large numbers may migrate or winter in the state, Pintails are very rare as a breeding bird in New York.

Class - **Aves** (birds)		
Order - **Anseriformes** (waterfowl)		
Family - **Anatidae** (ducks, geese, and swans)		

Gadwall
Anas strepera

Male

Female

Size: 20 inches.

Abundance: Fairly common.

Migratory Status: Summer resident, seasonal migrant.

Presumed range in New York

Variation: Significant sexual dimorphism (see photos above).

Habitat: Marshes and potholes of the great plains in summer. Uses all aquatic habitats in winter.

Breeding: Nests among thick vegetation near water, often on islands in marshes or lakes. Lays 7 to 12 eggs.

Natural History: Gadwalls breed and summer largely in the great plains region. In winter they are seen all across the southern half of America, with the greatest numbers wintering along the West Gulf Coastal Plain. Populations of this duck can fluctuate significantly depending upon water levels in the prairies of Canada and the north-central United States Droughts and poor agricultural practices that eliminate habitat can cause populations to plummet. Conversely, good rainfall and good wildlife conservation practices by farmers have shown to be a real boon to this and many other duck species that depend on the marshes and potholes on the great plains for nesting habitat. Adult Gadwalls feed mostly on plant material. Ducklings rely heavily upon high-protein invertebrates for growth and development. The Gadwall is a rare breeder in New York in widely scattered localities.

American Wigeon
Anas americana

Male

Female

Size: 19 inches.

Abundance: Fairly common.

Migratory Status: Mostly a winter resident and seasonal migrant.

Presumed range in New York

Variation: Significant sexual variation. See photos above.

Habitat: Range includes all types of aquatic habitats in the state (swamps, marshes, lakes, ponds, etc.).

Breeding: Nests near shallow freshwater wetlands and potholes mostly in the North American prairie. 3 to 12 eggs.

Natural History: The American Wigeon also goes by the name "Baldpate," a reference to the white crown of the male. This duck has a very similar old world counter part, the Eurasian Wigeon, which ranges throughout much of Europe and Asia. American birds feed mostly on plant material, but females when breeding opt for a higher protein diet of invertebrates. One of the more northerly ranging members of the "puddle duck" group, some individuals will summer as far north as the Arctic Coastal Plain of Alaska. These ducks are seen in the state mostly from September through April, but some breeding does occur in northern New York. Some merely pass through the state during north-south migrations, but some will overwinter in coastal regions. As with other puddle ducks, this species is susceptible to population declines during droughts, but overall the species appears healthy.

Green-winged Teal
Anas crecca

Male

Female

Size: 14 inches.

Abundance: Fairly common.

Migratory Status: Summer, winter, and migratory.

Presumed range in New York

Variation: Significant sexual variation. See photos above.

Habitat: Includes all types of aquatic/ wetland habitats in the state (swamps, marshes, salt marsh, lakes, ponds, etc.).

Breeding: Nest is in dense vegetation in wetland habitats. Some nesting occurs in New York. 6 to 9 eggs are laid in May.

Natural History: This is the smallest of America's "puddle ducks," and also one of the more common. They range throughout the northern hemisphere, with a distinct subspecies being found in Eurasia. They are fast and agile fliers and flocks of Green-winged Teal move back and forth across the southern half of the continent all winter in response to weather patterns. Populations of this duck appear stable and may even be increasing. About 90 percent of the population breeds in Canada and Alaska where they favor river deltas and boreal wetlands over the typical "pothole" habitats used by many puddle ducks. Some widely scattered nesting occurs in New York. Their main nesting habitat is the far north and thus largely undisturbed by man, which may account in part for this species' abundance. As with many species, the increasing daylight hours of spring triggers migration and breeding instincts.

Class - **Aves** (birds)

Order - **Anseriformes** (waterfowl)

Family - **Anatidae** (ducks, geese, and swans)

Blue-winged Teal *Anas discors*	**Shoveler** *Anas clypeata*	**Wood Duck** *Aix sponsa*
		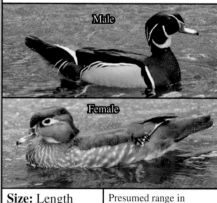

Blue-winged Teal	Shoveler	Wood Duck
Size: Length 15.5 inches.	**Size:** Length 19 inches.	**Size:** Length 18.5 inches.
Abundance: Fairly common.	**Abundance:** Fairly common.	**Abundance:** Common.
Migratory Status: Spring through fall.	**Migratory Status:** Year-round.	**Migratory Status:** Spring through fall.
Presumed range in New York	*Presumed range in New York*	*Presumed range in New York*
Variation: Significant sexual dimorphism (see photos above).	**Variation:** Significant sexual dimorphism (see photos above).	**Variation:** Significant sexual dimorphism (see photos above).
Habitat: Marshes, beaver ponds, bays, and other shallow water habitats.	**Habitat:** Prefers shallow habitats. Swamps, marshes, flooded fields, bays.	**Habitat:** Beaver ponds, swamps, flooded woodlands, and farm ponds.
Breeding: Nest is concealed in dense vegetation near water but above high waterline. Lays 6–12 eggs.	**Breeding:** Breeds mostly in northern and western United States (including Alaska) and in Canada. Averages 10 to 12 eggs.	**Breeding:** Nests in tree hollows and takes readily to artificial nest boxes. Lays about 8 to 12 eggs typically.
Natural History: The food of this species is mostly plant material including algae and aquatic greenery. Many seeds and grains are also eaten, especially in winter when they converge on rice fields and other flooded agricultural areas in America's lower coastal plain. Breeding females will consume large amounts of invertebrates during the breeding season. These ducks are early fall migrators and one of the last to migrate back north in the spring. Many will winter as far south as South America, but substantial numbers can be seen along the lower coastal plain of North America all winter. Most breed and spend the summer on the central prairies of the United States and Canada. But widespread breeding occurs in northern and western New York. The most breeding in New York probably occurs in the St. Lawrence River Valley. Young ducks are typically highly precocial, and babies will leave the nest within hours of hatching.	**Natural History:** The Shoveler's name is derived from the unique shape of its bill, which is a highly effective sieve for straining tiny organisms from water. They are often observed swimming along with the bill held under water or skimming the surface. Like several of America's duck species, the Shoveler is holarctic in distribution and it breeds in Europe and Asia as well as North America. Eurasian birds winter southward to north Africa and the pacific region. All ground-nesting birds are vulnerable to mammalian predators and the Shoveler is no exception. Red Foxes and Mink are significant predators on the nesting females, while skunks are a major threat to the eggs. A few Shovlers will breed in western New York but they are most common in the state during fall migration from late August through September. The nationwide population of these ducks seems to be on the increase, but waterfowl populations tend to be subject to significant annual variations.	**Natural History:** Male Wood Ducks are one of the most brilliantly colored birds in America. The bulk of the Wood Duck population in America occurs in the forested eastern half of the country. Populations plummeted during the latter half of the 19th century as America's forests were felled and swamplands drained. Populations began to recover by the 1950s and today the species is thriving. Most state wildlife agencies in America began placing Wood Duck nest boxes in suitable habitat many decades ago. The ducks responded favorably and a very high percentage of babies hatch in the man-made nests annually. Wood Ducks are widely hunted and make up a significant number of ducks killed by hunters annually. Although they are a small duck, they are considered by many as highly palatable. Along with the Mallard, the Wood Duck is one of the most common breeding ducks in New York.

Class - **Aves** (birds)

Order - **Anseriformes** (waterfowl)

Family - **Anatidae** (ducks, geese, and swans)

Lesser Scaup *Aythya affinis*	**Ring-necked Duck** *Aythya collaris*	**Redhead** *Aythya americana*

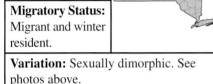

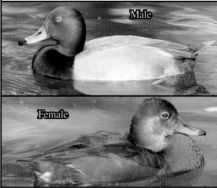

Size: Length 16.5 inches.

Presumed range in New York

Abundance: Fairly common.

Migratory Status: Migrant and winter resident.

Variation: Sexually dimorphic. See photos above.

Habitat: Likes larger bodies of water and deeper water than many other ducks. Regularly uses large lakes and rivers in the state as well as flooded river bottoms and coastal areas.

Breeding: 8 to 10 eggs is typical. Nests in west-central United States, Canada and in Alaska.

Natural History: These ducks are the most widespread and common of the "diving ducks." Diving ducks are capable of diving deeper and prefer deeper waters than the "puddle ducks." They are also more clumsy on land and need a running start on the water to get airborne. They thus favor larger lakes and rivers over small ponds and swamplands. These ducks often gather in large flocks on open water. These large flocks are called "rafts." Rafts of Lesser Scaup are a common sight on large lakes in winter. A slightly larger version of the Lesser Scaup, known as the **Greater Scaup** (*Aythya marila*) can also be seen in New York in winter. Both species like open water. The Greater Scaup tends to favor coastal areas and salt or brackish marshes, but it does migrate through much of the state. In New York the Greater may be the most common of the two.

Size: Length 17 inches.

Presumed range in New York

Abundance: Uncommon.

Migratory Status: Winter and migratory.

Variation: Pronounced sexual dimorphism. See photos above.

Habitat: Open-water habitats including shallow bays and flooded river bottoms. Also uses open marshes and large rivers and lakes, where it tends to use mostly shallow-water areas.

Breeding: Nests in subarctic regions of Canada and the northern Rockies in the United States. Lays 6 to 14 eggs.

Natural History: Closely related to and very similar in appearance to the scaups, the Ring-necked Duck should be called the Ring-billed duck. Although there is a brownish ring around the neck of the male, it is only visible when the bird is in the hand. The broad white ring near the tip of the bill and the narrow white ring at the base of the bill are both readily discernible on birds in the field. Unlike its relatives the scaups, which will feed on crustaceans, insects, and other aquatic invertebrates, the diet of the Ring-necked Duck is mostly vegetarian. Also unlike scaups, Ring-necked Ducks favor small lakes, ponds, and swamps over large rivers and lakes. Like other North American ducks, their movements in winter are determined by weather. Freeze-ups of open water will instigate massive movements.

Size: Length 19 inches.

Presumed range in New York

Abundance: Fairly common.

Migratory Status: Mostly a winter resident.

Variation: Pronounced sexual dimorphism. See photos above.

Habitat: Primarily a marshland species that alternates between prairie potholes and gulf coastal marshes. In migration they will use a variety of wetland habitats, especially the bays of large lakes.

Breeding: Breeds almost entirely in the "prairie pothole" region. Females often lay their eggs in other ducks nests.

Natural History: An entirely North American species, the Redhead is mostly a vegetarian and feeds heavily on tubers and aquatic vegetation. Most Redheads congregate in winter on the western Gulf Coast of Louisiana, Texas, and northwest Mexico. In fact hundreds of thousands will concentrate in this region each winter. Here they feed mostly on the roots of shoalgrass. They will also eat some animal matter, mostly aquatic invertebrates. Redheads are easily decoyed and during the days of market hunting their populations suffered dramatic declines. Recovery in the last few decades has been significant and in a good year the population may reach a million birds. The Redhead is a very rare breeding bird in New York but is fairly common in winter. They favor freshwater habitats along the Lake Erie shoreline or the lower Hudson River during winter.

Class - **Aves** (birds)

Order - **Anseriformes** (waterfowl)

Family - **Anatidae** (ducks, geese, and swans)

Canvasback *Aythya valisineria*	**Bufflehead** *Bucephala albeola*	**Common Goldeneye** *Bucephala clangula*

Size: Length 21 inches.	**Size:** Length 13.5 inches.	**Size:** Length 18.5 inches.
Abundance: Uncommon.	**Abundance:** Common.	**Abundance:** Uncommon.
Migratory Status: Winter resident.	**Migratory Status:** Winter resident.	**Migratory Status:** Mostly a winter resident.

Presumed range in New York (all three columns)

Variation: Strong sexual variation. See photos above.

Variation: Significant sexual variation. See photos above.

Variation: Significant sexual variation. See photos above. Juvenile like female.

Habitat: The primary breeding habitat for this species is known as "Aspen Parkland" habitat, which is found mostly in Canada. Winters mostly in marshes and bays along both coasts.

Habitat: Many winter in salt water habitats on the coast but a few overwinter on inland lakes and rivers in New York. In summer they use boreal forests and parklands in Canada.

Habitat: Freshwater habitats are large lakes and rivers. They are also fairly common in winter in coastal regions. In summer they are a bird of the boreal forests.

Breeding: The large nest is built from grasses and hidden vegetation. Clutch size averages around 7 or 8.

Breeding: Cavity nester. Nest is often an old woodpecker hole. Clutch size ranges from a few to over a dozen eggs.

Breeding: Cavity nester that will use artificial nest boxes. May nest over a mile from water. 7 to 12 eggs.

Natural History: One of the most adept of the diving ducks, Canvasbacks have been known to dive to a depth of 30 feet. Feeds mostly on plant material including roots and rhizomes, but will also eat mud-dwelling invertebrates. This is strictly a North American species and is one of the least common duck species in America. They are vulnerable to droughts, habitat loss (mostly from agriculture), and water pollution that can impact the abundance of aquatic food plants. The Canvasback population is closely monitored by the United States Fish and Wildlife Service and in years of low numbers hunting of this species may be banned. Even in years when hunting is allowed, the bag limits are typically very low (one per day). They can be seen in coastal bays in winter as well as in freshwater situations such as the Great Lakes, Finger Lakes, and the Hudson River.

Natural History: America's smallest of the diving ducks, the Bufflehead is one of the few duck species that will remain with the same mate year after year. Breeding pairs usually return to the same pond or marsh to breed each year as well. With the exception of some seeds, these ducks are mostly carnivorous, feeding on aquatic insects, crustaceans, mollusks, and small fish. Unlike the puddle ducks which often feed on the surface, the Bufflehead finds all its food by diving. Although they are often seen on deep-water lakes, they feed in the shallows along the banks or in the backs of bays. Almost always seen in small flocks, this is one of the few duck species that has actually increased in numbers in the last few decades. In New York they can be seen on almost any body of water from late October through early April, including small ponds on Long Island.

Natural History: As with other diving ducks the Common Goldeneye is an excellent swimmer that feeds by diving beneath the surface. They propel through the water using only the feet, with the wings held tight against the body. They are mostly carnivorous but they do eat some plant material in the form of tubers and seeds. Aquatic invertebrates are the main food and include (in order of importance) crustaceans, insects, and mollusks. Fish constitute only a small portion of the diet. Male Common Goldeneyes engage in a complex courtship display to attract females or reinforce the pair bond. These ducks are holarctic in distribution, breeding in boreal forests throughout the northern hemisphere. Although they are mostly a winter resident, some breeding has been recorded in upstate New York on Lake Champlain and in the Adirondacks.

Class - **Aves** (birds)

Order - **Anseriformes** (waterfowl)

Family - **Anatidae** (ducks, geese, and swans)

Ruddy Duck *Oxyura jamaicensis*	**Long-tailed Duck** *Clangula hyemalis*	**Common Eider** *Somateria mollissima*

Size: 15 inches.

Abundance: Fairly common.

Migratory Status: Winter resident mostly.

Presumed range in New York

Size: 21 inches.

Abundance: Fairly common.

Migratory Status: Winter resident.

Presumed range in New York

Size: 24 inches.

Abundance: Rare in New York.

Migratory Status: Winter resident.

Presumed range in New York

Variation: Significant sexual variation. See photos above.

Variation: Males have very long tails and are more strikingly colored.

Variation: Significant sexual variation. Female mottled brown.

Habitat: Marshes, ponds, lakes, and to a lesser extent rivers. This is a true "Prairie Pothole" species and nearly 90 percent of nesting occurs in the prairie pothole habitats in the northern plains.

Habitat: Summer habitat is arctic wetlands and seashores and deep-water lakes. Winter habitat is mostly coastal marine environments, but also large fresh-water lakes, especially the Great Lakes.

Habitat: The Common Eider is a marine species that inhabits rocky coastlines. In New York they are seen in coastal areas. Mostly a duck of northern waters.

Breeding: Nest is usually built in cattails or other aquatic vegetation. 7 or 8 eggs is average.

Breeding: Nests in the arctic region on islands and peninsulas of freshwater lakes or in wetland tundra. 6 to 8 eggs.

Breeding: Nest is usually fairly close to water. Nest site often in crevice or beneath overhang or shrub. 3 to 5 eggs.

Natural History: Ruddy Ducks are primarliy western birds that range generally from the Great Plains to the west coast. Winter range includes most of the eastern United States and they are regularly seen in New York in winter. Although they may rarely appear statewide, these ducks are more common-ly seen in New York in the coastal regions and on Long Island. They are very rare in upstate New York. The larva of aquatic insects of the order Diptera (flies, mosquitos, midges) are the primary food of these ducks. Although these are small ducks, their eggs are quite large and are in fact the largest eggs (relative to body size) of any North American duck. This species seems to be expanding its breeding range eastward into the Great Lakes region and a few Ruddy Ducks have nested in western New York. Congregates in large "rafts" on open water.

Natural History: Also known as "Oldsquaw" these are primarily northern ducks that often wander far south in winter. Although they have been recorded in a variety of localities around the state, in New York they are most likely to be seen around the Great Lakes or along the coast. These little ducks are great divers, and can dive to depths over 150 feet to reach marine invertebrate foods consisting mostly of benthic crustaceans. They also eat insects and their larva and to a lesser extent fish and fish eggs. This is one of the most northerly breeding ducks in the world and they nest well into the arctic. There is some evidence that populations on the west coast are in decline. Status of eastern populations unknown but believed stable. Often roosts in large "rafts" well offshore along coastlines or in large inland lakes.

Natural History: These ducks are cold tolerant species that nest as far north as the shores of the Arctic Ocean and in winter move only as far south as the northern United States coastline. In habits they are decidedly salt water birds but they tend to remain near the coast. They show a preference for rocky coasts where they locate their primary food of shellfish by diving to depth of up to 30 feet. Most feeding is done in shallower water with dives lasting up to a minute. Food items include mollusks, echinoderms, and crustaceans. Strong, chisel-like beak is used to pluck attached mollusks from rocks and to crush shells. Nests in colonies and forms large flocks in winter which may "raft up" off the shores of Long Island. Although uncommon in New York, this species has been increasing in the state in recent decades.

Class - **Aves** (birds)

Order - **Anseriformes** (waterfowl)

Family - **Anatidae** (ducks, geese, and swans)

Surf Scoter *Melanitta perspicillata*	**Black Scoter** *Melanitta americana*	**White-winged Scoter** *Melanitta fusca*

Size: 20 inches.	**Size:** 19 inches.	**Size:** 21 inches.
Abundance: Common.	**Abundance:** Common.	**Abundance:** Common.
Migratory Status: Migrant and winter resident.	**Migratory Status:** Migrant and winter resident.	**Migratory Status:** Migrant and winter resident.

 Presumed range in New York

 Presumed range in New York

 Presumed range in New York

Variation: Significant sexual dimorphism. See photo above.

Variation: Significant sexual dimorphism. See photos above.

Variation: Significant sexual dimorphism.

Habitat: Summer habitat is small lakes or ponds in the taiga forests of northern Canada. Winters along the North American coastline. Inland migrant use large lakes and rivers.

Habitat: Winters in marine environments along both coasts of North America. Summer habitat includes shallow freshwater lakes. Apparently not inclined to use rivers very much.

Habitat: Summer habitat is lakes and wetlands in western Canada and northern Alaska. Winter habitat is coastal waters of both coasts and large inland lakes and rivers.

Breeding: Nests in northern Canada in shallow wetland areas. Lays 6 to 9 eggs in a hollowed out nest on the ground that is lined with the mothers down.

Breeding: Breeds in northern Alaska, nothern Yukon, northern Quebec, and northernmost Ontario around Hudson Bay. Lays 8 or 9 eggs in a ground nest.

Breeding: Nest is on the ground and concealed by dense vegetation. Sometimes nests in close proximity to shorebirds. Lays 8 to 10 eggs per clutch.

Natural History: Unlike the other two Scoters on this page, the Surf Scoter is a resident of North America only. In New York migrants are common along the coast in October and November, and they are also seen inland on lakes and rivers. During winter they restrict their movements to marine environments mainly, where they can be seen in large flocks mixed with our other scoter species. The food is mostly mud-dwelling invertebrates and includes small bivalves like mussels. They are also known to eat the eggs of one of the most common marine fishes, the Herring. Scoter populations apprear to be in decline in recent decades. As with all sea birds they are highly susceptible to oil spills. The world's oceans are under assault and the decline of sea-going birds is a warning that should not go unheeded.

Natural History: In spite of the species name "americana," the range of the Black Scoter is not confined to the western hemisphere. A few range across the north pacific into eastern Russia. Food is invertebrates including large amounts of mussels. In freshwater environments will also eat insects and some plant material. Insects are reported to be a crucial element in the diet of yound ducklings. In winter adult birds wintering along the coast feed mostly by diving and foraging for mollusks, crustaceans, etc. These can be abundant birds along the northern coastlines of America in winter and they may be quite common along New York's coastline from late October through March. They are also frequently seen on Lake Ontario in winter, as well as other lakes during migration.

Natural History: Like the other two scoter species they usually associate in winter with coastal waters and all scoters are often collectively referred to as "Sea Ducks." All hunted in winter along the Atlantic coast where there is an established tradition of hunting "sea ducks." A long-term downward trend in populations of all three scoters brings into question the liberal harvests of these ducks by waterfowl hunters. Additional threats come from the fact the the favorite food of scoters (mussels) are filter-feeding organisms that absorb and concentrate pollutants and toxins in sea water. Studies have shown White-winged Scoters to have measurable levels of lead, cadmium, and PCBs. Once again, a warning sign that the world's oceans are being dangerously degraded.

Class - **Aves** (birds)

Order - **Anseriformes** (waterfowl)

Family - **Anatidae** (ducks, geese, and swans)

Common Merganser *Mergus merganser*	Red-breasted Merganser *Mergus serrator*	Hooded Merganser *Lophodytes cucullatus*
 Non-breeding male	 Male  Female	 Male  Female

Size: Length 25 inches.	**Size:** Length 23 inches.	**Size:** Length 18 inches.
Abundance: Fairly common.	**Abundance:** Fairly common.	**Abundance:** Fairly common.
Migratory Status: Year-round resident.	**Migratory Status:** Winter resident.	**Migratory Status:** Year-round resident.

Presumed range in New York (shown for each species)

Variation: Exhibits pronounced sexual dimorphism in breeding plumage with males having dark greenish head and white breast. Both plumages may be seen in New York.	**Variation:** Significant plumage variations between the sexes during the breeding season. Also exhibits seasonal variation with winter males (and juveniles) resembling females.	**Variation:** Shows strong sexual dimorphism. Males are strikingly marked, having black heads with white "hood" and black wings and back. Females are more subdued (see above).
Habitat: In winter uses large lakes and rivers and larger reservoirs.	**Habitat:** Uses larger lakes and rivers as well as salt water habitats on the coast.	**Habitat:** Uses swamps, shallow bays of lakes, and river floodplains.
Breeding: Nests in tree cavities or sometimes in root crevices on the ground. 10 or 12 eggs is average. Nests in the northern portion of New York.	**Breeding:** Nests on the ground. Nest is well hidden beneath overhanging vegetation or in cavities. 5 to 24 eggs. Very rare nester in New York state.	**Breeding:** Cavity nester. Most nesting in New York is in the Adirondacks, but nesting also occurs across the northern half of the state. Lays up to 12 eggs.
Natural History: A bird of northern climates and cold waters, the Common Merganser spends the summer on lakes in the boreal forests of Canada, Alaska, and in the cold water streams of the Rocky Mountains as well as in the Adirondack and Lake Champlain regions of New York. They are also found throughout Eurasia. Fish is the primary food for this species. Their bill is serrated for holding slippery prey and they are excellent divers and underwater swimmers. They are excellent fishermen and can dive to a depth of tens of yards and have been known to stay submerged up to two minutes. They use their bill to probe in mud or gravel for aquatic insects, mollusks, crustaceans, and worms.	**Natural History:** During winter these birds show a preference for coastal regions where they use estuaries and salt water bays and salt/brackish water marshes. Like its larger relative the Common Merganser, the Red-breasted has a holarctic distribution and is found in Europe and Asia as well as North America. In summer this species ranges even farther north than its larger cousin, being found as far north as the Arctic Ocean and southern Greenland. Food is mostly small fish that are grasped with the serrated bill. Also eats aquatic invertebrates and amphibians. Feeds both in shallow water and in deep water up to at least 25 feet deep. Flocks may feed cooperatively, with all the birds diving together to corral schools of minnows.	**Natural History:** Unlike our other two merganser ducks, both of which are holarctic in distribution, the Hooded Merganser is strictly a North American duck. Another odd distributional trait is the fact that these birds are rare in the great plains region, where many North American duck species are most common. They have a more diverse diet than the larger mergansers, feeding less on fish and more on aquatic invertebrates that are located by means of well-developed underwater vision capability. Winter waterfowl surveys indicate that over 50 percent of the population winters in the Mississippi flyway. Most birds winter to the south of New York, but this species can be seen year-round throughout the state.

Class - **Aves** (birds)

Order - **Anseriformes** (waterfowl)

Family - **Anatidae** (ducks, geese, and swans)

Snow Goose *Chen caerulescens*	**Canada Goose** *Branta canadensis*	**Brant** *Branta bernicla*

Snow Goose	Canada Goose	Brant
Size: 30 inches. **Abundance:** Common. **Migratory Status:** Winter resident and seasonal migrant. Presumed range in New York	**Size:** 45 inches. **Abundance:** Very common. **Migratory Status:** Year-round resident and seasonal migrant. Presumed range in New York	**Size:** 24 inches. **Abundance:** Fairly common. **Migratory Status:** Winter resident and migrant. Presumed range in New York
Variation: Two distinct color phases occur. Juveniles are uniformly gray.	**Variation:** No variation. Sexes and juveniles are all alike.	**Variation:** No variation in New York. A darker morph occurs in western United States.
Habitat: Uses large open areas such as large crop fields for resting and feeding. Winters in New York on Jamaica Bay Wildlife Refuge. Migrant statewide.	**Habitat:** Habitat includes all types of aquatic situations, from urban parks to remote and inaccessible marshes, swamps, or beaver ponds.	**Habitat:** Summers on the tundra regions along the Arctic Coastal Plain. Winter habitat is coastal marshes and bays along both coasts.
Breeding: Nests only in the high arctic tundra of Canada and Alaska.	**Breeding:** Nests above the waterline but near water. 4 to 8 eggs is typical.	**Breeding:** Breeds on Arctic Coastal Plain. 3 to 5 eggs in down-lined nest.

Natural History: Snow Goose populations have exploded in the last few decades, probably as a result of having so much habitat and food available throughout migration routes and on wintering grounds. The grain fields of Midwestern and southern United States provide more than an adequate food source. Mid-continent populations are expanding their migration routes eastward from their historical range west of the Mississippi River. Snow geese seen in New York are part of the east coast population that winters the along the Atlantic coast from New Jersey to the Carolinas. Snow Geese often occur in huge flocks that number hundreds or even thousands of birds. The **Ross's Goose** (*C. rossii*) is a is a smaller version of the Snow Goose that may rarely be seen in New York in the company of Snow Geese.

Natural History: This is the most recognized wild goose in America, due in large part to the fact that tame and semi-tame populations are found in parks and on rivers, ponds, and lakes in both urban and rural regions. Resident Canada Geese numbers are swelled dramatically during winter, as birds from farther north visit the state for either a brief stopover or a months long stay. The characteristic "V formation" of Canada Geese in flight is a familiar sight and their musical, honking call is to many a symbol of wild America. They are heavily hunted throughout America and many tens of thousands are killed by hunters each year. They are long-lived birds and have been known to survive over 40 years. There are several races of Canada Goose and they vary in size. An identical dwarf species of goose called the **Cackling Goose** (*B. hutchinsii*) is the size of a Mallard.

Natural History: There are two distinct color morphs of Brant, but only the pale-bellied Atlantic morph occurs in New York. Darker "Black Brant" is seen along the west coast. They are fairly common in coastal areas of New York in winter and they may be seen as migrants flying across much of the state during migration. They are also widely distributed in the old world in the northern hemisphere where they are known by the name "Brent Goose." East coast populations winter as far south as North Carolina. West coast birds may go as far south as the Baja Peninsula in winter. Food is strictly plant material, mostly salt marsh plants in winter. Eelgrass is listed as a primary food item and some grazing on "dry land" grasses may also occur. The greatest threat is loss of habitat in wintering areas. Summer habitats are mostly remote and fairly secure.

Class - **Aves** (birds)

Order - **Anseriformes** (waterfowl)

Family - **Anatidae** (ducks, geese, and swans)

Mute Swan *Cygnus olor*	**Tundra Swan** *Cygnus columbianus*	**Trumpeter Swan** *Cygnus buccinator*

Mute Swan
Cygnus olor

Size: 60 inches.

Abundance: Fairly common.

Migratory Status: Year-round resident.

Presumed range in New York

Variation: Some juveniles are brownish for the first year.

Habitat: Ponds, lakes, marshes, and swamps in both urban and rural areas. Most often seen in urban parks.

Breeding: Nest is platform of grasses up to 6 ft. wide. Near water but above floodplain. About 6 eggs per clutch.

Natural History: The Mute Swan is a Eurasian species that is common in parks, zoos, farms, and private preserves all across America. Many have become feral or semi-feral and the species seems to be increasing in the wild in America. The impact of this exotic species on native wildlife populations is unclear, but some state wildlife agencies (including NYSDEC) regard them as a nuisance animal. Many state wildlife agencies have active removal programs. In some other states they are protected. These large waterfowl are primarily vegetarians, but they will eat small amounts of animal matter. When threatened Mute Swans arch the wings over the back and pull the long neck back between the wings in a display known as "busking." They are graceful and elegant in flight or on the water, but rather clumsy on land due to the fact that the legs are located so far back on the body.

Tundra Swan
Cygnus columbianus

Size: 52 inches.

Abundance: Rare in New York.

Migratory Status: Mostly a seasonal migrant.

Presumed range in New York

Variation: Juveniles are "dingy" white with orange bill.

Habitat: Large lakes and large, open agricultural fields are used in migration. In New York often seen in Finger Lakes.

Breeding: Breeds on the tundra of the Arctic Coastal Plain. 3 to 5 eggs are laid.

Natural History: Although the Tundra Swan is America's most common swan species, these large swans are rare in New York. But they do pass through the state during migration. Most winter along the Atlantic coast from the Chesapeake Bay south to North Carolina and on the Pacific Coast from Washington to central California. In winter they use coastal estuaries and will fly inland to forage on waste grain in agricultural fields. Young swans stay with the parents throughout the first year until returning to their arctic breeding grounds the following spring. Prior to the passage of the first migratory bird protection legislation in 1918, these birds had become quite rare. Today their numbers have recovered substantially and a few states now allow a limited harvest during waterfowl season. Migratory flights over New York may include flocks numbering hundreds of swans, but smaller groups of one or two dozen is more common.

Trumpeter Swan
Cygnus buccinator

Size: 60 inches.

Abundance: Very rare in New York.

Migratory Status: Year-round resident.

Presumed range in New York

Variation: None in adults. Juveniles are grayish.

Habitat: In New York uses wetlands, lakes, etc. In western United States found on rivers, lakes, and freshwater marshes.

Breeding: Nest is a hummock in wetland area. May use muskrat house or beaver lodge. 4 to 6 eggs.

Natural History: Trumpeter Swans were eradicated from the eastern United States by European settlers about 200 years ago. They managed to cling to existance in northern and western North America but were highly endangered until recent decades. Today the species has recovered significantly and populations in the western half of North America appear secure. In New York they are still quite rare but efforts are underway to re-establish the species in New York and in nearby Ontario. Despite the fact that this species is increasing in numbers it still faces an uncertain future. The main threats to the species today are probably loss of habitat, pollution, and ingestion of lead sinkers used by fishermen. Food is mostly plant material, mainly aquatic plants but also some terrestrial plants. Adult birds often show a reddish wash on the head and neck as a result of foraging for tubers in mud that is rich in iron.

CHAPTER 5

THE TURTLES OF NEW YORK

— THE ORDERS AND FAMILIES OF NEW YORK TURTLES —

Note: The arrangement below is a reflection of how the orders and families of turtles appear in this book and may not be an accurate representation of the phylogentic relationship of the turtles.

Class - **Chelonia** (turtles)

Order - **Cryptodira** (straightneck turtles)

Family	**Chelydridae** (snapping turtles)
Family	**Kinosternidae** (mud and musk turtles)
Family	**Emydidae** (sliders and box turtles)
Family	**Trionychidae** (softshell turtles)

Class - **Chelonia** (turtles)

Order - **Cryptodira** (straightneck turtles)

Family - **Chelydridae** (snapping turtles)	Family - **Kinosternidae** (mud and musk turtles)	
Common Snapping Turtle *Chelydra serpentina*	**Common Musk Turtle** *Sternotherus odoratus*	**Eastern Mud Turtle** *Kinosternon subrubrum*

Common Snapping Turtle
Chelydra serpentina

Common Musk Turtle
Sternotherus odoratus

Eastern Mud Turtle
Kinosternon subrubrum

Size: Maximum length 20 inches. Record weight 86 pounds.

Abundance: Very common.

Presumed range in New York

Size: About 4 inches. Record length nearly 6 inches.

Abundance: Fairly common.

Presumed range in New York

Size: Adults range from 4 to 4.75 inches in length.

Abundance: Rare in New York.

Presumed range in New York

Variation: No variation in New York.

Variation: Female is slightly larger.

Variation: No variation in New York.

Habitat: Found in virtually every freshwater aquatic environment in the state. Ponds, lakes, rivers, creeks, swamps, and marshes.

Habitat: Primarily a stream dweller, but can be found in a variety of aquatic habitats including swamps, marshes, lakes.

Habitat: Found in all aquatic habitats withing its range, but prefers shallow water areas with abundant aquatic vegetation.

Breeding: Eggs are deposited in underground chambers excavated by the female turtle. A typical clutch contains 25 to 50 eggs. Hatchlings are about the size of a quarter. Hatchlings may overwinter in nest chamber and emerge the following spring.

Breeding: Female lays 2 to 5 eggs under leaf litter or sometimes merely on top of the ground. Unlike many aquatic turtles that make long excursions into upland areas to lay their eggs, the Common Musk Turtle deposits its eggs in the vicinity of water.

Breeding: Reaches breeding age at about 5 to 7 years old. Breeds in the spring. Females dig a hole and deposit an average of 2–4 eggs, sometimes as many as 8. Newly hatched babies are about one inch in length and weigh about 4 grams.

Natural History: These common turtles can be found in any aquatic habitat in the state, including tiny farm ponds or tributaries narrow enough for a person to step across. They even can exist in waters that are heavily polluted. They will feed on some plant material but are mainly carnivorous and will eat virtually anything they can swallow. Fish, frogs, tadpoles, small mammals, baby ducks, crayfish, and carrion are all listed as food items. The ferociousness of a captured snapping turtle is legendary and their sharp, powerful jaws can inflict a serious wound. When cornered on land they will face an enemy and extend the long neck in a lunging strike and so energetic that it may cause the entire turtle to move forward several inches. By contrast they rarely bite when under the water.

Natural History: Nocturnal and crepuscular and completely aquatic in habits. Unlike most aquatic turtles, Common Musk Turtle rarely basks, but when it does it may climb several feet up into branches that overhang the water. Since they seldom leave the water, the carapace is often covered with a thick growth of algae. Their name comes from the presence of musk-producing glands that emit an unpleas-ant odor when the turtles are handled. This musk also accounts for their other common name "Stinkpot." They are an omnivorous species that feeds on a variety of aquatic plant and animal matter. Like many turtles, the Eastern Musk Turtle is a long-lived species and a captive zoo specimen lived for 55 years. The plastron (lower shell) of this turtle has a single hinge.

Natural History: Although they are very aquatic turtles, Mud Turtles sometimes embark on overland treks, presumably to find new habitats or seek a mate. These are the only *aquatic* turtles in New York that have a double-hinged plastron, a characteristic that is rare in North American turtles. Their diet is omnivorous. A variety of aquatic plants are eaten and animal foods include crustaceans, aquatic insects, mollusks, amphibians, and carrion. Locates food by "bottom walking" when in water, but may also feed on land near the waters edge. They can remain under water for up to twenty minutes. These small turtles have been known to live up to 40 years and perhaps can survive even longer. This is one of New York's rarest turtles and they are regarded as an Endangered Species by NYSDEC.

Class - **Chelonia** (turtles)

Order - **Cryptodira** (straightneck turtles)

Family - **Emydidae** (sliders and box turtles)

Pond Slider *Trachemys scripta*	**Diamondback Terrapin** *Malaclemys terrapin*	**Painted Turtle** *Chrysemys picta*

Size: 6–8 inches.  Presumed range in New York	**Size:** 6–9 inches.  Presumed range in New York	**Size:** 4–6 inches.  Presumed range in New York
Abundance: Fairly common.	**Abundance:** Uncommon.	**Abundance:** Very common.
Variation: Males smaller with longer claws on the front feet.	**Variation:** Male is smaller. 7 subspecies, only one in New York.	**Variation:** There are 2 subspecies in New York. Eastern and Midland.

Habitat: Most common in large bodies of water but can be found in any aquatic habitat in the state except for very small streams.

Habitat: Coastal marshes. Uses both salt and brackish water marsh, estuaries, and intercoastal areas between barrier islands and mainland.

Habitat: Avoids fast-flowing streams in favor of still or slow-moving waters. Common in swamps, marshes, ponds, and lakes throughout its range.

Breeding: Females leave the safety of the water and crawl hundreds of yards to upland areas to deposit their eggs in an underground nest chamber dug with the hind legs. Large females may lay 20 eggs, younger females lay fewer.

Breeding: Nests on barrier islands well above the high tide mark. Up to 15 eggs are laid in an undergroud chamber. As with many turtles and also crocodilians, the ambient temparture in the nest determines the sex of the young.

Breeding: Females lay 10–15 eggs within a flask-shaped underground nest chamber dug with the turtles hind legs. Egg laying occurs from late May to early July. Eggs hatch in about 10 weeks. Hatchlings are the size of a quarter.

Natural History: Highly aquatic but sometimes seen far from water. Omnivorous. Eats a variety of water plants as well as mollusks, minnows, dead fish, aquatic insects, crustaceans, etc. Young are more carnivorous, while mature turtles will consume more plants. Old specimens tend to darken with age and very old specimens can be nearly all black (see inset). These are hardy turtles that will emerge from the mud to bask on logs on warm, sunny days throughout the winter. There are three subspecies of slider turtles in America, two of which, the **Red-eared Slider** (subspecies *elegans*) and **Yellow-bellied Slider** (subspecies *scripta),* are found in New York. For decades baby Pond Sliders were sold in pet stores across America with many turtles being released into the wild. All New York populations are apparently introduced.

Natural History: The Diamondback Terrapin was once heavily hunted for food, and they are still regarded as a delicacy by some New Yorkers. Prior to 1990 unregulated harvest of Terrapins had dramatically reduced populations in New York. Today harvest requires a license and is strictly regulated. They still face threats from pollution, loss of habitat, and human-induced hazards such as crab traps. This is the only North American turtle species that is endemic to brackish water environments and they may also be seen in salt water on occasion (note the barnacles attached to the shell of the specimen shown above). Diamondback Terrapins range along the eastern coastline of America from Massachussets to Texas and a total of seven subspecies are recognized. New York's subspecies is the Northern Diamonback Terrapin (*M. t. terrapin*).

Natural History: The Painted Turtles are among the most common and widespread of the Emydidae turtles in America. There are three subspecies recognized in North America and they range from the Atlantic coast well into the Great Plains. The races that are native to New York are the Midland Painted Turtle (*C. p. marginata*), and the Eastern Painted Turtle (*C. p. picta*) Like other members of their family they spend a great deal of time basking on floating logs and they are quick to slide into the water if approached too closely. They are omnivorous turtles that eat a very wide array of plant and animal foods as well as carrion such as fish heads and entrails discarded by fishermen. Hatchlings grow rapidly and can double in size their first year. Growth slows with size and age. Longevity in the wild may be as much as forty years.

Class - **Chelonia** (turtles)

Order - **Cryptodira** (straightneck turtles)

Family - **Emydidae** (sliders and box turtles)

Blanding's Turtle *Emydoidea blandingii*	**Common Map Turtle** *Graptemys geographica*	**Eastern Redbelly Turtle** *Pseudemys rubriventris*

Size: Maximum of 11 inches. Average of 5 to 7 inches.	Presumed range in New York 	**Size:** Males up to 6.5 inches. Females reach 11 inches.	Presumed range in New York 	**Size:** Averages 10 to 12 inches. Maximum of 15.75 inches.	Presumed range in New York 
Abundance: Uncommon.		**Abundance:** Fairly common.		**Abundance:** Uncommon.	

Variation: Amount of light, irregular spots, and lines on carapace is variable. Some individual have spots significantly faded or no spots at all. | **Variation:** In mature adults, females are larger and have larger heads. Hatchlings are miniature replicas of the adult but more vivid in color and pattern. | **Variation:** Highly variable. Old males may be reddish brown. Nearly solid black individuals also occur. Most show some red on the carapace.

Habitat: In Ohio the habitat is marshes and wetlands along the margins of Lake Erie. Also uses wet meadows and is commonly seen on land. | **Habitat:** Primarily found in larger rivers and lakes, but also found in smaller tributaries near their confluence with larger streams. | **Habitat:** Rivers, lakes, ponds, and marshes. Mainly a freshwater species but does use brackish estuaries. Needs basking sites and soft substrate.

Breeding: 10 to 15 eggs are laid by the female in an underground nest chamber that she digs at night. Only one clutch per year is produced. | **Breeding:** Breeds in early spring and eggs are laid in June. Most egg laying occurs in the morning. The average clutch size is about 10 eggs. | **Breeding:** 10 to 12 eggs are laid in an underground nest chamber dug by the female. Most nesting is in June and multiple clutches have been recorded.

Natural History: The oldest known wild specimen of Blanding's Turtle was calculated to be 77 years old. Crayfish are reported to be the favorite food item. Among aquatic foods listed are insects, fish, fish eggs, and frogs along with algae. On land they will eat earthworms, slugs, insect larva, leaves, grasses, and berries. It is thought that the Blanding's Turtle is closely related to the more terrestrial Box Turtle. Like the Box Turtle the Blanding's does posses a hinged plastron. Like their cousin the Box Turtle, the greatest threat to adult Blanding's Turtles is the automobile. Their nests are raided by a variety of predators including foxes, Opossums, Raccoons, and especially Striped Skunks. The epicenter of the range is in the Great Lakes region. Threatened. | **Natural History:** Diurnal and crepuscular in activity. These turtles are fond of basking on logs but are very wary and will disappear into the water if approached. Food items include, crustaceans, fish, insects, and aquatic plants. They also eat mollusks and the thick, crushing surface of the jaws suggests that small mussels may be an important element in the diet. Most of this turtles relatives in the genus *Graptemys* are southern animals. The Common Map Turtle is one of the more widely distributed of the map turtles and can be found from the Great Lakes southward into Arkansas and Alabama. In New York they can be near both Great Lakes and in the larger rivers such as the Hudson and St. Lawrence Rivers. They have a lifespan in the wild of at least twenty years. | **Natural History:** The Eastern Redbelly Turtle is found mainly in the Lower Atlantic Coastal Plain from Massachusetts southward to North Carolina. In New York isolated populations exist well inland. These inland locations probably represent introductions by man rather than naturally occuring populations. As is the case with most other turtles in the family Emydidae, the Eastern Redbelly Turtle is primarily diurnal in habits. Adults feed on a variety of aquatic plants, but young turtles are omnivorous and cat a variety of aquatic animals including both invertebrates and small vertebrate prey. This age-related change in dietary habits is explained by the fact that rapidly growing young turtles benefit from the added protein obtained by eating animals.

Class - **Chelonia** (turtles)

Order - **Cryptodira** (straightneck turtles)

Family - **Emydidae** (sliders and box turtles)

Bog Turtle *Clemmys mulhenbergii*	**Spotted Turtle** *Clemmys guttata*	**Wood Turtle** *Clemmys insculpta*

Bog Turtle
Clemmys mulhenbergii

Size: Up to 4.5 inches.

Abundance: Rare.

Variation: Males average larger than females.

Presumed range in New York

Habitat: Bogs, fens, wet meadows, and marshes, swamps, and smaller creeks with slow-moving waters and soft, mucky bottoms.

Breeding: Eggs are often laid in the top of a grass tussock exposed to sunlight amid wetland habitats. 3 eggs is average with a high of 6. Young turtles that later in the fall may overwinter in the nest chamber.

Natural History: New York's smallest turtle species, and perhaps one of its most threatened. Found only in the eastern United States surviving populations are today are fragmented and widely disjunct. Loss of wetland habitat and over collecting by the pet trade are two of the major reasons for the decline of the species. Adequate habitat must have some direct sunlight for basking and incubating eggs and invasive plants like the widespread alien reed *Phragmites* can overwhelm suitable habitat and render it useless to the turtles. Today the Bog Turtle is protected throughout its range, including in New York. These little turtles are omnivores and will eat insects and other invertebrates as well as vegetation. Unusual food items include berries and seeds. Sexual maturity is reach at about 5 years and longevity is at least 23 years. An Endangered Species in New York.

Spotted Turtle
Clemmys guttata

Size: 4.5 inches.

Abundance: Uncommon.

Variation: Spots fade with age. Old turtles may be solid black.

Presumed range in New York

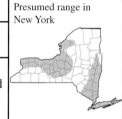

Habitat: Prefers sluggish waters. In inhabits lakes, marshes, swamps, and slow-moving rivers. Sometimes found in wet meadows or wet woods.

Breeding: Mating takes place in early spring through early summer with eggs being laid from May to July. Female digs a flask-shaped hole and deposits from 1 to 8 eggs. Two clutches per year is not uncommon.

Natural History: These handsome little turtles range throughout the Atlantic slope of the eastern United States from southern Maine to northern Florida. A disjunct population is found throughout the Great Lakes region. They are sometimes captured as pets, but collecting of this species is ill-advised as many populations are in decline. Loss of habitat and pollution are blamed for the loss of this turtle in many regions, including in New York where they were once much more common. Modern highways create impassible barriers that kill incredibly high numbers of turtles. The Spotted Turtle is both an omnivore and a scavenger. Aquatic grasses and algea make up the vegetarian diet with insects, crustaceans, snails, amphibian larva, and fish listed as food items. Opportunistic feeding on carrrion is also reported. A species of Special Concern in New York.

Wood Turtle
Clemmys insculpta

Size: Up to 9.5 inches.

Abundance: Uncommon.

Variation: No variation in New York specimens.

Presumed range in New York

Habitat: As its name implies this is a woodland species. Usually closely associated with streams. Also swamps, bogs, and nearby terrestrial habitats.

Breeding: Nest site is an underground chamber excavated by the female using her hind feet in the manner common to all turtles. One clutch per year of up to 18 eggs but often less than .25 that number. Nest site requires ample sun.

Natural History: One of the most northerly ranging turtles in the Emydidae family. Individuals in the northernmost part of their range may spend over half the year in hibernation. As is the case with other aquatic turtles, hibernation takes place underwater. They are primarily diurnal in habits but when excavating a nest females are known to dig well into the night. Wood Turtles are omnivores will consume plants, animals, and fungi. Like the other turtles on this page the Wood Turtle is in decline. Once again the triple threat of habitat loss, pollution, and over collecting for the pet trade is blamed for this decline. Most turtles mature slowly and have rather low reproductive rates, leaving them especially vulnerable to the rapid changes being wrought on their environment by humans. Listed as a Species of Concern by NYSDEC.

Class - **Chelonia** (turtles)

Order - **Cryptodira** (straightneck turtles)

Family - **Emydidae** (sliders and box turtles)	Family - **Trionychidae** (softshells)

Box Turtle
Terrapene carolina

Spiny Softshell
Apalone spinifera

Size: Averages 4 to 6 inches in length. Record length just under 8 inches.

Abundance: Quite common in much of the eastern United States but is less common in New York.

Variation: There are four subspecies. Only the eastern race occurs in New York. Highly variable. The color and pattern on each specimen is as individual as a fingerprint. Males have a concave plastron, tend to be larger than females.

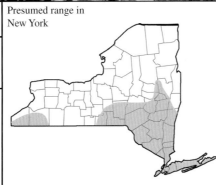
Presumed range in New York

Habitat: Occupies a wide variety of habitats from open fields to deep woods. Found in both upland and lowlands, but is most common in damp woods, edge areas near creeks and streams, and wooded bottom lands.

Breeding: Breeding takes place in spring with egg deposition in summer. 2 or 3 eggs is common. Eggs hatch in late fall and young may overwinter in their underground nest before emerging the following spring. Newly hatched babies do not possess the hinged plastron and are thus unable to tightly close themselves within their shell.

Natural History: Box Turtles are primarily diurnal and are most active in the morning and the late afternoon. They sometimes burrow into the mud during hot weather, and overwinter by burrowing themselves into loose soil or deep leaf litter. The hibernation burrow is quite shallow, only a few inches deep. Studies have shown that they are tolerant of some freezing, a trait that enables survival of such a shallow hibernator. Still, hibernation is a significant source of mortality among adults. Their diet is omnivorous and they consume berries, fruits, and mushrooms as well as a wide variety of insect prey and other invertebrates. Earthworms and snails are a favorite animal food and blackberries and mulberries are among the favorite plant foods. Box Turtles are known for their longevity and reports of their living up to a century are common but difficult to verify. Some researchers report a lifespan of 80 years, while others say 30 to 40 years is probably the average in the wild. When threatened they will retract the head and feet into the shell which can then close tightly by means of hinges on the front and back of the plastron. The muscles that close the shell are remarkably strong and efforts to pry open the shell of a frightened Box Turtle are futile. They are tough little turtles that can sometimes survive serious injury such as the shell being cracked open by a glancing blow from an automobile tire. Turtles with badly deformed but completely healed shells are sometimes found. In regions where wildfires are common many are seen with shells that are completely scarred by fire. Habitat degradation is a much more imminent threat, and automobiles take a fearful toll throughout their range each summer.

Size: Maximum of 18 inches.

Abundance: Uncommon in New York.

Variation: Female larger.

Presumed range in New York

Habitat: Occurs in both large and small streams and in impoundments. May also be found in farm ponds in some areas. Shows a preference for habitats with sandy substrates to facilitate burying the body with only the head exposed. Will frequent sandbars in larger streams.

Breeding: A dozen or more eggs are laid between May and August (most in June or July). Nests are often on sandbars of creeks or rivers.

Natural History: Crayfish, fish, and insects are the primary food items, but dead fish and other carrion can be an important food item, especially in lakes where fishing is common. Spiny Softshells are active from spring into early fall New York. They hunt both by ambush and by active pursuit. When immobile they can remain under water or several hours. Because of the soft, permeable shells and skin, softshells are more susceptible to dehydration than other turtle species and thus they seldom stray far from water. These turtles are harvested as food in many parts of their range, and much of this harvest is to date unregulated. Some believe this practice may pose a long-term threat to the species. Their long and flexible neck makes handling without being bitten difficult.

THE REPTILES
OF NEW YORK

PART 1: LIZARDS

CHAPTER 6
THE REPTILES OF NEW YORK

Note: The arrangement below is a reflection of how the orders and families of Reptiles appear in this book and many not be an accurate description of the phylogentic relationship of the reptiles.

— THE ORDERS AND FAMILIES
OF NEW YORK REPTILES —

Class - **Reptilia** (reptiles)

Order - **Squamata** (lizards and snakes)
Suborder - **Lacertilia** (lizards)

Family	**Phrynosomatidae** (spiny lizards)
Family	**Scincidae** (skinks)

Suborder - **Serpentes** (snakes)

Family	**Colubridae** (typical harmless snakes)
Family	**Dipsadidae** (rear-fanged snakes)
Family	**Natricidae** (harmless live-bearers)
Family	**Crotalidae** (pit vipers)

Class - **Reptilia** (reptiles)

Order - **Squamata** (lizards and snakes)

Family - **Phrynosomatidae** (spiny lizards)

Family - **Scincidae** (skinks)

Fence Lizard *Sceloporus undulatus*	**Five-lined Skink** *Plestiodon fasciatus*	**Coal Skink** *Plestiodon anthracinus*

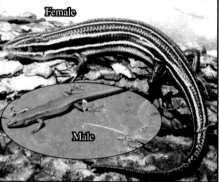

Size: Up to 7.25 inches.

Presumed range in New York

Abundance: Rare in New York.

Variation: Males have blue patches on the throat and belly.

Size: 4 to 6 inches.

Presumed range in New York

Abundance: Uncommon.

Variation: Young with pale yellow stripes and bright blue tails.

Size: 5 to 7 inches.

Presumed range in New York

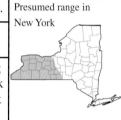

Abundance: Uncommon.

Variation: Young darker on the back with blue or black tail.

Habitat: Dry, upland woods. Found in both pure deciduous woods and in pine-dominated woodlands. Dry rocky hillsides and ridgetops are favored.

Habitat: Most common in damp woodlands but also found in swamps and in drier upland areas. The presence of sunlite places is important for micro-habitat.

Habitat: Coal Skinks inhabit the forest floor in damp woodlands. They are frequently found near creeks or springs. Also wooded hillsides with sunlite areas.

Breeding: Egg layer. Deposits 6 to 15 eggs in rotted logs, stumps, etc. Two clutches per year are common in the southern portions of the range.

Breeding: Eggs (6 to 12) are laid in May or early June in rotted logs, stumps, sawdust, mulch, or other moisture-retaining material. Female may remain with eggs.

Breeding: From 6 to 12 eggs are laid under rocks, logs, or other sheltering structures. Females will remain with and guard the eggs until hatching.

Natural History: A woodland species, the Eastern Fence Lizard spends much of its time on tree trunks and fallen logs. Its color and pattern perfectly matches the bark of most trees within its range. This is a very common lizard in much of the eastern United States. In New York they are restricted to the extreme southeastern tip of the state. They are quite arboreal in habits and will regularly climb trees to great heights. Food is insects, spiders, etc. Both sexes are often seen perched on rocks, logs, or stumps in wooded areas. Breeding males are especially conspicuous as they attempt to attract females by sitting atop rocks or stumps and methodically raising and lowering their body to show off the bright blue patches on the undersides. This is the only representative of its family in the northeastern United States, but the spiny lizard family is a large and diverse group in the deserts and grasslands of America's arid southwest.

Natural History: The young of this species are strikingly colored with bright blue tails and they sometimes are mistaken by laypeople as being another species going by the name "Blue-tailed Skink." These lizards are fond of sunning on decks, porches, sidewalks, and patios of homes in rural areas. They can often be found in suburban environments as well, particularly older neighborhoods with abundant large trees and shrubbery. They feed on a wide variety of insects, spiders, and arthropods and they are a useful species in controlling invertebrate pests around the home. Unfortunately they are highly vulnerable to pesticides and are easily killed by exterminators who commonly spray around the foundation of houses. These lizards do a much safer job of controlling insects and spiders around the outside of the home and exterminators should be encouraged to avoid spraying outside foundations and yards. Adult males have reddish heads.

Natural History: Termites, ant larva and pupae, and earthworms are listed as known food items. Probably feeds on a wide variety of small insects and other tiny invertebrates encountered among leaf litter on the forest floor. As with all lizards found in New York, they are diurnal. They shelter at night beneath logs, stones, or loose bark on dead snags, stumps, etc. The range of the Coal Skink today is patchy and discontinuous throughout the eastern United States. It appears that remaining populations are remnants of what was once a much larger contiguous range that encompassed much of the Eastern Temperate Forest Level I Ecoregion. Large contiguous populations still exist in parts of the southern United States but populations in the northeastern United States are highly fragmented. The southern populations are recognized as a seperate subspecies. New York populations are the northern subspecies (*P. a. anthracinus*).

THE REPTILES OF NEW YORK

PART 2: SNAKES

Class - **Reptilia** (reptiles)

Order - **Squamata** (lizards and snakes)

Family - **Colubridae** (typical harmless snakes)

Racer *Coluber constrictor*	**Midland Rat Snake** *Pantherophis spiloides*	**Milk Snake** *Lampropeltis triangulum*

Racer		**Midland Rat Snake**		**Milk Snake**	
Size: 4 to 6 feet. **Abundance:** Common. **Variation:** Juveniles are blotched (see inset photo).	 Presumed range in New York	**Size:** Up to 7 feet. **Abundance:** Fairly common. **Variation:** Young are light gray with dark blotches (see inset photo).	 Presumed range in New York	**Size:** Up to 4 feet. **Abundance:** Common. **Variation:** Young have reddish dorsal blotches.	 Presumed range in New York

Habitat: Black Racers are habitat generalists. They favor dry upland woods and overgrown fields and like many predators they are most common in edge areas where two habitats meet.	**Habitat:** Found in woodland and regenerative areas. They are least common in areas of intensive agriculture or urbanized areas, but they can persists in urban regions if there is cover and large trees.	**Habitat:** Eastern Milk Snakes are habitat generalists. They may be found in swamps, marshes, and bogs as well as in drier habitats like rocky hillsides. Upland woods may be their favorite habitat.
Breeding: Females lay from 5 to 20 eggs in rotted logs, humus, or frequently in sawdust piles around old sawmills. Eggs are laid in early summer and hatch in about two months. Like most egg layers, the Black Racer reproduces annually.	**Breeding:** An egg layer that breeds in the spring and lays up to 20 eggs. Eggs are laid in old woodpecker holes or hollow limbs above ground or on the ground in rotted stumps, beneath logs, or any sheltered place where some form of humus is present to prevent dessication.	**Breeding:** Egg layer. Eggs are deposited in rotten logs, stumps, or beneath a flat rock. Lays from 6 to 24 eggs. Hatchlings are about 8 or 9 inches in length and resemble adults but are much brighter in color. Saddles may be bright red with light areas in between whitish.
Natural History: Racers are alert, active snakes that relentlessly prowl in search of almost any type of animal prey that can be swallowed. They will eat insects, amphibians, lizards, other snakes (including the young of venomous species), nestling birds, eggs, and small mammals. They are also adept at catching fish trapped in drying pools of streams and swamps. Unlike many snake species, the Racer is a diurnal animal and may be active even during the heat of the day in mid-summer. When threatened, these snakes can use their speed to literally disappear into thick cover. When hard pressed out in the open they will climb into bushes or shrubs to escape. If captured they will bite viciously and spray the attacker with foul-smelling musk.	**Natural History:** This is the most arboreal snake species in New York and adults spend a great deal of time in trees. They often choose a regular den site in old woodpecker holes or hollows of trees and may be seen sunning with the forepart of the body emerged from a hole. Excellent climbers, they can ascend straight up a tree trunk using only the bark to gain a purchase with their belly scales. They will climb to great heights in search of bird nests. In addition to baby birds and eggs they will also eat rodents, squirrels, and other small mammals up to the size of a rabbit. They are fond of derelict buildings and abandoned barns where they search for rodents. They sometimes enter older houses that are still inhabited. Though they may bite if handled, they are harmless to humans.	**Natural History:** The name comes from the habit these snakes have of entering stock barns in search of mice. Early settlers erroneously thought the snakes were there to suckle from the milk cow (that every pioneer family kept on the farm). These snakes eat many lizards and will also consume other, smaller snakes. Reptile eggs may also be eaten along with amphibians and small mammals like mice. Milk Snakes enjoy a resistance to snake venom and baby copperheads or rattlesnakes may be eaten by large adults. Although they are presumed to occur statewide, documentation is missing from a few areas of the state, especially in the Adirondacks. Milk Snake may become nocturnal during warm summer months and will remain hidden during the day.

Class - **Reptilia** (reptiles)		
Order - **Squamata** (lizards and snakes)		
Family - **Colubridae**	Family - **Dipsadidae** (rear-fanged snakes)	

Smooth Green Snake *Opheodrys vernalis*	Ringneck Snake *Diadophis punctatus*	Wormsnake *Carphophis amoenus*

Size: Average 2–3 feet. Record 3 feet 11 inches.  Presumed range in New York	**Size:** Average about 14 inches. Maximum 2 feet.  Presumed range in New York	**Size:** 8 to 11 inches. Record length 13.5 inches.  Presumed range in New York
Abundance: Common.	**Abundance:** Very common.	**Abundance:** Rare in New York.
Variation: None.	**Variation:** None.	**Variation:** None.

Habitat: Open fields, pastures, meadows, and edges of lakes, ponds, or marshes. Generally a snake of open habitats but may be found in open woods.	**Habitat:** A woodland species that lives in rotted logs, stumps, and beneath rocks and leaf litter on the forest floor. Often seen in rural lawns in wooded areas.	**Habitat:** Found in a variety of habitats, but mostly in woodlands. Like other small terrestrial snakes its micro-habitat is beneath the leaf litter, logs, rocks, etc.
Breeding: Clutch size is relatively small and may be as few as 3 or 4 eggs or as high as a dozen. Egg laying has been reported from June to August.	**Breeding:** Lays up to a dozen eggs, usually fewer in rotted logs or other moisture retaining places. Young are about five inches long at hatching.	**Breeding:** From 1 to 12 eggs are laid in late June or July and hatch in two or three months. Hatchlings are only about three inches in length.

Natural History: The Smooth Green Snake often goes by the common name "Grass Snake" or "Green Grass Snake." An appropriate moniker as they favor open fields and grassy areas and sometimes appear in rural lawns. These small snakes eat a variety of invertebrate prey including slugs, spiders, millipedes, crickets, grasshoppers, and caterpillars, to name a few. This diet makes them exceptionally vulnerable to insecticides and widespread applications of chemicals on agricultural fields or around the home may pose a serious threat to this handsome little snake. Unlike the larger Rough Green Snake of the southern United States that climbs into bushes and small trees, the Smooth Green Snake tends to stay close to the ground. Although there are a few areas of the state where this species has not been documented it is presumed to occur statewide. Despite being widespread, they are easily overlooked as they are nearly invisible in tall, green grass.

Natural History: With its uniformly charcoal gray body and bright yellow ring around the neck, the Ringneck Snake is one of the most recognizable snakes in New York. In some areas it is also one of the most abundant snake species in the state. Especially in the Appalachian Plateau Province. These small snakes are often uncovered by humans beneath boards, stones, leaves, or other debris. The distinctive yellow or cream-colored collar around the neck readily identifies them, and even those unfamiliar with reptiles have no trouble recognizing this species. They feed mostly on soft-bodied insects and other invertebrates. Earthworms are a favorite food. When threatened they will often hold aloft the tightly curled-up tip of the underside of their bright yellow tail to distract a predator. This defense mechanism is probably designed to direct an attacker's attention away from the vulnerable head to the less vulnerable tail. They will also curl the lip and give an impression of a snarl, but rarely bite.

Natural History: A confirmed burrower that lives under leaf litter, logs, rocks, and even man-made debris such as old boards, discarded shingles, etc. Feeds on tiny soft-bodied invertebrates such as insect larva, termites, and earthworms. The aptly named worm snakes do in fact resemble earthworms. Their tiny, conical head and smooth glossy scales help to facilitate burrowing through tiny tunnels created by earthworms, termites, or insect larva. These snakes are often turned up in backyards by people gardening, raking leaves, or doing other types of yard work. Like the ringneck snakes, worm snakes possess tiny grooved teeth in the rear of the jaw that serve to introduce a mild venom into the bodies of prey. These tiny teeth are too small to penetrate human skin and these snakes are thus completely harmless to man. Their range in New York is restricted to the extreme southern tip of the state. However, they are quite common in the southeastern United States.

Class - **Reptilia** (reptiles)

Order - **Squamata** (lizards and snakes)

Family - **Dipsadidae** (rear-fanged snakes)	Family - **Natricidae** (harmless live-bearers)

Eastern Hognose Snake
Heterodon platirhinos

Hooding

Presumed range in New York

Northern Water Snake
Nerodia sipedon

Size: Average about 3.5 feet. Record is 59 inches.

Abundance: Common.

Presumed range in New York

Size: Average about 2.5 to 3 feet. Record is 50 inches.

Abundance: Can be fairly common in areas of suitable habitat.

Variation: Higly variable. See photos above for some common color morphs.

Habitat: Hognose Snakes are most common in habitats with sandy soils which facilitate easy burrowing. They tend to be more common in sandy creek bottoms and river valleys. They prefer areas with moist soils but can also be found in upland woods and fields.

Breeding: Hognose Snakes breed in early spring and lay up to two dozen eggs. Nests are probably in an underground chamber in sandy soil. Young snakes are about eight inches in length and always have a spotted pattern. Babies are grayish brown with well-defined dark gray or black blotches.

Natural History: The Eastern Hognose Snake is famous for the elaborate performance it puts on when threatened. First, they will spread the neck like a cobra (hence the nickname "Spreading Adder"), and with the mouth wide open they will strike repeatedly. They always intentionally miss with the strike and never bite even when picked up and handled. The initial "cobra display" is always accompanied by loud hissing. When their complicated bluff fails to deter the threat they will roll onto their backs, stick out their tongues, and give a convincing impression of being dead. Their primary food is frogs and toads. They have enlarged teeth in the rear of the upper jaw and the saliva of these snakes is mildly toxic, but is not considered to be a threat to humans. The food of these snake is almost entirely toads and frogs, making them one of the more specialized feeders among New York's snakes. Salamanders are reported to have been found in the stomachs of a few individuals as well. Anecdotal evidence suggests theses snakes may be declining. Their habit of feeding on toads and frogs almost exclusively may make them vulnerable to insecticides, as frog and toads are primarily insect eaters. To the uninformed or "snake phobic" persons, an Eastern Hognose Snake performing its "cobra" mimicry can be a frigthening sight. To early pioneers this snake must have seemed a real threat. The extent to which it has been misunderstood is evidenced in the array of ominous nicknames which has been assigned this species, such as "Hissing Viper," "Hognose Viper," and "Puff Adder."

Variation: Ranges from brown, tan, or reddish brown to gray-brown. Almost always exhibits a pattern of darker bands across the back that contrasts with the lighter color between the bands.

Habitat: Although aquatic animals they do sometimes wander away from water. They are fond of small farm ponds or small streams as habitat, but they can also be found in large lakes and in swamps and marshes.

Breeding: Live-born young can number two or three dozen and the largest females may produce nearly 100 babies.

Natural History: Northern Water Snakes adapt well to man-made environments like large lake impoundments where they can thrive in the rip-rap of dams and levees. Frogs and fish are the two favorite food items for these snakes. Around man-made impoundments they can become very numerous near boat docks and fishing areas where they scavenge on dead or dying fish and fish heads left behind by fishermen. Like most other water snake species, they are fond of basking in the sun atop debris and limbs overhanging water. They are commonly confused with the venomous Cottonmouth, even though the Cottonmouth does not occur in New York.

Class - **Reptilia** (reptiles)
Order - **Squamata** (lizards and snakes)
Family - **Natricidae** (harmless live-bearers)

Queen Snake *Regina septemvittata*	**Redbelly Snake** *Storeria occipitomaculata*	**Brown Snake** *Storeria dekayi*

Size: 2 feet is average with a maximum of 3 feet.

Abundance: Uncommon.

Variation: No variation.

Presumed range in New York

Size: 10 to 12 inches is average. Record 16 inches.

Abundance: Common.

Variation: Not variable.

Presumed range in New York

Size: Average about 12 inches. Record 19 inches.

Abundance: Very common.

Variation: Not variable.

Presumed range in New York

Habitat: Found mostly in limestone creeks but also in lakes and large rivers. Most common in creeks with flat stones for hiding beneath.

Habitat: Mostly found in wooded areas, in both lowland and uplands. They can also be found in fields around the edges of woods.

Habitat: Woodlands, grassy fields, and wetlands. May sometimes be found even in urban areas, especially vacant lots littered with old boards or scrap tin.

Breeding: The Queen Snake is a live-bearer that will produce up to a dozen young per litter, a relatively small number for an aquatic snake. Young are typically born in late summer/early fall.

Breeding: Live-bearer. Litters number from 5 to 15. Newborn babies are only about three inches in length and no bigger around than a matchstick.

Breeding: Gives birth to 5 to 20 young (rarely more, as many as 40). Baby snakes are about three inches long with the girth of a toothpick.

Natural History: The Queen Snake is a specialized feeder that preys almost exclusively on recently molted, soft-bodied crayfish. As a result their distribution is limited to areas where this common crustacean is abundant. Other known food items include dragonfly nymps, small fish, amphibians, and snails, but by far the bulk of their diet is crayfish. These snakes are often found hiding beneath flat stones in limestone creeks throughout their range. Like other water snakes they may be seen basking from limbs and branches overhanging water. A habit which has lead to the nickname "Willow Snake" in some parts of their range. This species occurs in New York only in the western end of the state. In ideal habitats (limestone creeks with abundant crayfish), this can be a very common snake. Baby Snakes are about seven inches in length.

Natural History: Redbelly Snakes usually remain hidden by day beneath rocks, logs, etc., and emerge at night to hunt insects and small soft-bodied invertebrates such as earthworms, slugs, beetle larva, isopods, etc. These snakes sometimes exhibit a peculiar behavior when threatened. If voiding of feces and musk fails to discourage a handler, they will curl their upper lip in a strange expression of apparent ferocity. It is a purely fallacious display however as their tiny teeth could never penetrate human skin. There are three subspecies of Redbelly Snake in America. New York's is the Northern Redbelly Snake (subspecies *occipitomaculata*). The Redbelly Snake is rarely seen due to mainly to its secretive habits. They are sometimes uncovered by people doing yard work in spring and summer months, and they can be found beneath stones and logs in wooded regions.

Natural History: This diminutive snake is often found in vacant lots of large cities and towns, where it hides beneath boards, trash, even small pieces of cardboard. It feeds primarily on earthworms and slugs, but also reportedly eats insects, amphibians eggs, and tiny fishes. Brown Snakes are known to hibernate communally, an odd behavior for a tiny snake that should have no trouble finding adequate crevices in which to spend the colder months. These snakes are sometimes called "Dekay's Snake," in honor of an early American naturalist. Brown Snakes can be very common snakes in some areas of New York, while they may be completely absent in other areas. They have probably fared better than most other New York snakes in adapting to the changes man has brought to the original habitats of the state.

Class - **Reptilia** (reptiles)

Order - **Squamata** (snakes and lizards)

Suborder - **Serpentes** (snakes)

Family - **Natricinae** (live-bearers)

Shorthead Garter Snake *Thamnophis brachystoma*	**Ribbon Snake** *Thamnophis sauritus*	**Eastern Garter Snake** *Thamnophis sirtalis*

Size: Averages 14 to 18 inches with a maximum recorded length of 23 inches.

Abundance: Uncommon.

Presumed range in New York

Size: Averages about 18 to 28 inches. Record length is 38 inches.

Abundance: Common.

Presumed range in New York

Size: Averages 2 feet with a maximum recorded length of 51 inches.

Abundance: Very common.

Presumed range in New York

Variation: For all practical purposes this species shows no real variation among individuals. Lateral stripes may vary a little from whitish to yellow.

Variation: A total of three subspecies are found in the eastern United States. Two, the Eastern Ribbon Snake and the Northern Ribbon Snake, occur in New York.

Variation: There are seven subspecies of this widespread snake in the United States. The eastern subspecies (*T. s. sirtalis*) is the only one in New York.

Habitat: Often associates with streamside habitats. Overgrown fields, meadows, fence rows, rock piles, and sedge-dominated habitats are listed as haunts.

Habitat: Occupies aquatic and semi-aquatic habitats from swamps and marshes to streams, stream edges, and mesic bottomland woodlands.

Habitat: A habitat generalist that favors pastures, fields, and rural yards. Can be seen almost anywhere, including vacant lots in urban areas.

Breeding: Like all garter snakes, this species is a live-bearer. Up to 14 young are born in late summer.

Breeding: 10 to 20 young is typical. Birthing occurs in late summer following breeding in the early spring.

Breeding: Garter Snakes are live-bearers that give birth to enormous litters of up to 60 babies.

Natural History: This is a small garter snake with an exceptionally small head. This unusual little garter snake has a very small range, being found only in western New York and western Pennslyvania with a small population in northeastern Ohio. Their range is contained entirely within the Appalachian Plateaus Province. There is not much information available on the natural history of this species. They are reported to feed mainly on earthworms. Other listed food items include insects and small amphibians. Although they are uncommon in New York due to the rather restricted range in the state, they are reported by some authors to be quite common in areas where they are found (Allen 1992, Kruitbosch 2014).

Natural History: Ribbon Snakes are both diurnal and nocturnal in habits. They often climb into low shrubs and vines. They are alert snakes that hunt by both smell and with their excellent eyesight that is attuned to quick movements of fleeing prey. Food items include insects, frogs, minnows, crayfish, and tadpoles. Although these snakes are nearly always found near water, they tend to live near the edges of wetlands rather than within them. In many ways the ribbon snakes occupy a niche that is halfway between an aquatic and a terrestrial species. The Common Ribbon Snake (subspecies *sauritus*) is found in southeastern New York while the Northern Ribbon Snake (subspecies *septentrionalis*) can be found in northern and western New York.

Natural History: The Eastern Garter Snake is the one snake that everyone knows. They are one of the most common snakes in the eastern United States. They are non-specialized feeders that will eat insects, earthworms, frogs, toads, salamanders, fish, and rarely small mammals such as baby mice or voles. Their name is derived from their resemblance to the old fashioned "garters" that were used to hold up men's socks. The name has been widely familiarized to "Garden Snake" in many places. Still appropriate as they are often encountered in people's gardens. They are a ubiquitous species that may be found in both wilderness or urban regions. They range throughout the entire eastern United States from southern Florida to the maritme provinces in Canada.

Class - **Reptilia** (reptiles)
Order - **Squamata** (snakes and lizards)
Suborder - **Serpentes** (snakes)
Family - **Crotalidae** (pit vipers)

Copperhead *Agkistrodon contortrix*	**Timber Rattlesnake** *Crotalus horridus*	**Eastern Massasauga** *Sistrurus catenatus*
	 Light morph / Dark morph	

Size: Average adult size 2.5 to 3 feet. The record length is 58 inches. Presumed range in New York 	**Size:** Averages about 3 to 4 feet in New York. Record is 6 feet 2 inches. Presumed range in New York	**Size:** Average adult size for New York is about 2 feet. The record 39.5 inches. Presumed range in New York
Abundance: Uncommon.	**Abundance:** Rare.	**Abundance:** Very rare.
Variation: Colors between bands varies from tan, brown, or purplish to reddish brown. Bands are dark brown or grayish. Males are larger than females.	**Variation:** Two color morphs occur in New York. A yellowish phase and a much darker melanistic form. See photos above.	**Variation:** Two color morphs (light and dark) are known to occur, but there is no significant variation among New York populations.
Habitat: Copperheads are primarily woodland animals, but they do wander into overgrown fields and thickets where rodent prey is abundant. Edge areas and small woodland openings chocked with briers, saplings, and weeds are prime habitat.	**Habitat:** As their name implies Timber Rattlesnakes are forest animals. Within their woodland habitats they are most common in upland areas with rocky outcrops and talus slopes. They inhabit both mature forests and second growth woodlands, as well as forest edges.	**Habitat:** Wetlands primarily. Inhabits swamps, marshes, wooded floodplains. In New York there are only two disjunct populations remaining (Cicero Swamp WMA and Bergon-Byron Swamp). Wetlands or bogs with openings for sunlight to penetrate seems to be a requirement.
Breeding: Breeds in spring or in the fall. From 4 to 12 young are born in late August through September. The resources required to produce a litter by a live-bearing snake are considerable and can be quite stressful on the female. Thus many copperheads likely produce litters only ever other year.	**Breeding:** Timber Rattlesnakes typically breed in August and the females delay implantation of embryos until the following spring. The young snakes are then born in late summer or early fall, about a year after breeding. Females will produce young only every other year. Average litter is 6 to 12.	**Breeding:** Young are born in late July, August or September. 5 or 6 babies is common but can be as many as 14. Baby snakes are eight to ten inches in length and are miniature replicas of the adults except for possessing the bright yellow tail tip seen on some other baby crotalid snakes like the Copperhead.
Natural History: Copperheads are primarily nocturnal, especially during hotter months. In early spring and fall they may be seen abroad during the day. Young eat some invertebrates and young frogs, lizards, and small snakes. Larger snakes prey on small mammals (mice and voles) and the young of ground nesting birds. Insects are also taken. In areas of undisturbed habitat these can be fairly common snakes but they are secretive and discreet.	**Natural History:** This is one of the largest rattlesnake species in America and their bite is quite capable of killing a human. Fortunately they are peace-loving animals that only strike as a last resort. Timber Rattlesnake populations have declined significantly in many areas of their range, including in New York. Today they are absent from vast areas of their former range shown on the map above. They are today a protected species in New York.	**Natural History:** The name Massasauga comes from the Chippewa Indian name for a marshy area at the mouth of a river. This is New York's rarest snake species. They were probably once much more widespread in the state, but their populations throughout the United States have been in decline since European settlement. Surviving populations are often widely separated. Food items include rodents, amphibians, birds, crayfish, and insects.

THE AMPHIBIANS OF NEW YORK

PART 1: FROGS AND TOADS

CHAPTER 7
THE AMPHIBIANS OF NEW YORK

— THE ORDERS AND FAMILIES OF NEW YORK AMPHIBIANS —

Note: The arrangement below is a reflection of how the orders and families of amphibians appear in this book and may not be an accurate representation of the phylogentic relationship of the amphibians.

Class - **Amphibia** (amphibians)

Order - **Anura** (frogs and toads)

Family	**Ranidae** (true frogs)
Family	**Hylidae** (treefrogs)
Family	**Scaphiopodidae** (spadefoots)
Family	**Bufonidae** (true toads)

Order - **Caudata** (salamanders)

Family	**Ambystomatidae** (mole salamanders)
Family	**Salamandridae** (newts)
Family	**Plethodontidae** (lungless salamanders)
Family	**Cryptobranchidae** (giant salamanders)
Family	**Proteidae** (mudpuppies)

Class - **Amphibia** (amphibians)

Order - **Anura** (frogs and toads)

Family - **Ranidae** (true frogs)

Wood Frog *Lithobates sylvaticus*	Northern Leopard Frog *Lithobates pipiens*	Green Frog *Lithobates clamitans*

Wood Frog		Northern Leopard Frog		Green Frog	
Size: 2–3 inches. **Abundance:** Common. **Variation:** May vary from light tan to dark brown.	Presumed range in New York	**Size:** 3–4 inches. **Abundance:** Fairly common. **Variation:** Skin between spots varies from green to brown or tan.	Presumed range in New York	**Size:** 2–4 inches. **Abundance:** Very common. **Variation:** Color varies from brownish to greenish.	Presumed range in New York

Habitat: This is a forest species that is most common in mountainous regions. It prefers mesic woods near streams. Found statewide in New York.

Breeding: Breeds in winter. This is one of the earliest breeding frogs in New York and they may breed as early as February. Eggs are laid in ephemeral pools and small fishless bodies of water.

Natural History: Despite the fact that this is the most widespread frog species in America, there are no subspecies and it shows little variation. Wood frogs from Canada and Alaska are identical to those found northern Alabama or northern Georgia. This is one of the most cold-tolerant frog species in America and it ranges farther to the north than any of its kin. They can be frozen solid and recover without harm when thawed. Food is a variety of small invertebrates. Like many frogs, Wood Frogs migrate overland during periods of heavy rainfall. They can be commonly seen on roadways at night during the breeding season. New York Herpetological Atlas data gathered from 1990 to 2007 shows this species to have been documented from 780 of the states 979 geographical quadrangles (source NYSDEC website).

Habitat: Wet meadows, vegetated fields, wetlands, and stream edges. This species wanders extensively into grassy fields in bottom lands.

Breeding: Breeding occurs in the early spring in ponds, marshes, and swamps. Females will lay 2 to 5 thousand eggs. Tadpoles grow from less than an inch to nearly four inches before transforming.

Natural History: Insects and spiders are the mainstay of this frog's diet. It is not uncommon for these frogs to be seen far from water during the summer months. But they return to ponds and wetlands in the late fall to hibernate in the mud underwater. These are familiar animals to anyone who has dissected frogs in a biology class. In recent years their numbers in the wild have experienced an unexplained decline. In many regions specimens are being found with deformities to limbs. Some possible causes include chemical pollutants, acid rain, a pathogenic fungus that attacks frogs, or a combination of these and other, as yet unknown factors. The number one threat is habitat destruction. Most notably the draining of beaver ponds, swamps, and marshes. Agricultural practices that result in the draining of farm ponds destroys breeding habitat.

Habitat: Found in virtually every aquatic habitat within the state, from small ponds and large lakes to streams and wetlands.

Breeding: Breeding can begin as early as May and continue until August. Up to 4000 eggs may be deposited. Two clutches per year can occur. Eggs hatch in as little as a week.

Natural History: A drive through a wetland on a rainy night in late summer when the tadpoles of *Lithobates clamitans* are emerging onto land will reveal astounding numbers of small frogs crossing the roadway as they disperse into new territories. Adult frogs feed on insects primarily but other arthropods including small crayfish are frequently eaten. Minnows and other small aquatic vertebrates are also potential prey. These frogs are easily confused with the much larger Bullfrog, but are distinguished by the presence of a fold of skin (known as a dorso-lateral fold) that runs along each side of the back. These frogs require smaller bodies of water than the larger Bullfrog and they can be found in almost any moist environment, including temporary puddles. Like other aquatic frogs they sometimes wander away from water on rainy nights to forage for insects in grassy areas.

Class - **Amphibia** (amphibians)

Order - **Anura** (frogs and toads)

Family - **Ranidae** (true frogs)

Bullfrog *Lithobates catesbeianus*	**Pickerel Frog** *Lithobates palustris*	**Southern Leopard Frog** *Lithobates sphenocephalus*

Size: 4–8 inches.  Presumed range in New York	**Size:** 3 inches. 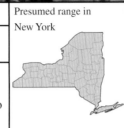 Presumed range in New York	**Size:** 3–5 inches.  Presumed range in New York
Abundance: Common.	**Abundance:** Fairly common.	**Abundance:** Uncommon.
Variation: Male has larger tympanum yellow throat.	**Variation:** Ground color varies from tan to brown.	**Variation:** Varies from bright green to light tan (see photos above).
Habitat: Ponds, lakes, and streams as well as swamps and marshes. May travel overland between ponds or wetland areas during rainy weather.	**Habitat:** Prefers spring-fed streams and clear, cool waters in woodland areas. Also found in swamps and marshes. May occur in fields near streams.	**Habitat:** Found in virtually all fresh-water aquatic habitats within its range. They often wander in to grassy fields far from water.
Breeding: Breeding and egg laying occurs from late spring through mid-summer. Several thousand eggs can be laid and two clutches per year is not uncommon.	**Breeding:** Breeds in ponds, ditches, or permanent streams. Beaver Ponds are reported as a favorite breeding site. Lays 2000 to 4000 eggs. Tadpoles transform in about three months.	**Breeding:** Breeds mostly in April and May. Breeding localities are ponds, ditches, marshes, and swamps. Lays up to 5000 eggs in several clumps. Young frogs emerge in mid-summer.
Natural History: These are the largest frogs in New York (and in fact in the United States). Their hind legs are considered to be a delicacy by many. They are regarded as a game animal and are hunted for food during the annual "frog season." In some places they are raised commercially for food and for research or teaching laboratories. They may venture far from water and will travel from pond to pond during rainy weather. Bullfrogs hunt mostly by utilizing a "sit and wait" ambush strategy. Food is almost any animal small enough to be swallowed, including other frogs. There is even a record of a large Bullfrog eating a baby rattlesnake! Bullfrog tadpoles can take up to two or rarely three years to transform into froglets. Populations in the north have shorter growing seasons and thus tadpoles take longer to mature into frogs.	**Natural History:** Pickerel Frogs are distinguished from Leopard Frogs by their square rather than round spots. These frogs secrete a toxin from the skin that protects them from many predators and is strong enough to kill other frogs kept with them in a small container. Among the predators that are able to eat them, however, is another frog species, the Bullfrog. These are hardy frogs that may be active from April through October in New York. Northern populations of Pickerel Frogs show a preference for clean water and seem to be suceptible to pollution. In this respect the Pickerel Frog may be an indicator species that can provide an early warning regarding environmental threats like water pollution. The status of New York populations appears stable and these frogs are widespread throughout the state.	**Natural History:** Leopard frogs are frequently found some distance from permanent water sources in meadows and overgrown fields. They can even be seen in rural lawns on occasion, especially in late summer. Southern Leopard Frogs can be told from their northern cousin by the lack of a dark spot on the snout. They are easily discerned from the Pickeral Frog by their round rather than squarish spots. A wide variety of insects, spiders, and other invertebrates are eaten. Like most frogs, they spend the winter in the mud at the bottom of a pond, creek, or other permanent water. As their name implies, these are mostly southern animals that are widespread and common throughout the southern United States. Extreme southeastern New York state represents the northernmost extension of this species' range in America.

Class - **Amphibia** (amphibians)

Order - **Anura** (frogs and toads)

| Family - **Ranidae** (true frogs) | Family - **Hylidae** (treefrogs) | |

Mink Frog
Lithobates septentrionalis

Chorus Frogs
Pseudacris triseriata and Pseudacris maculata

Spring Peeper
Pseudacris crucifer

Midland Chorus Frog

Size: Up to 3 inches.

Abundance: Fairly common.

Variation: Variable-shaped dark markings.

Presumed range in New York

Size: Up to 1.5 inches.

Abundance: Uncommon.

Variation: Two similar species in New York.

Presumed range in New York

Size: 1 inch.

Abundance: Common.

Variation: Tan, brown, grayish, or reddish.

Presumed range in New York

Habitat: Lakes shores, pond edges, bogs, and creeks. A boreal, cold-tolerant species that actually prefers cold water environments. Shallow areas with abundant aquatic vegation are favored.

Breeding: Breeds in summer (June into August). As many as 4000 eggs are encased in a jelly-like mass that is attached to underwater vegetation.

Natural History: These frogs some-times pose in a classic fashion atop floating lily pads. Their name comes from the musky odor they produce when stressed, which resembles the musk of a mink. This odor may serve to deter some predators. Still, Mink Frogs are preyed upon by snakes, skunks, and raccoons. Their food is insects, minnows, milli-peds, leeches, snails, and spiders and probably any other small organism that can be swallowed. They are highly aquatic and often rest submerged with just the eyes and nostrils above the surface. These frogs spend much of their lives in hibernation beneath the mud and muck of bogs and ponds in boreal regions. Emergence is usually not until May. In New York this northern species is found only in the Adirondack region. The tadpoles may take two years to metamorph into adult frogs.

Habitat: Low wet fields, bottomland woods, swamps, marshes, ponds, or bogs. Also found in uplands that are in close proximity to bottomlands, creeks, or other permanent water.

Breeding: Very early breeders that may begin breeding as early as February. Breeding is in ephemeral pools in flooded fields, roadside ditches, etc.

Natural History: Until recently all Chorus Frogs in New York were designat-ed as the Western Chorus Frog. Recent investigations suggest that there are two species of Chorus Frogs in New York, and the species once known as the Western Chorus Frog is now called the Midland Chorus Frog. It is found in western New York (light gray on map above). Chorus frog populations in extreme northeast New York are now known to belong to the species known as the Boreal Chorus Frog (dark gray on map). These are small frogs that are only about an inch and half in length when fully grown. They are thus easily overlooked. They make their presence known in early spring when their chorus of breeding calls will emanate from flooded crop fields, roadside ditches, and small ponds. Their trilling call is surpris-ingly loud and resonant for such a tiny frog and it can be hear for long distances.

Habitat: Woodlands and thickets, usually near water. Most common in lowlands (swamps, marshes, etc.), but also found in upland areas adjacent to creek bottoms or wetlands.

Breeding: Spring Peepers begin breeding activity as early as late winter and continue into early spring. Several hundred eggs are laid in shallow water.

Natural History: Another dimunitive frog that is heard more often than seen. The name comes from the sound made when breeding frogs are calling. The call is a rapidly repeated "peep, peep, peep." Despite their small size, a chorus of calling spring peepers can be heard for a distance of up to a mile. Although members of the treefrog family, they live mostly on the ground. The species name "*crucifer*" is latin for "cross bearer" and refers to the x-shaped mark that is always present on this frog's back. These little frogs, along with their cousins the Chorus Frogs, are a true harbinger of spring throughout much of the eastern United States. They may breed in the same flooded field pools with Chorus Frogs or even in the same pool. They feed on tiny insects and arthropods. Spring Peepers are found from sea level to the highest elevations in New York and are one of our most ubiqutous frogs.

Class - **Amphibia** (amphibians)

Order - **Anura** (frogs and toads)

| Family - **Hylidae** (treefrogs) | | Family - **Scaphiopodidae** (spadefoots) |

Eastern Cricket Frog
Acris crepitans

Gray Treefrog
Hyla versicolor

Eastern Spadefoot
Scaphiopus holbrookii

Size: 1.375 inches.

Presumed range in New York

Abundance: Uncommon.

Variation: Brown, reddish tan, or grayish green.

Habitat: Shorelines of ponds, along creeks, temporary pools, marshes, swamps, wet meadows, and uplands. Can be found in woodlands in summer.

Breeding: Breeds from spring through late summer in permenant or ephemeral waters. Up to 400 eggs per clutch.

Natural History: These tiny frogs are most commonly seen along the receding shorelines of ponds and lakes in late summer or early fall. When startled they will often jump into the water and then immediately swim back to shore. This may be an "out of the frying pan into the fire" behavior intended to keep them from the jaws of hungry fish. They are often seen far from water in fields and woodlands, but are always more common in wetland habitats and permanently damp areas. Their name comes from their call which resembles that of a cricket, but a group of Cricket Frogs calling in chorus is more accurately described as sounding like the sound of many small stones being rapidly clicked together. There are three morphologically indistinguishable cricket frog species found in the eastern United States. Each is determined to be a distinct species based on laboratory analysis of DNA.

Size: 2.5 inches.

Presumed range in New York

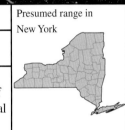

Abundance: Common.

Variation: Varying shades of gray from charcoal to smokey gray.

Habitat: These treefrogs are more adapted to dry uplands than most members of their genus and they can be found far from water in upland woods.

Breeding: Breeds from late spring through summer in small bodies of water. Up to 2000 eggs are laid.

Natural History: These highly arboreal treefrogs are rarely seen on the ground and they often climb high into treetops to forage for insects. They are mainly nocturnal but they may be active by day on cloudy or rainy days. They shelter by day in small hollows in tree trunks or limbs and have been known to take up residence in small bird nest boxes such as a wren box. They will also live in the rain gutters of house roofs. They can sometimes be seen sitting in the opening of their hiding place with the head and front feet exposed. They possess remarkable camouflage abilities and the gray, lichen-like pattern of their skin will perfectly match the bark of the tree they occupy. They can produce a natural anti-freeze in the blood which allows them to hibernate in tree hollows above the ground, or in leaf litter on the forest floor. Most members of the genus *Hyla* are southern animals, but these frogs range far into the northern states and even into parts of southern Canada.

Size: 2.25 inches.

Presumed range in New York

Abundance: Uncommon.

Variation: Varies from brown or olive through dark gray.

Habitat: The main habitat requirement is loose, sandy soil that facilitates easy burrowing. In New York restricted to the Coastal Plain and Husdon Valley.

Breeding: Breeds explosively during periods of heavy rainfall. Up to 5000 eggs hatch will within a few days.

Natural History: The name "Spade-foot" come from a sickle-shaped horny structure on the hind feet that is used for digging into the ground. They spend much of their lives in burrows only a few inches deep and emerge only on rainy nights. During dry weather they may spend weeks in the burrow without feeding. They secrete a toxic substance which is highly irritant to mucus membranes, thus making these anurans unpalatable to many potential predators. Touching the face or other sensitive skin after handling a Spadefoot will result in an uncomfortable burning sensation. Although widespread and quite common farther to the south, in New York the Spadefoot is sporadically distributed and may be absent from many areas shown on the range map above. The spadefoots are a unique and specialized group anurans. Most members of this genus are found in the southwestern United States and Mexico. Another group lives in Eurasia.

Class - **Amphibia** (amphibians)

Order - **Anura** (frogs and toads)

Family - **Bufonidae** (true toads)

American Toad *Bufo americanus*	**Fowler's Toad** *Bufo fowleri*

Size: 2 to 4 inches. Record 6.125 inches.

Abundance: Very common.

Variation: Varies from light tan to very dark brown, olive brown, reddish, or grayish.

Presumed range in New York

Habitat: Virtually anywhere. Inhabits dry uplands and moist lowlands from remote wilderness to urban lawns.

Breeding: Breeding in New York usually begins in April. Eggs are laid in long strings of clear gelationous material. Breeding sites are small ponds, water-filled ditches, or temporary pools in seasonally flooded lowlands. Eggs hatch in about one week into tiny black tadpoles that metamorph into quarter-inch toadlets in mid-summer.

Natural History: American Toads eat a wide variety of insects and other small arthropods. They are adept burrowers and like other toads possess hardened spade-like structures on the hind feet that are used for digging. These toads can be told from the similar and sympatrically occuring Fowler's Toad by the their larger warts and the fact that the dark spots on the back never have more than two warts per spot. The similar Fowler's Toad may have up to six warts per dark spot. Although they are sometimes active by day, these toads are primarily nocturnal in habits. They usually spend the day at least partially buried in loose soil or beneath leaf litter or other debris. When attacked by a predator they will inflate their bodies by gulping air. This behavior sometimes works if the predator is an animal like a snake that must swallow its food whole. The common Eastern Garter Snake along with the Eastern Hognose Snake are two of their major predators. Like most other toads the American Toad likes loose soils that facilitate easy burrowing.

Size: Average of 2 to 3 inches. Record 3.75 inches.

Abundance: Common.

Variation: Varies in color from dark brown to reddish brown, tan, or grayish brown.

Presumed range in New York

Habitat: Shows a preference for sandy, loose soils in bottomlands, lake shores, river valleys, etc.

Breeding: Breeding begins shortly after emerging from hibernation. In New York most breeding is about a month later than with the American Toad, usually begining in early May. Shallow ponds, ditches, creeks, flooded fields, etc. are all used as breeding sites but this species is also likely to breed in streams. From 5000 to 10000 eggs are laid.

Natural History: The natural history of the Fowler's Toad is similar to that of the American Toad. Fowler's Toads emerge from hibernation later in the spring and breed later in the spring. Young toadlets do not emerge from the tadpole stage until late summer. Fowler's Toads like open habitats and sandy soils. They often take up residence in gardens that are kept well tilled and thus maintain loose soils that facilitate easy burrowing. Encouraging toads in the garden provides an all-natural and benign form of pest control. Placing a half buried water dish in the center of the garden that is kept filled during the dry summer months will make life more pleasant for garden toads. Fowler's Toads avoid the deep woods in favor of more semi-open habitats. Like many toads (and many treefrogs) the Fowler's Toad secretes a toxic substance from the skin when threatened. While this toxin can cause irritation to sensitive areas and membranes, the old wives' tale that toads cause warts is a fallacy. Skin secretions are protection against some predators, but by no means all.

THE AMPHIBIANS OF NEW YORK

PART 2: SALAMANDERS

Class - **Amphibia** (amphibians)

Order - **Caudata** (salamanders)

Family - **Ambystomatidae** (mole salamanders)

Tiger Salamander *Ambystoma tigrinum*	Spotted Salamander *Ambystoma maculatum*	Marbled Salamander *Ambystoma opacum*

Size: Averages about 8 inches. Max 14 inches.

Abundance: Very rare in New York.

Presumed range in New York

Size: Average 6 inches. Maximum of 9 inches.

Abundance: Common but may be declining.

Presumed range in New York

Size: 3 to 4 inches. Record 5.3 inches.

Abundance: Uncommon in New York.

Presumed range in New York

Variation: The light markings can appear as irregular spots, blotches, or stripes. The color of the light pigments can vary as well and may be yellow, orange, or greenish. Spotted Salamander has spots that are more rounded.

Variation: The polka dot spots on the Spotted Salamander may be yellow or orange. The number of spots varies widely, and a few individuals may lack spots altogether. Tiger Salamander's spots are more irregular, less round.

Variation: Sexually dimorphic when breeding. Light colors are gray or silver in the female and white in the male.

Habitat: Woodlands and fields, in both upland an lowland areas. In New York found only on eastern Long Island (Suffolk and Nassau Counties) where it lives mainly in the central pine barrens.

Habitat: Primarily woodland areas, but also found in overgrown fields and edges bordering agricultural lands. Favors upland woods bordering floodplains. They are found statewide in New York.

Habitat: Most fond of bottomlands and stream floodplains (especially during breeding) but they can also common in upland woods adjacent to lowlands.

Breeding: Breeds in small, fishless bodies of water like stock ponds, vernal pools, and "borrow pits." Breeding occurs in mid-winter with a few hundred to several thousand eggs produced by the female. Males and females migrate to breeding ponds where breeding takes place. Eggs are encased in a ball of jelly-like material and hatch in about a month.

Breeding: Breeds in the same types of aquatic habitats as the Tiger Salamander (ponds, ditches, etc). Migration to breeding sites occurs during periods of heavy rainfall in late winter. Eggs are deposited in large gelatinous masses in ponds or wetland pools. Eggs hatch in a few weeks and larva transform into minature adults in two to four months. Young adults are about 2–3 inches long.

Breeding: Breeds in the fall during rainy weather. Overland migration is common. Eggs are laid on land under rocks, logs, etc. in low-lying areas subject to flooding. Hatching is delayed until eggs are flooded by fall rains.

Natural History: The large size of the Tiger Salamander allows it to feed on much larger prey than most salamander species. Although invertebrates such as earthworms and insect larva are the major foods, small vertebrates may also eaten and captive specimens will eat baby mice. Despite their large size, Tiger Salamanders are rarely seen except during the late winter breeding season when they travel to breeding ponds.

Natural History: Primarily subterranean in habits. Lives in underground burrows and beneath rocks, logs, or leaf litter on the forest floor. During periods of hot dry weather retreats deeper underground or stays in the vicinity's perennially wet areas. Feeds on a wide variety of insects and invertebrates as well as a few small vertebrates. In the late winter they may be observed on rural roads at night during rainy weather.

Natural History: This is one of the few salamanders to exhibit sexual dimorphism. The light markings are wider and whiter on the male and narrower and more silver or grayish on the female. These sexual differences manifest during breeding. Like other members of the "mole salamander" family, Marbled Salamanders are fossorial in habits. In fact, this species may be even more secretive than many of its kin. Thus, even where they are fairly common they are not readily observed. They can reportedly produce a noxious secretion from the tail which may help to ward off some predators. Adults probably feed on most any small animal they can swallow. Larva have been known to eat the eggs of small frogs.

Class - **Amphibia** (amphibians)

Order - **Caudata** (salamanders)

Family - **Ambystomatidae** (mole salamanders)		Family - **Salamandridae** (newts)

Jefferson's Salamander *Ambystoma jeffersonianum*	Blue-spotted Salamander *Ambystoma laterale*	Red-spotted Newt *Notophthalmus viridescens*

Size: Average 4 to 5 inches. Max up to 8 inches.	Presumed range in New York 	**Size:** 4 to 5 inches average. Record 6.25.	Presumed range in New York 	**Size:** Average 3 to 4 inches. Record 5.5 inches.	Presumed range in New York 
Abundance: Locally common to uncommon.		**Abundance:** Widespread but uncommon.		**Abundance:** Common and widespread.	

Variation: There is some variation in the amount of light blue flecking that is present. Older adults tend to lose their spots and become darker. "Unisexual" specimens can be confusingly variable (see Natural History below).

Variation: Considerable variation in the amount of blue spotting present. Hybrid unisexual forms can resemble either species or neither one. Any unidentifiable specimen is likely a unisexual hybrid.

Variation: No significant geographic variation. Significant ontogenetic variation involves three stages to the life cycle following hatching from the egg. Larva, eft (intermediate adult stage), and adult (see Natural History section).

Habitat: An upland forest species. Both deciduos and mixed forests are used. Likes closed canopy forests.

Habitat: Another forest species. May also be found in wet meadows and swamps. Favors areas with loamy soils.

Habitat: Adults are found in ponds, swamps, or other permanent water. Eft stage is a terrestrial animal of woods.

Breeding: Breeding occurs in late winter or early spring, with eggs being deposited in woodland ponds. Eggs hatch into larva that spend up to a year as thoroughly aquatic, gilled salamanders before transforming into adults.

Breeding: Breeds in early spring. Courtship activity involves the male grasping the female from above and rubbing the nose across her body. The male then deposits sperm packets which are picked up by the females cloaca.

Breeding: Breeds in spring. Males deposit packages of sperm which are taken up by the female into the cloaca where fertilization occurs internally before eggs are then laid. Hatchlings metamorph into efts in 4–5 months.

Natural History: Although primarily nocturnal, Jefferson's Salamanders are sometimes seen abroad on rainy, heavily overcast days. These salamanders have an unnamed "sister species" that represents an enigma for biologists. Throughout much of the Great Lakes region exists a unique population of salamanders known as "unisexual salamanders." They are similar in appearance to the Jefferson's Salamander but they are a hybrid population that incorporates genetic material from two or more (up to five) different *Ambystoma* species. Hybridization with the following species (Blue-spotted Salamander) is common and widespread in New York, and these hybrids are always females.

Natural History: Hybridization with the Jefferson's Salamander regularly occurs. All hybrids have triploid chromosones and all are females, hence the term "unisexual." Hybrids were once regarded as distinct species. Those with more chromosones from the Blue-spotted were known as "Tremblay's Salamander." Hybird individuals with more chromosones from the Jefferon's were called "Silvery Salamander." Food is small insects and other invertebrates such as worms, sow bugs, snails, spiders, etc. The Blue-spotted is a boreal salamander that ranges well to the north in eastern Canada. It is the most northerly ranging of the "mole salamander" group.

Natural History: Newts are unique among New York salamanders in having an extra stage in their life cycle. Following hatching the young spend the summer as gill-breathing larva then undergo a transformation to an air-breathing semi-adult that lives on land for up to three years. Newts in this terrestrial stage are call "efts." After one to three years the eft returns to the water and undergoes another metmorphosis into a totally aquatic adult. After returning to the water the coarse skin of the eft becomes smooth and the round tail flattens vertically to become fin-like. Their lifespan can be up to 15 years. Newts produce a neurotoxin in their skin that protects them from many predators.

Class - **Amphibia** (amphibians)		
Order - **Caudata** (salamandridae)		
Family - **Plethodontidae** (lungless salamanders)		

Four-toed Salamander *Hemidactylium scutatum*	Northern Dusky Salamander *Desmognathus fuscus*	Allegheny Dusky Salamander *Desmognathus ochrophaeus*

Size: 2–3 inches.	Presumed range in New York	**Size:** 3–4 inches.	Presumed range in New York	**Size:** 3–4 inches.	Presumed range in New York
Abundance: Uncommon.		**Abundance:** Common.	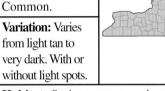	**Abundance:** Common.	
Variation: Color varies from brown to gray or orange.		**Variation:** Varies from light tan to very dark. With or without light spots.		**Variation:** May show a light stripe dorsally or may be uniformly dark.	

Habitat: Mature woodlands, usually near woodland bogs, springs, and seeps, or small woodland ponds.	**Habitat:** Springs, seeps, and spring-fed brooks in wooded areas. Beneath rocks, detritus, or in the muck of forest streams.	**Habitat:** A forest species found in mesic woodlands. Favors hemlock ravines or the vicinity of streams and seeps.
Breeding: Eggs are laid in winter at the edge of streams, ponds, etc. Females remain with the eggs until hatching in about four weeks.	**Breeding:** Eggs are laid under rocks in the vicinity of streams. The eggs (average 15–30) are laid in clusters of individual eggs rather than in a mass of jelly.	**Breeding:** Gravid females lay one to two dozen eggs in areas where there is a constant moisture little temparture variation.
Natural History: The name comes from the fact that they have only four toes on the hind foot (other terrestrial salamanders in New York have five). There is also an obvious constriction at the base of the tail that is unique to this species. It is at this constricted location that the tail will be broken off as a defensive manuever. The most readily identifiable characteristic of this species is its white belly with black spots. No other salamander in New York is similarly colored and patterned. This salamander has a greater geographic range than any other in America. It is found from Nova Scotia, Canada, to the Gulf Coast and west to Minnesota and Arkansas. But like many amphibians this species is threatened by habitat destruction and has been in decline for decades. The disappearance of vernal pools, bogs, and streamside habitat to agriculture and urban development is probably the most significant threat.	**Natural History:** The Northern Dusky and its kin are salamanders that are often well known to rural folk. Many a youngster has amused themselves on a hot summer day by rolling stones and logs in mountain streams to try and catch these slippery and quick moving sala- manders. They are often collected for fish bait in many areas within their range and sometimes go by the name "Spring Lizards." They are frequently sold in bait stores in the Appalachian region. Although this practice probably has no significant impact on this common species, accidental "by catch" of some rarer species may have an negative impact on those less common species. Mainly nocturnal, they will emerge at night to forage. Northern Duskys occur sypatrically with their close relative the Allegheny Dusky. They can be differenti- ated by examining the tail, which has a sharp "knife edge" on the Northern Dusky. Allegheny Dusky has round tail.	**Natural History:** Several studies suggest that within ideal habitat these small salamanders can be so numerous as to outnumber all other vertebrate life forms in the area. When a species is this common, it usually means that it is a highly valuable member of the local ecosystem. It is known that salamanders are food for a very wide array of predators, including snakes, shrews, probably every type mammalian carni- vore in the area, and a wide array of bird species (including some songbirds). Being prey for so many predators, these little salamanders are remarkable quick and agile. When uncovered from beneath a flat rock of log on the forest floor they can dissappear with surprising speed. They are very similar to the preceding species from which they can be separated by examing the tail. Allegheny Duskys have a rounded tail. Northern Dusky has a tail that is laterally flattened into a sharp edge.

Class - **Amphibia** (amphibians)
Order - **Caudata** (salamandridae)
Family - **Plethodontidae** (lungless salamanders)

Northern Redback Salamander *Plethodon cinereeus*	Northern Slimy Salamander *Plethodon glutinosus*	Wehrle's Salamander *Plethodon wehrlei*
 	 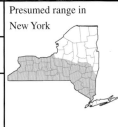	 

Size: 3–4 inches.	Presumed range in New York	**Size:** Up to 8 inches.	Presumed range in New York	**Size:** Up to 6.75 inches.	Presumed range in New York
Abundance: Very common.		**Abundance:** Common.		**Abundance:** Uncommon.	
Variation: Highly variable in both ground color and color of stripes.		**Variation:** Varies considerably in the amount of light flecking.		**Variation:** Size, amount and color of light spots and flecking variable.	

Habitat: Chiefly woodlands. This is another terrestrial but retiring species that hides beneath leaf litter, logs, etc.	**Habitat:** Another woodland species. More common in upland woods and hillsides than in bottomlands.	**Habitat:** Damp upland forests in mountainous areas. Shows a preference for wooded, rocky slopes.
Breeding: Female lays about 10 eggs on land and guards them until they hatch. Babies hatch fully formed.	**Breeding:** 12 to 15 eggs seems to be the average. As with other *Plethodon* Salamanders, young hatch fully formed.	**Breeding:** Little is known. Presumably it is similar to other Plethodontidae (i.e., eggs laid on land, no larva).
Natural History: Shows considerable variation in the dorsal pattern. The color of the dorsal strip varies from yellow, red, or orange. Some Redback Salamanders are not red on the back at all, but uniformly gray. This color morph is known as the "lead-backed phase." This is one of the most northerly ranging salamanders in eastern North America and can be found as far north as the Canadian provinces of Quebec, Nova Scotia, and New Brunswick. In the heart of its range this is not only the most common salamander species, but one of the most common vertebrate species. In ideal habitats it seems that every rock or log will have one of these small salamanders hiding beneath it. Savvy environmental educators around the state often use this salamander to introduce children to the wonders of nature. Watching a group of kids hunt for salamanders in a nearby park or nature preserve is a testament to the inherent interest humans show for nature.	**Natural History:** The name is derived from the fact that slimy salamanders exude a thick, sticky mucus from the skin when handled. This material is difficult to wash off and once dried becomes black and crusty. Herpetologists capturing slimy salamanders sometimes wear the residue of salamander mucus on their hands for days before it finally wears off. The food of these woodland species is undoubtedly a wide variety of soft-bodied insects, insect larva, annelids, small crustaceans, and other tiny invertebrate life found among the leaf litter on the forest floor. Until the advent of DNA technology there was only one ubiquitous species of Slimy Salamander that ranged across most of the eastern United States. There are now over dozen individual species. Most are southern animals and only one species (Northern Slimy) ranges northward into New York. Mostly subterranean and nocturnal in habits but may venture out on heavily overcast days.	**Natural History:** The species name (*wehrlei*) honors the naturalist who first discovered this salamander. Although this species is not widely distributed in the state, it is apparently fairly common in the regions where it does occur. Some researches in Pennsylvania report high poulation densities in areas of prime habitat (Hall and Stafford 1972). In New York this salamander is restricted to the southwestern part of the state in the Level III Ecoregion known as the Northern Appalachian Plateau (see Figure 9). Like many other members of its family this is a terrestrial salamander that lives in mature forests on mountain slopes. As with other salamanders they can be very hard to find during hot, dry summer months as they will retreat into underground burrows beneath large rocks and boulders and aestivate. The members of the *Plethodon* genus of salamanders are often referred to by biologists as "Woodland Salamanders," a reference to their preferred habitat.

Class - **Amphibia** (amphibians)

Order - **Caudata** (salamandridae)

Family - **Plethodontidae** (lungless salamanders)

Spring Salamander *Gyrinophilus porphyriticus*	Red Salamander *Pseudotriton ruber*	Northern Two-lined Salamander *Eurycea bislineata*
	 Old adult 	

Size: Up to 9 inches.	**Size:** 3 inches.	**Size:** Up to 4 inches.
Abundance: Common.	**Abundance:** Failry common.	**Abundance:** Very common.
Variation: Color varies from pinkish or light red to reddish brown or purplish.	**Variation:** Adults tend to darken with age (ontogenetic melanism).	**Variation:** Ground color varies from bright yellow to dingy brown.

Presumed range in New York  Presumed range in New York  Presumed range in New York

Habitat: Springs, seeps, and spring-fed streams as well as caves. Also on the forest floor near water. Ranges throughout the entire Appalachian Plateau.	**Habitat:** Found within and in the vicinity of springs and spring feed brooks. Found both in the water and under moss, logs, etc., in the vicinity of water.	**Habitat:** Streams, wetlands, and seeps. Mostly a lowland animal but also found in mesic upland environments. Usually in the vicinity of permenant moisture.
Breeding: Eggs are laid in water (stream or spring) during summer and hatch in the fall. The aquatic larval stage can be exceedingly long, lasting on average four to five years. Rarely up to 10 years in cave-dwelling populations.	**Breeding:** Several dozen eggs are laid in the water in spring-fed streams during late summer/fall. Females will guard the eggs until they hatch in the winter. Totally aquatic larva can take one and a half to three years to transform into adults.	**Breeding:** Several dozen eggs are attached to the underside of rocks and brooks. Eggs hatch in accordance with stream temperature (two to four weeks). Aquatic larva transform into adults in one or two years.
Natural History: This is one of the more diurnal salamander species, and adults have been observed prowling on the forest floor during daylight hours. In some areas of their range they are reportedly very common in cave habitats. These are large salamanders and they are fierce predators of a wide variety of small animal life, including other salamanders which can make up as much as 50 percent of their diet. They are reported to secrete a noxious substance from the skin that deters some predators. There are four very similar subspecies, but only one ranges into New York (Northern Spring Salamander, *G. p. porphyriticus*). These salamanders don't seem to tolerate human alterations to their habitats and they are thus vulnerable to development projects, strip mining, etc.	**Natural History:** Adult Red Salamanders will wander away from water and may be found in moist environments a good distance from springs or streams. Young adults are bright, fire-engine red with scattered black specks throughout the body. As they age they tend to become darker on the back and very old individuals may be uniformly dark gray or deep purple dorsally. There are four subspecies. Only the northern subspecies (*P. r. ruber*) occurs in New York. As with most other salamanders they are mostly nocturnal. On rainy summer nights they will prowl the forest floor in search of prey and it is at this time that they are most easily observed. "Road cruising" on little-traveled roads through forested regions on rainy nights will often produce numerous sightings.	**Natural History:** Like most of its kin this is a secretive salamander that is easily overlooked. Turning flat stones or logs in the vicinity of water however will frequently reveal one or more of these agile and quick-moving little salamanders. They may have rather small home ranges that encompass only a few square meters. They do make forays into the surrounding habitats on rainy nights and are usually easy to find by driving slowly and looking closely for salamanders crossing the roadway. One of their favorite habitats are clear, cold streams which in the northern regions are also home to trout and other fishes that are known to eat these smallish salamanders. Food for the Two-line Salamander is mostly soft-bodied invertebrates such as insect larva.

Class - **Amphibia** (amphibians)

Order - **Caudata** (salamanders)

Family - **Plethodontidae** (lungless salamanders)	Family - **Cryptobranchidae** (giant salamanders)	Family - **Proteidae** (mudpuppies)

Longtail Salamander
Eurycea longicauda

Hellbender
Eurycea longicauda

Mudpuppy
Necturus maculosus

Size: Up to 7.75 inches.

Abundance: Uncommon.

Variation: Ground color varies from yellow to orange.

Presumed range in New York

Size: Up to 30 inches.

Abundance: Rare.

Variation: Varies from reddish, brown, tan, or chocolate.

Presumed range in New York

Size: Up to 19 inches.

Abundance: Uncommon.

Variation: No significant variation in New York specimens.

Presumed range in New York

Habitat: Spring runs, small clear creeks, in the vicinity of seeps, and near cave openings.

Breeding: Breeds in late winter or early spring. Eggs are deposited in streams and springs or often in caves. Larva metamorphose in about a year.

Natural History: These salamanders can often be found beneath rocks within small clear streams. They also live in mesic woodland environments, usually in the vicinity of a permanent stream. Here they may be found hiding beneath or within rotted logs or stumps. On rainy nights they can be encountered on roads as they roam around in search of tiny invertebrate prey. Although they can reach an impressive length of over seven inches, they are a slim-bodied animal and over most of their length is tail. In New York these are animals of the Appalachian Plateau and Ridge and Valley Provinces, but they do not range throughout these regions. Rather they barely enter the southern portion of New York, which represents the northernmost extension of their range in America. Food items listed for this species include insects, spiders, worms, snails, millipedes, and crustaceans.

Habitat: Restricted to remote, unpolluted streams. Large underwater rocks are used as a refuge.

Breeding: Fertilization is external and eggs are laid in a nest guarded by the male. Lays over 400 eggs in a large mass about the size of a grapefruit.

Natural History: These huge, totally aquatic salamanders have deep folds and wrinkles in the skin. They have very large, dorso-ventrally flattened heads and laterally flattened, fin-like tails. They are completely aquatic and feed on crustaceans, minnows, and invertebrates with crayfish reported as a primary prey. They require clean, unpolluted flowing waters and they are in decline throughout their range due to stream degradation, impoundments, and chemical pollutants. This is one of America's largest salamander species, but it is dwarfed by it larger relative from Japan. The world's largest salamander, the Pacific Giant Salamander, is native to pristine streams in the mountains of Japan where it can reach five feet in length. Many streams within their range now lack the water quality to continue to support this species. They are listed as a Species of Concern by NYSDEC.

Habitat: Female Mudpuppies hollow out a nest beneath a sunken log or rock where they will lay up to 100 eggs.

Breeding: Natural lakes and man-made impoundments, larger creeks and rivers, and canals. Shows a preference for water with some current.

Natural History: Mudpuppies have extensive external gills that resemble downy feathers. Some think the gills are reminiscent of the ears of a dog, thus the name "Mudpuppy." These are totally aquatic salamanders that never lose the gills of the larva. This condition of permanent larval characteristics is known scientifically as "neotony" and is a phenomena that is not rare in salamanders of several species. Mudpuppies prey on fish eggs, insects, mollusks, small crustaceans, and annelids. They are strictly aquatic animals and are mainly nocturnal in habits. They may remain active in colder months if in deep water. They tend to stay on the bottom and are thus not easily observed unless in shallow water. They are sometimes caught by fishermen using worms or other types of live bait.

CHAPTER 8
THE RIVERS AND STREAMS OF NEW YORK

As a preface to the next chapter (Chapter 9, The Fishes of New York), this short chapter is intended to provide a brief introduction into the waterways of New York, which are home to the state's fish species. The state of New York boasts over 70000 miles of named rivers and streams. The largest of which, the St. Lawrence River, is shared with Canada and makes up a portion of the state's northern border. In addition to the state's rivers and streams, numerous natural lakes and man-made impoundments (about 7600 smaller lakes, resevoirs and ponds) provide habitat for the state's fish species. The most significant of these of course are Lakes Erie and Ontario, whose shorelines provide the western border for much of the state (actually the state line extends well out into the lakes and thus many islands in the northeastern portion of Lake Ontario are part New York).

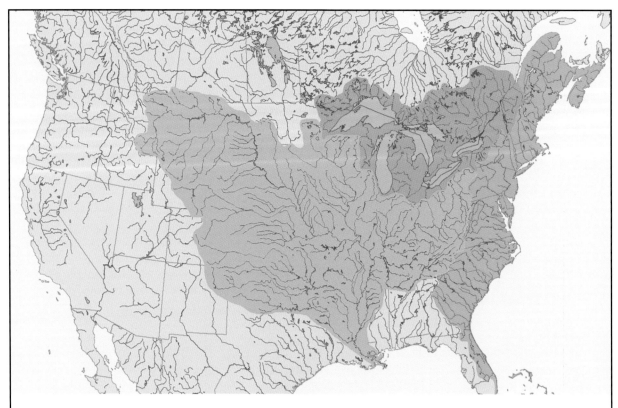

Figure 10.
The map above shows the major rivers and streams of North America. The shaded areas depict the major watersheds that affect the state of New York. Gray is the Mississippi River Watershed, green is the St. Lawrence Watershed, and blue denotes the Atlantic Seaboard Watershed area.

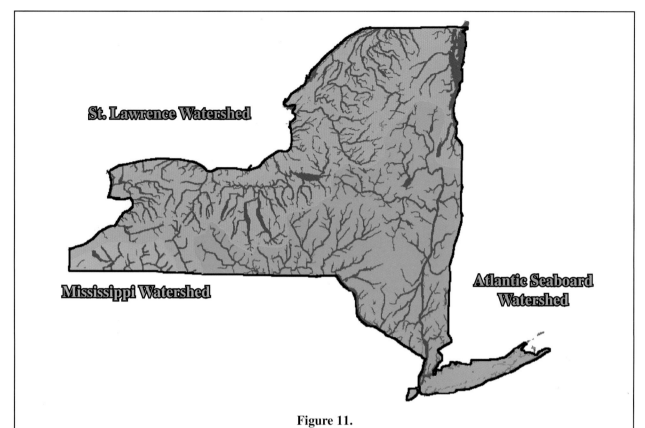

Figure 11.
The map above shows the major rivers and streams of New York with color-shaded areas showing where the major watersheds that affect the state of New York occur in the state. Gray is the Mississippi River Watershed, green is the St. Lawrence Watershed, and blue denotes the Atlantic Seaboard Watershed area.

Most of New York's rivers and streams drain into Lakes Erie and Ontario which are in turn a part of the much larger St. Lawrence River watershed. Most of the land area of western and northern New York is within the St. Lawrence Watershed. In extreme southwestern New York a small area of the state's land mass is in the Mississippi River Watershed via the Allegheny River. All the rest of the state is within the greater watershed known as the Atlantic Seaboard. Figure 10 on page 166 shows a map of the major watersheds in North America that impact the state of New York.

All three of the major watershed areas shown above consist of increasingly smaller tributaries, each of which constitutes its own drainage (watershed) area. The map below shows how the large watersheds in the state are comprised of smaller drainage basins (watersheds).

The distribution of fishes often coincides with one or more watershed areas, thus some understanding of the natural geograpic divisions which constitute the different watersheds is insightful information when considering the distribution of the state's freshwater fish species. All three of the major watershed areas above can be further divided into smaller watershed (drainage) areas as large river systems are downgraded into the smaller rivers that make up their tributaries. Each of these smaller tributaries and the areas they drain (watersheds) can subsequently be divided into smaller and smaller tributaries, each with its smaller and smaller accompanying drainage area (watershed).

Some widespread fish species may occur throughout an entire major watershed, or even several major watersheds. Other species may be confined to a single creek and thus restricted to a relatively tiny geographic area. Natural scientists in general and ichthyologists in particular find the hierarchal arrangement of increasingly smaller watershed maps to be useful tools to understanding the distribution, evolutionary history, and ecosystem requirements of aquatic organisms.

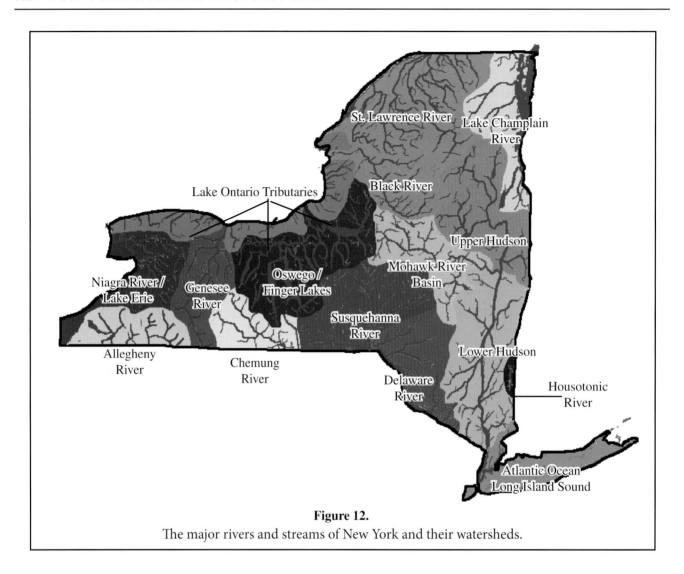

Figure 12.
The major rivers and streams of New York and their watersheds.

Like all other habitat types within the eastern United States, the waterways of New York have been highly altered by man. In addition to numerous dams, impoundments, and canals, the waterways of New York have also suffered severe insults from both pollution and siltation.

Direct pollution from industry and resource extraction is an important source of stream degradation across much of America. But of equal importance is indirect contamination from agriculture. Agricultural-related pollution and stream degradation can come in the form of chemical runoff or the destruction of vegetated buffer zones by farmers needing to maximize the production area of their land. Erosion and siltation from row cropping operations impact nearly every watershed in the eastern United States. To a lesser extent, livestock operations can also have negative impacts as cattle destroy creek banks and stir up silt from stream bottoms.

Today many of America's streams no longer support the high diversity of fish and other aquatic species that once were abundant within their banks. A total of 19 of New York's 165 freshwater fish species are now regarded by the New State Department of Environmental Conservation as threatened or endangered. Five more are considered to be species of concern. The future for many of America's fish species is, frankly, quite grim. If we regard this fact as a warning sign relating to the health of our aquatic ecosystems, and surely they are just that, then all Americans should be acutely concerned about the future of our waterways. We often hear reasonable people argue against stringent protections of our environment. But few things are more important than these protections. Humans can survive for a maximum of four minutes without air and maximum of four days without water. It follows then that our paramount priorities should be to ensure that we all always have clean air to breathe and pure water to drink!

The series of maps shown on the previous pages gives a good representation of how smaller streams and their watersheds are integrated into larger streams and larger watersheds. What also becomes apparent from these maps is that when it comes water, everything (and everyone) downstream is affected by the quality of the water and the overall environmental health of the waters upstream. The environmental quality of that tiny creek in your backyard or on your farm affects not only the life of organisms living within that stream, but also organisms within the larger aquatic ecosystems into which it flows. And ultimately, the aquatic wildlife living in the Great Lakes and the North Atlantic, or in the Mississippi River, in Louisiana's coastal marshes, the depths of the Gulf of Mexico, and the magnificent coral ecosystems of the great reefs of the Caribbean.

The following chapter is an introduction to the 165 freshwater fish species that call the state of New York home. Some are familiar, many others are largely unknown to most New Yorkers. All are important members of the state's wild fauna and each plays a role in an ecological scheme so complex that we have just begun to understand it.

It should be noted here that the range maps for New York's fishes that appear in the following chapter may not always accurately depict that species range within the state. While a number of reliable sources were referenced in the creation of the maps, in some cases the sources reviewed reflected some disparities. Although most of the maps are believed to be fairly accurate, the reader should keep in mind that creating range maps is always problematic and some range maps may represent "presumptions" of a particular species range within New York.

CHAPTER 9

THE FISHES OF NEW YORK

— THE ORDERS AND FAMILIES OF NEW YORK FISHES —

Note: The arrangement below is a reflection of how the orders and families of fishes appear in this book and is not an accurate representation of the phylogentic relationship of the fishes.

Class - **Actinopterygii** (ray-finned fishes)

Order - **Perciformes** (typical fishes)

Family	**Centrarchidae** (sunfishes)
Family	**Moronidae** (true basses)
Family	**Scianidae** (drums)
Family	**Percidae** (perch and darters)
Family	**Gobiidae** (gobies)

Order - **Salmoniformes**

Family	**Esocidae** (pikes)
Family	**Salmonidae** (trouts)
Family	**Osmeridae** (smelts)
Family	**Umbridae** (mudminnows)

Order - **Anguilliformes** (eels)

Family	**Anguillidae** (freshwater eels)

Order - **Amiiformes** (bowfin)

Family	**Amiidae** (bowfin)

Order - **Gadiformes**

Family	**Gadidae** (codfish)

Order - **Atheriniformes**

Family	**Atherinidae** (silversides)

Order - **Lepisosteiformes** (gar)

Family	**Lepisosteidae** (gars)

Order - **Osteoglossiformes** (bonytongues)

Family	**Hiodontidae** (mooneyes)

Order - **Gasterosteiformes** (small marine fishes)

Family	**Gasterosteidae** (sticklebacks)

Order - **Scorpaeniformes** (scorpion fish)

Family	**Cottidae** (sculpins)

Order - **Clupeiformes** (sardines, herrings, and shads)

Family	**Clupeidae** (herring and shad)

Order - **Cyprinodontiformes** (topminnows and livebearers)

Family	**Fundulidae** (topminnows)
Family	**Fundulidae** -Family Poeciliidae (live-bearers)

Order - **Percopsiformes** (pirate perch and cavefish)

Family	**Aphredoderus** (pirate perch)
Family	**Percopsidae** (trout perch)

Order - **Siluriformes** (catfishes)

Family	**Ictaluridae** (American catfishes)

Order - **Acipenseriformes** (primitive fishes)

Family	**Acipenseridae** (sturgeons)
Family	**Polyodontidae** (paddlefish)

Order - **Cypriniformes** (minnows and suckers)

Family	**Catostomidae** (suckers)
Family	**Cyprinidae** (minnows)

Class - **Actinopterygii** (ray-finned fishes)

Order - **Perciformes** (typical fishes)

Family - **Centrarchidae** (sunfishes)

Largemouth Bass	Smallmouth Bass	Redbreast Sunfish
Micropterus salmoides	*Micropterus dolomieu*	*Lepomis auritus*

Size: May reach 38 inches and 22 pounds. Record size for New York is just over 11 pounds 4 ounces and 25.5 inches.

Presumed range in New York

Size: Maximum of up to 11 pounds. New York record size is 8 pounds 4 ounces and 20.5 inches.

Presumed range in New York

Size: The maximum size attained by this sunfish is about 1.5 pounds. No known records for New York.

Presumed range in New York

Abundance: Very common.

Abundance: Very common.

Abundance: Common.

Natural History: This is probably America's most popular freshwater game fish, pursued by anglers throughout the country. Indeed an entire sporting industry has evolved around the pursuit of this fish. Found in virtually any large body of water in the state. Also in smaller streams and small farm ponds. Produced in captivity for stocking.

Natural History: Prefers clearer, cooler, more highly oxygenated waters than the Largemouth Bass. Crayfish are a preferred prey, especially for stream-dwelling Smallmouth Bass. Like its cousin the Largemouth Bass, this is an important game species. It is renowned among sport fishermen for its tenacious fighting abilities when hooked.

Natural History: The natural range of the Redbreast Sunfish is the Atlantic Seaboard from Maine to Florida. Today this species has been widely introduced into other areas of New York as well as much of the eastern United States. This is a popular game fish along the eastern seaboard where it is fairly common. Most are only about four to five inches in length.

Bluegill	Northern Sunfish	Warmouth
Lepomis macrochirus	*Lepomis peltastes*	*Lepomis gulosus*

Size: Record of 4 pounds 12 ounces. New York record is 2 pounds 8 ounces and 12 inches. Most are under .5 pounds.

Presumed range in New York

Size: Maximum size for this species is about 5 inches total length. No known size records for New York.

Presumed range in New York

Size: Record of 2 pounds 7 ounces. No known size records for New York. Most are about 6–7 inches.

Presumed range in New York

Abundance: Very common.

Abundance: Rare in New York.

Abundance: Rare in New York.

Natural History: The Bluegill is America's best-known sunfish. This is the first fish caught on hook and line by many a young angler. It is an important game fish throughout the state. They are regularly stocked in new impoundments and are found in virtually every significant body of water in New York, including most farm ponds.

Natural History: Breeding males are one of the most brilliantly colored of the sunfishes. Clear streams with gravelly or sandy substrates are the primary habitat. In New York this species is restricted to the Niagra River/Lake Erie and the Lake Ontario Tributaries watersheds. This is a threatened species in New York and re-stocking efforts are underway.

Natural History: A fish of lowland creeks and swamps, the Warmouth is most common in the southern United States. In New York it is restricted to the Lower Hudson River watershed area. It prefers waters with thick growths of aquatic plants. The name comes from a patch of teeth that are present on the tongue. Introduced.

Class - **Actinopterygii** (ray-finned fishes)

Order - **Perciformes** (typical fishes)

Family - **Centrarchidae** (sunfishes)

Green Sunfish *Lepomis cyanellus*	Pumpkinseed *Lepomis gibbosus*	Bluespotted Sunfish *Enneacanthus gloriosus*

Size: Maximum recorded size is 2 lb. 2 oz. and 12 inches in length. No known size records for New York.  Presumed range in New York

Size: New York record 1 lb. 9 oz. and 11.5 inches. The maximum length for this species is 16 inches.  Presumed range in New York

Size: Maximum length 3.75 inches. Most are much smaller, averaging only about 2 to 2.5 inches.  Presumed range in New York

Abundance: Very common.

Abundance: Very common.

Abundance: Uncommon in New York.

Natural History: Introduced but becoming a fairly common fish in New York. It may be found in ponds and lakes, but its natural habitat is quite pools of slow-moving streams. It is known to hybridize readily with other *Lepomis* sunfishes, especially the Bluegill. Tolerates warm, low oxygen, muddy waters better than most other sunfishes.

Natural History: Found mainly in the northern United States and along the eastern seaboard. Inhabits still or slow-moving waters. Snails and bivalves are a major food source. The Pumpkinseed is similar to the Redear Sunfish of the southern United States. It also resembles the Redear Sunfish and could be considered the northern counterpart of that species.

Natural History: This handsome little sunfish is endemic to the Atlantic Seaboard and eastern Gulf Coastal Plain drainages from southern New York to Mississippi. Inhabits quiet waters of rivers and lakes having abundant aquatic vegetation that are often stained with tannins from decaying organic matter. Mucky substrates are preferred.

Banded Sunfish *Enneacanthus obesus*	Rock Bass *Ambloplites rupestris*	White Croppie and Black Croppie *Pomoxis annularis* and *Pomoxis nigromaculatus*

Size: Reaches a maximum length of only about 3.25 inches. Most are smaller.  Presumed range in New York

Size: Record size 3 pounds 10 ounces and 13.25 inches. in length. New York record 1 pound 5 ounces.  Presumed range in New York

Size: Record for White 5 lb. 3 oz. For Black 6 lbs. New York record is 3 lb. 6 oz. for Black. White 3 lbs. 3 oz.  Presumed range in New York

Abundance: Very rare in New York.

Abundance: Rare in New York.

Abundance: Common.

Natural History: This is New York's rarest sunfish species, currently found in only a few localities on Long Island. Though regarded as a Threatened Species in New York, it can be quite common along the Atlantic Seaboard much farther to south. Ranges from Long Island south to Florida. Inhabits quite, vegetated, mud-bottomed habitats.

Natural History: Also known as the "Goggle Eye," the Rock Bass is a fish of clear, cool waters. They are primarily a stream fish that is found in clear streams and lakes with good water quality throughout the state. The natural distribution is from the Great Lakes region west to the Dakotas and south into northern Alabama.

Natural History: The Black Croppie likes clearer waters than the White Croppie, though both are often found in the same waters. Popular game fishes, both species have been widely introduced across America. Positive ID can be made by counting the stiff spines on the dorsal fin. White Croppie has only six, Black has seven or eight.

Class - **Actinopterygii** (ray-finned fishes)

Order - **Perciformes** (typical fishes)

Family - **Moronidae** (true basses)

White Perch *Morone americana*	**White Bass** *Morone chrysops*	**Striped Bass** *Morone saxatilis*

White Perch
Morone americana

Size: New York record size is 3 lb. 1 oz. and 17.5 inches. Maximum size attained is about 22 inches.

Presumed range in New York

Abundance: Common.

Natural History: The White Perch is native to streams and brackish waters east of the Appalachian Plateau. They have been introduced into Lake Erie and now also occur in the lower portions of most of the lakes lower drainages. Introduction into a few other inland lakes in New York may have occurred as well.

White Bass
Morone chrysops

Size: World record 5 lb. 9 oz. Averages 10–14 inches and about a pound. New York record 3 pounds 6 ounces.

Presumed range in New York

Abundance: Generally uncommon.

Natural History: These important game fish are famous for forcing schools of bait fish to the surface then attacking them in a feeding frenzy. Bait fish leaping from the water create a visible indicator of the presence of feeding bass. Savvy fishermen look for these eruptions of bait fish known as "jumps."

Striped Bass
Morone saxatilis

Size: World record of 78.5 pounds is from salt water. New York record is 60 pounds and 53 inches in length.

Presumed range in New York

Abundance: Uncommon.

Natural History: Striped Bass are anadromous fish (lives in salt water but migrates into freshwater rivers to spawn). They are widely stocked in lakes by wildlife agencies across America and "landlocked" freshwater populations are now common in many areas of the country.

Family - **Sciaenidae** (drums)

Freshwater Drum
Aplodinotus grunniens

Presumed range in New York

Size: Record size is 54 pounds. New York record is 29 pounds 14 ounces and 36 inches in length. About 10 pounds is average.

Abundance: Generally common. They can become very common in some lake environments.

Natural History: This is the only member of the drum family that lives in freshwater. Most are salt water fishes and several are important food and sport fishes. By contrast the Freshwater Drum is not highly regarded by sport anglers despite the fact that they obtain an impressive size and will sometimes strike artificial lures meant for bass, trout, or other "game fishes." The flesh of the Freswater Drum is edible, but not very palatable. In some places they often go by the name "Sheephead." They are also sometimes called "grunt" or "croaker" in reference to the fact that they are capable of emitting grunting sounds from the air bladder. They feed heavily on small bivalves and have likely benefited from the invasion of the Zebra Mussel.

Class - **Actinopterygii** (ray-finned fishes)
Order - **Perciformes** (typical fishes)
Family - **Percidae** (perch and darters)

Yellow Perch *Perca flavescens*	**Walleye** *Sander vitreus*	**Sauger** *Sander canadensis*
		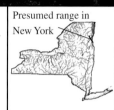
Size: World record 4 pounds 3 ounces. The New York record 3 pounds 8 ounces. Averages less than a pound. *Presumed range in New York*	**Size:** World record is 25 pounds. Average is 2 to 4 pounds. New York record is 16 pounds 9 ounces. *Presumed range in New York*	**Size:** World record 8 pounds 12 ounces. Average about a pound. New York record is 4 pounds 8 ounces and 22 inches. *Presumed range in New York*
Abundance: Very common.	**Abundance:** Fairly common.	**Abundance:** Very rare in New York.
Natural History: Native to the northern and eastern United States, Yellow Perch have recently expanded their range into more southerly regions. They are a popular pan fish throughout New York. They are found in both man-made and natural lakes throughout the region, including the Great Lakes.	**Natural History:** Walleye live in larger rivers, impoundments, and natural lakes where deep water provides the cool temperatures these fish require. They are regarded as one of the most palatable of the game fishes. Today they are found statewide but they are not native in the Atlantic Seaboard watershed.	**Natural History:** The Sauger is a smaller relative of the Walleye that is more adapted to turbid waters. Originally found throughout much of Great Lakes region, the Sauger today has largely disappeared from New York. Plans for re-introduction are underway by the fisheries componant of the NYSDEC.

Eastern Sand Darter
Ammocrypta pellucida

Size: A tiny fish, the Eastern Sand Darter can reach a maximum of 3.25 inches. The average size is usually just under 3 inches. Photo above is nearly three times life-size.

Presumed range in New York

Abundance: Relatively uncommon today. Siltation of streams is a major threat. A Threatened Species in New York.

Natural History: The aptly named Sand Darter is associated with sandy substrates of medium to large streams. When not swimming about in search of food or a mate they stay buried in the sand except for the top of head. Their translucent-colored bodies render them effectively invisible under these conditions. They require relatively clean waters with clean sandy bottoms. Unfortunately, due to siltation, these are conditions that no longer exist in vast stretches of many rivers and streams. These unusual little fish are virtually unknown to most New Yorkers.

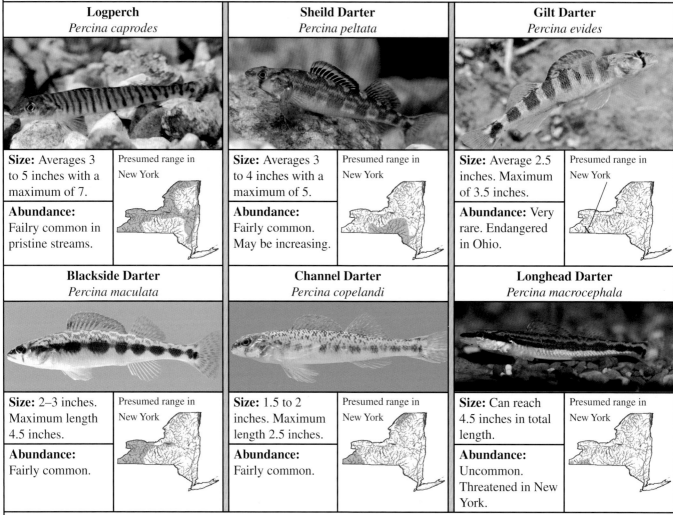

Class - **Actinopterygii** (ray-finned fishes)

Order - **Perciformes** (typical fishes)

Family - **Percidae** (perch and darters)

The Logperch Darters - genus *Percina* - six species in New York

Logperch *Percina caprodes*	**Sheild Darter** *Percina peltata*	**Gilt Darter** *Percina evides*

Logperch
Percina caprodes

Size: Averages 3 to 5 inches with a maximum of 7.

Abundance: Failry common in pristine streams.

Presumed range in New York

Sheild Darter
Percina peltata

Size: Averages 3 to 4 inches with a maximum of 5.

Abundance: Fairly common. May be increasing.

Presumed range in New York

Gilt Darter
Percina evides

Size: Average 2.5 inches. Maximum of 3.5 inches.

Abundance: Very rare. Endangered in Ohio.

Presumed range in New York

Blackside Darter
Percina maculata

Size: 2–3 inches. Maximum length 4.5 inches.

Abundance: Fairly common.

Presumed range in New York

Channel Darter
Percina copelandi

Size: 1.5 to 2 inches. Maximum length 2.5 inches.

Abundance: Fairly common.

Presumed range in New York

Longhead Darter
Percina macrocephala

Size: Can reach 4.5 inches in total length.

Abundance: Uncommon. Threatened in New York.

Presumed range in New York

Natural History: The darters of the genus *Percina* are represented by a total of six species in New York. Today one (Gilt Darter- *P. evides*) is extremely rare and endangered (re-stocking has been attempted by NYSDEC fisheries component). The Longhead Darter is also in trouble in New York and is regarded as a threatened species. There as many as 40 *Percina* species in the United States and collectively they range throughout much of the eastern United States. All occur east of the Rocky Mountains and most are found east of the Great Plains. The infamous Snail Darter, which was the subject of a great environmental controversy that arose over the construction of the Tellico Dam in Tennessee, is a member of this genus. Most of these fishes tend to inhabit the larger creeks (or even rivers), but some can be found in small (even tiny) creeks. A few species have adapted to lake life in reservoirs that have inundated their former riverine habitats, but all must return to streams to lay their eggs in flowing waters. Their habitats range from deep pools to shallow riffle areas, and all species spawn in the shallow gravel riffles of small or medium-sized creeks. The dependance upon clean, unaltered streams for breeding means these fishes face serious threats in America. In New York the invasive Round Goby is threat to species around Lake Erie. Along with their smaller relatives the *Etheostoma* darters (next two pages), these are some of New York's most interesting and colorful fishes. Both groups have become popular with aquarists, and in fact the darters have helped usher in a new style of fish keeping that focuses on native freshwater fishes of North America. Many aquarists, once introduced to the darters, will abandon the keeping of exotic tropical fishes for these beautiful "home grown" aquarium fishes. The diet of these fishes consists mostly of tiny aquatic insects and their larva, which makes keeping them in captivity quite challenging for the aquarist. For those interested in keeping these fascinating fish in captivity, the book *American Aquarium Fishes* from Texas A&M University Press is a handy reference. Another great source on information is the North American Native Fish Association (NANFA). Longevity in the wild for these fish is probably no more than a few years. Generally the darters of this genus are larger than their relatives in the *Etheostoma* genus which begin on the next page. The two groups can be told apart by the presence of a row of enlarged scales on the belly of the *Percina* group. The six representatives of New York's *Percina* darters are shown above.

Class - **Actinopterygii** (ray-finned fishes)

Order - **Perciformes** (typical fishes)

Family - **Percidae** (perch and darters)

The True Darters - genus *Etheostoma* - 11 species in New York (eight shown below and three on next page)

Banded Darter *Etheostoma zonale*	**Johnny Darter** *Etheostoma nigrum*	**Greenside Darter** *Etheostoma blennioides*

Male

Winter

Summer

Size: Maximum total length 3 inches.

Abundance: Fairly common.

Presumed range in New York

Size: Averages 2 to 2.75 inches. Max of 3 inches.

Abundance: Common within its range in New York.

Presumed range in New York

Size: Largest of the *Etheostoma*. Reaches 6.5 inches.

Abundance: Fairly common to common.

Presumed range in New York

Bluebreast Darter *Etheostoma camurum*	**Fantail Darter** *Etheostoma flabellare*	**Iowa Darter** *Etheostoma exile*

Male breeding

Male non-breeding

Size: Maximum total length is 3.5 inches.

Abundance: Very rare in New York. Endangered.

Presumed range in New York

Size: Maximum length of 3.3 inches.

Abundance: Common and widespread in New York.

Presumed range in New York

Size: One of America's smallest fish. Max 1.75 inches.

Abundance: Uncommon and declining in New York.

Presumed range in New York

Spotted Darter *Etheostoma maculatum*	**Rainbow Darter** *Etheostoma caeruleum*

Male

Female

Non-breeding male

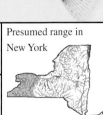
Breeding male

Female

Size: Maximum length just under 3 inches.

Abundance: Rare in New York. A threatened species.

Presumed range in New York

Size: Maximum length is just over 3 inches.

Abundance: Common in western New York.

Presumed range in New York

Class - **Actinopterygii** (ray-finned fishes)

Order - **Perciformes** (typical fishes)

Family - **Percidae** (perch and darters)

Tesselated Darter *Etheostoma olmstedi*	**Swamp Darter** *Etheostoma fusiforme*	**Variagate Darter** *Etheostoma variatum*

Size: Very small. Maximum length 2.75 inches. **Abundance:** New York's most common darter.	Presumed range in New York	**Size:** Can reach a maximum length 3.5 inches. **Abundance:** New York range is Long Island only.	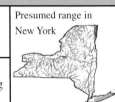Presumed range in New York	**Size:** Very small. Averages 1.5 inches. Max 1.7 inches. **Abundance:** NY range is Allegheny Watershed only.	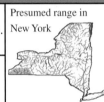Presumed range in New York

Natural History: With at least 148 species distributed across North America, the genus *Etheostoma* boasts more species than any other genus of freshwater fish in the United States. Among them are some of America's rarest fish and some of our most common. In coloration they range from a camouflaging mottled brown to remarkably colorful. Sexual dimorphism is common and is especially pronounced during the breeding season. In many species the breeding males rival the most colorful of tropical aquarium fishes. Most species are strongly sexually dimorphic, with the females being more subdued in color and sometimes outright drab. The stunning breeding color of the male is usually temporary and replaced by a much more faded appearance through the rest of the year following spring breeding. The females of these fishes are often so similar that even expert ichthyologists can have difficulty identifying them. New species have been recently described and there are most likely new species yet to be discovered. Unlike most fishes, they lack air bladders for flotation and they are mostly bottom dwellers that hug the sand and gravel bottoms of flowing streams. When startled they will move in quick, short dashes, hence the common name "darter." New York is home to 11 species of *Etheostoma*. Tennessee has the most of any state, at least 70 species! Collectively their habitats in include all the major watersheds in the state. They are found in waterways ranging from the Great Lakes to swamps, large rivers, and small creeks. Most species associate with flowing streams and many favor places with robust current. In these riffle areas they hug the substrate in water that may be only a couple of inches deep. Deep pools are used by other types of darters, and all may retreat to deeper pools in winter. A few species have a very restrictive distribution, being confined to a small area of drainage. Many species require pristine water conditions and these little fish can be a barometer to help determine the quality of New York's waterways. Like "the canary in the coal mine" they are often the first fishes to suffer from the effects of water pollution, siltation, and other forms of stream degradation. Before the passage of the Clean Water Act and other environmental legislation in the 1970s, many of America's darters had dissappeared from vast stretches of the nations waterways. Efforts to restore rivers and streams to more natural conditions in recent years has paid off with a resurgence of fish populations, including many of the darters. However several species are still regarded as threatened or endangered and recent presidential excutive orders relaxing protection of streams from mineral extraction activities may spell doom for some species.

Family - **Gobiidae** (gobies)

Round Goby (*Neogobius melanostomus*) and **Tubnose Goby** (*Proterorhinus semilunaris*)

Size: Averages about 5 or 6 inches but can reach a maximum length of 10 inches. **Abundance:** They are quite common in Lake Erie and within the lower portions of its tributaries.	Round Goby	Presumed range in New York

Natural History: The Round Goby is an exotic invasive species native to Eurasia that appeared in the Great Lakes sometime around 1990 and were first discovered in Lake Erie in 1995. As is often the case with exotic species, these fish have not been good for the Great Lakes. Though relatively small, they are voracious predators of the fry and eggs of game fish as well as smaller fish species such as darters and minnows. They are prolific reproducers that breed several times per year and they are blamed for the depletion of many native species throughout the Great Lakes region, especially the native darters and sculpins. It is believed they arrived in the Great Lakes in the ballast water of the many container ships that ply the waters of the Great Lakes.

Class - **Actinopterygii** (ray-finned fishes)

Order - **Salmoniformes**

Family - **Esocidae** (pikes)

Northern Pike *Esox lucius*	Grass Pickerel/Redfin Pickeral *Esox americanus*

Grass Pickeral

Size: Record size of 62.5 pounds is from Europe. North American record is 46 pounds 2 ounces and was a fish from NY.

Abundance: Common. Found statewide except for Long Island.

Presumed range in New York

Size: Average 8 to 10 inches. Maximum about 15 inches and 2 pounds. New York state record is 2 pounds and 1 ounce.

Abundance: Map shows Grass Pickerel as light gray, Redfin as dark gray.

Presumed range in New York

Natural History: The Northern Pike is a fish of clear waters with abundant aquatic vegetation. Inhabits lakes and large rivers. Its natural range in New York is the Great Lakes and the Allegheny Watershed, but it has been widely introduced and now occurs in all the state's watersheds except the Atlantic Ocean/Long Island Sound Watershed (see Figure 12). A voracious predator on fish, baby ducks, rodents, and just about any small animal that lives in or enters its aquatic habits. Like all members of the pike family, it has a large mouth lined with sharp, dagger-like teeth.

Natural History: Two distinct races of *E. americanus* are found in New York. The Redfin Pickerel (subspecies *americanus*) occurs in the eastern half of the state. As implied by the name it is recognized by its red fins. The Grass Pickerel (subspecies *vermiculatus*) is found in western New York and the Great Lakes. Inhabits swamps and streams. In smaller creeks it usually is found in quiet pools. Likes clear waters and avoids muddy streams. This is the smallest of the pike family and thus feeds on smaller prey. Minnows and other small fish are the principal prey.

Chain Pickerel *Esox niger*	Muskellunge *Esox masquinongy*

Size: Record size 9 pounds 6 ounces. New York record is 8 pounds 1 ounces. Average size about 3–4 pounds.

Abundance: Common. Widely introduced and today probably found statewide.

Presumed range in New York

Size: Record size 69 pounds 15 ounces was a specimen caught in New York from the St. Lawrence River in 1957.

Abundance: Uncommon to fairly common. Declining in the St. Lawrence River.

Presumed range in New York

Natural History: The Chain Pickerel is a fish of clear waters with abundant aquatic vegetation. Like all members of the pike family it is a highly carnivorous ambush predator with a very large mouth. The shape of the jaws is like a duck bill, and the jaws are equipped with rows of sharp, barracuda-like teeth. Feeds mostly on fish but will eat almost anything it can swallow.

Natural History: Known as the "Musky" by fishermen, this largest of the pikes is a prized game fish and one of the most difficult fishes to catch. They live in both man-made lakes and clear water rivers where they favor the deep pools containing boulders, logs, and other types of hiding places. The "Tiger Musky" is a hybrid between the Muskellunge and the Northern Pike.

Class - **Actinopterygii** (ray-finned fishes)

Order - **Salmoniformes**

Family - **Salmonidae** (trouts)

Rainbow Trout	Chinook Salmon	Pink Salmon
Oncorhynchus mykiss	*Oncorhynchus tshawytscha*	*Oncorhynchus gorbuscha*

Size: World record 42 lb. 2 oz. New York record 31 lb. 3 oz.

Presumed range in New York

Abundance: Common statewide in New York.

Size: New York's largest Salmon. Record from Alaska is 126 pounds.

Presumed range in New York

Abundance: Fairly common in Lake Ontario.

Size: New York record 4 pounds 15 ounces.

Presumed range in New York

Abundance: Very rare in New York. Great Lakes only.

Natural History: The Rainbow Trout was originally native to pacific drainages of the northwest. Today they have been widely introduced across much of America. They require cold, clear waters and thus are limited in distribution to the regions and watersheds with streams or lakes that met these criteria. Stocked annually by NYSDEC fisheries division.

Natural History: This species is popular game fish and it has been stocked regularly in New York waters since the early 1970s. Like most American Salmon they are naturally anadromous fishes of the pacific northwest. They are an introduced species that has adpated well to life in the Great Lakes. The record for New York is 47 pounds, 13 ounces and 48 inches in length.

Natural History: An anadromous species native to the pacific northwest of America. Has been introduced into the Great Lakes. First seen in Lake Erie in 1979 and has now adapted to a freshwater existance. Adults move out of the lake and into the lower reaches of some eastern Great Lakes drainages to spawn. Sometimes called "Humpback Salmon." This salmon is rather rare in New York waters.

Coho Salmon	Sockeye Salmon
Oncorhynchus kisutch	*Oncorhynchus nerka*

Size: New York record is 33 pounds 7 ounces. That is also the world record for hook and line. Can reach at least 38 inches total length. Most are between 12 and 20 pounds as adults.

Presumed range in New York

Abundance: Rare in New York.

Size: Can reach 33 inches in total length and weigh over 15 pounds. No records are available for New York. "Landlocked" freshwater forms are much smaller.

Presumed range in New York

Abundance: Rare in New York.

Natural History: Another anadromous species native to the pacific. Has been stocked in the Great Lakes since the 1970s and now enjoys a limited amount of spawning in New York waters in the tributaries of lakes Erie and Ontario. The sport fishery for this and other non-native salmon in New York is maintained by continuous re-stocking by NYDEC. These fish often go by the name "Silver Salmon" a reference to the color of non-spawning fishes. This is an important commercial fish species, but its flesh is not as highly rated as the Sockeye.

Natural History: Another anadromous species from the pacific that has been stocked in northern and eastern New York. Natural reproduction (if it occurs at all) is very rare in New York populations. Breeders on the pacific coast turn bright red when spawning in freshwaters of the pacific northwest. Thus these fish also go by the name "Red Salmon." The landlocked freshwater form is called "Kokanee Salmon." They are regarded by many as the most palatable species of salmon and they are an important commercial species.

Class - **Actinopterygii** (ray-finned fishes)

Order - **Perciformes** (typical fishes)

Family - **Salmonidae** (trouts)

Atlantic Salmon *Salmo salar*	**Brown Trout** *Salmo trutta*	**Brook Trout** *Salvelinus fontinalis*

Size: The New York state record is 24 lb. 15 oz. and 35 inches in length. Max 55 inches.	 **Size:** World record 40 lb. 4 oz. New York record 33 lb. 2 oz. and 38 inches in length.	**Size:** World record 14.5 lb. Most are much smaller and the New York state record is 6 lb.

Abundance: Generally uncommon.

Abundance: Common.

Abundance: Very common.

Natural History: The Atlantic Salmon is another primarily anadromous fish that has become landlocked in many of fresh the state's water environments. Unlike New York's other salmon specis, the Atlantic Salmon, as its name idicates is native to the east coast and is New York's only native salmon species. Today's populations are supported by stocking.

Natural History: A native of Europe, the Brown Trout this species has been introduced ithroughout America where cool, clear waters allow for its survival. In the most ideal waters natural repro- duction occurs, but but these fish are regularly stocked. In some areas they may outcompete and become a threat to native Brook Trout populations.

Natural History: The Brook Trout is the only stream trout native to the eastern United States. This fish requires cooler water temperatures than our other trouts, and is less tolerant of changes in stream conditions. It is widespread throughout the state but its range in some streams has decreased due to competion with the introduced Brown Trout.

Lake Trout *Salvelinus namaycush*	**Cisco** *Coregonus artedi*	**Lake Whitefish** and **Round Whitefish** *Coregonus clupeaformis* and *Prosopium cylindraceum*

 **Size:** New York record is 41 pounds 8 ounces and 43 inches in length. Maximum length is 4 feet.	 **Size:** Maximum length of 20 inches and up to 3 pounds. New York record is 5 pounds 7 ounces.	  **Size:** Lake White- fish reaches 31 inches. (New York record 10 pounds) Round Whitefish to 22 inches.

Abundance: Generally uncommon.

Abundance: Uncommon, declining.

Abundance: Uncommon.

Natural History: The Lake Trout is a native to the New York's Great Lakes. It was once the dominant trout in both Lake Erie and Lake Ontario but populations of this fish have declined significantly. They are regularly stocked in many of the state's inland lakes and it is an important game fish in New York. Restricted to lakes.

Natural History: These fish were once so common that a single fisherman might catch over a hundred in days fishing on Lake Erie. A northern species that reaches the southernmost limits of its range in Lake Erie. Inhabits deep, cold waters of natural lakes from the arctic to the Great Lakes region. Sometimes goes by the name "Lake Herring."

Natural History: Whitefish inhabit deep, cold waters with high dissolved oxygen content. In summer these fish retreat to the depths, often more than 40 feet deep. Although not rare, they are much less common than in historical times before the impact of human activities. Lake Whitefish is the most widespread of the two in New York.

Class - **Actinopterygii** (ray-finned fishes)

Order - **Perciformes** (typical fishes)		Order - **Anguilliformes** (eels)

Family - **Osmeridae** (smelts) · Family - **Umbridae** (mudminnows) · Family - **Anguillidae** (freshwater eels)

Rainbow Smelt
Osmerus mordax

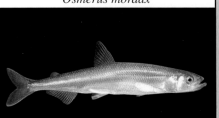

Size: Adults average 8 to 10 inches with a maximum length of about 14 inches.

Presumed range in New York

Abundance: Fairly common.

Natural History: In New York this anadromous fish naturally occurs in Lake Champlain, the lower Hudson, and the Great Lakes. It has been introduced and now occurs as a landlocked fish in many other watersheds across the state. The map above may not represent a completely accurate depiction of this fish's range in New York.

Mudminnows
Umbra lima and *Umbra pygmaea*

Central Mudminnow

Size: Average about 2–3 inches. Central Mudminnow can reach 6 inches, Eastern is smaller.

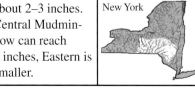
Presumed range in New York

Abundance: Common.

Natural History: New York's two *Umbra* species are very similar. The Central Mudminnow (*U. lima*) is the most widespread. The Eastern Mudminnow (*U. pygmaea*) occurs only in the lower Hudson, Long Island, and in the Delaware River watersheds. The Central Mudminnow occupies most of the rest of the state.

American Eel
Anguilla rostrata

Size: Adults frequently may reach 4 feet in length. The maximum recorded lenth is 60 inches.

Presumed range in New York

Abundance: Uncommon in New York

Natural History: Eels have one of the most remarkable life cycles of any fish. After hatching far out in the Atlantic Ocean tiny larva migrate to the coast and swim hundreds of miles upstream in inland rivers. After as many as 15 years adults return to the sea to spawn and die. Dams can hinder dispersal and the occurrence of eels today is sporadic.

Order - **Amiiformes**	Order - **Gadiformes**	Order - **Atheriniformes**

Family - **Amiidae** (bowfin) · Family - **Gadidae** (codfish) · Family - **Atherinidae** (silversides)

Bowfin
Amia calva

Size: Record size 21.5 pounds. New York record 12 pounds 14 ounces.

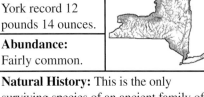
Presumed range in New York

Abundance: Fairly common.

Natural History: This is the only surviving species of an ancient family of primitive fishes that dates back to the age of the dinosaurs. Favors shallow waters. These fish are capable of gulping air into the swim bladder and burrowing into the mud during droughts.

Burbot
Lota lota

Size: Record size 18.5 pounds. New York record 16 pounds 2 ounces.

Presumed range in New York

Abundance: Uncommon.

Natural History: A relative of the salt water cod, haddock, and pollock. The Burbot is the single freshwater species of the entire order. They are cold-water fish that inhabit large rivers. They are usually confined to deep waters. Also found in Europe and Asia.

Brook Silverside
Labidesthes sicculus

Size: About 3 to 4 inches is average. Can reach 5 inches.

Presumed range in New York

Abundance: Fairly common.

Natural History: Silversides travel in large schools near the surface of lakes and rivers and are important prey for larger fish, including many game fish. They require clear water with abundant aquatic vegetation. Most members of this family are marine fishes.

Class - **Actinopterygii** (ray-finned fishes)

Order - **Lepisosteiformes** (gar)

Family - **Lepisosteidae** (gars)

Longnose Gar
Lepisosteus osseus

Presumed range in New York

Size: Maximum of about 5 pounds and 33 inches. New York record 13 pounds 3 ounces.

Abundance: Fairly common in western New York.

Natural History: Longnose Gar can be found in rivers, lakes, large creeks, and man-made impoundments. Uses quiet pools, backwaters, and shallow bays. Has the ability to obtain oxygen directly from the air via the air bladder, allowing it to survive droughts conditions that are fatal to most other fish species.

Order - **Gasterosteiformes** (small marine fishes)

Family - **Gasterosteidae** (sticklebacks)

Brook Stickleback
Culaea inconstans

Size: Average about 2.5 inches, maximum of 3.5 inches.

Abundance: Brook Stickleback is fairly common everywhere except southeast New York where it is replaced by the Fourspine Stickleback. Threespine is found only in Lake Ontario.

Presumed range in New York

Natural History: Most members of their order (Gasterosteiformes) are marine and include such strange fishes as the pipefish, tubenoses, and trumpetfishes to name a few. There are a total of four stickleback species and all once occured in New York. Today the Ninespine Stickleback is considered extirpated in the state. The Brook Stickleback (*Culea inconstans*, shown above) is the most widespread. The other two species are the **Threespine Stickleback** (*C. aculeatus*) found in Lake Ontario, and the **Fourspine Stickleback** (*Apeltes quadracus*) of the Lower Hudson River Watershed. Collectively their ranges include most of the state.

Order - **Osteoglossiformes** (bonytongues)

Family - **Hiodontidae** (mooneyes)

Mooneye
Hiodon tergisus

Presumed range in New York

Size: Average adult size is about 12 to 15 inches. Maximum of 17 inches and 2.5 pounds.

Abundance: Rare in New York and in decline everywhere.

Natural History: The Mooneye is one of only two species in the family Hiodontidae, which is a family that is endemic to North America. Their appearance is very similar to their distant relatives the shads and herrings. They live in large rivers and lakes and feed on a wide variety of invertebrate and small vertebrate prey.

Order - **Scorpaeniformes** (scorpion fish)

Family - **Cottidae** (sculpins)

Mottled Sculpin
Cottus bairdi

Size: Can reach a maximum of 6 inches in length.

Abundance: Mottled Sculpin is common in western New York. Slimy Sculpin is common to uncommon. Deep Water Sculpin is rare in New York and confined mostly to Lake Ontario.

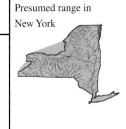

Presumed range in New York

Natural History: The Mottled Sculpin is typically a fish of upland streams and spring-fed runs where they inhabit the fast-flowing regions with gravel or rocky substrates. They are highly cryptic and nearly impossible to see when motionless on the gravel of stream beds. It is found mostly in western New York. In addition two other Sculpin species occur in the state. The **Slimy Sculpin** (*C. cognatus*) is widespread except for Long Island while the **Deep Water Sculpin** (*Myoxocephalus thompsonii*) lives only in Lake Ontario. All Sculpins have large mouths that enable them to take larger prey than would be suspected for such a small fish.

Class - **Actinopterygii** (ray-finned fishes)

Order - **Clupeiformes** (sardines, herrings, and shads)

Family - **Clupeidae** (herring and shad)

Alewife	American Shad

Alewife
Alosa pseudoharengus

Presumed range in New York

Size: Can reach about 15 inches.

Abundance: Common and widespread in New York.

Natural History: Alewife are anadromous fishes by nature, but they have been introduced into lakes such as the Finger Lakes where they have adapted to a year-round life in freshwater. Alewife in eastern New York (Long Island, Hudson River, Delaware River, Susquehanna River, and Chemung River) are sea-run fish that return to inland rivers to spawn.

American Shad
Alosa sapidissima

Presumed range in New York

Size: Up to 30 inches.

Abundance: Uncommon and in decline.

Natural History: As is the case with many other fish species that spawn in freshwater rivers but spend the rest of their lives in salt water, populations of American Shad have been negatively impacted by human alteration of natural waterways. Dams impede the ability to migrate upstream to spawning grounds. Once an important game fish.

Blueback Herring
Alosa aestivalis

Presumed range in New York

Size: Can reach about 16 inches.

Abundance: Uncommon and in decline in New York waters.

Natural History: An anadromous species. Found throughout the Atlantic coast from Nova Scotia to northern Florida and still fairly common in some areas. But dams have impeded spawning runs and negatively impacted populations in some areas. The range today has diminished as a result of these impacts. Adults migrate into freshwater in late spring to spawn. Young migrate back to the ocean within a few weeks when only about two inches long. In New York they are found mainly in the Hudson and Mohawk rivers.

Gizzard Shad
Dorosoma cepedianum

Presumed range in New York

Size: Can reach 20 inches and 3.5 pounds.

Abundance: Common within its range.

Natural History: Gizzard Shad are plankton feeders that filter tiny organisms from the water through specialized gill rakers. These fish occur in major rivers, natural lakes, and large impoundments throughout the eastern United States, including most of the larger rivers in New York as well as in the Great Lakes. Also lives in brackish waters in the lower Hudson River. The young and immatures are an important forage species for many other fish, including many game species. Even adults are prey for larger fish.

Class - **Actinopterygii** (ray-finned fishes)

Order - **Cyprinodontiformes** (topminnows and livebearers)

Family - **Fundulidae** (topminnows)	Family - **Poeciliidae** (livebearers)

Banded Killifish
Fundulus diaphanus

Size: Maximum of 5 inches.

Abundance: Common.

Natural History: A small fish that hunts the surface of shallow waters for tiny invertebrate prey. A similar species, the **Mummichog** (*F. heroclitus*), occurs on Long Island and in the Lower Hudson River drainage.

Presumed range in New York

Eastern Mosquitofish
Gambusia holbrooki

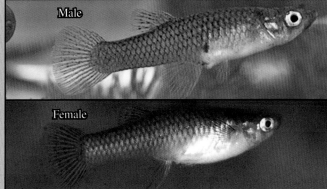

Male

Female

Size: Females 2.5 inches, males 1.25 inches.

Abundance: Uncommon in New York.

Natural History: True to their name, these tiny fish eat large numbers of mosquito larva. Uniquely among New York fishes, they give birth to fully formed young. They live in the shallows and forage in water less than an inch deep.

Presumed range in New York

Order - **Percopsiformes**

Family- **Aphredoderus** (pirate perch)	Family- **Percopsidae** (trout perch)

Pirate Perch
Aphredoderus sayanus

Size: Maximum 5.5 inches. Average adult is around 3 to 4 inches.

Presumed range in New York

Abundance: The western race found in tributaries of Lake Ontario is rare. The population inhabiting Long Island is fairly common.

Natural History: The Pirate Perch is endemic to North America. It lives in swamps and spring-fed wetlands among heavy aquatic vegetation. May also be found in backwaters of large creeks and small rivers. Although they are small fishes, they have rather large mouths and they are quite predaceous on insects, crustaceans, and small fishes.

Trout Perch
Percopsis omiscomaycus

Size: Adults average about 3 or 4 inches. Maximum length 6 inches.

Presumed range in New York

Abundance: Fairly common in Ohio. Most common in Lake Erie and its lower tributaries but also found in most other river systems in the state.

Natural History: The Trout Perch lives in lakes and quiet pools of larger streams. It feeds on insects, crustaceans, and small fish. Mainly nocturnal, it spends the day in deep water and moves into the shallows at night to feed. This is a species of high latitudes that approaches the southernmost limits of its range in the Great Lakes region.

Class - **Actinopterygii** (ray-finned fishes)

Order - **Siluriformes** (catfishes)

Family - **Ictaluridae** (American catfishes)

Yellow Bullhead *Ameiurus natalis*	**Black Bullhead** *Ameiurus melas*	**Brown Bullhead** *Ameiurus nebulosus*

Size: Maximum of 19 inches. Record weight 3 pounds 10 ounces.

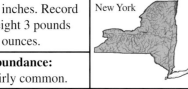
Presumed range in New York

Abundance: Fairly common.

Natural History: Widespread, common, and easily caught on hook and line the Yellow Bullhead is a familiar fish to many Americans. They are often known by the nickname "Mudcat." Ranges from the central Great Plains eastward, including all of New York except Long Island. Told from other bullheads by yellow-colored chin barbels.

Size: Record weight is 8 pounds but few will ever exceed 3 pounds.

Presumed range in New York

Abundance: Uncommon.

Natural History: Black Bullheads are mainly nocturnal fishes that do not feed during the day. They live in still-water pools in streams or in natural lakes and man-made impoundments. They can be distinguished from the Yellow Bullhead by their dark chin barbels. From the Brown Bullhead by the lighter color of the caudal fin.

Size: Maximum length 21 inches. May rarely reach 6–8 pounds.

Presumed range in New York

Abundance: Common.

Natural History: Very similar to the Black Bullhead. The most common of the New York's *Ameiurus* catfishes. As with other bullheads, the parent fish stay with the eggs until hatching and the newly hatched young swim in schools near the surface with the mother bullhead in attendance. Found in ponds, lakes, sloughs, creeks, and small rivers.

White Catfish *Ameiurus catus*	**Channel Catfish** *Ictalurus punctatus*	**Stonecat** *Noturus flavus*

Size: Maximum size attained is just over 2 feet. New York record is 10 pounds 5 ounces.

Presumed range in New York

Abundance: Uncommon.

Natural History: Favors sluggish streams and backwaters. The largest member of its genus but still small compared to many members of the catfish family, some of which can exceed 100 pounds. Endemic to the Atlantic Coastal Plain of America from southern New England southward into Florida. Though closely related to the Bullheads it resembles the Channel Catfish.

Size: Maximum of about 65 pounds. New York record 35 pounds and 38.25 inches.

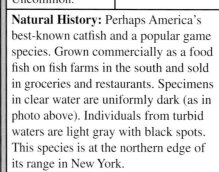
Presumed range in New York

Abundance: Uncommon.

Natural History: Perhaps America's best-known catfish and a popular game species. Grown commercially as a food fish on fish farms in the south and sold in groceries and restaurants. Specimens in clear water are uniformly dark (as in photo above). Individuals from turbid waters are light gray with black spots. This species is at the northern edge of its range in New York.

Size: Maximum of about 12 inches. Average around 7–8 inches.

Presumed range in New York

Abundance: Fairly common.

Natural History: The Stonecat is the largest member of the Madtom group (genus *Noturus*). Most Madtoms are diminutive catfishes that are only a few inches in length. All are stream fishes and the Stonecat prefers streams with rocky substrates. Like other members of it's genus it is a nocturnal predator of a wide variety of aquatic invertebrate and small vertebrate prey.

Class - **Actinopterygii** (ray-finned fishes)

Order - **Siluriformes** (catfishes)

Family - **Ictaluridae** (American catfishes)

Madtoms - genus *Noturus* (four species in New York)

Margined Madtom *Noturus insignis*	**Brindled Madtom** *Noturus miurus*	**Tadpole Madtom** *Noturus gyrinus*

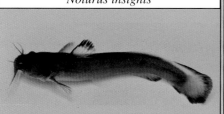  

Size: Maximum length 5.25 inches. Average 2–4 inches.  Presumed range in New York	**Size:** Maximum length 5.25 inches. Average 3 inches. 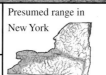 Presumed range in New York	**Size:** Maximum length 5 inches. 2–3 inches average. 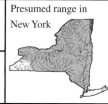 Presumed range in New York
Abundance: Fairly common in central New York.	**Abundance:** Uncommon in New York.	**Abundance:** Fairly common and widespread.

Natural History: These are small catfishes that average only a few inches in length. There are 26 species total in this genus. A total of four species occur in New York. All Madtoms are secretive and nocturnal, and are thus relatively unknown to the general public. Like other American catfishes the Madtoms have spiny dorsal and pectoral fins that produce a mild venom. A puncture from one of these spines can result in a significant amount of pain and swelling, but it is not life threatening. Like all catfishes, madtoms have a fleshy fin between the dorsal fin and the tail known as an "adipose fin." These are predaceous fish that feed on a wide variety of aquatic life consisting of both invertebrates and very small fishes. They feed and are active mostly at night, and spend the days hidden beneath overhanging root wads or burrowed into detritus of deep pools. Human refuse is also used as a refugia, with old tires and even beer cans reportedly used as daytime hiding places. New York's fourth madtom species (not shown) is the Stonecat (*N. flavus*).

Order - **Acipenseriformes** (primitive fishes)

Family - **Acipenseridae** (sturgeons)		Family - **Polyodontidae** (paddlefish)
Shortnose Sturgeon *Acipenser brevirostrum*	**Lake Sturgeon** *Acipenser fulvescens*	**Paddlefish** *Polyodon spathula*

Size: Record weight 8 pounds. No records available for New York.  Presumed range in New York	**Size:** Record 310 pounds. Maximum length 8 feet.  Presumed range in New York	**Size:** Can reach at least 180 lb. and over 7 ft. No records for New York. Presumed range in New York
Abundance: Rare in New York.	**Abundance:** Maximum of 43 inches.	**Abundance:** Very rare in New York.

| **Natural History:** The Shortnose Sturgeon is an endangered species in New York. It occurs in New York only in the lower Hudson River. A similar species, the **Atlantic Sturgeon** (*A. oxyrhincus*) is also found in the lower Hudson and is also endangered. Atlantic Sturgeon can reach 10 feet in length and weigh several hundred pounds. | **Natural History:** The Lake Sturgeon inhabits the deep channels of the large rivers draining the middle of America as well as the Great Lakes and the St. Lawrence Watershed. They may live for up to 150 years. Large females will lay up to three million eggs. Females attain a greater size than males. Despite being widespread, they are rare. | **Natural History:** Paddlefish often go by the name "Spoonbill Catfish," but in fact they are not related to the catfishes. They are a member of a very small, primitive order of fishes that have skeletons that are mostly cartilage. Like the other fish on this page they have been impacted by dams which prohibit movement. |

Class - **Actinopterygii** (ray-finned fishes)

Order - **Cypriniformes** (minnows and suckers)

Family - **Catostomidae** (suckers)

Quillback *Carpiodes cyprinus*	**Largemouth Buffalo** *Ictiobus cyprinellus*	**Spotted Sucker** *Minytrema melanops*

Quillback
Carpiodes cyprinus

Size: Maximum about 2 feet and 12 pounds.

Abundance: Fairly common in larger streams.

Presumed range in New York
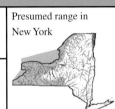

Natural History: The Quillback is most common in slow-moving streams. Food is benthic invertebrates sucked from the substrate. Occurs both in rivers and natural lakes or impoundments but may be less tolerant of turbid conditions than many other members of the sucker family. Like many large suckers, this is a commercial food fish in some areas.

Largemouth Buffalo
Ictiobus cyprinellus

Size: Can reach a maximum of 80 pounds.

Abundance: Very rare in New York.

Presumed range in New York

Natural History: Largemouth Buffalo are important commercial food fishes. Found in large rivers and their backwaters and in impoundments. This species is more accepting of silt-laden waters than others of its family. Breeds during spring in flooded fields and backwaters. May be negatively impacted in flood controlled rivers and streams.

Spotted Sucker
Minytrema melanops

Size: Maximum of about 18 inches.

Abundance: Very rare in New York. Restricted to two locations.

Presumed range in New York

Natural History: Lives in pools and slow-moving waters of large and small rivers, as well as larger creeks. Moves into smaller creeks in spring to spawn over gravel or rocks. Feeds on small aquatic invertebrates. Although fairly widespread in the eastern United States, this is a rare fish in New York. It was not discovered in the state until recently.

Eastern Creek Chubsucker *Erimyzon oblongus*	**Northern Hogsucker** *Hypentelium nigricans*

Eastern Creek Chubsucker
Erimyzon oblongus

Presumed range in New York

Size: Maximum size 16.5 inches.

Abundance: Fairly common in streams except in southwestern and northeastern New York.

Natural History: The Creek Chubsucker is widespread throughout southeastern and central New York. It is fairly common in small and large creeks in areas with sand or gravel substrate. They eat tiny crustaceans, insects, and algae. A very simialr species, the Lake Chubsucker, was once found in New York's Great Lakes, but that species is believed to now be extirpated in the state. In New York it often inhabits swampy, dark-water streams.

Northern Hogsucker
Hypentelium nigricans

Presumed range in New York
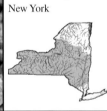

Size: Maximum size 22.5 inches.

Abundance: Fairly common in suitable habitats throughout its range. In New York most common in western region.

Natural History: This species is found mostly in large, clear creeks with rocky substrates. Also inhabits clear lakes with gravel or rocky bottoms. This is a bottom dweller that hugs the substrate and sucks small aquatic invertebrates from sand or gravel. The name "Hogsucker" comes from their method of feeding that entails "rooting" in the substrate like a hog. They are very cryptically patterned and blend in well with gravel bottoms.

Class - **Actinopterygii** (ray-finned fishes)
Order - **Cypriniformes** (minnows and suckers)
Family - **Catostomidae** (suckers)
Redhorse Suckers - genus *Moxostoma* (seven species in New York, five shown)

Golden Redhorse
Moxostoma erythrurum

Size: Maximum of about 26 inches. and 4.5 pounds.

Abundance: The most common redhorse in Ohio.

Presumed range in New York

Black Redhorse
Moxostoma duquesnii

Size: Record size 26 inches and 7 pounds.

Abundance: Fairly common in unpolluted streams.

Presumed range in New York

Shorthead Redhorse
Moxostoma macrolepidotum

Size: Can reach 19 inches and 3 pounds.

Abundance: Fairly common in larger rivers.

Presumed range in New York

River Redhorse - *Moxostoma carinatum*

Size: The largest of the redhorse suckers. Reaches at least 29 inches and 10.5 pounds.

Abundance: Uncommon. Restricted to larger rivers. Listed as a Species of Concern by ODNR.

Presumed range in New York

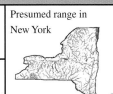

Silver Redhorse - *Moxostoma anisurum*

Size: Official record 25 inches and 8.25 pounds. Unconfirmed reports of up to 10 pounds.

Abundance: Restricted to large and medium size rivers. Vulnerable to pollution and siltation.

Presumed range in New York

Natural History: The Redhorse Suckers are the most diverse group within the sucker family, with 20 species found in North America. The genus ranges across much of the eastern United States and their are seven species that range into New York. All are similar in appearance and can be difficult to properly identify. Collectively, they range throughout most of the state and nearly ever major drainage has at least one species. Their flesh is described as good but bony, and they are sometimes pursued by anglers both for food and sport. In some regions of their range there are "gigging seasons" for these species, and they are hunted at night with lights and gigs from specialized boats. This practice is fairly common in the clear rivers of the Ozark Plateau in Missouri. Some anglers will use bow-fishing techniques for these species as well. Although they will persist in reservoirs they always spawn in small to medium-sized streams with gravel substrates. These are stream fishes that are typically found in clear waters. Pictured above are five of New York's *Moxostoma* species. The other species (not shown) are the **Greater Redhorse** (*M. valenciennesi*) and the **Smallmouth Redhorse** (*M. breviceps*). The Greater Redhorse is a northern fish that occurs in New York only in the St. Lawrence watershed . The Smallmouth Redhorse is very similar to the Shorthead Redhorse (shown above). The Smallmouth Redhorse is widespread and can be found in both the St. Lawrence and the Atlantic Seaboard watersheds. Collectively, these fishes are often mistaken for Carp. Unlike the Carp, which is a non-native species from the old world that can live in waters of poor quality, the Redhorse Suckers require unpolluted waters. In this manner their presence is an indicator of the overall health of a stream.

Class - **Actinopterygii** (ray-finned fishes)

Order - **Cypriniformes** (minnows and suckers)

Family - **Catostomidae** (suckers)

White Sucker *Catostomus commersoni*	Longnose Sucker *Catostomus catostomus*

Size: Maximum 25 inches and 7 pounds.

Abundance: Common. The White Sucker is found throughout the state in virtually all major drainages.

Presumed range in New York

Size: Maximum length 25 inches.

Abundance: Uncommon. Although found nearly statewide, the Longnose Sucker is generally an uncommon fish.

Presumed range in New York

Natural History: There are a total of three similar sucker species found in New York state. The White Sucker is the most common. It inhabits a wide variety of small rivers and creeks as well as natural and man-made lakes. In New York they are common everywhere except perhaps on Long Island. Although bony, their flesh is quite palatable and they are sought for food and sport in some regions, including in New York where they are often caught on hook and line. The Longnose Sucker was historically more common and widespread in the state, but today populations appear to be in decline or even extirpated from many of its former habitats. In New York this fish favors cool streams and lakes with gravel substrates. Its range includes most of Canada and all of Alaska as far north as the arctic, so though it may be declining in New York, as a species it appears secure. Finally, the **Summer Sucker** (*C. utawana*) is New York's only endemic sucker. Somewhat rare and poorly known the Summer Sucker has disappeared from some former watersheds and is now restricted to a few small creeks in the Adirondacks region. It is similar to the more common White Sucker, but is much smaller and inhabits smaller streams and creeks.

Family - **Cyprinidae** (minnows)

Common Carp *Cyprinus carpio*	Goldfish *Carassius auratus*	Golden Shiner *Notemigonus crysoleucas*

Size: Angling record is 55 pounds.

Abundance: Common and widespread except in Adirondacks.

Presumed range in New York

Size: Maximum 20 inches and 5 pounds.

Abundance: Uncommon but widely distributed in suitable habitat.

Presumed range in New York

Size: Maximum size 14.5 inches.

Abundance: Common and widespread.

Presumed range in New York

Natural History: Many people are surprised to learn that the Common Carp is an invasive species in America. Native to Eurasia, they were first brought to the United States in the early 1800s. They are now widespread and common in most aquatic habitats in America. A benthic feeder that "roots" like a hog in muddy bottoms and increases water turbidity.

Natural History: Native to Asia, the Goldfish is now widely established across most of North America. The gaudy colors commonly seen in fish ponds and pet stores rarely survive in wild populations. Found in most rivers and lakes and can survive in tiny ponds. More tolerant of pollution and siltation than many native species.

Natural History: This minnow is well known among fishermen and is sold as a bait fish in many regions of the United States. In their natural habitat they are fish of still-water pools of streams and backwaters of rivers. They will also thrive in impoundments and small farm ponds. Millions are raised commercially each year to be sold in bait stores.

Class - **Actinopterygii** (ray-finned fishes)

Order - **Cypriniformes** (minnows and suckers)

Family - **Cyprinidae** (minnows)

Redside Dace	**Common Shiner**	**Striped Shiner**
Clinostomus elongatus	*Luxilus cornutus*	*Luxilus chrysocephalus*

Size: Can reach 4.5 inches.

Abundance: Fairly common within its range in the state.

Presumed range in New York

Size: Can reach 8 inches.

Abundance: Common and widespread throughout New York.

Presumed range in New York

Size: Can reach 8 inches.

Abundance: Fairly comon but in western New York only.

Presumed range in New York

Natural History: Lives in clear-water creeks or small, clear rivers with gravel, sand, or rock substrates. Often found in very small streams. Usually seen in large schools hanging out in small pools. Food is small aquatic insects. Absent from the Adirondacks and southeastern New York.

Natural History: Two very similar species that often hybridize where their range overlaps. Both are stream fishes that live in small to medium-sized creeks with clear water and sand or gravel substrates. Small individuals of both species are frequently trapped by fishermen to use as bait and both are common prey species for larger fish. As with many minnow species, the color and pattern of these shiners can change with age and significant sexual dimorphism also occurs (shown above are mature males). Miscellaneous invertebrates including aquatic insect larva are eaten along with algae.

Northern Redbelly Dace	**Finescale Dace**	**Central Stoneroller**
Chrosomus eos	*Chrosomus neogaeus*	*Campostoma anomalum*

Size: Maximum of 4.5 inches.

Abundance: Common in small, clear, flowing streams.

Presumed range in New York

Size: Maximum of 4.5 inches.

Abundance: Fairly common to uncommon. Declining in places.

Presumed range in New York

Size: Maximum of about 11 inches.

Abundance: One of the more common stream fish within its range.

Presumed range in New York

Natural History: The Northern Redbelly Dace can be found in very small streams only a few feet across. Both species require clean, unpolluted waters with moderate to fast current and abundant riffles and pools. The preferred substrate for both is a silt bottom. The Northern Redbelly Dace is often very common in small streams in forested regions, especially those that are fed by springs or seeps and this species is an indicator of good water quality. The breeding males are one of the most colorful minnows in America. Food is mostly insects, some caught by leaping into the air. Also eats some plant material. Finescale Dace uses sluggish swampy streams with abundant vegetation. Insects and small crustaceans are reported as food items for this species. In New York the Northern Redbelly Dace is more widespread, with the Finescale Dace being restricted to the Adirondack region of the state. Both spawn in the spring and the Northern Redbelly Dace may spawn again in summer. Some hybridization occurs where the ranges of the two similar species overlap.

Natural History: Nearly every stream within their range capable of supporting fish life will have a population of Stonerollers. Their name comes from their habit of aggressive bottom-feeding in gravelly stream beds, moving small stones in the process. Male Stonerollers will also move pebbles with their mouths in the construction of the spawning bed. They use their lower mandibles to scrape algae and tiny organisms from gravel, stones, submerged logs, etc.

Class - **Actinopterygii** (ray-finned fishes)
Order - **Cypriniformes** (minnows and suckers)
Family - **Cyprinidae** (minnows)

Grass Carp
Ctenopharyngodon idella

Size: Maximum 4 feet and 100 pounds.

Abundance: Uncommon in New York. Introduced.

Presumed range in New York

Natural History: The Grass Carp is a non-native species introduced to control the growth of invasive aquatic plants. These huge members of the minnow family are strictly vegetarian. Specimens released into New York waters are sterilized to prevent natural reproduction of a species that might become detrimental if allowed to reproduce.

Creek Chub
Semotilus atromaculatus

Breeding Male

Size: Maximum length 12 inches.

Abundance: Very common. Found in almost every creek in New York.

Presumed range in New York

Natural History: The Creek Chub is of the most widespread and common creek fishes in America and it probably inhabits nearly every stream in the state that is capable of supporting fish life (except for on Long Island). Like many minnows, breeding males develop tubercles on the head and snout, leading to the common nickname "Hornyhead" (see inset photo above). The Fallfish is a much larger version of the Creek Chub that is less common in the state. Creek Chubs can inhabit small creeks where they are sometimes the stream's top fish predator. Fallfish are found in larger creeks with sandy substrates. Both have large mouths and prey on a wide variety of insects, small crustaceans, and tiny fishes.

Fallfish
Semotilus corporalis

Size: Can reach 20 inches.

Abundance: Uncommon in New York. Western New York only.

Presumed range in New York

Lake Chub
Couesius plumbeus

Size: Maximum of 9 inches.

Abundance: Uncommon and has declined in many former drainages.

Presumed range in New York

Natural History: The Lake Chub is the most northerly ranging minnow species in America and is the only Cyprinid fish found in Alaska. It lives in both lakes and streams but needs cold, clean waters with gravel bottoms. It is widespread and common across much of Canada's uspoiled wilderness. In New York the species has declined significantly in much of its former range but still thrives in most of the Adirondack region of the state.

Northern Pearl Dace
Margariscus nachtriebi

Size: Maximum of about 6.5 inches.

Abundance: Fairly common within its rather restricted range in New York.

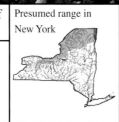
Presumed range in New York

Natural History: Inhabits pools in creeks and small rivers as well as ponds and lakes. Favors small cold water streams with clean gravel bottoms. A very similar species known as the **Allegheny Pearl Dace** (*M. margarita*) is found in western and central New York. The habitat requirements are the same as for the Northern Pearl Dace and the Allegheny Pearl Dace can be regarded as a more southerly counterpart to the Northern Pearl Dace.

Rudd
Scardinius erythrophthalmus

Size: Maximum of 19 inches.

Abundance: Fairly common and increasing in some watersheds.

Presumed range in New York

Natural History: The Rudd is one of three non-native invasive minnows originally native to Europe that have now become established in parts of New York. Rudd are similar in appearance to the Golden Shiner and are widespread across the state. The other two invasives are the **Tench**, a carp-like minnow that can reach 33 inches established in Lake Champlain, and the **Bitterling**, a small, deep-bodied minnow established near the mouth of the Hudson River.

Class - **Actinopterygii** (ray-finned fishes)

Order - **Cypriniformes** (minnows and suckers)

Family - **Cyprinidae** (minnows)

Bigeye Chub *Hybopsis amblops*	**Eastern Silvery Minnow** *Hybognathus regius*	**Silver Chub** *Macrhybopsis storeianna*

Size: May reach 4 inches in length.

Abundance: Rare. NYSDEC Species of Greatest Conservation Need.

Presumed range in New York

Natural History: A fish of small rivers and large creeks. Declining over much of its range, due mainly to siltation. This fish requires clean gravel or stones in the stream substrate and excessive runoff from agricultural lands or non-vegetated areas can result in siltation of stream bottoms. Restricted to the western portion of New York.

Size: May reach 4.75 inches.

Abundance: Fairly common but declining in some areas of the state.

Presumed range in New York

Natural History: *Hybognathus* minnows are bottom feeders that ingest tiny algae and detritus from silt. Two species occur in New York. The **Brassy Minnow** (*H. hankinsoni*) ranges across most of northern New York. Its range overlaps that of the Eastern Silvery Minnow in that region, but it prefers to inhabit smaller streams.

Size: Can reach 9 inches in length.

Abundance: Very rare. An Endangered Species.

Presumed range in New York

Natural History: This species is good example of the fact that many of the state's fishes are completely unknown to most New York residents. The Silver Chub inhabits the deep waters of large rivers and lakes. In New York it occurs only in Lake Erie and in the mouths of lake tributaries. It is an important forage species for many larger game fish.

Fathead Minnow *Pimephales promelas*	**Bluntnose Minnow** *Pimephales notatus*	**Cutlip Minnow** *Exoglossum maxillingua*

Size: Males can reach 4 inches. Females smaller.

Abundance: Common and widespread.

Presumed range in New York

Size: Males can reach 4.25 inches. Females smaller.

Abundance: Very common except on Long Island.

Presumed range in New York

Size: Can reach at least 6 inches in length.

Abundance: Fairly common.

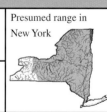
Presumed range in New York

Natural History: These are very common minnows that may be found in rivers, creeks, reservoirs, and even ponds occasionally. They are tough little fishes that can survive warm, low-oxygen waters and waters with high turbidity. Breeding males of both species have very dark, nearly black heads and tubercles on the snout. Their resilience, rapid reproductive capacity, and ease in rearing in captivity has led to their being widely used as bait minnows, where they are often sold under the nickname "Tuffy." A reddish-colored strain of the Fathead Minnow known as "Rosy Red" has also been bred for sale in bait stores. Because of their prolific use for bait, these minnows have become widely established across the United States and Canada and they are today perhaps the most common fish species in North America. They are mostly bottom feeders that both tiny invertebrates as well as algae.

Natural History: A stream fish that prefers areas with clean gravel sub-strate. This unique genus (*Exoglossum*) contains only two species and both occur in New York. Both have similar habitat requirements. The other species is known as the **Tonguetied Minnow** (*E. laura*). It is fouind in New York only in the Allegheny watershed of the extreme southwestern part of the state. The Cutlip Minnow is more widespread.

Class - **Actinopterygii** (ray-finned fishes)
Order - **Cypriniformes** (minnows and suckers)
Family - **Cyprinidae** (minnows)

Streamlined Chub *Erimystax dissimilis*	**River Chub** *Nocomis micropogon*	**Hornyhead Chub** *Nocomis biguttatus*

Size: Up to 5.5 inches.

Presumed range in New York

Abundance: Rare. Found in New York only in the Allegheny Watershed.

Size: Can exceed 12 inches.

Presumed range in New York

Abundance: Fairly common within its limited range in the state.

Size: Can exceed 10 inches.

Presumed range in New York

Abundance: Fairly common. May not occur in all areas shown.

Natural History: Another stream fish that favors clear streams with gravel or rocky bottoms. Usually found in stream portions with significant current. Inhabits medium-sized to large streams and rivers. The only remaining member of its genus in New York. One other species (Gravel Chub, *E. x-punctatus*) once also occured in the Allegheny watershed.

Natural History: Habitat is clear creeks and small rivers with sandy or gravel bottoms. These large minnows are both herbivorous and invertivorous in diet. All species have well-developed tubercles on the head. The head tubercles are especially apparent on the breeding males, who will also have small tubercles on their pectoral fins. Males build elaborate spawning nests by moving pebbles with their mouth. Large adults are quite carnivorous and feed on small crayfish, snails, and aquatic insects. They will readily take worms on hook and line and many a young fishermen learned their trade by catching *Nocomis* chubs from nearby rivers and streams in rural areas.

Blacknose Dace *Rhinichthys atratulus*	**Longnose Dace** *Rhinichthys cataractae*	**Silverjaw Minnow** *Ericymba buccata*

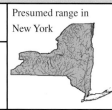

Size: Up to 4 inches.

Presumed range in

Abundance: Very common except on Long Island.

Size: Up to 5 inches.

Presumed range in New York

Abundance: Very common. Less common in the Adirondacks.

Size: About 3.75 inches.

Presumed range in New York

Abundance: Rare in New York. Far western New York only.

Natural History: Both species like small to medium-sized streams with gravel bottoms. Blacknose can be found in tiny creeks and will sometimes inhabit lakes that have feeder streams. Longnose Dace likes areas with significant currents and will inhabit rivers as well as lakes with feeder streams. The food for these fish is tiny aquatic insects (especially the larva of aquatic dipterans), amphipods, isopods, and small worms. Although both species occur throughout the state, they usually partition the habitat with the Longnose Dace inhabiting colder, more swiftly moving waters. Where they occur in the same streams they avoid interbreeding by spawning at different times. Some experts now split the Blacknose Dace into two distinct species (Eastern and Western Blacknose Dace).

Natural History: The Silverjaw Minnow is unique among New York minnows in having a series of visible cavities within the upper jaw below the eye. The function of these cavities may be tactile or sensory. Some experts place this species in the *Notropis* genus, while others argue the unique morphological character of its jaws warrant its placement in a different genus.

Class - **Actinopterygii** (ray-finned fishes)

Order - **Cypriniformes** (minnows and suckers)

Family - **Cyprinidae** (minnows)

Redfin Shiner *Lythrurus umbratilis*	**Spotfin Shiner** *Cyprinella spiloptera*	**Satinfin Shiner** *Cyprinella analostana*

Size: Maximum of 3.5 inches.	**Size:** Can reach nearly 5 inches.	**Size:** Maximum of 4.5 inches.
Abundance: Rare in New York. A Species of Special Concern. 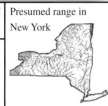 Presumed range in New York	**Abundance:** Fairly common and possibly increasing.  Presumed range in New York	**Abundance:** Uncommon. Possibly declining in New York. 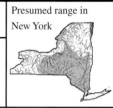 Presumed range in New York

Natural History: The Redfin Shiner is mostly a fish of small to medium creeks. They are more tolerant of poor water quality than many other stream fishes. The breeding males are among our most colorful minnows, but they lose their dramatic colors following breeding.

Natural History: Unlike some stream fishes that require flowing waters, the adaptable Spotfin Shiner can also thrive in man-made watersheds. Lives in both medium-sized streams and large rivers. Food is tiny invertebrates and algae. Breeding males have yellowish fins.

Natural History: The Satinfin Shiner is the only member of its genus that is endemic to the Atlantic Seaboard. The Satinfin Shiner inhabits small to medium-sized creeks with rocky or sandy substrates. Very similar to the Spotfin Shiner but has black pigment.

Genus - *Notropis* (true minnows - 14 species in New York, 12 shown below and on next page)

Blackchin Shiner *Notropis heterodon*	**Pugnose Shiner** *Notropis anogenus*	**Bigmouth Shiner** *Notropis dorsalis*

Size: Small. Maximum 2.75 inches.	**Size:** Tiny. Maximum 2.25 inches.	**Size:** Maximum of only 3 inches.
Abundance: Uncommon. Species of Greatest Conservation Need. Presumed range in New York	**Abundance:** Very rare in New York. An Endangered Species.  Presumed range in New York	**Abundance:** Fairly common in western New York but in decline.  Presumed range in New York

Emerald Shiner *Notropis atherinoides*	**Ironcolor Shiner** *Notropis chalybaeus*	**Mimic Shiner** *Notropis volucellus*

Size: Maximum about 5 inches.	**Size:** Small. Maximum 2.5 inches.	**Size:** Maximum of only 3 inches.
Abundance: Common and widespread except Long Island.  Presumed range in New York	**Abundance:** Very rare in New York. A species of Special Concern. 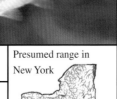 Presumed range in New York	**Abundance:** Common. One of the few *Notropis* that is increasing.  Presumed range in New York

| Class - **Actinopterygii** (ray-finned fishes) |
| Order - **Cypriniformes** (minnows and suckers) |
| Family - **Cyprinidae** (minnows) |
| Genus - *Notropis* (true minnows - continued) |

Blacknose Shiner *Notropis heterolepis*	**Rosyface Shiner** *Notropis rubellus*	**Sand Shiner** *Notropis stramineus*
Size: Up to 3.75 inches.	**Size:** Up to 3.75 inches.	**Size:** Maximum about 3.5 inches.
Abundance: Fairly common but declining in some areas.	Presumed range in New York	**Abundance:** Common and increasing in some areas of New York.	Presumed range in New York	**Abundance:** Fairly common and possibly increasing.	Presumed range in New York

Silver Shiner *Notropis photogenis*	**Spottail Shiner** *Notropis hudsonius*	**Swallowtail Shiner** *Notropis procne*
Size: Maximum about 5.5 inches.	**Size:** Maximum of 5.75 inches.	**Size:** Up to 2.75 inches.
Abundance: Fairly common in the Allegheny Watershed.	Presumed range in New York	**Abundance:** One of the most common *Notropis* minnows in New York.	Presumed range in New York	**Abundance:** Un-common. Species of Greatest Conservation Need.	Presumed range in New York

Natural History: *Notropis* is the largest genus of minnows in North America with as many as 83 species across the continent. In fact, this is the second largest generic group of fishes in North America, surpassed only by the darters of the *Etheostoma* genus. The exact status of some species included in this genus is problematic and taxonomic changes occur frequently within the group, with occasional species being re-assigned to another genus and some being added from other genera. These are confusingly similar fishes (except for breeding males) and most laypeople will find identifying individual species to be quite challenging. Consulting the accompanying range maps will allow elimination of some species. The distribution of this group is generally east of the Rocky Mountain Continental Divide, and most species occur within the Gulf of Mexico Drainage Basin. In addition to the 12 species shown here, two other *Notropis* minnows can be seen in New York. Those two species are the **Comely Shiner** (*N. amoenus*) and the **Bridle Shiner** (*N. bifrenatus*). The breeding males of many *Notropis* species are quite colorful. Even those species that don't acquire significant color on the body will typically acquire yellow, orange, or red color in the fins of nuptial males. Collectively, the Shiner Minnows are found in virtually all aquatic habitats within the state and their combined ranges encompass nearly all of New York. At least one species, the Emerald Shiner (*N. atherinoides*), is used as a bait minnow and has been introduced widely. There are 14 species extant in New York but several species have experienced population declines. Three are regarded as Species of Special Concern, two more as Species of Greatest Conservation Need, and one as an Endangered Species. If we consider population declines of widespread and once common fishes to be a warning about the health of America's waterways, then there is cause for great concern regarding the condition of America's streams. The condition of our waterways is analogous to "the canary in the coal mine" regarding the overall health of our environment and few things are more important than maintaining the environmental health of our planet. Indeed what could be more important. A good job and a thriving economy are useless withouth clean air to breathe and clean water to drink!

REFERENCES

Chapters 1 and 2

Print

Bailey, Robert G. 2009. *Ecosystem Geography, From Ecoregions to Sites.* Springer Science and Business Media, New York, NY.

Edinger, G. J., D. J. Evans, S. Gebauer, T. G. Howard, D. M. Hunt, and A. M. Olivero (editors). 2014. *Ecological Communities of New York State.* Second Edition. A revised and expanded edition of Carol Reschke's Ecological Communities of New York State. New York Natural Heritage Program, New York State Department of Environmental Conservation, Albany, NY.

Hunt, Charles B. 1974. *Natural Regions of the United States and Canada.* W.H. Freeman and Company, San Francisco, CA.

Ricketts, Taylor, H., Eric Dinerstein, David M. Olson, and ColJ Loucks, et al. 1999. *Terrestrial Ecoregions of North America.* World Wildlife Fund and Island Press. Washington, DC.

New York State Department of Environmental Conservation. 2015. *Keeping New Yorks Forest as Forests.*

Internet

New York Department of Environmental Conservation—www.dec.ny.gov

Mammals

Print

Bauer, Erwin A. and Peggy Bauer. 1993. *Whitetails: behavior, ecology and conservation.* Voyageur Press, Inc., Stillwater, MN.

Bowers, Nora, Rick Bowers and Kenn Kafuman. 2004. *Mammals of North America.* Houghton Mifflin Company. NY, NY.

DeGraaf, Richard M and Mariko Yamasaki. 2000. *New England Wildlife: Habitat, Natural History and Distribution.* UPNE

Godin, A.J. *Wild Mammals of New England.* 1977. The Johns Hopkins University Press, Baltimore and London.

Kays, Roland W. and Don. E. Wilson. 2009. *Mammals of North America.* Princeton University Press. Princeton, NJ.

New York Department of Enviornmental Conservation, Division of Fish, Wildlife and Marine Resources.

2010. *Checklist of Amphbians, Reptiles, Birds and Mammals of New York State.*

Walker, E.P. 1983. *Walkers Mammals of the World.* The John's Hopkins University Press. Baltimore, MD.

Whitaker, John O. Jr. and W. J. Hamilton Jr. 1998. *Mammals of the Eastern United States.* Cornell University Press. Ithaca, NY.

Wilson, Don E. and Sue Ruff. 1999. *North American Mammals.* Smithsonian Institution.

Internet

New York State Department of Environmental Conservation—www.dec.ny.gov

International Union of Concerned Naturalists—www.iucnredlist.org

Nature Serve Explorer—www.natureserve.org

Smithsonian National Museum of Natural History—www.mnh.si.edu

Mammalian Species, American Society of Mammalogists species accounts—www.science.smith.edu

State University of New York, College of Environmental Science and Forestry—www.esf.edu

Birds

Print

Clark, William S. and Brian K. Wheeler. 1987. *A Field Guide to Hawks-North America.* Peterson Field Guides, Houghton Mifflin Co. Boston, MA.

Carroll, Dan and Brian L Smith. 2000. *Status of the Trumpeter Swan in New York State.* Kingbird 50: 232–236.

Dunn, John L., Kimball Garret, Thomas Shultz, and Cindy House. *A Field Guide to Warblers of North America.* Peterson Field Guides, Houghton Mifflin Co. Boston, MA.

DeGraaf, Richard M. and Mariko Yamasaki. 2000. *New England Wildlife: Habitat, Natural History and Distribution.* UPNE.

Farrand, John, Jr. 1998. *An Audubon Handbook, Eastern Birds.* McGraw Hill Book Co. New York, NY.

Finger, Corey and Brian Small. 2016. *Field Guide to the Birds of New York.* Scott and Nix, Inc., New York, NY.

Floyd, Ted. 2008. *Smithsonian Field Guide to the Birds of North America.* Harper Collins Publishers. New York, NY.

Johnsgard, Paul A. 1988. *North American Owls, Biology and Natural History.* Smithsonian Institution Press, Washington, DC.

Kaufman, Ken. 2000. *The Birds of North America.* Houghton Mifflin Co., New York, NY.

New York Department of Enviornmental Conservation, Division of Fish, Wildlife and Marine Resources. 2010. *Checklist of Amphbians, Reptiles, Birds and Mammals of New York State.*

Peterson, Roger T. 1980. *A Field Guide to the Birds, Eastern Birds.* Houghton Mifflin Co., Boston, MA.

Sherony, Dominic and Jeffrey S. Bolsinger. 2007. *Status of the Trumpeter Swan in New York State in 2007.* Kingbird 57(1).

Vanner, Micheal. 2003. *The Encyclopedia of North American Birds.* Parragon Publishing, Bath, UK.

Internet

Cornell University Lab of Ornithology-Birds of North America Online—http://birds.bna.cornell.edu.bna/species.

New York State Department of Environmental Conservation—www.dec.ny.gov

State University of New York, College of Environmental Science and Forestry—www.esf.edu

McGill Bird Observatory—www.migrationresearch.org

Environment Canada—www.ec.gc.ca

Ebird—www.ebird.org

Waterfowl Hunting Management in North America—www.flyways.us

NatureServe Explorer—www.natureserve.org

Turtles

Print

Buhlmann, Kurt. Tracey Tuberville, and Whit Gibbons. 2008. *Turtles of the Southeast.* The University of Georgia Press, Athens, GA.

Collins, Joseph T. and Travis W. Taggart. 2009. *Standard Common and Scientific Names for North American Amphibians, Turtles, Reptiles and Crocodilians.* The Center for North American Herpetology, Hays, KS.

Conant Roger, and Joseph T. Collins. 1998. *Reptiles and Amphibians of Eastern/Central North America.* Houghton Mifflin Co., Boston-New York.

Ernst, Carl H., Jeffrey E. Lovich, and Roger W. Barbour. 1994. *Turtles of the United States and Canada.* Smithsonian Institution Press, Washington and London.

Niemiller, Matthew L., R. Graham Reynolds, and Brian T. Miller. 2013. *The Reptiles of Tennessee.* The University of Tennessee Press, Knoxville, TN.

Trauth, Stanley E., Henry W. Robison, and Michael V. Plummer. 2004. *The Amphibians and Reptiles of Arkansas.* The University of Arkansas Press, Fayetteville, AR.

Internet

NatureServe Explorer—www.natureserve.org

New York State Department of Environmental Conservation—www.dec.ny.gov

Reptiles

Print

Allen, William B. 1992. *The Snakes of Pennslyvania.* Reptile and Amphibian Magazine.

Collins, Joseph T. and Travis W. Taggart. 2009. *Standard Common and Scientific Names for North American Amphibians, Turtles, Reptiles and Crocodilians.* The Center for North American Herpetology, Hays, KS.

Conant Roger, and Joseph T. Collins. 1998. *Reptiles and Amphibians of Eastern/Central North America.* Houghton Mifflin Co., Boston-New York.

DeGraaf, Richard M and Mariko Yamasaki. 2000. *New England Wildlife: Habitat, Natural History and Distribution.* UPNE.

Hall, Russell J and Duane P. Stafford. 1972. *Studies in the Life History of the Wehrle's Salamander.* Herpetologica. 28: 300–309.

Meade, Les. 2005. *Kentucky Snakes. Their Identification, Variation, and Distribution.* Kentucky State Nature Preserves Commission.

Niemiller, Matthew L., R. Graham Reynolds, and Brian T. Miller. 2013. *The Reptiles of Tennessee.* The University of Tennessee Press, Knoxville, TN.

Mitchell, Joseph C. 1994. *The Reptiles of Virginia.* Smithsonian Institute Press, Washington and London.

Shupe, Scott. 2005. *U.S. Guide To Venomous Snakes And Their Mimics.* Skyhorse Publishing, New York, NY.

Shupe, Scott. 2012. *Venomous Snakes of the World, A Manual For Use By U.S. Amphibious Forces.* Skyhorse Publishing, New York, NY.

Tennant, Alan and Richard D. Bartlett. 2000. *Snakes of North America, Eastern and Central Regions.* Gulf Publishg Company, Houston, TX.

Trauth, Stanley E., Henry W. Robison, and Michael V. Plummer. 2004. *The Amphibians and Reptiles of Arkansas.* The University of Arkansas Press, Fayetteville, AR.

Wynn, Douglas E. and Scott M. Moody. 2006. *Ohio Turtle, Lizard, and Snake Atlas.* Ohio Biological Survey., Columbus, OH.

Wright, Albert Hazen and Anna Allen Wright. 1957. *Handbook of Snakes of the United States and Canada.* Comstock Publishing, Ithaca, NY.

Internet

NatureServe Explorer—www.natureserve.org

New York State Department of Environmental Conservation (Herp Atlas Project)—www.dec.ny.gov

Ohio Department of Natural Resources—www.wildlife.ohiodnr.gov

The Center for North American Herpetology—www.naherpetology.org

NatureServe Explorer—www.natureserve.org

Roger T. Peterson Institute of Natural History—www.rtpi.org

Fish

Print

Clay, William M. 1974. *The Fishes of Kentucky.* Kentucky Department of Fish and Wildlife Resources, Frankfort, KY.

Eddy, Samuel. 1969. *How to Know the Fresh Water Fishes.* Wm. C. Brown Company Publishers, Dubuque, IA.

Etnier, David A. and Wayne C. Starnes. 1993. *The Fishes of Tennessee.* The University of Tennessee Press, Knoxville, TN.

Goldstein, Robert J. with Rodney Harper and Ridchard Edwards. 2000. *American Aquarium Fishes.* Texas A&M University Press, College Station, TX.

Miller, Rudolph J. 2004. *The Fishes of Oklahoma.* The University of Oklahoma Press, Norman, OK.

Page, Lawrence M. and Brooks M. Burr. 2011. *Peterson Field Guide to Freshwater Fishes of North America North of Mexico.* Houghton Mifflin Harcourt, Boston - New York.

Pflieger, William L. 1975. *The Fishes of Missouri.* Missouri Department of Conservation, Springfield, MO.

Rice, Daniel L. and Gary Meszaros. 2014. *The Native Fishes of Ohio.* The Kent State University Press. Kent, OH.

Internet

FishBase—www.fishbase.org

North American Native Fish Association—www.nanfa.org

National Fish Habitat Action Plan—www.fishhabitat.org

NatureServe Explorer—www.natureserve.org

Ohio Department of Natural Resources—www.wildlife.ohiodnr.gov

USGS Fact Sheets—www.search.usgs.gov

International Union of Concerned Naturalists—www.iucnredlist.org

Kentucky Department of Fish and Wildlife Resources—www.kdfwr.state.ky.us

Encyclopedia of Life—www.eol.org

New York State Department of Environmental Conservation (Fish Atlas Maps)—www.dec.ny.gov

International Game Fish Association—www.igfa.org

Inland Fishes of New York (online)—www.fish.dnr.cornell.edu

GLOSSARY

Aestivate / Aestivation	Dormant state of inactivity usually brought on by hot, dry conditions. The opposite of hibernation, which is a winter-time dormancy.
Amphipod	A crustacean of the order Amphipoda. Includes the freshwater shrimps.
Anadromous	Ascending into freshwater rivers to spawn.
Annelid / Annalida	A class of invertebrate organisms commonly known as worms.
Anuran	A member of the amphibian order Anura (the frogs and toads).
Arboreal	Pertaining to trees.
Arthropod	A member of the invertebrate phylum Arthropoda.
Aspen Parkland	An open or semi-open area (usually grassland) that is intermingled with groves of Aspen.
Barbel	A long "whisker-like" appendage orginating near the mouth of fishes, often sensory.
Barrens	Open areas within normally forested or brusy habitats.
Benthic	Pertaining to the bottom of a stream or lake.
Bivalve	An organism of the phylum Molluska (mollusks) or Branchiopoda having a shell consisting of two halves.
Boreal	Northern.
Borrow Pit	Shallow ditches and ponds created by road construction when earth is "borrowed" from a nearby area to build up road beds.
Buteo	A hawk belonging to the genus Buteo. Also known as the "Broad-winged Hawks."
Cache	The act of storing or hiding food for future use.
Carapace	The top half of the shell of a turtle.
Carnivore	A meat eater.
Caudal	Pertaining to the tail.
Chromosone	Long strand of proteins and DNA found within the nucleus of a cell.
Circumpolar	Literally, around the poles. Usually used in reference to the geographic range of an organism that is found throughout the northern hemisphere.
Cryptic Species	The condition of two or more species being so similar in appearance that they might be mistaken for being the same species.
Cloaca	A common opening for reproductive and excretory functions in an organism. Typical for all vertebrate animals except mammals.
Congeneric	Belonging to the same genus.
Conspecific	Belonging to the same species.
Contiguous	In contact with or adjoining.
Copepod	A group of tiny crustaceans belonging to the suborder Copapoda. Many are microscopic and aquatic and are important food for tiny fishes and other small aquatic organisms.

CRP	Conservation Reserve Program.
Crustacean	A member of the class Crustacea. A class of Arthropod organisms that includes the crayfish, lobsters, crabs, shrimps, barnacles, copepods, and water fleas.
Cryptic	Pertaining to concealment.
Dipteran	An insect of the order Diptera. Includes flies, mosquitos, gnats, and midges.
Disjunct	Not attached to or not adjoining.
Dessicate / Dissication	Dry out.
Diurnal	Pertaining to day. Being active by day.
Dorsal	The top or back of an organism.
Dorso-ventral	The region between the side and the belly of an organism, or along the lower side adjacent to the belly.
Echolocate / echolocation	The use of sound waves to navigate or move about. As in bats.
Ecoregion	A large unit of land or water containing a geographically distinct assemblage of species, natural communities, and environmental conditions.
Ecotone	The region where one or more habitats converge.
Embryo	A young animal that is developing from a fertilized egg. Embryonic stage ends at birth or hatching.
Endemic	Native to a particular area.
Endotherm / Endothermic	A organism that regulates its body tempaerature internally. Warm blooded.
Ephemeral	Fleeting. Temporary.
Extirpated	No longer found within a given area.
Extant	Still present. Opposite of extirpated.
Fecund / Fecundity	Capable of producing abundant offspring.
Fin Rays	The bony structures that support the membranes of a fishes fin.
Fossorial	Burrowing or living in underground burrows.
Gastropod	A class of the animal phylum Molluska. Includes snails and slugs.
Herbaceous	A type of flowering plant which does not develop woody tissue.
Holarctic	The circumpolar region that includes North America, Europe, and Asia.
Homogeneous	Of the same kind.
Insectivorus	Insect eating.
Invertivorous	Feeding on invertebrates.
Intergrade	An organism which possess morphological characteristics that are intermediate between two distinctly different forms.
Irruptive	The sudden movement of animals from one portion of their range to another, often very distant portion of their range. As in when Snowy Owls occasionally move down from the arctic region into the southern half of North America.
Isopod	An order of Crustaceans that includes the familiar pillbugs.
Keeled Scales	The presence of a small ridge down the middle of the dorsal scales on snakes.
Lentic	Non-flowing bodies of water, lakes, swamps, ponds, etc.
Mandible	The lower jaw of an animal or the bill of a bird.
Marine	Pertaining to living in a salt water environment.
Mast	Seeds produced by plants in a deciduous forest. Usually means the cumulative production of acorns, nuts, berries, seeds, etc., which are widely utilized by wildlife as food.

Melanistic	A predominance of the dark pigment known as melanin. The opposite of Albinistic.
Mesic	Damp or moist.
Metabolic / Metabolism	The sum of the chemical activity that occurs within a living organism. Usually relates to the digestion of food and utilization of food compounds within the body.
Metamorphose	Change of the body. Usually refers to the change from an immature stage to a more mature stage (as in a tadpole to a frog).
Metamorphosis	Abrupt physical change of body form.
NYSDEC	New York State Department of Environmental Conservation.
Millinery Trade	The sale of bird feathers.
Molt	The shedding of and renewal (replacement) of skin, hair, or feathers.
Moraine	Large mass of earth, sand, gravels, and rock bulldozed by glacial movement. Moraines usually accumulate along the sides and in the front of glaciers.
Morphology	The study of the body form, shape, and structure of organisms, including colors or patterns.
Muskeg	A Sphagnum bog occuring the boreal (northern) regions of North America.
Neotropical	Pertaining to the tropical regions of the western hemisphere.
Nuptial	Pertaining to breeding.
Obligate	In biology means occuring within a restricted environment.
ODNR	Ohio Department of Natural Resources.
Omnivore	Eats both plant and animal matter.
Ontogenetic	Related to the development or age of an organism.
Opercle Flap	The bony structure on the side of a fishes head that covers the gills. Also sometimes called gill cover.
Organism	A living thing.
Orthopteran	A member of the insect order Orthoptera. Includes such well-known insects as crickets and grasshoppers.
Ossification	The formation of bone.
Palearctic	The geographic region that includes Europe and northern Asia.
Parthenogenesis	The development of an ovum (egg) without fertilization.
Passage Migrant	Refers to birds that merely migrate through an area without staying any appreciable amount of time.
Pectoral	Pertaining to or located in the chest area.
Pelage	Fur.
Pelvic	Pertaining to or located in the region of the pelvis (hips).
Phylogeny	The evolutionary relationships and/or evolutionary history of organisms.
Physiography	Refers to the natural features of a landscape, e.g., mountains, rivers, plains, etc.
Piscivorous	Fish eating.
Plastron	The ventral (bottom) portion of a turtles shell.
Plumage	The feathers of a bird.
Polychaete Worms	Annelid worms (Phylum Annelida) belonging to the class Polychaeta. Mostly marine but some are freshwater.
Precocious	Having adult (or highly developed) characteristics in the young. Precocial being highly precocious.
Predaceous	Feeding on other animals, being a predator.

Piscivorous	Fish eating.
Puddle Duck	Ducks belonging to the genus *Anas*.
Prehensile	Grasping. As in a prehensile tail that is able to wrap around and grasp a tree limb.
Regenerative	Refers to the ability to repair or replace damage or destroyed tissues or structures.
Riparian	Pertaining to the bank of a stream or river.
Sexual Dimorphism	Morphological differences between the sexes.
Species of Concern	A species or subspecies which might become threatened in New York under continued or increased stress.
Species of Special Interest	A species that occurs periodically and is capable of breeding in New York.
Successional Woodlands / Areas	Landscape areas (usually woodlands) that are undergoing change from an early stage of development to an older stage. As in woodlands regenerating following logging operations.
Sympatric / Sympatrically	A condition where more than one species occurs in the same or overlapping area or habitat.
Taiga	A type of forest occuring in the far north. Usually dominated by dwarfed spruces.
Topography	The configuration of the land surface. Literally, "the lay of the land."
Troglodyte	Cave dwelling. Usually refers to organisms that live in caves.
Turbid	Water that is opaque due to the high amount of suspended silt particles.
Tympanum	The circular ear structure on the side of the head of frogs and toads.
USF&WS	Acronym for the United States Fish and Wildlife Service.
Ventral	Pertaining to the belly or bottom side of and organism.
Vernal	Pertaining to spring. Also frequently used to describe temporary ponds and pools that hold water only during the wet season.
Vestigial	A rudimentary structure. Usually a remnant, degenerative structure that was once (in the evolutionary history of the organism) a fully functioning structure.
Xeric	Dry.
Zygote	A fertilized egg that has not yet begun to divide.

INDEX

PHOTO CREDITS

John R. MacGregor

Meadow Jumping Mouse, Southern Bog Lemming, Southern Red-backed Vole, Masked Shrew, Northern Bat, Eastern Small-footed Bat, Silver-haired Bat, Hoary Bat, Eastern Red Bat, Four-toed Salamander, Northern Redback Salamander, Wehrle's Salamander, Hellbender

Matthew R. Thomas

Eastern Sand Darter, Blackside Darter, Banded Darter, Variagate Darter, Channel Darter, Stonecat, Tadpole Madtom, Spotted Sucker, River Redhorse, Streamlined Chub, Rosyface Shiner, Mimic Shiner, Silver Shiner

David Speiser www.lilibirds.com

Alder Flycatcher, Yellow-bellied Flycatcher, Northern Shrike, Sedge Wren, Wilson's Warbler (male), Golden-winged Warbler (male), Connectcut Warbler, Mourning Warbler, Saltmarsh Sparrow, Snow Bunting, Long-tailed Duck (male and female), Surf Scoters, Black Scoter (male and female)

Don Martin Bird Photograpy

Olive-sided Flycatcher, Least Flycatcher, Willow Flycatcher, Ruby-crowned Kinglet (male), Clay-colored Sparrow, Henslow's Sparrow, White-winged Crossbill, Virginia Rail, Baird's Sandpiper, Western Sandpiper, White-winged Scoter

Konrad Schmidt

Iowa Darter, Rainbow Smelt, Trout Perch, Silver Redhorse, Common Shiner, Finescale Dace, Northern Pearl Dace, Blackchin Shiner, Blacknose Shiner, Bigmouth Shiner, Spottail Shiner

Brian Zimmerman

Spotted Darter (male), Spotted Darter (female), Swamp Darter, Brook Stickleback, Swamp Darter, Margined Madtom, Redside Dace, Northern Redbelly Dace, Cutlip Minnow, Pugnose Shiner, Longhead Darter

James Harding

Bog Turtle, Wood Turtle, Mink Frog, Blue-spotted Salamander

Dave Neely

Sockeye Salmon, Fallfish, Eastern Silvery Minnow, Satinfin Shiner

James Kiser

Northern Short-tailed Shrew, Bluebreast Darter

Robert Morin

Snowy Owl, Black-backed Woodpecker, Three-toed Woodpecker

Twan Leenders
Common Eider, Shorthead Garter Snake

Jeff Poklen
Little Gull, Great Cormorant, Brant

Fishingwithpole
American Shad, Alewife, Blueback Herring

Greg Lavaty
Short-eared Owl, Purple Sandpiper

Phil Myers
Meadow Vole, Smoky Shrew

Missy Mandel
Marten, Boreal Chckadee

Nate Tessler
White Perch, Pink Salmon

Chris Crippen
Shortnose Sturgeon, Shield Darter

Jeffrey Offerman
Long-tailed Weasel

Sterling Daniels
Hairy-tailed Mole
T. Travis Brown
Mottled Sculpin

Wayne Helfrich
Star-nosed Mole

Tom Murray
Goshawk

Uland Thomas
Mooneye

Dave Frymire
Brook Silverside

Margaret Novak
Rudd

United States Forest Service, Pacifc Southwest Region
Fisher

United States Fish and Wildlife Service, Roger Tabor
Chinook Salmon

United States Fish and Wildlife Service, Peter Steenstra
Atlantic Salmon

* All other photos are by Scott Shupe.

ABOUT THE AUTHOR

Naturalist Scott Shupe began his professional career in 1971 at the famed Ross Allen Reptile Institute and Venom Laboratory in Silver Springs, Florida. He later worked at the St. Augustine Alligator Farm in St. Augustine, Florida, and with Reptile Gardens in Rapid City, South Dakota. From 1992 to 2002 he enjoyed an association with the Knight and Hale Game Call company in Cadiz, Kentucky, where he served as director of The Woods and Wetlands Wildlife Center, a private zoo/nature center. He is the founder and original owner of the Natural History Educational Company, an organization of professional naturalists that provided live-animal wildlife education programs to thousands of schools throughout the United States.

He has served as a host and narrator for wildlife-related television programming (In the Wild-Outdoor Channel), produced educational life science videos, and has appeared as a guest naturalist on a number of public television programs and satellite networks. He has been recognized for his contributions to conservation education by the United States Fish and Wildlife Service, named naturalist of the year by the Kentucky Society of Naturalists, awarded the Jesse Stuart Media Award for his educational video productions, and received the Environmental Stewardship Award from the Kentucky Environmental Quality Commission. Since 1987 he has contracted annually with the Kentucky Department of Parks to provide naturalist programming in state parks across Kentucky.

He has written for outdoor and nature periodicals and scientific journals and his wildlife photographs have appeared in dozens of nature magazines and books. This is his sixth book on nature and wildlife and his third in a series of state wildlife encyclopedias being produced for Skyhorse Publishing. He also authored *Kentucky Wildlife Encyclopedia*, *Ohio Wildlife Encyclopedia*, *U.S. Guide to Venomous Snakes and their Mimics*, *Venomous Snakes of the World: A Manuel for Use by U.S. Amphibious Forces*, and *Life List of North American Birds*. He is a native of Kentucky who today describes himself as a dedicated wanderer and a citizen of the world.

Contact Scott Shupe at kscottshupe@gmail.com.